THE ECOLOGY OF PRESCHOOL BEHAVIOUR

THE ECOLOGY OF PRESCHOOL BEHAVIOUR

PETER K. SMITH

Lecturer in Psychology, University of Sheffield

AND

KEVIN J. CONNOLLY

Professor of Psychology, University of Sheffield

CAMBRIDGE UNIVERSITY PRESS

Cambridge
London   New York   New Rochelle
Melbourne   Sydney

Published by the Press Syndicate of the University of Cambridge
The Pitt Building, Trumpington Street, Cambridge CB2 1RP
32 East 57th Street, New York, NY 10022, USA
296 Beaconsfield Parade, Middle Park, Melbourne 3206, Australia

First published 1980

Printed in Great Britain at the
University Press, Cambridge

British Library Cataloguing in Publication Data
Smith, Peter K.
The ecology of preschool behaviour.
1. Child psychology
2. Play groups
I. Title II. Connolly, Kevin J.
155.4'23   BF721   79-42647
ISBN 0 521 22331 8

Contents

Appendices

Preface

Ethological methods and concepts have played an important role in the recent history of the behavioural sciences. Ethology has its roots in evolutionary biology and often gives rise to functional questions about behaviour. The methods have been characterised by careful and detailed descriptive work along with a paramount concern for ecological validity. In contrast, much of psychology has been characterised by the careful experimental analysis of behaviour which has led to the search for immediate antecedent causes of behaviours. In the study of animal behaviour these once separate approaches have come together over the last 25 years, so that it is often impossible to discover an author's intellectual origins from an account of his or her typical research style and approach.

Both of us have been interested in child behaviour and development throughout our professional careers. The use of sophisticated observational methods for studying the behaviour of children suggested itself to KJC after attending an International Ethological Conference in the early 1960s. These methods were used first in work with the human newborn and then in studies with preschool children. About that time PKS came to Sheffield to work on a doctoral thesis under KJC's supervision. This research took the form of detailed observational studies of the behaviour of young children in day nurseries, nursery schools, and playgroups. At that time simply watching and recording behaviour seemed a dangerously new idea compared with the laboratory traditions in which we had both been educated. It is interesting that now it seems quite commonplace and unremarkable. During the late 1960s and early 1970s we had fruitful meetings with a small number of other research workers with similar interests, often in Nick Blurton Jones's rooms in the Institute of Child Health in London.

It was generally our view that the initial observational studies should be seen as laying the groundwork for more structured research. Many of the factors we believed to be important influences on the behaviour of preschool children could be clearly investigated only by using some form of experimental manipulation and control. This book documents our attempt to combine experimental rigour with ecological validity and to explore at least some practically important issues concerning how the preschool environment influences children's behaviour. Thus work with children begins to show the merging of traditions that is evident in research on animal behaviour.

The research was supported by grant number HR 1414/2 from the Social Science Research Council, London, to KJC. Amongst our colleagues we should like especially to thank Mrs Dorothy Fleming, who provided invaluable help in the early stages of setting up and running the playgroup, and Dr Margaret Martlew, whose own doctoral work was based upon 'the playgroup' and who has provided help and support in organisation and in discussing our findings. We are indebted to the staff who ran the playgroup over the three years. Mrs Patricia Blanchard, Mrs Maureen Gascoyne, Mrs Janet King, Mrs Winifred Froggatt, Mrs Susan Laughlin, Mrs Wendy Wilkinson, and the late Mrs Margaret Perkins. We thank also the children who made up the playgroups. We are especially grateful to Mrs Audrey Rixham for many things, not least of which was the masterly typing of an exceptionally complex manuscript. Finally, our thanks to the staff of Cambridge University Press for their care and thoroughness in seeing the book through to publication and to Sarah Connolly who made the indexes.

Department of Psychology   PETER SMITH, KEVIN CONNOLLY
University of Sheffield
April 1980

1   Introduction: research perspectives

In industrialised societies children generally begin their formal schooling between the ages of 4 and 7. In Britain formal schooling is mandatory from the age of 5. Before this age many children attend 'preschools' – a general term which we use to cover the variety of settings in which children receive collective caretaking before school age. Nursery schools and classes, day nurseries, and playgroups are the principal kinds of large-scale preschool institution in Britain. These institutions have different aims and backgrounds and reflect to differing extents the needs of children, their parents, and the wider society.

Nursery schools are open during school hours and terms, and each class is the responsibility of at least one trained teacher. They are administered by local education authorities and aim to be a transitional setting between home and school, with an emphasis on educational objectives. Children are usually accepted from the age of 3, though this depends on the availability of places in a given locality. Nursery classes are similar, but are attached directly to infant or first schools.

Day nurseries are open for longer hours and throughout the year. They are staffed by nursery nurses and administered by departments of social or family and community services. Their aim is more one of providing full day care for one-parent families, or where both parents are working full-time, and the emphasis tends to be more on physical health and well-being than on educational objectives *per se*. Children may be accepted from the age of 9 months.

Playgroups are private organisations run by groups of parents, or sometimes commercially. In Britain many are affiliated to the Preschool Playgroups Association and they are registered with local authorities who prescribe certain minimum conditions and standards. The training of staff varies considerably and often the playgroup is staffed by a rota of parents. Playgroups also vary considerably in their aims and daily routine. Many open only for certain weekdays, usually on a half-day basis, and rarely are meals provided. Children are usually accepted from the age of 2 or 3.

In England and Wales in the mid-1970s there were some $3\frac{1}{2}$ million children below school age and over 2 million between 2 and 4 years old. State-maintained nursery schools and classes provided about 50,000 full-time places and 100,000 part-time places for preschool children. Day nurseries provided about 25,000 full-time places, and approximately an equal number were provided by private or voluntary nurseries. Preschool playgroups provided for many more children – around 300,000 – but these were mainly part-time (Chazan, 1975; Tizard, 1975; Van der Eyken, 1977). Altogether, places were available for about 15 per cent of the under-fives; full-time places were available for only about 100,000 children, or 3 per cent of the total preschool population.

It was estimated that during this same period some 600,000 mothers of preschool age children were engaged in paid employment, and that there were over 200,000 children under 5 with mothers working more than 30 hours per week (Tizard, 1975). The shortfall of institutional provision for working mothers is obvious, and many young children are in fact cared for by childminders – often parents themselves who take in several other young children. Over 50,000 childminders were registered in the mid-1970s, but in addition much 'illegal' childminding is carried on – perhaps two or three times as much (Mayall and Petrie, 1977). In Britain and in several other European countries (Council of Europe, 1975) there is considerable feeling that a policy of increasing organised preschool provision should be pursued. Financial considerations have tended to curtail any large-scale implementation of such policies, but in the future preschool facilities may accommodate many more young children than they do at present.

While differing in several respects, nursery schools and classes, day nurseries, and playgroups are all similar in that large numbers of children between 2 and 5 years old are grouped together with a few adults and a variety of play apparatus and equipment for an appreciable part of the day. In this book we are concerned with examining aspects of the preschool environment and its impact on the children's behaviour – in short, the behavioural ecology of the preschool.

The preschool is an important behaviour setting for many children, and it is a setting in which observation combined with experimental manipulation are at least relatively easy to carry out. Much is going on in the preschool. There are the fleeting friendships, the early tussles, the beginnings of cooperation and hostility in social interaction. There is a high rate of general physical activity. There are a variety of toys, tasks, and equipment to challenge the child's intellectual skills and curiosity. The amount of skill development between 2 and 5 years is enormous. In language, simple two-or three-word utterances give way to a close approximation to adult speech. Socially, the child moves from predominantly solitary play to cooperative play with several other children. Both general motor coordination and dextrous manual skills show great improvement. The child masters the concepts of number, colour, and shape. Sex identity is established, and with it the beginnings of awareness of sex-appropriate behaviour. Thus in the preschool we have a context of richness of behaviour, where important developmental changes are taking place. The preschool is also a planned environment. The planning is sometimes haphazard, and certainly individual preschools differ greatly in the environmental experiences they present to their children. We may expect such differences to affect the way the children develop. Admittedly the preschool is only one component in the child's life at the time, and this period is only one component in the individual's life history. Nevertheless it is a component, and whatever its ultimate significance relative to the family home and other behaviour settings, it is important that it be carefully studied.

The development of research into the behaviour of children at preschools, and the effects of different types of preschools, is reviewed further below. We now have much more knowledge relevant to the planning of preschool provision than was available twenty or even ten years ago. One may wonder why a further book of research findings, entitled *The Ecology of Preschool Behaviour*, should be necessary. In fact, because of the unique facilities which our experimental playgroup provided and the unusual combination of detailed observation together with precise experimental change which it permitted, several studies reported in this book are the first of their kind; the facilities and methodology are described in the next chapter.

How much space is necessary for adequate provision in a playgroup? Does the amount of play equipment affect social and aggressive behaviour? Does it make any difference to children's play patterns if ten, twenty, or thirty children gather together in the playgroup? Apart from a few studies of spatial density, the influence of physical parameters in the preschool environment has been grossly neglected. The research reported in Chapters 3–7 of the book is, to the best of our knowledge, breaking new ground in this respect.

The role of the adult in the preschool, and the contrast between structured, educational settings and non-structured, free-play settings continues to be a matter of contrast and controversy. Of the many studies on the impact of different kinds of preschool organisation on the participating children, few have looked at the *processes* involved rather than the *product*. The research reported in Chapter 9 is of necessity a pilot study, given its restricted size, but its emphasis on process as well as product, and on socio-emotional as well as cognitive measures, provides distinctive features which will be of wider interest.

In any kind of educational setting, the ratio of staff to children is a matter of planning and policy debate. There is virtually no experimental research evidence on which to base decisions. We examined the effects of experimental variations in staff: child ratios on the quality and inequality of communication patterns in playgroups, in a structured, educational setting. This is reported in Chapter 10.

Development of research on preschool children and of observational studies in preschool settings

Research on the behaviour of young children in preschool settings has a long history – long at least so far as psychological research is concerned. As early as the 1920s and 1930s a great deal of systematic research was being carried out, mostly in the USA; and although the impetus for naturalistic studies in preschools declined during the 1940s and 1950s, the last decade has seen a revival of interest, fired by new outlooks and methodologies.

The precursors of this interest in young children in general, and in preschool education and care in particular, can be found in the last century. In mediaeval society the young child was seen as a miniature adult, whose needs were not thought to merit special attention (Aries, 1962; Blackstone, 1971), but during the nineteenth century a substantial literature on child-rearing and the moral training of children began to appear. Attitudes became more 'child centred'. Froebel (1782–1852) was perhaps the first person to delineate in a systematic way how very young children should be educated (Froebel, 1826), and in 1837 he established the first kindergarten in Blankenburg in Germany. The first English kindergarten was founded in 1851. The nursery school and kindergarten movement spread, although slowly, through the latter half of the nineteenth century. The trend of preschool provision especially was influenced by the need parents felt to prepare the child, through education and play, for further schooling and for adult life in an increasingly industrial and technological society. This predominantly middle-class concern contrasted somewhat with another trend of provision for working-class children, designed to provide full day care whilst mothers worked in the factories. Here the emphasis was more on physical health than on education, although the development of child psychology and of educational psychology had some impact on all these aspects of preschool care and provision.

G. S. Hall (1844–1924) has been described as 'without qualification the founder of child psychology in the United States' (Kessen, 1965). Hall's emphasis on orientating education to the natural stages of children's growth reinforced the trend towards programmes and curricula specifically for the preschool period. Much of the ferment of ideas in child psychology and preschool education by the end of the nineteenth century was centred in the USA, with the writings of Hall, Dewey, Thorndike, and later Watson and Gesell in the 1920s. Burt and Isaacs in England, Binkler in Germany (later in the USA), Binet in France, and Piaget in Switzerland were also influential (Senn, 1975).

The period after the First World War brought many of these trends to fruition. At centres such as Teachers' College at Columbia University, the University of Iowa Child Welfare Center, the University of Toronto Child Development Service, and others, a phase of naturalistic behaviour observation in nursery schools flourished during the later 1920s and through the 1930s. By now, the nursery school movement had established itself in a number of industrialised countries, and the practical problems of how to organise such schools and what methods to use with the children posed a challenge to psychological and educational research and thinking. In the serial publications of institutes such as those mentioned above, as well as in other journals such as the *Pedagogical Seminary* (founded in 1891, renamed *Journal of Genetic Psychology* in 1927) *Genetic Psychology Monographs*, and the recently started *Child Development* (founded in 1930), a spate of research articles and observations relevant to the development and needs of young children appeared (Anderson, 1956).

The observational work of the 1920s and 1930s provides a fascinating preview of many of the problems and purposes of later work in the 1960s and 1970s. On the whole, this considerable body of research reports is now neglected. But perhaps more than the actual results obtained, the problems tackled and methods of study well deserve some attention from present-day researchers. This is despite, indeed partly because of, the conceptual and historical limitations of much of this research; contemporary research too will presently become dated.

The development of observational research during this period and its strengths and weaknesses have been reviewed by Smith and Connolly (1972). In part, this work seems to have been laying down basic knowledge about the behaviour of young children in preschools – comparable to the sort of basic information being obtained by Gesell and by Piaget in their contemporaneous studies of infant development. Some, such as Mildred Parten's classic descriptions of the kinds of social participation and leadership found in preschool children (1932, 1933), have formed a basis for much future work. Her basic distinctions between solitary, parallel, and group activities are indeed utilised in the research described in this book. Parten's work is perhaps the best-known example of a genre which included studies of physical and skill development, friendship patterns, choice of toys, cognitive and linguistic abilities, and age and sex differences in behaviour. Besides this gathering of basic knowledge, and inextricably interwoven with it, was a concern to give advice on the practical problems of institutional preschool care for young children. There were studies of training procedures for eating, sleeping, and toilet habits; of coping with aggressive behaviour and behaviour problems; of children's adjustment to preschool; of the possible benefits of nursery attendance; of teacher–child contacts; and the effectiveness of different kinds of preschool experience.

Thus this was far from being ivory tower research; indeed in retrospect some of this concern for practical problems seems even to detract from the scientific relevance of the work for us, forty years later. The reasons for this are in the main methodological. The categories used for the description of behaviour are often too bound up with specific ideas of what practitioners at that time considered to be important. For example, there are temporal and cultural bounds on what are considered to be 'behaviour disturbances'. In addition, there seemed to be relatively little interest in seeking deeper explanations for the behaviour patterns observed – whether in terms of the child's motivational structure or of the influence of the environment on his behavioural development – or in seeking a more embracing theoretical approach to the growth of competence in the young child. While there were attempts in some reports to use finer and more objectively defined behaviour categories, these were in part frustrated by the lack of inexpensive filming equipment, or of video recording equipment. (Gesell was one of the first to employ filming techniques, at Yale; it was little used elsewhere at this time.) Even in the case of substantive and valuable research such as Parten's, further work on the detailed development of early social interactions has really had to await the use of videotape and slow-motion playback (e.g. Lewis and Rosenblum, 1975). Another important technological development is the availability of the computer for large and complex data analyses.

However, one's reservations concerning the scientific merit of this work should lie not with its concern with practical problems, but rather with the frequent failure of the investigator to 'distance' him- or herself sufficiently from a problem to allow a more independent approach – one in which the methods (conceptualisation of the problem, categories used, etc.) were not in effect dictated by the preconceptions of teachers and parents at the time. In other words, the drawback lies not in the concern with practical ends, but with the limitations inherent in the methods chosen.

The main methodological issues publicly debated at the time were techniques of observation, particularly the use of different kinds of time sampling (Olson and Cunningham, 1934), and the reliability of data and of observers (Arrington, 1939, 1943). Much of this discussion was very thorough. It was not until the influence of ethological studies of primates was felt in the late 1960s that further methodological advances in the observation and description of behaviour of young children were made.

A few of the pre-war studies will be reviewed in more detail in relation to the particular research areas dealt with in later chapters. Despite the originality of the issues, some of these studies are of limited value. For example, Johnson's paper (1935) on the effects on behaviour of varying the amount of play equipment had clear limitations due to the small-scale design which confounded amount and variety of equipment, inadequate categorisation of behaviour, and the lack of statistical analysis of the data. In contrast, a later monograph by Thompson (1944) on the social and emotional development of preschool age children in relation to the educational programme provides one of the best examples of the pre-war work with its fairly wide scope of assessment and the care with which inferences are made from the results.

Many other journals besides *Child Development* had been started by 1930; for example, in the USA there were *Child Welfare* (1922), *Childhood Education* (1924), and *Genetic Psychology Monographs* (1926); in Britain *Nursery World* (1925), and in Switzerland the *International Child Welfare Review* (1926). These journals were fed by the research generated by the new interest in childhood in general, and in the welfare and education of young children in particular. Observational studies of preschool children formed one major component of this stream of research, summarised in books such as Thorpe's *Child Psychology and Development* (1946) or Carmichael's *Manual of Child Psychology* (1946). By the 1940s, however, things were changing. The reasons for the change are difficult to ascertain, but the facts are clear enough. The phase of observational work and naturalistic study came more or less to an end, perhaps because with the assumptions and techniques prevailing at the time the field had exhausted itself. However, it would scarcely be true to say that this work was used as a basis for subsequent experiment and theory construction. Even if it had been wholly adequate as such a basis, which seems unlikely, the change in the main was due to a shift in orientation away from what were seen as uncontrolled descriptive studies towards studies of particular abilities in particular experimental situations. The theoretical perspective when present was predominantly a behaviourist one, in the United States at least. Experimental investigations of discrimination learning, the effectiveness of reinforcers, and so on, were not based on studies of how children learnt or behaved in the nursery, but were, on the whole, designed and carried out in a tight experimental laboratory tradition. The emphasis turned more to experimental rigour and the exclusion of uncontrolled variables, at the expense, it may now seem, of the reality of the problems investigated and relevance to real-life situations.

With the turning away from naturalistic observation came also an increased emphasis on testing, and the use of standard assessment techniques (such as doll play for assessing aggression), interviews, and questionnaires. While 'objective' in the sense of standardised, such techniques have difficulties and limitations in terms of their validity with respect to what they purport to measure. However, the few observational studies still carried out certainly show no improvement on the pre-war research. For example, Body (1955) and Walters *et al.* (1957) reported observational studies of aggressive behaviour in nursery schools, but in the former case an objective definition of aggressive behaviour is not even attempted. Heathers (1954) and Heinicke (1956) described the effects of separation from parents when the child first went to nursery school; but these authors use broad categories such as 'seeks reassurance', 'shows negativism', and 'gives affection', which are just as complex, subjective, and culture-bound as any of the examples from the 1930s.

Perhaps the most valuable observational studies made during this period were on choice of play companions, in the tradition of Challman (1932) and Hagman (1933). Even these, however, were largely done to validate the alternative techniques of teacher judgements and sociometric tests (Biehler, 1954; McCandless and Marshall, 1957; Marshall, 1957; Marshall and McCandless, 1957). There was increased sophistication in data analysis in some observation-based studies (e.g. Cattell and Peterson, 1958; Rafferty *et al.*, 1960; Martin, 1964) vitiated, however, by the lack of sophistication in the behaviour categorisation and techniques of observation and recording (Smith, 1973). Some of the lessons of the 1930s were already being forgotten.

Not only was there little observational research in the 1950s and early 1960s, but the overall volume of publication in child development declined in the immediate post-war years (Anderson, 1956; Brackbill, 1967). Developmental psychology was no longer such an important focus of psychological research. Very few new journals were launched between 1930 and 1960. The only major exception, admittedly a prestigious one, is the *Merrill-Palmer Quarterly* (1954). In Britain the *Journal of Child Psychology and Psychiatry* was started in 1960. At this time, these and older journals were on the whole little concerned with preschool research. This changed during the 1960s, largely because of the increasing attention paid to educational disadvantage and the importance of intervention in the preschool years, culminating in the USA in the nationwide Headstart Program of 1965–7.

In considering the factors leading to the resurgence of scientific interest in preschool education, one must certainly take into account the important focus, in post-war psychological research, on early experience. This was believed to be of great importance in determining the paths of future development. Studies on animals had a decisive role in strengthening this viewpoint. Hebb's book, *The Organisation of Behaviour* (1949), was particularly influential with its emphasis on central nervous system plasticity in higher mammalian species and the development of 'cell assemblies' to match features of the external environment. These ideas provided great impetus to much subsequent work. Although Hebb's specific ideas were not greatly developed by others, a number of studies on various species in the next decade or so suggested that early experience could indeed have important and profound effects. Much of this work was summarised in Hunt's book, *Intelligence and Experience* (1961). Bloom's monograph, *Stability and Change in Human Characteristics* (1964), promoted the view that early experience was as crucial in human as in animal infancy. Originating in but going beyond the psychoanalytic tradition, the views of Bowlby (1951) on maternal deprivation also contributed strongly to this view.

It now seems clear that the deterministic aspect of early experience was over-emphasised; the apparent continuity often found in development could frequently be explained in terms of continuing environmental circumstances (Clarke and Clarke, 1976). If such circumstances were changed dramatically, so was a child's developmental prognosis (e.g. Koluchova, 1976). The emphasis on early experience should certainly not lead to complacency or resignation in the case of children whose early experience has been adverse or unfortunate. Nor should it lead to an undue weighting of society's resources towards very young children, relative to those for later childhood. Nevertheless there is a case to be made that some changes in early experience may be made more easily and be more readily effective than changes made later on. A more sophisticated analysis of early experience which draws on notions from developmental genetics should be developed.

Another factor must also be considered. The idealism of wartime and the years immediately after the Second World War had brought about educational reforms, such as universal free schooling, designed to give equality of educational opportunity to children from all racial and socio-economic groups, and a climate of opinion in which equality of opportunity was expected to lead to equality of achievement. And yet, during the 1950s, it became apparent that equality of achievement was far from being a reality. The Coleman report in the USA (Coleman *et al.*, 1966) and the results of national surveys in Britain (Douglas, 1964; Douglas *et al.*, 1968; Davie *et al.*, 1972) amply documented the still massive failure, in general, of children from lower socio-economic classes and racial minority groups to succeed at middle-class white levels within the educational system.

Concern amongst educational and child psychologists at this failure meshed in with the interest in the effects of early experience, to suggest that these children were 'deficient' in early experience, specifically during the preschool years. Reisman's book, *The Culturally Deprived Child* (1962), coined a phrase whose extreme and value-laden connotations have subsequently been largely rejected, but which at the time was widely used and accepted. Bernstein's early publications (1959, 1960, 1962) offered support for the view that there were specifically linguistic deficits in mother–child interaction in lower working-class homes, and that this could lead to cognitive deficits and to failure in school. Bernstein's views influenced Hess and Shipman (1965), and led to an outburst of research in the USA which purported to show deficits in the early experience and abilities of children from lower socio-economic classes and from racial minority groups.

In retrospect, it is clear that this work had far too inadequate a data base to justify the assumptions made by the researchers. Much of it also had a white middle-class bias in the situations 'and tests used, which were insensitive to the cultural and subcultural differences they were supposedly investigating. Nevertheless the findings fitted in closely with prevailing professional assumptions at the time. To reject a 'deficit in early experience' model seemed to lead to a 'genetic' model, which was not generally acceptable. Accordingly, the 'deficit' model gained acceptance, and individually funded preschool programmes were developed in an attempt to improve children's early cognitive and linguistic skills, *before* school entry. Well-known examples in the USA are seen in the work of Gray and Klaus (1965), Bereiter and Engelmann (1966), Deutsch (1967), and Blank and Solomon (1968).

At first these programmes seemed to be having some success (Weikart, 1967). Pressure had been building up for more nationwide action in the USA and President Johnson's administration started the Headstart Program in 1965. By 1967 some 2 million children had participated in Headstart in a wide variety of programmes, short and long, structured and less structured, across the length and breadth of the USA. In Britain, following the Plowden Report of 1967, similar steps were taken on a much smaller scale, notably in the 'Educational Priority Areas' designed in 1972. By this time, however, longer-term evaluations of the intervention programmes in the USA suggested less permanent success than psychologists had hoped for; and the Westinghouse Report (Cicirelli, 1969) and evaluation of results achieved at a hundred Headstart centres documented reasonably conclusively the failure of Headstart to give any permanent benefit to the children experiencing the programmes. Compared with matched controls, the children in general showed some benefit in the first grade at school, but none at all by the third grade.

The failure of Headstart shattered the pre-existing consensus in the USA and led to a fragmentation of aims and ideals in compensatory education and educational reform. Jensen (1969) claimed that the failure of intervention made a genetic theory of educational disadvantage more plausible. Other psychologists decided that the Headstart intervention programmes had not been early enough, intensive enough, or sustained enough (Hellmuth, 1970). Early day-care programmes for disadvantaged children were advocated, together with Follow Through programmes after the preschool intervention period. The deficit model now also received a fundamental challenge from those who claimed that lower-income or minority group children had a *different* subculture, expressed in a different set of competences, which should not be regarded as a deficient. The work of Labov (1970) on non-standard negro English dialect and on aspects of negro society in the ghetto was one of the inspirations for this viewpoint, expressed forcibly also by Baratz and Baratz (1970).

Other writers accepted many criticisms made by the difference theorists, without completely rejecting a deficit model and thereby according equal valuation to all conditions of child-rearing in contemporary industrial society. Whatever failing there was, however, was now located as much in wider aspects of society, such as the inequality of housing conditions and income, as in aspects of mother–child interaction. Furthermore, as subcultural differences were indeed a reality, any intervention programme would have to be very cautiously and carefully initiated to avoid charges of paternalism and authoritarianism (Cole and Bruner, 1971; Tulkin, 1972). This viewpoint also focussed on the need to approach directly other societal aspects of inequality, rather than simply rely on compensatory education as a universal panacea. Indeed Jencks *et al.* (1972) claimed that educational reform to bring about equality of school achievement would have little effect on other aspects of inequality, which must be tackled separately. However, as Jencks admits, as yet there is consensus only on the need to move towards equality in school achievement, and this may still be the most malleable area for change in the near future.

There is no scope in this introductory chapter to pursue further the implications of these different viewpoints. The relevant point here is that through the last two decades this debate led directly to renewed consideration of the value of different kinds of preschool experience and institutionalised programmes, and the setting up of many preschool centres. More indirectly, it probably helped to bring about a refocussing on child development as an important field of research. Certainly during the later 1960s developmental psychology experienced an upswing in productivity as well as a revitalisation from different sources. In the USA, for example, a number of new journals appeared – the *Journal of Experimental Child Psychology* (1964), *Headstart Newsletter* (1966), *Child Study Journal* (1970), *Child Psychology and Human Development* (1970), *Child Care Quarterly* (1971), *Day Care and Child Development Reports* (1971), *Journal of Clinical Child Psychology* (1972), *Journal of Abnormal Child Psychology* (1973) *History of Childhood Quarterly* (1973), and *Journal of Child Language* (1974); and outside the USA, the *International Journal of Early Childhood* (1969), and *Early Child Development and Care* (1971). In Britain the Developmental Section of the British Psychological Society was founded in 1973 and quickly became an important and lively focus of activity.

Much of the new work in child development, and especially within the preschool age range, was concerned either with the different abilities of children from different backgrounds, or with the effects of different preschool environments. The latter were evaluated by a conventional pre-test–post-test paradigm, using tests of cognitive and linguistic achievement. The limitations of this approach will be discussed later in a consideration of post-war classroom research. In some of the studies on children's abilities, however, there was a gradual reintroduction of naturalistic observational methods. For example, Smilansky (1968) and Eifermann (1970) used direct observation of children's play in kindergarten and school playgrounds in Israel in investigations of social class differences in fantasy and sociodramatic play. Studies began of young children's language, using recordings of natural language in the home context (e.g. Nelson, 1973; Martlew *et al.*, 1978). Some such investigations are directly concerned with social class differences (e.g. Wootton, 1974). More general observational studies of social class and racial differences in mother–child interaction in the home were made (Lewis and Wilson, 1972; Tulkin and Kagan, 1972; Clarke-Stewart, 1973).

Another major debate which helped to revitalise developmental psychology and also encouraged naturalistic methodology was started with the publication of Bowlby's important monograph *Maternal Care and Mental Health* (1951). Again a wartime phenomenon, the experience of homeless and refugee children separated from their parents, or of orphans placed into institutionalised care, led to renewed concern with early childhood experience – in this case with early social and emotional experience rather than with the early cognitive and linguistic experience emphasised in the compensatory education debate. Bowlby's early statements about the essential need for a young child to have a continuous relationship with one permanent mother-figure is now widely believed to be an over-statement (Rutter, 1972; Tizard and Rees, 1975); but it was only shown to be so on the basis of further detailed research on mother–child interaction and on institutional care, which Bowlby's work did much to stimulate. A combination of experimental method and naturalistic home observation has been used by Ainsworth and her co-workers (Ainsworth, 1973; Ainsworth *et al.*, 1974) in their programme of research on the nature of early attachment relationships. And similarly, observation of ongoing interactions, as well as the use of standardised tests, has been employed by the Tizards in a comparison of the experiences and abilities of children in different residential children's homes (Tizard *et al.*, 1972, Tizard, J., 1974). These are only examples in a great body of research in these areas.

Yet another influence in contemporary child development research has been that of ethological methodology. In fact Bowlby (1957) was one of the first to suggest the use of ethological approaches to child development, though primarily thinking of the use of concepts such as 'innate releasing mechanism' and 'imprinting'. These ideas were taken up by others, such as Gray (1958) and Freedman (1961). However, some of these earlier ethological concepts were already being superseded, especially in the study of mammalian behaviour (Hinde, 1959a; Brown, 1964). More significant was the importance the ethologists gave to an initial phase of naturalistic observation, before controlled experiments could usefully be conducted to provide meaningful and relevant results. In an initial phase of unstructured observation the typical behaviour patterns of species could be identified, and a behaviour catalogue or *ethogram* constructed. More systematic observation, perhaps combined with experiment, could elucidate the way behaviours were combined in temporal sequence, the situational context of behaviours, and their motivational significance. Also important was an emphasis on the evolution of behaviour and the function of behaviour patterns in the adaptation of species members to their habitat (Hinde, 1959b; Tinbergen, 1969).

The later 1950s and the 1960s saw a rapid, indeed exponential, growth in ethological studies of primates (Altmann, 1965). Two specialist journals, *Primates* and *Folia Primatologica*, were started in 1957 and 1963 respectively. Here, ethological methods were proving useful in the understanding of social structure and communication in species with a high degree of behavioural complexity. The relation of social structure to ecology was also receiving attention (Crook, 1970). The utilisation of ethological techniques for the study of human beings seemed a natural development; and it is perhaps not surprising that the majority of ethological studies of human behaviour have been with young children (Smith, 1974a). Groups of preschool children are easy to observe, and they have to be watched (rather than interviewed) for social structure and motivation to be really understood.

Child ethology has had several strands which soon became interwoven. In Britain, Blurton Jones (1967) commenced observations of nursery school children, and a few years later (1972) was able to edit a book, *Ethological Studies of Children's Behaviour*, which brought together contributions from a number of British research workers. In Germany, Eibl-Eibesfeldt (1970) was developing ethological studies, and in the USA, Ainsworth and others were adopting an explicitly ethological approach in their observation of mother–child interaction.

In the 1970s communication between human ethologists in different countries became more organised. 1973 saw the first of a series of International Human Ethology Workshops, and 1974 the start of the informal *Human Ethology Newsletter*. *Behavioural Ecology and Sociobiology* started publication in 1976, and *Ethology and Sociobiology* in 1979. It became clear that human ethology was potentially a wide, multi-disciplinary area of investigation, with close links with biosocial anthropology and with sociobiology (Fox and Fleising, 1976; Barkow, 1977). Nevertheless much of the ongoing research still involved observational work with young children. Particularly relevant here were the ethologists' attempts to categorise behaviour in well-defined physical terms, and the use once again of systematic behaviour-sampling techniques.

Two other areas of research might have interacted with ethological – developmental methodology, but to date have done so to a very limited extent, if at all. These are classroom research within educational psychology, and ecological psychology.

One possible approach in educational research is to make direct observations of classroom behaviour. Clearly many of the methodological problems in observing behaviour in primary school classrooms would be similar to those of observing behaviour in nursery schools. In fact the two practices have very different traditions lying behind them. As mentioned earlier, observations in nursery schools were carried out by child psychologists in the 1930s, and again by child psychologists and ethologists in the 1970s. In both cases perhaps the major emphasis was on social and emotional relationships among the children, and the relatively unstructured regime of nursery schools was conducive to making such investigations. By contrast, most observational classroom research by psychologists interested in education has, until recently, been carried out in primary schools in the United States. During the 1960s, when methodologies were being developed, teaching was by traditional 'chalk and talk' or teacher-focussed methods. The main interest was not on children's experience or social life in school, but on the efficiency of the school in terms of educational productivity. Most observational research was on the related problems of teacher effectiveness and classroom climate (Bealing, 1973; Gordon and Jester, 1973). A series of publications (Simon and Boyer, 1967, 1970a, b) details 92 observational systems which have been developed, 73 of which are for use in classrooms; but only seven of these focus on pupils, as distinct from teachers or teacher–pupil contacts (Boydell, 1975).

Observational classroom research has been reviewed comprehensively by Medley and Mitzel (1963), and Rosenshine and Furst (1973); clearly much thought has gone into devising methods of behaviour sampling and categorisation, quite independently of similar work by ethologists (e.g. Smith and Connolly, 1972; Altmann, 1974). Many of the observational systems use 'high- inference' categories; one example, Flander's influential interaction analysis model of teacher behaviour, uses categories such as 'teacher accepts pupil feeling', or 'silence or confusion'. As with the observational categories employed by child psychologists in the 1930s, these categories seem to be insufficiently distanced from the phenomena to allow much possibility of new insights, and are unlikely to be well understood by observers in different cultural contexts (Smith and Connolly, 1972). Other criticisms of interaction analysis have been made by Hamilton and Delamont (1974), who point out that there has been another tradition in American classroom research which they label 'anthropological'. Whereas interaction analysis involves non-participant observation using a behaviour-category system, an anthropological approach (e.g. Smith and Geoffrey, 1968) generally involves participant observation, and aims at a wider and more perceptive account of the total classroom experience. 'The observer immerses himself in their world, discovering how they see it' (Hamilton and Delamont, 1974, p. 7).

From an ethological perspective, it might seem that an 'anthropological' approach would be an optimal first stage in classroom description, to be followed by a more detailed analysis of selected aspects by means of categorising and sampling behaviour, and by other means such as interviews and self-reports. As Hamilton and Delamont point out, however, the two traditions in the USA have remained almost entirely separate, with no debate going on between them. In Britain approaches have been less polarised, and in addition British infant schools have been less structured and more 'child centred' than their American counterparts. Classroom research in British schools has recently been diverse, but receptive to new influences and methodologies (Chanan and Delamont, 1975).

A great deal of the nursery school and kindergarten research instigated by the Headstart movement in the USA was, however, influenced by the interests of classroom researchers there at the time. Of the many evaluations of differing preschool programmes and regimes in the 1960s, almost all followed a pre-test–post-test paradigm. The pre- and post-tests were of cognitive and linguistic abilities as measured by standard tests. There were generally no ongoing observations of the experiences of children and teachers during the programmes, and little or no assessment of the impact of the programmes on children's social or emotional development. Such work may appear satisfactory in terms of an *educational productivity* assessment, but appear deficient by wider criteria. In a review of early education programmes, Beller (1973) notes that important and neglected methodological points have been: the need for long-term follow up, the use of multiple criteria in evaluation, and the taking into account of individual differences between children in evaluating the effects of preschool experience. He particularly notes that very little research has related teacher technique or preschool regime to measures of socio-emotional functioning in the children.

Not all American classroom research has been concerned with productivity measures, and in addition to the 'anthropological' tradition, and related to it, has been work influenced by the methods of ecological psychology. As proposed by Wright (1967) and Barker (1968), ecological psychology involves the delineation of behaviour settings and the descriptions of behaviour within these settings, primarily using diary or narrative records to record the 'stream of behaviour'.

Some applications of ecological psychology to education have concentrated on comparisons between school settings. For example, Barker and Gump (1964) compared large and small schools in this way. For smaller-scale studies a weakness of some of the ecological psychology research has been a lack of techniques for recording behaviour sequences, as compared with recording behaviour settings. Narrative or diary records cannot cope with the total behaviour of even one person, and must therefore be selective. This being so, it is desirable to have an explicit system of behaviour categories so that the inevitable selection of behaviours is clearly appreciated. Indeed diary records were rejected by child psychologists as early as the 1920s for just these reasons (Arrington, 1931). Nevertheless more detailed techniques are being developed, and the approach has been usefully applied in studies in classrooms, for example, in characterising lesson settings and in examining the influence of classroom design (Kounin and Gump, 1974). One strength of the ecological approach has been its emphasis on the influence of the environment (both physical and social) on behaviour, appreciably before 'environmental psychology' became a strong focus of interest (Proshansky *et al.*, 1970). However, relatively little research has been carried out on the physical environment as it affects behaviour in the preschool. Much of the research that has been done has been on the effects of space and crowding on nursery school children (Smith, 1974b). This work was influenced not only by environmental psychology, but also by research on the effects of crowding on animals, and in some cases ethological recording techniques were employed.

Preschool provision: the present situation in Britain

It has been recent government policy in Britain to expand nursery and preschool provision (Department of Education and Science, 1973), and there is general public and professional consensus on the desirability of doing so, although at present progress has been halted on economic grounds. The increasing trend for more married women, including more women with young children, to seek part- or full-time employment (Social Trends, 1974) can only reinfoce this consensus, leaving aside the arguments concerning compensatory education on which much of the professional case for nursery school expansion rested until recently. Where consensus is markedly lacking is on what kind of preschool facilities should be provided. A review by Tizard (1975) identified a number of areas of current controversy. The general aims of group institutional care for preschool children are still in doubt and are still being questioned. Is the main aim one of social development, as suggested by a sample of nursery school teachers (Taylor *et al.*, 1972)? Is it one of cognitive stimulation? Is it mainly to relieve harrassed mothers in confined housing quarters (Brown *et al.*, 1975), or to involve mothers (and fathers) in 'parent education'? Should preschool care be 'professionalised', or parental involvement welcomed? Would neighbourhood groups, or nursery schools, or comprehensive preschool centres be most desirable? How important is the structuring of activities in the preschool, compared with letting children have free rein in the choice of activities? How important is 'play' compared with 'instruction' in development? What kinds of physical resources and staffing ratios does a preschool institution need? These are all real and serious problems which interrelate with one another, with the values of our society and of different groups within it, and with the needs, abilities, and interests of children with different personalities and different backgrounds.

In our opinion preschool research will continue to demand and deserve concentrated effort on the part of child psychologists and educationalists until at least some greater degree of consensus and knowledge is obtained than prevails at present. In the rest of this book we present research which bears on some of these issues, necessarily only a few since the field is vast.

Plan of the book

The research we report was carried out with the help of a play-group for preschool age children which we established in Sheffield. In most respects this was an ordinary preschool playgroup, but it was possible for us to alter systematically aspects of the physical and social environment in the playgroup, and monitor the effects of these changes on the children. This possibility lent itself to certain kinds of enquiry and certain kinds of methodology. The general methodological outlook we adopted, together with details of the playgroup organisation, are given in Chapter 2. Briefly, we used what we believe to be a fruitful and unusual combination of quite precise experimental manipulations with a broad range of assessment, including a pronounced emphasis on the direct observation of behaviour in the different environments created for the children. The ability to vary environmental conditions in a much more closely controlled fashion than has usually been possible in preschool research implies a much enhanced possibility of making precise causal inferences from the particular environmental change, to the changes in the children's behaviour. However, because we were testing for the general effects of environmental variation rather than for very specific hypotheses, a wide-ranging assessment seemed desirable. The assessment was in the main ongoing; that is, it monitored the immediate changes in the children's experience and behaviour when placed in differing environments. It was of wide range in the sense that we intended to collect information on changes in the children's social groupings, their friendly and aggressive behaviours, kinds of motor activity, choices of toys or activities, and where appropriate on measures such as attention span and cognitive and linguistic performance. In making observations we mainly used low-inference categories, aiming to build up an overall picture of the effects of environmental variation from the resultant pattern of effects on a wide range of simple, but clearly defined, behaviour units. Here we have been greatly influenced by the ethological approach and indeed have utilised behaviour units which other ethological investigators have also used. In this sense the method of behaviour categorisation was highly structured, but hopefully the range of possible inferences from the results has not been too narrowly determined. There is admittedly a corresponding risk of missing out more subtle or complex processes, where observer inference plays a more important and subjective part. We believe, however, that in the preschool situation, and for the kinds of experimental variables we were investigating, the procedure adopted was the most satisfactory, given the inevitable constraints of time and manpower within which any investigation is carried out.

The most substantial investigation – actually a combination of two studies – concerns the relative influence of number of children and resources available to them on behaviour in the playgroup. In free play we took the most important resources to be the amount of space available for the children to play in and the amount of play equipment for them to play with. Previous work on these variables is reviewed in Chapter 3. As part of our research programme we carried out a study in which the number of children attending the playgroup on different days was varied, while holding the resources per child constant. This is described in Chapter 4. We also investigated the effects of the amounts of space and play equipment in playgroups of constant size, and these studies are described in Chapter 5. The combination of these two sets of studies allows inferences to be made about the effect of three variables – number of children, amount of resources, and resource density.

Two smaller studies complemented these larger ones. In one we compared the behavioural consequences of a sharp contrast in the kind of play equipment available to the children; on some sessions mostly small manipulative toys were available, on others, mainly large apparatus. A second study examined the effects at different group size levels of more extreme spatial variations than were carried out in our initial study. This was in response to a lack of marked effects of spatial variation in the first investigation, coupled with a published report (Loo, 1972) suggesting that more extreme variations might have greater consequences. These studies are all described in Chapter 6. The results of all these studies on the physical environment of the preschool are put together and compared with previous work in Chapter 7.

All the above-mentioned research was carried out in a free-play setting in which the children were allowed to choose their own activities without direction from the playgroup staff. We considered that this setting offered the greatest potential for finding and assessing immediate behavioural effects on the children of variations in numbers of other children and resources available. However, many nurseries and preschools adopt a more structured or directive approach to children's activities, and this difference in itself is a matter of controversy. The history of research in this area is reviewed in Chapter 8. As another facet of our research programme, we made a sustained attempt to compare and assess these two kinds of preschool organisation. Two separate but closely matched groups of children experienced the two kinds of regime, with the same staff and premises and broadly the same equipment. The experiment was continued for two terms. Pre- and post-testing of cognitive and linguistic skills in the children were carried out, but even more attention was paid to the immediate effects of the two programmes on the children – on the process as much as on the product. Besides observing the children's social groupings, behaviours, and choice of activities as before, special attention was also paid to aggressive behaviour, fantasy play, and the attention span of the children at activities. In addition, observations were made of staff verbalisations to children, and ratings of the staff's impressions of the two systems were obtained. This research is described in Chapter 9.

The structured kind of preschool setting was used again in combination with the variations in number of children mentioned earlier. In this more instructional setting, the interest focussed more logically on staff–child interaction at different staff:child ratios, rather than on the children's own social groupings. Therefore, experimental variations in the number of staff present were also introduced. Data collection in the main concentrated on the amount, kind, and distribution of verbal contacts between staff and children, although child-focussed records were also obtained, as well as staff ratings of the different conditions. A number of different staff:child ratios were examined over the two terms of investigation. The results are discussed in Chapter 10. The findings of this and the previous study are put together and compared with earlier work in Chapter 11.

We believe that this body of research should be of considerable interest and relevance to child psychologists and those interested in preschool education. Some of the work will also be of particular interest to those psychologists concerned with the effects of crowding on behaviour. In most of the investigation we endeavoured to make the results more generalisable by duplicating the research with two independent groups of children – a procedure which generally gave satisfactory and consistent results. Nevertheless there are clearly limitations to the extent to which any research findings can be generalised, and this is important in evaluating the implications for preschool practice and design. There are also issues to be discussed in the interpretation of findings, particularly with reference to theory, and the design of future investigations. Together with a summary of the research findings, these will be found in Chapter 12.

2 Research philosophy and methods

This chapter describes the setting up of the experimental preschool playgroup on which the research was carried out. Before presenting the details of the experimental design and observation techniques, two questions which governed our choice of them must be considered. How natural are the setting and the behaviour observed in it, and what inferences and generalisations can be made from the results?

Observation and experiment

With much psychological research, a compromise has to be sought between a realistic, ecologically valid setting, and the well-defined experimental control of variables. This is especially so in social and in developmental psychology. Only precise experimental manipulation of one or a few independent variables can allow a clear causal inference to changes in the dependent variables, but often this experimental control means that the research is carried out in unnatural circumstances with a highly selected subject population. For example, when student volunteers participate in an experiment in a university laboratory, generalisation to real-life phenomena, however clear the inferences from the experiment itself, remains questionable (Chapanis, 1967). The experimenter may have examined only a small subset of the important dependent variables. In consequence, the obtained results may not hold true outside the particular limited range of variation of the independent variables, in the experimental conditions. Also, the subjects in the experiment may not be representative of the wider population to which generalisation is being attempted. Indeed the subjects' awareness of being part of an experiment may lead to their producing responses or behaviours which they feel are required or are appropriate (Orne, 1962).

On the other hand, non-interventive research has its own draw-backs. While the dangers of prematurely delimiting the field of enquiry or obtaining artificial results are avoided, there is a limit to the extent to which one can make sound inferences about cause–effect relationships in the

21

phenomena under investigation. This is important when one is seeking to make generalisations. For example, Galle *et al.* (1972) sought to relate indicators of social pathology to indicators of crowding in urban areas. The correlational data obtained were subjected to very sophisticated analysis, such that the final conclusions were a complex reinterpretation of the raw correlations; yet still further analysis can produce further reinterpretation (McPherson, 1975). Generally, data gathered from a variety of real-life situations which vary in numerous and uncontrolled ways give a confused picture of causal relationships; there is consequently more danger of the researcher getting the results he 'expects', given the variety of different analytic techniques which he can apply to the data.

This dilemma is just as troublesome in research with young children as in other areas of psychology. Much experimental work on aggression in children, for instance, has used rather artificial situations. For example, one child in a laboratory can press a button to prevent another child doing well in a marble game (Hoving *et al.*, 1974). This assures tight control of some variables, but the situation is remote from natural contexts in which aggression occurs. Furthermore, some such experimental investigations may not even be studying aggression. Blurton Jones (1972b) has suggested that studies of the imitation of aggression in children, such as those by Bandura *et al.* (1961, 1963) and Nelson *et al.* (1969), may be eliciting rough-and-tumble play rather than aggression.

Much can be learnt about aggression in children by simply observing and recording in nurseries and playgroups, as was done in the 1930s and again, using more highly developed ethological techniques, in the last few years. In particular, the typical patterns and contexts of aggressive behaviour and the relationship of aggression to dominance and other aspects of the social structure of a children's group can be established (McGrew, 1972; Abramovich, 1976; Hold, 1976; Sluckin and Smith, 1977). However, the influence of other factors is difficult to ascertain.

Jersild and Markey (1935), in a classic study of aggression in children, made a detailed study of three nursery schools. The frequency of aggressive behaviour differed considerably in the three settings. The three schools differed in several respects – the amount of space provided, the background of the children, the age–sex composition of the group, and the behaviour of the adult staff. In Jersild and Markey's book, and more especially in some later texts, it is implied if not definitely stated that, for example, their results showed aggression to be greater in a smaller space. However, as space was confounded with several other factors this is not a legitimate inference.

In the work reported here we have sought to escape this particular dilemma. A study of environmental differences and behavioural differences among a wide variety of preschool institutions would have been possible, but, as with Jersild and Markey's study (1935), drawing precise conclusions would have been difficult. Indeed, some of our earlier work had come up against just this difficulty (Connolly and Smith, 1972; Smith, 1972). Some years before this research project, we started work on developing techniques of observing and recording behaviour in preschool children and on obtaining baseline data on the kinds of behaviour and activities seen in children of different sexes and ages. We found interesting differences in the behaviour of children both within preschools (according to whether they played indoors or outdoors) and between different kinds of preschools (day nurseries, nursery schools, and playgroups). But the differences could have been due to a variety of factors, such as the space and equipment provided, staff training and behaviour, number of children, their home background, length of stay in the nursery, and so on. It was impossible to sort out the individual influences of these different factors.

Some of these variables – such as resources provided and numbers of children – are clearly very amenable to planned variation, and this can also be attempted with other factors such as the behaviour of the staff with the children. However, it would be difficult if not impossible to attempt tight experimental control of such factors in pre-existing preschool institutions. We therefore decided to start a preschool playgroup in which such experimental variations could be carried out. In doing so, we attempted to make the playgroup as natural a setting as possible, to avoid the usual limitations of experimental studies. In most respects the playgroup which we started was an entirely typical one. Children from mixed socio-economic backgrounds met in a church hall, under the supervision of three trained staff, and with the usual selection of nursery equipment. Two independent playgroups were established, meeting on different weekdays. Apart from the variations in space, equipment, numbers of children, and patterns of staff interaction with children, the research was non-interventive, with data being gathered by non-participant observers. The parents of the children were regularly informed of our research plans by a newsletter and through parents' meetings, but, as with many preschools, they did not stay with the children during their mornings at the playgroup. The children themselves seemed to accept the playgroup as it was in each session, and seldom if ever commented to the staff on changes introduced. While clearly there are still possible drawbacks to this experimental arrangement (discussed further in Chapter 12), we feel confident that we succeeded in running two playgroups which in all important respects were natural ones, while still retaining experimental control over the variables we were interested in.

Setting up the playgroup

The first year

The experimental playgroup was established in a church hall, situated about one mile from the University in Sheffield, and was named St Augustine's after the church. It was registered with the Local Authority, regularly visited by a playgroup advisor, and affiliated to the Preschool Playgroups Association. The hall was large (about 2,000 sq. ft), rectangular, and most suitable for the spatial variations which were planned. The vicar of St Augustine's felt that there was a need for a playgroup in the area, and indeed there had been some attempts to start one earlier, but these had failed because of lack of funds. It seemed unlikely that there would be difficulty in finding sufficient local children to enable the playgroup to run. On one side lay a densely populated district of terraced housing, on the other side an area of semi-detached and detached housing.

For the first year of the research programme we intended to vary the space and equipment available. Given the area of the hall and the recommended minimum spatial density of 25 sq. ft per child suggested by the Local Authority, we were able, with 24 children in each of our two groups, to vary the space available to provide 25, 50, or 75 sq. ft per child (see Chapter 5).

The establishment of the playgroup was widely announced by local advertisements in shops, doctors' surgeries, and in the parish newsletter. Parents answering the advertisements were sent a standard registration form, and a letter explaining the research purposes of the playgroup. Children whose parents returned the form were put on the waiting list. During the summer of 1971, when the programme began, there were about eighty children on the waiting list. Their home backgrounds were quite varied, although few, if any, would have been classed as severely disadvantaged or coming from problem homes. Having received a research grant from the Social Science Research Council, we were able to obtain equipment for the playgroup, employ experienced staff, and charge parents only a nominal fee of 5 pence a morning to cover the cost of milk and biscuits. (Usual playgroup charges at the time were 15–25 pence a morning.) We were thus able to offer attractive facilities at a cost which few parents would have found a deterrent.

From the eighty children on the waiting list two groups of 24 children were selected to start the playgroup in September 1971. Since none of these children was known to us, the selection from the waiting list was essentially random. Tight constraints were exercised, however, on the age and sex distributions in the two groups. Children below the age of 2 years 4 months were not accepted, and nor were children older than 4 years, as we did not want to take children who would leave for school before the end of the first year. (Sheffield at the time had a 'rising fives' policy – children started school at the beginning of the term in which their fifth birthday fell.) Each group of 24 children was to consist of 12 boys and 12 girls, and we endeavoured to match for age across the sexes, and across the two groups, to within one or two months. The ages of the children, together with further details obtained from the registration form (occupation of parents, number of siblings), are given in Appendix A.

One group (Group One) met on Tuesday and Thursday mornings, and the other group (Group Two) on Wednesday and Friday mornings during school terms. Like many other playgroups, St Augustine's Playgroup was open from 9.00 a.m. to 12.00 noon. A regular routine was followed. Parents and children arrived between 9.00 and 9.25. Apart from any settling in required for new children at the beginning of a year, parents were asked to leave by 9.30. From 9.30 until 10.15 the children were engaged in 'free play' with the equipment provided, and observations were made. From 10.15 until 11.00 there was a milk break for the children; they formed a circle with the staff, who handed out milk and biscuits, told stories, and sang songs. After a visit to the toilet, children were back for 11.00. From 11.00 to 11.45 there was another free-play period during which more observations were made. Parents collected their children between 11.45 and 12 noon. This routine continued largely unchanged throughout the three years, although the precise nature of the play periods was subject to variation.

The Local Authority regulations required that three adults be present to supervise the 24 children in each group. Three women were recruited through advertisement and interview. One was appointed supervisor, the other two as assistants. All had some previous experience with playgroups or teaching in schools, although none had specific nursery training.

A variety of equipment was purchased for the playgroup. These were the usual kinds of playgroup equipment – climbing-frames, Wendy houses, tricycles, prams and dolls, jigsaws, blocks, and so on. Further details of the equipment used in each project are given in later chapters.

The second year

The investigations carried out during the second year of the project were designed to examine the effects of differences in the typical manner of interaction between staff and children (Chapter 9). By the summer of 1972, however, the playgroup had to vacate the old church hall, because the land was being redeveloped for housing. We were offered the use of a Scout hut a few hundred yards away. These premises were somewhat smaller – about 1,200 sq. ft – but this was not important since no further spatial variations were planned for this year. In other respects the premises were very suitable, being lighter and more modern than the church hall.

Our supervisor of the first year resigned to take a teacher-training course. We appointed a new supervisor who had had specific nursery school training and experience; we judged this to be important for the effective execution of the variations in regime which were planned. The two assistants employed during the first year remained, though one had to leave during the second term (March 1973) because she was expecting a baby. A new assistant was appointed for the remainder of the school year.

Since some children had left for school at the end of the summer (1972), new children were recruited for September 1972 when the second year of the programme began. A few children left at Christmas 1972, and these were not included in our main sample which consisted of 22 children in each group. Further details of the children are given in Appendix A. The project ran over the first two terms of the year. At Easter 1973 more children left for school, and further children were recruited so that they would settle in for the research planned during the third year.

In order to cover increased costs, and especially to get new toys and equipment needed this year, the daily fee was raised to 10 pence. This was still very cheap compared with the charges at other playgroups.

The third year

During the third school year, studies were made on the effects of varying the number of children in the playgroup (Chapters 4 and 10). Children left each term for school, and the naturally falling size of the groups was utilised in the experimental design. In addition to the two original groups of children, other children (Group Three) attended on Wednesday and Thursday mornings, to give the requisite variations in size of group. Further details of this design are given in Chapter 4.

As we intended to vary space and equipment commensurately with group size, it was important to use large premises again. Fortunately the conversion work on the church was completed and the new church hall was available to us. The new hall had a spacious design with an area of over 2,000 sq. ft, so large groups could be accommodated in the experimental design.

During the first term of the third year (September–December 1973)

Table 2.1. *Timetable of research projects*

First year		
September 1971–June 1972	Old church hall	Variations in amounts of space and of play equipment (Chapter 5)
June 1972	Old church hall	Variations in kinds of play equipment (Chapter 6)
July 1972	Old church hall	Further variations in amount of play equipment (Chapter 6)
Second year		
September 1972–April 1973	Scout hut	Variations in patterns of staff interaction with children (Chapter 9)
May–July 1973	Scout hut	No active research. New children settled in prior to next project
Third year		
September–December 1973	New church hall	Variations in numbers of children (Chapter 4) and staff–child ratio (Chapter 10)
January–April 1974	New church hall	Variations in numbers of children (Chapter 4) and staff–child ratio (Chapter 10)
April–July 1974	New church hall	Variations in numbers of children (Chapter 4) and amount of space (Chapter 6)

Groups One and Two had 20 and 22 children respectively and Group Three had 12. During the second term (January–April 1974) each of the three groups had 14 children. During the third term (April–July 1974) Groups One, Two, and Three had 12, 11, and 23 children respectively. Further details of the children are given in Appendix A.

A new supervisor was appointed for the third year; she had previous experience in supervising a nursery class and held an NNEB[1] certificate. The temporary assistant appointed at the end of the second year left to take up a teaching appointment, and a new assistant was appointed. The third assistant remained with us over the whole three-year period.

The fee charged during the third year remained at 10 pence. Throughout the period we maintained a long waiting list, although during the third year

[1] Nursery Nurse Education Board.

it was much longer for girls; almost all the boys on the list were given places.

Throughout the three years of the research we were fortunate in maintaining high attendances by the children. These averaged 85–90 per cent; detailed figures are given in later sections. We attributed this to the low charge and to the good relationship between researchers, parents, and staff. Besides frequent informal meetings with the playgroup staff, we also held regular (usually termly) parents' evenings at which the researchers gave an account of their work, the research was discussed, refreshments were served, and videotapes of the children playing were shown.

During the last term of the third year, as the research drew to a close, we consulted with the vicar of the church and held a number of meetings with parents to discuss the future of the playgroup. We were pleased that the playgroup was able to continue, although a higher fee had to be charged. A committee was elected to run the playgroup, and it is now run successfully by the parents, while continuing to have close and friendly links with the University.

A summary of the timetabling of different projects is given in Table 2.1.

Two independent groups

In most of the projects reported here, the same series of environmental variations was presented to the two independent groups of children recruited to the playgroup. This was the case with the studies on numbers of children in the group (Chapter 4), and those on amount of space and amount of play equipment (Chapters 5 and 6). Only in the project investigating different modes of staff interaction with children (preschool regime) were the two groups in different experimental conditions (Chapter 9). This is one reason why, for this study more than for the others, the confidence with which we can generalise our findings to other contexts is limited.

Running two independent groups was a deliberate choice, designed to avoid a mistake which has often been made in the past. Many of the earlier studies on behaviour in playgroups, or in interacting groups generally, have examined *one* group, and tested for significance of differences in behaviour using children's scores as units for statistical analysis. For example, this approach has been a standard one in examining sex differences in behaviour. Children are observed in a nursery, and the separate scores of boys and of girls, on a category such as 'aggressive behaviour', are compared; the significance of any difference between the scores of boys and girls is examined using a *t* test or Mann–Whitney test. Similarly, a few earlier studies have examined effects of environmental variations on one group of preschool children, comparing children's scores in different environments (Hutt and Vaizey, 1966; Bates, 1970; McGrew, 1972; Preiser, 1972).

A 'significant' difference is generally taken to imply a degree of confidence with which a similar result could be expected, with different children selected from the same subject population as the original sample. However, this canot be done in studies of the kind just mentioned because statistical tests (such as the *t* test or Mann–Whitney test) embody the assumption that the unit scores fed into the analysis are themselves independent. In a social group, this assumption is certainly violated; by definition, the individuals in a group are interacting, and therefore the behaviour of one individual may influence that of another. A statistical test on data from children in a single group will therefore overestimate the degree of confidence with which to extrapolate to other groups. The theoretically more correct procedure is to study a large number of groups, and to use group means instead of (or as well as) individual means for the purposes of statistical analysis.

Sex differences in aggressive behaviour provide an illustrative example. Suppose a playgroup contains one very aggressive boy, whereas the other boys and girls in the group are, in his absence, only as aggressive as each other. Let us assume, fairly plausibly, that the aggressive boy plays more with other boys than with girls; and that his own aggressive behaviour potentiates aggressive behaviour in those children he plays with. We might well then obtain a 'significant' sex difference in aggressive behaviour, for which in fact one boy was, in a sense, responsible. While valid *for that group*, generalisation to other groups should not be at the level of confidence statistically predicted; another group might not contain a very aggressive boy (or might have a very aggressive girl instead) and the likelihood of these possibilities cannot be calculated from data on one group only.

In order to generalise about sex differences in this respect, it would be better to obtain data on a large number of groups, even at the cost of obtaining less data for each individual group. In essence, one would be looking for replications of the single-group experiment. In Lykken's (1968) terminology, these might be literal replications, operational replications, or constructive replications. Literal replications are cases where the experimenter examines more groups, using the same observational or experimental procedures. For example, Smith and Green (1974) examined sex differences in aggressive behaviour in 15 different English preschools, using group means for analysis. If another investigation attempted to replicate these results, following the methods reported in the published article, this would constitute an operational replication. By contrast, reviews such as Oetzel

(1966), Feshbach (1970), and Maccoby and Jacklin (1974) summarise the results of a large number of different studies which use different methods and which purport to bear on 'sex differences in aggressive behaviour in children'. These constitute constructive replications.

In any particular investigation, a balance must clearly be drawn between looking at many groups superficially, or at one or a few groups in detail. Given constraints on time and manpower, this was a problem we faced at the beginning of our project. Above all, we wished to avoid a narrow or superficial choice of observational variables. We considered it essential to examine the effects of environmental change on a wide variety of indices. We thought it likely (and indeed found) that when finally evaluating the effects of playgroup environments, our results might indicate 'trade-offs' in terms of one kind of behavioural change against another.

Getting this kind of observational detail meant that it was not possible to utilise a large number of groups in this study. Such a possibility would also have been very difficult on organisational grounds. However, for the reasons given earlier, we also considered it highly desirable to avoid a situation where we had results for only one group of children. We arrived at a suitable compromise by taking two independent groups. The children were drawn from the same subject pool, and experienced the same conditions in all but one study. In Lykken's (1968) terms therefore this is a 'literal replication'.

Two groups are not many, certainly if one is taking group means as a statistic for behavioural analysis. However, although statistics derived from individual child means *do* overestimate generalisability, as indicated earlier, this does not mean that they are valueless. Especially in large groups, the effects of interactions between children are likely to be only moderate. This is because many preschool children engage in solitary or parallel play, in which there is very little interaction with, or influence on, another child's behaviour. When group play does occur, subgroups are usually of only two or three children.

The size of the groups studied was never less than ten children and was usually in excess of twenty. In these circumstances, the assumption of independence from one child to the next is not too grossly violated. It is unlikely that two children sampled in close succession will be interacting with each other. This assumption clearly holds best for those studies where the groups were largest. Our policy, then, was to treat 'significant' results seriously only when they were consistently obtained for *both* of the independent groups examined.

The importance of having two groups, although it doubled the work load, was borne out in practice in our observations that through much of the three years of the project, the two groups were perceived as different by staff and researchers, each having a distinct 'group character'. This difference was substantiated in terms of sex differences and friendship patterns in the two groups. Nevertheless, so far as environmental changes were concerned, the effects on the two groups were, more often than not, closely similar. That these same effects were obtained with two groups which in fact had different behaviour profiles contributes greatly to our confidence in the generalisability of our findings.

Data collection methods

Direct observation techniques were used as the primary means of data collection in all the studies reported in this book. In order to obtain precise quantitative data on the behaviour of individual children in the different conditions, no alternative was feasible. We have argued elsewhere (Smith and Connolly, 1972) that direct observation techniques can be a powerful research tool. However, there are a number of possible time-sampling procedures that can be followed. Altmann (1974) distinguishes seven such procedures, and we shall adopt her nomenclature here.

Ad libitum sampling consists of informal, non-systematic observations. While we did keep informal observations in a daily diary, these data were not used for analyses. This kind of sampling is sometimes supplemented by *sociometric matrix completion*, involving additional observations on certain individuals; this procedure was not necessary in our studies. Nor did we make use of *sequence sampling*, in which certain interaction sequences are watched from beginning to end, themselves determining the samples taken.

Four other kinds of procedure defined by Altmann were used. These were *focal-person sampling*, in which full details of all specified behaviours are obtained for one particular individual – the focal child or adult of that sample; *one–zero sampling*, in which only the occurrence or non-occurrence of behaviours within a sample period is noted for the child observed; *sampling all occurrences*, in which the whole group is watched and any occurrence of a particular behaviour recorded; this is also referred to as *incident sampling*; and *instantaneous scan sampling*, in which the whole group is scanned at regular intervals, particular behaviours of each individual child being sampled within a very brief time period. Further discussion of these techniques is provided in Altmann's review.

A standard method we chose was of collecting large numbers of short (40-second) modified focal-child samples on all of the children individually. A large number of behaviour categories, derived from ethological work, were used, as well as categories for choice of companions and activity. Most of the data were converted into an all-or-none or one–zero sampling form on transcription. This procedure was comprehensive and efficient, and was utilised in each of the studies we carried out, with the exception of the project on staff–child communication patterns at different staff:child ratios (Chapter 10). The choice of categories, and the rationale of the sampling technique, will be described more fully below. This method enabled us to build up average behaviour profiles on each individual, or group of children, in each kind of environmental setting, and thus to make sensitive comparisons between the behavioural effects of the settings. However, we also supplemented our data from other sources as appropriate for each of the projects. These additional methods will be summarised here, and described in more detail in connection with the particular studies where they were used.

Five supplementary observational techniques were used. In the study of amounts of space and play equipment (Chapter 5), spatial plots were made on standard record-sheets, showing the positions of children in the room, at regular intervals throughout a morning session. This enabled us to calculate the utilisation of space and the distribution of children in the different conditions.

In the project in which free-play and structured patterns of staff–child interaction were compared (Chapter 9), three additional observational techniques were used. Incident sampling (sampling all occurrences) was used to record both agonistic (aggressive and submissive) behaviour and examples of fantasy play on different occasions. Here, the whole group was watched, and any incidents of the particular behaviour were noted down in a diary-type fashion as they occurred. Categorisation was largely subsequent to observation. Although incident sampling is less reliable than focal sampling as an observational technique, it does have the advantage, for rarely occurring events such as agonistic encounters, of permitting much faster data collection.

Scan sampling was also used in this study. Regular scans (repeated at 2-minute intervals) were made of the whole group, with the choice of activity of each child recorded as rapidly as possible. This gave information on the number of activities engaged in and length of activity span for all children in the group.

Finally, focal-adult samples were made of individual playgroup staff members' conversation with children in the two regimes. We used these to check that the stated differences between the free-play and structured interaction patterns were indeed being put into practice by the staff.

In the final study on communication patterns at different staff:child ratios (Chapter 10), long and extensive focal-adult samples of staff conversations were obtained; this was indeed the primary source of data collection in this case. In addition, shorter focal-child samples were made on individual children.

Besides these additional observational techniques, three other kinds of data were obtained. These were staff reports on environmental settings, staff reports on children, and test data on the children.

In all the studies we obtained staff opinions on what they felt to be the effects of the different environmental settings on the children. In the final study (Chapter 10) some quantified ratings from the staff were also obtained.

Staff reports on the children were also quantified. At first we used repertory grid techniques, eliciting the staff's own constructs as to behavioural differences in the children. In subsequent projects we employed some of the constructs we had elicited in more standard rating procedures.

In the comparison of children in the free-play and structured settings (Chapter 9), standard tests were made on the children before and after the different staff–child interaction patterns were implemented. The tests were designed to measure cognitive and linguistic competence, and task performance.

More details of all these supplementary methods are given at relevant points in the book. The remainder of this chapter is devoted to an account of the primary source of data collection used throughout the research programme, namely, short observational samples of behaviour taken on individual children. First, direct observation and the effects of the observer will be considered. Second, the behaviour categories used will be described. Third, inter-observer agreement on the use of categories will be presented. Finally, sampling procedure will be discussed.

Direct observation and effects of observer

When short observational samples of individual children's behaviour were being obtained, it was possible to follow a child around or remain close, usually within a couple of feet. In addition, the observer could usually position himself so that the child's face and hands could be seen. The observer used a small portable cassette tape-recorder to record his observations on the child's behaviour. It was thus possible to make detailed records while continuously observing the child through the sample period.

While the use of a tape-recorder was found during pilot work to be essential for accuracy of data collection, it had the danger of being potentially more noticeable and obtrusive than pen and paper. This, together with the close following of individual children, clearly might have had effects on the behaviour one was trying to observe in the target child (the focal child for that sample). While this danger must always be borne in mind in observational studies, there are several cogent reasons for believing that the effects would be small in our research, as well as direct evidence that this was in fact the case.

The most important factor here was undoubtedly the fact that most of the data collection, and *all* the observations by the standard method of short samples on individual children, were made by one observer. The observer was therefore present at the playgroup every morning it met, almost without exception. Rather than being a stranger to the children, he was in fact very familiar to them. The word boring could be used here, because the observer deliberately tried to be uninteresting to the child, keeping interactions to a minimum. An earlier investigation of ours (Connolly and Smith, 1972) had shown that a passive observer might attract less continuing interest from children than an observer who smiled and talked to them, and that most children paid very little attention to a passive observer after five consecutive visits. Our own subsequent experience, and that of others, has suggested that being a *completely* passive observer may not be an optimal approach, as on occasion not responding to a child may cause the child to be more interested and persistent than if the observer had made a response. Complete passivity to verbal enquiry can be unnatural and unfriendly. However, it does seem true that the observer best becomes 'part of the furniture' by making only the minimal responses consistent with politeness, and not initiating any interactions himself with the children. In addition he can often convey, non-verbally, a non-interactive intent, for example, by avoiding eye contact with the children. This procedure was followed consistently in the present investigations.

The observer found that he could talk very quietly into the tape-recorder, holding the microphone close to his mouth. His speech was usually inaudible to the child he was watching. The children did of course see the observer engaged in this, indeed they were very familiar with it. One mother in fact told us that her son had been seen walking around at home, holding a stick to his mouth! However, it was very seldom that a child showed any signs of disturbance at being watched. Although an individual child might have become upset if he or she had been aware of being 'followed', the sample period – 40 seconds – was so short that this rarely if ever happened.

Generally speaking, then, the children were too busy getting on with their own activities to pay much attention to the observer. The lack of overt attention to the observer is borne out from the sample records themselves. Vocal, visual, and physical contacts with the observer were recorded, as were similar contacts with other children and with staff. Physical contacts with the observer were very infrequent indeed and vocal contacts were virtually non-existent.

The lack of contact with the observer does not of course prove that the observer's presence had no effect, although it is strong evidence for that contention. However, the observer was also able to gauge directly, as he approached a child from a distance to record a sample, whether his increased proximity seemed to alter the child's behaviour or interrupt the flow of activity. Amongst the thousands of samples obtained, this occasionally happened. In the odd sample, a child might suddenly notice the observer, stare at him for a few seconds, then either resume the activity or, very rarely, move off. Also, while the great majority of the children paid no attention to the observer whatsoever, a few were clearly somewhat more affected. This kind of individual difference has been reported previously (Connolly and Smith, 1972). The observer soon realised who these children were, and then took extra care when he was approaching them to make observations. Whereas most children could be approached rapidly and directly, the others – perhaps two or three each year – were approached more slowly and obliquely, and extra care was taken to avoid direct eye contact. This seemed to work well. Only with one child, in the first year of the project, was any consistent difficulty experienced. This child was the youngest in the group at the time, and rather solitary; he tended to monitor the observer's presence and keep some distance away. (This was also the child who walked around holding a stick to his mouth at home.) All that could be done here was to make observations from a greater distance, as unobtrusively as possible.

The few instances where the observer's presence did have an effect only serve to contrast with the vast majority of samples in which there is no reason to believe that the observer's presence had any impact on the child's behaviour. We are confident that the observer had only a very small effect on individual differences observed in the children (with perhaps the one exception mentioned above). Furthermore, there is no reason to believe that any such small effect would have differential consequences in the various environmental settings studied.

Behaviour categories

In observing the children's behaviour, three kinds of information were recorded. First, what the overall nature was of the child's social interactions, and who his companions were. Second, what toys he was using, or what general activity, if any, he was engaged in. Third, what specific behaviour the child was exhibiting or utilising in his social and non-social activities. Means of classifying and categorising these three kinds of information were developed, and in combination they provided three differing but related views of the child's overall response to his environment. Data on the child's companions and activities were recorded at the end of each short time sample. Information on the child's behaviours was recorded continuously through the sample period.

Companions

At the end of each time sample, the observer recorded the names of any children or adults with whom the target child had been engaged in group or parallel activity for the majority of the sample period. Other children were classified as 'group' companions if they interacted with the target child in the course of the activity. They were classified as 'parallel' companions if engaged in substantially the same activity as the target child, in close proximity, but without substantial interaction (Parten, 1932; Smith and Connolly, 1972). Both group and parallel companions would be noted in the same sample period. If there were no group or parallel companions for the greater part of the period, then the child was recorded as being 'alone'.

These data on companions could be used for sociometric purposes and for calculating the mean size of children's subgroups and the mean number of same-sex and opposite-sex companions. For further analysis, nine comprehensive and mutually exclusive categories were formulated. These are listed and defined in Appendix B.

Activities

At the end of each sample period, the observer recorded any toys or equipment the child had used, or any non-toy activities he or she had engaged in for any substantial time (about ten seconds or longer). For further analysis, the possible toys or activities were divided into 22 comprehensive but not mutually exclusive categories (see Appendix B). Sixteen of these categories simply referred to one toy (such as the toy telephone) or piece of equipment (such as the rocking-boat), or to a collection of similar toys (such as doll, pram, cradle, and teddy). Another category referred to the room fitments. In principle, any number of these categories could be scored in the same time sample.

Three categories – fantasy play, rough-and-tumble play, and unusual uses of apparatus – could be scored in addition to, or instead of, the other categories. Another category – miscellaneous play – was used a a 'dustbin' category for any sample period in which the child seemed actively engaged in an activity which did not fit any of the other categories. Finally, the child was scored as doing nothing if he or she was not using any toys or equipment, or was not engaged in any social interaction, for most or all of the sample period.

Behaviours

The recording of the child's behaviour posed a more difficult problem of categorisation than the recording of companions and activities. There is a myriad of ways of categorising the flow of a young child's behaviour, and many recording systems have been developed (e.g. Simon and Boyer, 1974). One requirement to be borne in mind was that the system should be reasonably comprehensive. We did not have preconceived ideas as to what the effects of the environmental changes would be; this was a fact-finding research programme, rather than the testing of specific hypotheses about particular behaviours. This suggested using quite a large number of behaviour categories, reflecting different facets of the behaviour flow such as social contacts, object use, body posture and locomotion, and so on.

Alternatively, fewer, more complex categories could have been used, such as measures of a child's cooperative behaviour or attention to tasks. In some ways this strategy seems more meaningful and appealing, but while there would have been some advantages, there were serious disadvantages as well which led us to abandon it. First, the use of more complex categories involves larger inferences on the part of the observer. It requires more time to decide whether a child has shown 'cooperative behaviour' or 'sustained task attention', than to record 'gives object to child' or 'manipulates object'. This means that, within the requirements of accurate recording, the observer can deal with many more of the simple categories than the complex ones. The use of complex categories would have meant largely sacrificing the goal of a wide and comprehensive system initially aimed for.

Second, the short sample of 40 seconds would have made it difficult to assess accurately and record more complex categories. There were other and cogent reasons for using short sample periods (see below, p. 44), so this was an important consideration.

Third, in our view it is in many ways more useful, and valid, to record a wide variety of simple behaviours and attempt to build up a more complex interpretative picture later, than to use complex categories in the first place. This is because the simple categories can be defined in more objective terms, and the reader can judge for himself whether the global interpretation subsequently made is a justifiable or plausible one. The use of more complex or inferential categories would probably mean lower levels of inter-observer agreement, unless observers were specifically trained for such agreement. As we have argued elsewhere (Smith and Connolly, 1972), the latter procedure is not entirely satisfactory. Specific training imparts more information on when a complex category (such as 'shows cooperation') is to be scored, than is presented in the written definition. But this additional information is not available to subsequent readers, and the complex categories will to that extent be less objective than the less inferential ones.

For these reasons a system of mainly simple, low-inference categories was used. Systems such as this had been developed much earlier in the United States (for example, Arrington, 1931), and several such systems had been developed and used by us in previous work in Sheffield (Smith and Connolly, 1972; Smith, 1973). Other research workers in Britain have also developed equally low-inference category lists for use with preschool children (Grant, 1969; McGrew, W. C., 1970, 1972; Blurton Jones, 1972b; Brannigan and Humphries, 1972). These lists, as well as our own, were influenced by ethological methods and by the approach to behaviour categorisation developed by researchers in animal behaviour. The animal ethologists, faced with the task of describing the behaviour of a species with which they could not communicate directly, attempted to delineate relatively invariant units of behaviour, described and defined in largely physical terms. In this way anthropomorphic interpretation by the observer could be minimised. The motivational significance of the behaviours can nevertheless be investigated by temporal, situational, and form analysis (Hinde, 1959a).

Amongst the several low-inference category lists devised for describing the behaviour of preschool children, there is some degree of consistency and overlap, although the systems differ somewhat in their level and detail of analysis and scope (Smith, 1974a). For example, Grant (1969) provides a very detailed list of facial expressions, but lacks scope in some other areas. In devising our own list of behaviour units, we endeavoured to make use of categories defined by other workers, on the basis that these distinctions had proved their utility. It seemed sensible and desirable to build on earlier established systems rather than work on devising an entirely new list. After some pilot work, the final list of behaviours – 114 in all – covered facial expressions, vocalisations, visual and physical contacts, postural and locomotor behaviours, object use, agonistic behaviours, and automanipulative and stereotypic behaviours. These behaviour 'units' were of a low-inference kind, and defined either in physical terms (e.g. open smile), or, in a few cases, in goal-orientated terms (e.g. follow adult). In some cases, noticeably with the agonistic behaviour units, some motivational inference was implicit in the definitions, but the inference was not at a high level, and the behaviours were identified on the basis of previous research, by ourselves and others, into the kinds of behaviours occurring in agonistic contexts.

The behaviour units and definitions are listed in Appendix B. Where appropriate, it has been indicated that the units are identical with, or simple composites of, units previous defined and employed by Grant (1969), McGrew, W. C. (1970), Blurton Jones (1972b), and Brannigan and Humphries (1972). Other units are similar or identical to those used previously by ourselves (Smith and Connolly, 1972; Smith, 1973). Particularly with the detailed facial expressions defined by Grant and by Branningan and Humphries, it was not found possible in pilot work with our sampling procedures to utilise the fine distinctions in their category lists. It was possible, however, to retain recording accuracy using compound units – for example, 'open smile', 'upper smile', and 'simple smile'. Here we lost the more detailed information implicit in categories such as Grant's 'wide smile' or 'lip in smile'. However, we retained what is probably the most meaningful first-order distinction between different smiles (Brannigan and Humphries, 1969), which is more useful than simply recording 'smile' as one global category.

The final list of 114 behaviour units covered a wide range of social and non-social behaviours on the part of the child. Even granted the low-inference status of the units, there would clearly be a considerable burden on the ability of the observer to deal accurately with all these units. However, several factors made this a feasible proposition.

First, the time-sample data were all recorded by one observer who became highly competent at using the category lists. Three weeks' intensive practice was carried out before data collection for the first project started.

Second, the nature of the units was such that most could be easily perceived, or reliably picked up, using the narrative record and subsequent all-or-none coding procedure. During the sample period, the observer provided a running narrative account of the child's behaviour. In providing the narrative account, the categories were borne in mind. That is, the observer made a point of incorporating in his narrative account the child's facial expressions, vocalisations, visual and physical contacts, postural or locomotor behaviour, object use, and automanipulative or stereotypic behaviours. With the exception of the last, these could all readily be incorporated in a natural narrative flow which did not unduly tax the observer's information-processing capacity. The narrative account was recorded on tape, and the behaviour units themselves were only scored subsequently, on playback and transcription.

The observer's task was eased by the fact that (with few exceptions) the occurrence of behaviour units was recorded on an all-or-none basis for the sample period. That is, a behaviour unit was checked for occurrence or non-occurrence; if a behaviour occurred, it made no difference whether it occurred once or ten times in the 40-second sample period. This meant that no decisions had to be made as to when a behaviour (such as 'open smile') finished or occurred again. For example, it was necessary to say that a child was 'sitting' or 'running' only once in a narrative commentary. In fact the commentaries generally contained redundant information – either repetitions of behaviours within a sample, or more detail than was in the behaviour unit lists; this was filtered out when transcriptions were made.

There were two modifications of the all-or-none transcription method. One concerned the other persons with whom contacts were made. Contacts here included verbal contacts, visual contacts, physical contacts, and contacts via showing, giving, or receiving objects. If the focal child made a contact with another child or an adult, the name of that child or adult was also recorded. Thus, for example, several visual contacts with different children might be recorded in one sample (though a visual contact with one particular child would not be noted more than once). In most cases we did not use this additional information, and further recoding to all-or-none occurrence of the behaviour was made. However, in Chapter 4 some analysis of these more detailed data is presented.

The other exception to the all-or-none transcription of the commentary was made in the case of agonistic encounters. The appropriate behaviour units were transcribed like the others on an all-or-none basis, but in addition, any other details of the circumstances of the encounter (such as who initiated it or why it occurred) which were on the narrative record were noted down. The occasional occurrence of two or more agonistic encounters in one sample period was thus recoverable from the transcription sheets.

Examples of the commentaries for two sets of four time samples on two different children are given in Appendix C, together with their transcriptions on to standard score-sheets.

Inter-observer agreement

Measures of inter-observer agreement were obtained for the categories of companions, activities, and behaviours, during the first year of the project. One hundred time samples were made independently and simultaneously by the principal and a second observer, to obtain the measures of agreement between them. The second observer had read the written definitions of the categories given in Appendix B, and had practiced independent recording for several hours prior to simultaneous records being made; but there was no specific training to increase agreement further. Fifty samples were made at the beginning of the first year, and fifty were made five months later. A rather similar pattern of concordance was obtained on the two occasions, and the results are presented for the total.

The standard definition of concordance used (as, for example, in Lytton, 1973) was

$$C = \frac{A}{A+D+\frac{1}{2}X},$$

where C = concordance, A = number of agreements, D = number of disagreements, and X = total number of omissions by either observer.

In the case of a comprehensive and mutually exclusive category list, such as for companions, there are no omissions, but only disagreement between the observers. The formula then becomes $C = A/(A+D)$. Conversely, for overlapping category lists, as with those for activities and behaviours, one observer may omit a behaviour recorded by another, but there was no definite disagreement as such. The formula then becomes $C = A/(A+\frac{1}{2}X)$, where the term $\frac{1}{2}X$ represents the average number of omissions by either observer.

The results showed that *overall* concordance (summing A, D, and X for all categories) was 82 per cent for companion categories (range: 59–87 per cent), 95 per cent for activity categories (range: 70–100 per cent), and 74 per cent for behaviour units (range: 23–100 per cent). Individual concordances are given in brackets in Appendix B.[1]

We have considered a concordance of 60 per cent or over to be satisfactory, given that the observers were not trained to reach higher agreement. It will be seen that concordance was generally satisfactory for the companion and activity categories. It varied considerably for the different behaviour units. In a shorter list of 27 units, including many composites, used for the principal data presentation, all concordances were over 65 per cent.

Concordance for the companion categories was reasonably good, with the exception of the categories *small parallel subgroup* and *large parallel subgroup*, which had concordances of 59 and 61 per cent respectively. Here

[1] Kerr (1976) used a slightly modified version of the coding scheme used here for a doctoral thesis on preschool children at three schools in Winnipeg, Manitoba. Twelve observers were trained for some time until stable performance was reached. Measures of inter-observer agreement were then obtained. Overall concordance between pairs of observers ranged from 68 to 100 per cent. For individual categories, mean agreement ranged from 80 to 100 per cent for companion categories, and 60 to 100 per cent for behaviour units. Activity categories were not scored.

The concordance figures are overall somewhat higher than our own, undoubtedly because of the observer training that preceded the measurements.

there were several disagreements between the observers as to the number of companions the child was in parallel with. The concordance for the combination of these two categories was appreciably higher, at 76 per cent.

All of the activity categories had a high concordance, with the exception of *fantasy play*. The initial concordance for this category was only 50 per cent. Subsequent discussion between the observers indicated that they had indeed been using different criteria for scoring this category. Unlike most of the other categories, this was a relatively high-inference one. The rather low concordance was probably due in part to the original written definition not providing a sufficiently objective criterion for judging the occurrence or non-occurrence of this activity. After expansion of the original definition, a further session with another observer produced a concordance of 80 per cent. This was based on a further fifty samples taken specifically to get another concordance figure for this category. While the final figure is satisfactory, it may be an overestimate compared with the conditions in which the other concordance figures were obtained. However, this should not affect the consistency of the recordings made by the main observer.

So far as the behaviour units are concerned, the concordance was more varied. For most of them it was satisfactory, and for some, including most of the vocalisations and postural and locomotor units, it was high. In calculating the inter-observer agreement it was possible to ascertain whether low concordance was likely to be due to complete omission by one observer, or to a disagreement as to whether, for example, a *look* was a *glance*, or a *groom* was a *brush hair*. The two cases where disagreement was very common were in fact visual contacts with other children or adults, and facial contacts by the child. Glances, looks, and stares differed only in terms of duration, and were quite often confused, especially glances and looks. The composite visual contact units had a higher concordance. There was similarly some disagreement about behaviours such as *groom* and *brush hair*, and *nose contact* and *hand to face*. Again, the composite *face contact* had a higher concordance.

Some agonistic behaviour units did not have very reliable individual concordance, owing to infrequent occurrence. The composite unit of *agonistic behaviour*, however, had a concordance of 77 per cent.

Concordance for some units was low, as a result of omission by one observer, probably due to failure to notice the behaviour occurring. This was true of units such as *sing* (often done very quietly), *shuffle*, and *turn round* (not well defined and easy to miss), and *clothes fumble*, *hand fumble*, and *mouth fumble*. The last three behaviours were unobtrusive and easy to miss, although the definitions seemed satisfactory.

Generally speaking, concordance for vocal contacts was high, and for visual and physical contacts it was satisfactory, especially if composite visual contact units were used. With a few exceptions, concordance for postural and locomotor units was good. For the composite *agonistic behaviour* it was reasonable; for automanipulative and stereotypic behaviours it was not so high, and in a few cases very poor; it was better for the more noticeable facial units, being high for *suck* and the composite *facial contact*. The composite unit of automanipulation had a concordance of only 66 per cent, however, because of observer omissions.

The concordances indicate the reliability with which another observer might expect to see the same behaviours in a target child. Low concordance could be due to poorly defined units (as probably with the initial definition of *fantasy play*) or to poor pick-up rate of occurrence (as with some automanipulative behaviours). If low concordance is due to poor definition (difficult for the second person to be sure of the criteria), this need not imply unreliability in the case of the single observer who made all the observations, especially if the interest is in comparing environmental settings; but it does make the finding more difficult for others to interpret. If low concordance is due to poor 'pick-up' rate of behaviours which are easy to miss, then it is quite conceivable that some behaviours might be missed more easily in certain conditions (e.g. small space) than others. It is certainly reasonable that results for units with low concordance figures should be treated with more caution than those for units with satisfactory or high figures.

Inter-observer agreement for the subsidiary data collection methods are summarised in the appropriate sections elsewhere.

Time-sampling procedures

Data were gathered, using the category lists for companions, activities, and behaviours, by obtaining a large number of time samples on individual children in each environmental setting. The samples were modified focal-child samples, but most of the data were transcribed in an all-or-none (one–zero) format. The samples were of 40 seconds' duration, with the exception of one study in which they lasted for 30 seconds (see Chapter 6). Children were sampled in a fixed order at each session.

The choice of procedures stemmed from the fact that we wished to generalise about the behavioural effects of different environmental settings. This meant that we needed a large number of independent samples in each setting. Also, the samples had to be dispersed through the different sessions in which a particular environmental setting was presented. Furthermore, we wished to have data on individual children's behavioural responses, in case individual differences (or age or sex differences) were an important factor in the results. These requirements in combination pointed to short, focal-child samples as the best solution. Focal-child samples would give the individual behaviour profiles required for each environment. Short samples would mean, given the overall time constraints, that a large number of independent and dispersed samples could be collected.

In fact, the shorter the duration of the sample, the more samples could be obtained per child, per condition. There were, however, practical constraints on how short they could be. First, a judgement was needed at the end of the sample as to the children's companions. Was the child engaged in group activity or parallel activity, or was he alone? It requires at least ten seconds of following a child's behaviour to make this kind of judgement accurately. Other aspects – the child's choice of activity and any agonistic behaviours – can be judged or recorded better given at least this minimum sample length. For these reasons, the instantaneous scan technique (Altmann, 1974) was rejected; every sample, even an 'instantaneous' one, requires some finite time of observation. Specifying a given sample period, long enough to enable accurate judgements to be made, was considered to be preferable.

Second, for statistical purposes, the samples obtained for an individual child needed to be independent. In other words, the time gap between two consecutive samples on the same child should be long enough for the probability of behaviour at one sample directly influencing behaviour at another sample time to be small. Given that activity spans are of the order of five to ten minutes for this age range (Smith, 1977; see also Chapter 9), this suggests that at least ten minutes should separate consecutive samples on a child. If there are about twenty children in a group being sampled consecutively, then a sample period of less than about thirty seconds does not allow more samples to be taken; having sampled each child once, the observer would need to wait before recommencing sampling, in order to preserve sample independence.

For these reasons, the sample period finally chosen was 40 seconds. In one study (see Chapter 6) this was reduced to 30 seconds, when overall time constraints were greater and more samples were required. A period of 40 seconds was long enough to enable the observer to appreciate the flow of the child's behaviour and make accurate judgements about companions and activities at the end of the period. Some reasonable details of agonistic encounters could also be gathered. The period was short enough to be compatible with gathering a large number of samples, while not so short as to compromise the independence of samples obtained on the same child.

The choice of sample length also influenced, and was influenced by, the decision to use all-or-none or one–zero transcriptions of most of the behavioural data. The use of one–zero coding was dictated by the need to avoid overburdening the observer, while maximising the number of behaviour units which could be used reliably. One–zero coding is also an efficient use of short, independent samples where each sample is essentially one unit for statistical purposes.

Alternatives to one–zero coding would have been either instantaneous scan sampling, or focal-child sampling in which the initiation and termination of behaviours was coded. The technique of sequential instantaneous scans was employed previously by us (Smith and Connolly, 1972), when ongoing behaviour of the target child was sampled every 10 seconds for a 5-minute sample period. Another example of its use is by Boydell (1975), who used five sequential instantaneous records of ongoing behaviour, at 25-second intervals. The disadvantage of this method (apart from the difficulty of making truly 'instantaneous' scans, referred to earlier) is that the sequential scans within the sample are very interdependent. If a child is playing with sand at the start of a 5-minute interval, it is highly likely that he will be playing there for many or all of the scans in that sample period. It is not really legitimate to obtain a total score for all the scans in the sample, add them to similar totals for other samples, and treat these as independent measures in statistical analysis. The only independent measures are the samples, not the scans within them. To be statistically correct, it would be better to separate the individual scans within a sample so that they are independent. This approximates to our own decision to use short samples, separated for a given child by an appreciable interval. The recording of more than one occurrence of a behaviour within the short sample would then be pointless.

The other alternative is carrying out focal-child sampling and coding the initiation, duration, and termination of each behaviour (Altmann, 1974). This would be possible only for a limited number of behaviour units. It would be desirable, for example, if it was thought important to measure behaviour durations or to record more about who initiated sequences. For our purposes, sampling a wider range of behaviours was more important than obtaining details of initiation and duration of each behaviour unit.

The use of a 30- or 40-second sample period in fact fits in well with one–zero sampling. Earlier research (Smith, 1973) had involved piloting different sample periods for observing preschool children. It turned out that a 30- or 40-second period was generally long enough to pick up the behaviour units characteristic of the activity the child was engaged in; if, say, the child was engaged in some kind of group activity, the sample was long enough to pick up the repertoire of social behaviour he or she was employing in the situation. On the other hand, periods of one minute or more seemed to be unnecessarily long, given one–zero coding. The observer was by now mostly noting items already checked, until the child substantially changed activity.

The use of one–zero sampling or coding procedures has been criticised by Altmann (1974) in her recent review of sampling methods in the observation of behaviour. Altmann quite correctly points out that the statistic obtained from one–zero coding, namely, the number of samples in which a behaviour occurs, does not give a precise measure either of number of occurrences of the behaviour, or of behaviour duration. Nor is it a precise measure of the amount of time spent in the behaviour, although it does provide an upper limit to this. Dunbar (1976) has since provided a quantitative demonstration of Altmann's points. As Altmann puts it (1974, p. 258), 'for those who consider frequency and duration of behaviours and percent of time spent in various states as variables of interest, alternative sampling methods should be considered'.

The alternative methods Altmann suggests are focal-child sampling, and instantaneous or scan sampling. These have already been discussed, and shown not to be suitable for our particular purposes. However, it still remains to argue that the one–zero coding we employed gives meaningful and useful results.

The main point here is that the variables of interest are *not* necessarily the frequency of behaviours, or their duration, or the percentage of time spent in the behaviour, although these are often the variables of interest in ethological studies such as those with which Altmann was primarily concerned. Our essential requirement was a sampling procedure which used a clear operational definition of what was measured, and which in some sense measured the 'amount' of behaviour in different environmental settings. The one–zero coding system satisfied this.

To take a concrete example (see Table 5.5, p. 122), for one group of children we recorded 220 samples in which 'run' occurred in a small space, and 399 in which 'run' occurred in a large space (out of a total of 1,728 samples in each case). This result is clearly operationally defined. The fact that the difference is significant ($p < 0.001$) implies that someone else taking similar 40-second all-or-none samples on similar children in similar conditions would get similar results. There would be more samples in which the observer would note running in the larger space than in the smaller space. *In this sense*, there is more running in the larger space. For our purposes, this seems almost as useful as to be able to say that 'there are more bouts of running', *or* that 'the bouts of running are of longer duration', *or* that 'there is more time spent running'. While it would have been nice to have had such extra information, it was not essential, and other constraints made the extra effort impracticable.

Having said this, it is clear that our own procedure of short, widely spaced time samples will reflect more the frequency of occurrence of behaviours than behaviour duration. Provided that the 'bunching together' of a particular behaviour unit is not affected greatly by the independent variable (environmental change), then the quantitative measure of number of samples in which a behaviour occurred should translate, at least on an ordinal scale, and often on an interval scale, to the number of instances of the behaviour (frequency of occurrence). These would in turn translate in time spent in behaviour, *provided* duration was not affected. These provisos are plausible for most of the behaviour units employed, but nevertheless they are not specifically tested. Therefore while the all-or-none scores probably give a reasonable indication of relative frequency of occurrence, and time spent, they can be confidently interpreted as 'more' or 'less' of a given behaviour only in terms of the operationally defined sampling methods.

While there would not be much reason to doubt significant relationships obtained between environmental changes and number of samples in which a behaviour unit occurred, Altmann's criticisms do bear on the inferences to be made from non-significant relationships. It is quite possible that a non-significant result might conceal relationships which were in fact there. For example, changes in behaviour duration with the independent variable would not be readily detected. It is also true of course that for many research purposes, precise details of frequency, duration, and/or time spent in a behaviour *are* necessary. In such cases Altmann is correct in suggesting that one–zero procedures should not be used.

Two final points on sampling procedure remain to be discussed: the number of samples obtained for each child in each setting, and the order of sampling children.

Clearly an appreciable number of independent samples are needed in order to give a reliable quantification for use in statistical analyses. The number of samples required will vary with the frequency of occurrence of the particular behaviour units concerned. The problem can be investigated by calculating split-half or split-third reliabilities for differences obtained with a given number of samples in each condition. In earlier work (Smith, 1973), we investigated the stability of differences between individual children. Generally high reliabilities were obtained with one hundred 30-second all-or-none samples for each child.

Unfortunately time constraints, such as the length of school terms and the duration of the research programme, meant that we could not obtain one hundred samples for each child in each environmental condition. However, our main interest was to obtain enough data to reveal reliable differences between environmental settings, rather than between children.

Table 2.2. *Number of children, environmental conditions, and time samples in the various studies*

	Number of children	Number of environmental conditions	Number of time samples/ child/ condition	Number of time samples/ condition
Number of children	20			500
(Chapter 4)	22	2	25	550
	14			350
	14	2	25	350
Number of children	12			240
and spatial density	11	4	20	220
(Chapters 4 and 6)				
Amount of space and	24			576
play equipment	24	9	24	576
(Chapter 5)				
Additional variations	23			184
in amount of play	21	2	8	168
equipment (Chapter 6)				
Variations in kind of	24			192
play equipment	22	3	8	176
(Chapter 6)				
Free play and	22			352
structured activities	22	2	16	352
(Chapter 9)				

It was clearly necessary to get well over one hundred samples per environment; in general we obtained two hundred or more, although it fell just below this for two small studies. The numbers of samples, children, and environmental settings are shown in Table 2.2. These numbers are good so far as comparing environmental settings are concerned. With the exception of the study on amount of space and play equipment, they are not so good for comparing individual children. Our main interest was environmental differences, and age and sex differences in relation to this; by these criteria the number of samples are adequate to good. With the exception of the above study, reliability of individual (as opposed to age and sex) differences in response to environmental settings is not so high.

In obtaining the samples, the target children were selected in the same fixed order on each session. The important consideration here was the effect of time of day – generally small but not insignificant (McGrew, 1972; and Chapter 5). Given that we were comparing the same children in different environments, any error due to time of day effects would be reduced by the fixed order of sampling; we would be comparing the same children at approximately the same times. On the other hand, error would be increased so far as comparisons of individual children were concerned; as already indicated, however, such comparison was not our intention, and the sampling procedure was not expected to be sensitive or highly reliable for this purpose. The fixed sampling order of children was designed so that boys and girls, and older and younger children, were alternated. By this means systematic effects of time of day on age and sex differences would be avoided, although they might still persist for individual differences.

If a child was absent on a certain day, his or her records were made up on the subsequent presentation of the environmental condition missed. At the end of each project, a few additional sessions and half-sessions ensured that a complete sample record was obtained for each child in each group.

3 Preschool behaviour and the physical environment: a review

Over the next five chapters an examination is made of how various aspects of the physical environment of the preschool affect children's activities and behaviour. In particular, the amounts of space and of play equipment are considered, and also the number of children in the group. Although not strictly a physical environment variable, the effect of the number of children on free-play behaviour is considered in this part (the number of children as it affects staff–child interaction is considered in Chapter 10). Some results of variations in the kinds of play equipment provided are also presented.

First, however, a review of previous work is provided. The field of enquiry broadly known as environmental psychology has gained strength in recent years, but research on physical environment factors in the preschool is still scanty. Two areas in which an appreciable amount of research has been done are the environmental design of play areas, and studies on the behavioural effects of crowding.

Choice of toys and the design of play environments

Research into play environments has consisted mainly of studies of toy design and preferences, research into types and provisioning of playgrounds, and studies of design features such as the shape and layout of nurseries and classrooms.

Studies of toy preferences were made as early as the 1920s and 1930s (e.g. Bridges, 1929; Farwell, 1930; Van Alstyne, 1932; McDowell, 1937). These investigated the popularity of different kinds of toys amongst young children of different ages and sexes. Studies were also made of attention or activity spans (see Chapter 8). Similar studies have been made more recently (Clark *et al.*, 1969), and they have also been supplemented by experimental investigations designed to examine the effects of making toys more complex (Gramza and Scholtz, 1974), and arranging them differently in the room (Witt and Gramza, 1970). The early studies of this kind helped to establish the popularity of certain toys and activities, such as modelling clay, painting, building blocks, materials for dressing up, and so on, which now constitute a fairly standard range of materials provided for children in the age range 2–5. Little detailed study has been made of the ways in which different kinds of materials may elicit different skills from the children, but one early exception is the report by Updegraff and Herbst (1933) comparing the different kinds of social behaviour encouraged by playing with clay and with wooden blocks. Another study of this kind was made by Shure (1963) who compared art corner, books, dolls, games, and blocks as relative facilitators of active social interchange and/or destructive behaviour.

Some larger-scale studies of the design and provisioning of playgrounds have been particularly concerned with the evaluation of play areas in cities. Studies of play area provision in modern medium- and high-rise housing estates have pinpointed the difficulties of mothers with young children in such situations, and the unimaginative design of many of the play facilities provided (Hole and Miller, 1966; Holme and Massie, 1970; Department of the Environment, 1973; Moore, 1974; Bjorklid-Chu, 1977). The use of immovable concrete structures has come in for particular criticism.

Studies of the popularity of different outdoor play areas (Dee and Liebman, 1970; Hayward *et al.*, 1974) are the macro-equivalents of the early studies on toy preference. In a more experimental study, Derman (1974) examined the effects of different pieces of large equipment in an outdoor play area.

Most of these studies have been of outdoor play areas. There are fewer macro-level studies of the design of indoor play spaces. Campbel (1972) carried out a small study in Vancouver, which demonstrated that small activity rooms were not likely to be used by preschool children for solitary play. Hutt and McGrew (1967) reported a study with a trefoil shaped playroom (see also Hutt and Hutt, 1970); on the basis of their results they suggested that the presence of partially bounded areas increased territorial and aggressive behaviours. This playroom was in a hospital with mentally handicapped or disturbed children, so it is not certain how relevant the finding may be to a normal playgroup. Another study in a clinical setting is that of Richer and Nicoll (1971), who designed a playroom and living area specifically for the needs of autistic children.

Many of the macro-level studies of interior areas for children have been made in schools, and in particular have been concerned with the open or traditional classroom design controversy. The studies so far (Brunetti, 1972; Durlak *et al.*, 1972; Clem *et al.*, 1974; Durlak and Lehman, 1974; Evans, 1974), mainly by architects, have concentrated on the description of existing practices and the documentation of how such measures as teacher perception and student achievement correlate with these. Few if any experimental studies in schools have been carried out.

Gump and James (1975), and Gump (1975, 1978), have reviewed the research on child development and the man-made environment. Their review covers some of the work in ecological psychology on child life in large and small communities; the effects of housing conditions; home versus day care, and day-care environments; and open versus traditional educational settings.

Behavioural effects of crowding

One specific concern in the general area of how the physical environment affects behaviour has been the consequences of crowding. Generally, crowding has been thought likely to have adverse effects. Usually, too, crowding has been considered as numbers of individuals in relation to spatial area. Research on crowding has been done on humans, and there is also a considerable body of evidence from animal work. Both experimental and correlational studies have been reported in some abundance. Choldin and McGinty (1972) have provided a review and bibliography, and Lawrence (1974) and Freedman (1975) give subsequent reviews.

Probably some initial impetus for the concern with crowding came from research with animal groups. Calhoun's dramatic experiments (1962) documented the breakdown of social behaviour in severely overcrowded rat populations – the so-called 'behavioural sink'. Other experimental studies with animals have also found effects of crowding on aggression and measures of social stress (Christian and Davis, 1964; Southwick, 1967; Alexander and Roth, 1971), although in more natural situations it seems that the effects of increased population density are complex, with stress and aggression being only one of several possible outcomes (Archer, 1970; Krebs *et al.*, 1973). Research on animal behaviour suggests that other aspects as well as mere spatial density should be considered. For example, Southwick (1967) found that halving the area in an enclosure did lead to increased aggression in a colony of monkeys, but that introduction of new group members had much more significant effects. So also did food deprivation. The more naturalistic ethological studies also point in this direction. It has become increasingly clear that aspects of the ecology of an animal species, in particular the types and distribution of food resources and sleeping or nesting sites, as well as aspects of predation, have profound formative influences on the social structure and behaviour of the species concerned (Alcock, 1975; Krebs and Davies, 1978). Attempts, so far only partially successful, have been made to construct a theoretical framework whereby social structure and behaviour could be deduced from ecological variables and broad species parameters (Crook *et al.*, 1976; Hamilton and Watt, 1970). These investigations, based on field studies of many species and particularly primates, are not of direct relevance to our research, but they do indicate the importance of considering ecological factors, and especially amounts and distribution of important resources, in observations of social structure and behaviour in natural group situations.

In research on the effects of crowding in humans, two main approaches have been adopted. These are, first, correlational studies of population density and social pathology; and second, experimental studies, usually in laboratory conditions.

Several investigations have been made in which indices of population density, such as person per unit area, or rooms per house, have been correlated with other indices such as mental hospital admissions, delinquency rates, public assistance rates, and so on. As with correlational studies generally, the difficulty in interpreting these results has been that other variables, such as social class, may be the cause of any positive correlations obtained. Studies by Schmitt (1957), Winsborough (1965), and Mitchell (1971) found correlations which largely disappeared once social class and income had been partialled out. Galle *et al.* (1972) succeed in finding correlations of persons per room with public assistance and delinquency rates, and rooms per house with mental hospital admission rates, after a complex multiple-partial correlation procedure to remove social class and income effects. This study used data obtained from Chicago in 1960. However, in a further analysis McPherson (1975) questioned this interpretation of the results on the basis of time-lag correlations between earlier 1950 data and the 1960 data. Other studies (Baldassare, 1975; Welch and Booth, 1975) also have found little to suggest that housing density and other similar variables reliably indicate stress or social pathology, and Freedman (1975) in his review is probably correct in his overall view of these studies when he suggests they are inconclusive. One investigation not mentioned by Freedman, however, is worth noting. Murray (1974), in a study carried out in Dundee, found correlations between an index relating to number of persons per house, and questionnaire and rating measures of neuroticism and aggression in children. Within-group comparisons found these results to be stable when family size, social class, housing quality, and neighbourhood status were held constant.

Other studies have looked at naturally existing differences in crowding in institutions and real-life behaviour settings, such as prisons (D'Atri, 1975; Paulus *et al.*, 1975; McCain *et al.*, 1976), naval vessels (Dean *et al.*, 1975), college dormitories and student residences (Baum *et al.*, 1975),

Table 3.1. *Summary of previous studies on behavioural effects of group size and density on young children* (For definition of study types, see p. 59.)

Reference	Study type	No. of groups	Ages of children (years)	Group sizes	Densities (sq. ft/child)	Effects of increased N or D on — Social interaction	Effects of increased N or D on — Aggressive behaviour
Hutt & Vaizey (1966)	$N(D_S+D_p)$	1	3–8	< 6, 7–11, > 12 (5 normal, 5 autistic and 5 brain-damaged children observed)	79, 53, 39	Decrease (Normal children)	Increase (Normal and brain-damaged children)
Bates (1970)	$N(D_S+D_p)$	1	2 and 3	10–15, 17–24, 25–30 (20 children observed)	83, 51, 40	Decrease (Girls only)	Increase
McGrew (1972)	$N(D_S+D_p)$ } D_SR_S	1	3 and 4	8, 16 (20 children observed)	86, 74, 52, 37	No change No change	No change No change }
Gilligan (1970)	D_SR_S	3	4 and 5	21, 22, 22	178, 130, 83	No change	—
Price (1971)	D_SR_S	22	3–6	19 (mean)	26, 9 (means)	Decrease	No change
Preiser (1972)	D_SR_S	1	3 and 4	15	40, 27	No change? (Only brief report available)	No change?
Loo (1972)	D_SR_S	10	4 and 5	6	44, 15	Decrease	Decrease (Boys only)
Johnson (1935)	D_pR_p	1	3–5	33	Play equipment reduced	Increase }	Increase
		2	4 and 5	29, 46	Play equipment added		

psychiatric hospital wards (Wolfe, 1975), and shopping centres (Saegert *et al.*, 1975). Generally, these studies have found links between crowded conditions and measures such as psychological arousal, negative affect, or social avoidance. Like Murray's study (1974), these also suggest that Freedman's generalisation (1975) that crowding *per se* lacks importance may be too rash. Although these studies are stronger than the purely correlational ones, in that it is assumed that the difference in crowding is the only relevant independent variable, there is still not the degree of control, and therefore of assured causal inference, found in experimental studies. For example, subject selection or allocation to the different conditions (such as dormitories of different size) may not be random.

The experimental studies of the effects of crowding on humans have also produced mixed results. These studies have mostly been carried out on students in university laboratories, and have, in the main, used measures of task performance, or ratings of friendliness or affect. Not being very realistic, they do not bear closely on real-life crowding situations. One of the first studies, by Freedman *et al.* (1971), failed to find any effects of group size or room size on task performance. However, as there was no social interaction in this setting it is not surprising that possible effects of crowding were minimised. Subsequent experimental studies, such as Freedman *et al.* (1972), Ross *et al.* (1973), Stokols *et al.* (1973), and Marshall and Heslin (1975), have tended to find effects on liking or competitiveness, with an interaction with sex of subjects, but the results are not very consistent. These studies have mainly involved room size rather than group size, and again social interaction has been minimised. Studies using doll figures in pictures (Baxter and Deanovich, 1970) or miniature models of rooms and figures (Desor, 1972) seem even further removed from reality. These researches have gained experimental control at the expense of losing relevance to real-life behaviour.

By contrast, some eight studies of crowding in children's playgroups have combined some degree of experimental control with a reasonably natural setting in which much social interaction took place. These studies relate closely to our own and will be discussed in some detail. They are summarised in Table 3.1.

Crowding in the preschool

The first study of this genre was by Hutt and Vaizey (1966) and was carried out in a hospital playroom. It was found that increased group size (more children in the playroom) led to more aggression, and, generally, less social interaction. However, the subjects, aged 3–8, were a heterogeneous group of normal, brain-damaged, and autistic children, and only one playgroup was observed. No firm generalisations can be made to other groups or to normal children. Nevertheless their findings suggested negative reactions to crowding, and set expectations for much subsequent work.

Two similar studies on normal children, in which group size was varied, have been made by Bates (1970) and by McGrew (1972). Bates observed 2-and 3-year old children in a nursery school in Oregon. Group size varied between 10 and 30 children, owing to natural fluctuations in attendance. More conflict interactions were observed in larger groups; girls played more in smaller subgroups, boys more in larger ones. Again, only one group was observed, and the group size variable was not well controlled experimentally. McGrew (1972) reported results from a study of one nursery class in Edinburgh. The class was made up of 20 children aged 3 and 4; the number of children observed indoors was varied by sending half the children outside on alternate sessions. Few significant results were obtained, and the method of event sampling which he employed was of doubtful reliability.

The research by W. C. McGrew (see also McGrew, P. L., 1970) represented a conceptual advance in its attempt to isolate two distinct crowding variables. McGrew uses the term *social density*, which is changed when more people are added to a given space, and *spatial density*, which is changed when space is varied for a given number of people. McGrew complemented his social density study with a spatial density study in which the space in the playroom was reduced by 20 per cent. Again, few significant results were obtained, but the concept of isolating the effects of different variables in the same setting is a valuable one.

Four other studies have, like McGrew's (1972), varied spatial density. Preiser (1972) reduced available space by one-third in a nursery class of 15 children in Virginia. His brief report suggests no effects on social interaction or aggression. Gilligan (1970) varied playground size for three groups of 4- and 5-year-old children in New York, and found no effects on social participation and leadership. Price (1971) examined 22 separate groups of preschool and first-grade children in New York, in crowded and uncrowded conditions, by blocking off areas of classrooms. A reduction in locomotor activity was observed in the crowded conditions. There was also less talking and playing with other children, and more solitary play and automanipulation. Thus in contrast to McGrew, Preiser, and Gilligan, Price obtained some negative effects of crowding.

The Price study differed from those of McGrew, Preiser, and Gilligan in the range of spatial densities studied (as well as in the age range of the children). Very crowded spatial densities of around 10 sq. ft per child were employed. Another study by Loo (1972) also used a very crowded condition of 15 sq. ft per child in comparison with a less crowded one of 45 sq. ft per child. Ten groups of 6 children were observed in the two conditions. Loo reported that children, especially boys, were *less* aggressive in the crowded conditions; and both sexes showed less group play and more solitary play. The latter finding agrees with Price (1971). However, the failure of both these studies to find increases in aggressive behaviour contrasts, superficially at least, with the results of Hutt and Vaizey (1966), and Bates (1970).

These studies all have the advantage of experimental control of the crowding variables. As pointed out earlier, this is an advantage, indeed almost an essential requirement, if confident causal inferences are to be made. Two non-experimental studies can be considered by way of contrast. Jersild and Markey (1935) examined three preschool groups, A, B, and C. Group C had the highest rate of conflicts, and also the smallest playground. This is sometimes cited (e.g. Swift, 1964) as indicating the effects of spatial density on aggression. However, the three groups also differed in respect of racial and class background of the children, mean IQ, age range, sex ratio, and staff behaviour, any of which variables might well affect the level of conflict behaviour.

Fagot (1977) has compared behaviour at three preschools in the Netherlands, with spatial densities of about 12.5 sq. ft per child, and two preschools in the USA, with densities of 25 and 113 sq. ft per child. She found no differences in aggressive behaviour, but more positive interaction and less solitary play in the high-density (Dutch) preschools. These preschools differed, however, in the overall culture (Dutch versus US), as well as in the group size and age composition of the institutions. Again, it is not possible to confidently ascribe differences to spatial density.

Although the experimental studies permit firmer causal inferences, there are certain disadvantages which pertain to some or all of them. Four points are considered below.

First, several of the studies have examined only one group of children (Hutt and Vaizey, Bates, McGrew, Preiser). The limitations of this strategy have been discussed in Chapter 2. Results may well be specific to the one particular group under study. This problem was best overcome by Loo and by Price.

Second, it is difficult to avoid novelty in some of the experimental conditions. For example, in McGrew's group size study, the smaller group size was novel in the sense that the children were not used to the group being divided in half. Similarly, the smaller space conditions were novel in the work of McGrew and of Price. In Loo's study both the small and large space conditions were equally novel, which overcomes this problem.

However, each group of children came only for two sessions, so the whole set-up was novel. This in itself limits generalisation to more long-term behaviour. It is well documented that children take some time to settle into a new environment, or with a new group of children, and that behaviour during such adjustment periods is not typical (McGrew, 1972; Smith, 1974c).

A third problem relates specifically to observations of aggressive behaviour. Here it is important to distinguish between 'real' aggression and rough-and-tumble play. This distinction is well established from primate studies (Poirier, 1972), and from ethological work on children (Blurton Jones, 1967; Smith, 1974a; Aldis, 1975). Rough-and-tumble play, or play-fighting, is easily confused with actual fighting by parents or teachers. However, it typically occurs in different contexts from aggressive behaviour, being a pleasurable activity which children seek to continue, often involving inhibition of responses such as hitting or biting, and role reversal as in chasing. Aggressive behaviour can sometimes be observed in rough-and-tumble play sequences, and in older children (11- and 12-year-olds) the two may intermingle (Neill, 1976); however, in younger children the two kinds of behaviour are usually quite separate.

Nevertheless aggression and rough-and-tumble were often lumped together in earlier psychological studies, including the studies by Loo and by Price reviewed here. Clearly, firm decisions as to how crowding affects aggression requires that these two kinds of behaviour be treated separately.

Finally, we may consider whether studies of group size and space provide in themselves an adequate conceptualisation of the density or crowding situation. In other words, how satisfactory is McGrew's separation of social density and spatial density as the two main variables? Further consideration of this has led us to reconceptualise the kinds of density or crowding experiments which can be carried out.

A reconceptualisation of crowding experiments

We consider that McGrew's formulation is unsatisfactory in two respects. First, it inadequately defines the resources to which density parameters may refer. Second, it does not embrace studies where group size is increased commensurately with resources.

The animal behaviour research mentioned above pointed to the importance of considering the amount and distribution of resources generally, not only space, when considering social behaviour. Clearly, a very important resource for preschool children is the amount of play equipment provided. Most of the time children spend in nurseries and playgroups they are using play materials, and they have definite preferences for particular types. Futhermore, the majority of conflicts are over toy possession (Smith and Green, 1974). A couple of experimental studies also point to the importance of the amount of play materials. An early study by Johnson (1935) found increases in social interaction and in aggression when playground equipment was reduced in three American preschools; and Ramey *et al.* (1976) found that infants aged 6–12 months interacted more with adults and peers when fewer toys were present.

Johnson's study (1935), included in Table 3.1, is not sufficiently sound methodologically to give a definitive answer as to how toy availability affects behaviour. However, it certainly suggests that if the number of children is varied while play equipment is held constant, changes in social interaction and aggression may be expected because of the changes in equipment available per child. This could apply to the studies of Hutt and Vaizey, Bates, and McGrew. McGrew's double study of social density and spatial density was designed to separate out group size and space as contributing variables. However, any results attributed to group size in these smaller studies could also be attributed to play equipment density. Although McGrew's technique of combining two kinds of study is a correct one, his definition of resources purely in spatial terms is clearly insufficient.

The following formulation leads to three kinds of study, of which a minimum of two should be done in combination.

We start by taking N as the number of children in a group, where a group is a collection of individuals who potentially can interact socially. This group has a certain area in which social and non-social activities can occur, but more generally we consider the amount of environmental resources, R, where this refers to any resources available for communal use by the group. Besides spatial area, we postulate that the other main important physical resource is the amount of play equipment available. These two resources we call R_s and R_p respectively.

We now define density (D) as N/R. (It could alternatively be defined as R/N, as common language use is ambiguous in this respect. However, the difference is immaterial for the present discussion.) We can define spatial density (D_s) as N/R_s, and equipment density (D_p) as N/R_p.

The three main variables N, D, and R yield three types of study. These are:

ND: both N and D are varied, R being constant;
DR: both D and R are varied, N being constant;
NR: both N and R are varied, D being constant.

The previous researches have all been of types ND and DR (see Table 3.1, where the previous studies are classed according to our terminology).

An *NR* study does not change densities. However, it should still be considered as a type of crowding study. A 'crowd' can mean a large group (and hence perhaps more social interaction, conflict, or frustration; e.g. Milgram, 1970) irrespective of the availability of resources. Logically, this type also complements the other two. At least two types of experiment should be carried out, in order to ascertain the separate effects of the *N*, *D*, and *R* factors. Also, both spatial and equipment densities and resources should be considered.

The classification of previous work in Table 3.1 also indicates which parameters may be responsible for the results. For example, the *ND* studies of Hutt and Vaizey, and Bates, gave results which may be due to *N*, D_s, or D_p. McGrew's second experiment enabled him to allow for effects of D_s or R_s, but D_p (or R_p) was not taken into account. As noted earlier, only Johnson's study (1935) had investigated this variable in the preschool age range.

Research programme

The research described in the next three chapters was designed with these critical points in mind. It was sufficiently controlled to enable causal inferences to be made, while attempting to retain a natural setting. Two separate groups of children were observed, so that generalisations could be made with some confidence. Where possible, relative novelty of different conditions was avoided and a wide range of behaviour and activities was monitored, with aggression and rough-and-tumble being carefully distinguished.

Chapter 4 describes a series of *NR* studies, and Chapter 5 a complementary *DR* study. In both cases play equipment was considered as an important resource, as well as spatial area. Chapter 6 describes additional *DR* studies, and also an investigation in which the *kind* of play equipment rather than the *amount* was varied. Chapter 7 reviews the overall results and the previous research and attempts to estimate the behavioural impact of the *N*, *D*, and *R* parameters.

4 Number of children in the group

Three separate studies of the effects of group size on behaviour were carried out during consecutive terms in the third year of the research programme (see Chapter 2). The results reported here concern effects of group size on the friendships, activities, and behaviours of children while they were engaged in free play. Studies were also made of differing staff:child ratios in more structured contexts; these are described in Chapter 10.

Population sample and group size variations

The series of group size variations was carried out independently on the two groups of children attending the experimental playgroup – Group One, which attended on Tuesday and Thursday mornings, and Group Two, which attended on Wednesday and Friday mornings. Two kinds of variations in group size were examined. Numbers decreased across consecutive terms as older children left to go to school, and this provided one kind of variation; however, this confounded group size variation with age and experience. The main variation in group size was brought about *within* each term, by the use of a third group of children, Group Three, who attended on Wednesday and Thursday mornings. This gave the following attendance pattern:

> Tuesday: Group One
> Thursday: Groups One and Three
> Friday: Group Two
> Wednesday: Groups Two and Three

This arrangement enabled us to compare the behaviour of the Group One and Two children when alone (Tuesdays and Fridays) and when in a larger overall group (Wednesdays and Thursdays). Thus the behaviour of particular children could be compared in two different group size conditions, avoiding the possible confounding of age and experience factors. In this design it was not necessary to make observations on the Group Three children, although some sociometric scans were made for purposes of examining friendship structure in the large and small groups.

Table 4.1. *Age and sex composition of groups*

	Number of children	Boys	Girls	Mean age at start of term (months)	Age range (months)
Term One					
Group One	20	9	11	44	28–56
Group Two	22	9	13	44	28–56
Group Three	12	6	6	42	32–53
Term Two					
Group One	14	8	6	42	32–54
Group Two	14	6	8	43	32–54
Group Three	14	7	7	44	32–54
Term Three					
Group One	12	6	6	43	34–55
Group Two	11	4	7	46	35–54
Group Three	23	11	12	42	32–53

During the first term there were 20, 22 and 12 children in Groups One, Two, and Three respectively. The ratio of small to large group size was thus 20:32 for Group One, and 22:34 for Group Two, or approximately 2:3 in each case.

At the end of the first term seven children left Group One and nine left Group Two. One new child was introduced to each group, both of which then had 14 children. Three children had left Group Three and five new children were introduced, also giving 14 children. The ratio of small to large group size was thus 14:28 or 1:2 for Groups One and Two during the second term.

At the end of the second term three children left both Group One and Group Two, and one new child was introduced to Group One. Thus Group One had 12 children and Group Two had 11. Three children left Group Three and 12 new ones were introduced, giving a total of 23. The ratio of small to large group size was thus 12:35 for Group One and 11:34 for Group Two, or approximately 1:3 in each case, during the third term.

Details of the age and sex composition of each group during each term, and of mean attendance figures, are given in Tables 4.1 and 4.2. Background details for each child are available in Appendix A.

The matching of behaviour of individual children in either a small or a large group context is an advantage of this design. However, two other aspects of the method should be mentioned. First, although the comparisons for Groups One and Two are independent, the children in both these groups

Table 4.2. *Mean attendance, and actual group size ratio*

	Attendance (percentage)	Mean number	Actual mean group size ratio
Term One			
Tuesdays	85	17.9	
Thursdays	85	27.9	0.64
Fridays	88	19.3	
Wednesdays	84	28.6	0.68
Term Two			
Tuesdays	88	12.3	
Thursdays	87	24.4	0.50
Fridays	87	12.2	
Wednesdays	89	25.0	0.49
Term Three			
Tuesdays	86	10.3	
Thursdays	84	29.5	0.35
Fridays	88	9.7	
Wednesdays	88	30.0	0.32

experienced the larger group size in the presence of the Group Three children. This aspect in common introduces some degree of non-independence into the design, which could not easily be avoided.

A second point to bear in mind is not necessarily disadvantageous. This is that the Group Three children in the larger group had less experience of the other (Group One or Group Two) children than they did of each other, and vice versa. Thus in the larger group the children on average had less experience of each other. In fact this reduced mutual experience would in most cases be a natural concomitant of larger groups compared with smaller ones (given equivalent length of existence of both groups), so that this is a realistic characteristic, but one that must be recognised. An apparently alternative strategy – breaking up a pre-existing group, as done by McGrew (1972) – has complementary limitations. If the pre-existing group is split on only a few occasions, the smaller groups are novel in that friendship patterns are broken and new ones must be made. If the pre-existing group is split the same way on many occasions, however, then the children in the smaller group will come to have more mutual experience than the children in the (pre-existing) larger group.

Although this factor of differential mutual experience in small and large groups was not – and, it is argued, could not – be avoided, steps were taken to ensure that the contrast was not unreasonably great. Clearly, when Group

Three was started some time would be needed for the children to settle into a pattern of mixing with two pre-existing groups. Group Three children were therefore introduced immediately after the end of the previous (Year Two) project, giving a two-month settling-in period in the summer. In addition, another three weeks of settling in was allowed at the beginning of the first term of this project (Autumn 1973) before observations commenced.

New children were also introduced at the beginning of the second and third terms. In both cases there was a settling-in period of three weeks before data collection began.

Commensurate resource variations

As discussed in Chapter 3, studies of numbers, densities, and resources can be of types *NR*, *DR*, or *ND*. Two different types of study had to be carried out to separate the effects of *N*, *D*, and *R*. This series of studies was intended to be of type *NR*, to complement the *DR* studies described in Chapter 5; so resources were varied commensurately with number of children in the group. Important resources were taken to be amount of space and amount of play equipment.

The amount of play equipment available was varied by having either one, two, or three basic sets of equipment available; thus the amount of equipment was not confused with the kinds of item provided. The basic set used in the first two terms was: two pairs of nursery tables placed together, with six chairs, and table toys (paper, crayons; plastic Meccano or Lego); a climbing-frame and slide with mat; a rocking-boat; a toy chest with lid; a Wendy house, with small table, two small stools, plastic tea set, iron, and ironing board; a pram with cushions and doll; a tricycle; a bowl containing sand or water; a bookcase with books and comics, surrounded by three chairs; a double-sided easel with paints, pots, and brushes; two jigsaws, one on a chair; a miniature doll's house, with figures and furniture; a bucket of wooden blocks; a teddy bear; a telephone; a few musical instruments.

The procedure during Term Three was more complicated than in Terms One and Two. This was because in Term Three the experiment was carried out at two different spatial density levels (see Table 4.3 and Chapter 6). The intention was to examine the effects of fairly extreme variations in spatial density, and the rationale for this is explained further in Chapter 6. A smaller basic set of play equipment had to be employed during this term, as not all the larger set could be fitted into the restricted spatial density condition (15 sq. ft per child). The smaller set was also used when

Table 4.3. *Spatial densities and equipment densities*

Small and large group size for Terms One and Two, and for all four group – space conditions in Term Three

Term	Group size ratio		Actual density (sq. ft/child) (relative to mean attendance of children)				Equipment density (approx.)
			Small group size		Large group size		
			Tues.	Fri.	Thurs.	Wed.	
One	2:3		70	65	65	64	1 set/10 children
Two	1:2		74	75	75	73	1 set/12 children
Three	1:3	Small space	15	15	15	15	
		Large space	61	65	62	61	1 reduced set/ 10 children

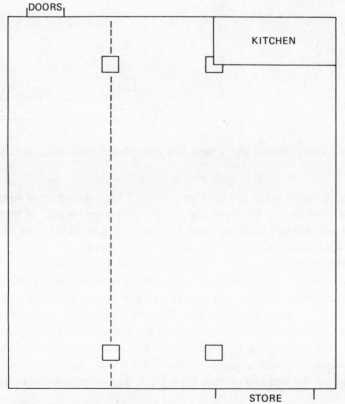

Figure 4.1. Plan of the hall during the first term (Broken line indicates curtain screen.)

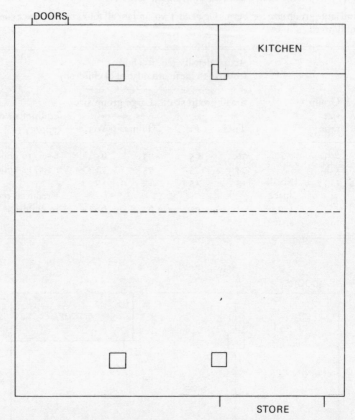

Figure 4.2. Plan of the hall during the second term (Broken line indicates curtain screen.)

the density was relaxed (60 sq. ft per child). This reduced set of equipment was the same as the basic set above, but omitting one pair of tables, the climbing-frame and slide with mat, the tricycle, the rocking-boat, the doll's house with accessories, and the musical instruments.

As the group size ratios were 2:3, 1:2, and 1:3 in successive terms, it was possible to vary the amount of equipment commensurately with group size, thus holding the amount of play equipment per child constant within each term, as shown in Table 4.3. The actual spatial densities each term, based on mean attendance of children, are also shown in Table 4.3.

The amount of space available was varied by means of movable screens. Space variations were achieved in the first term by using a curtain screen hung across the hall as shown in Figure 4.1. The large group condition had

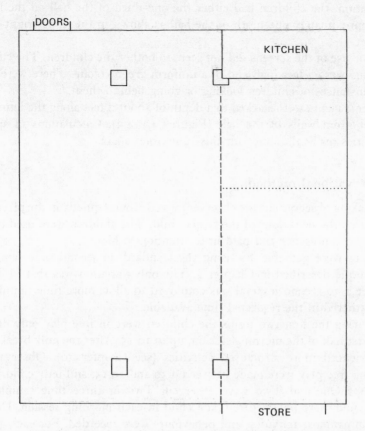

Figure 4.3. Plan of the hall during the third term (Broken line indicates curtain screen.)

all the hall (no screen), and in the smaller group condition only two-thirds of the hall (to the right of the screen) was used.

In the second term the hall was divided in half as shown in Figure 4.2. In this case it was possible to use folding floor-to-ceiling screens which were among the fixtures in the hall. Two screens folded out from the walls to meet in the centre. The large group condition had all the hall, and in the smaller group condition only the half of the hall in the upper part of Figure 4.2 was used.

In the third term the hall was divided by curtain screens hung as shown in Figure 4.3. During this term spatial density was covaried with group size. In the large group condition, the children either had all the hall or the one-third of the hall on the right in Figure 4.3. In the smaller group condition, the children had either the one-third of the hall on the right, or approximately one-ninth of the hall as shown in the upper right-hand corner.

The use of the screens did not seem to bother the children. The curtain screens were 7 feet high and of a uniform green colour. There were very few instances of children looking or going behind them.

Some chairs were stacked to a depth of about 2 feet along the left-hand and bottom walls of the hall (Figures 4.1–4.3). Calculations of spatial densities made allowance for this 'unusable' space.

Observational methods

In making observations the observer moved around quietly in the playroom to watch the behaviour of the target child. The children were used to the observer's presence and paid little attention to him.

Data were gathered by using the standard 40-second time-sampling technique described in Chapter 2. The only variation was that in Term Three a 30-second interval was employed to allow more time samples to be gathered in the restricted time available.

During the first two terms the children were in free play only during the first half of the morning session, up to 10.15. After the milk break they experienced more structured activities (see Chapter 10). Observations during free play were made between 9.30 and 10.15, and only children in Groups One and Two were observed. Two or three time samples of behaviour were obtained for each child in each morning session. Details of companions, activities, and behaviours were recorded. For each group size there were ten sessions of observation, giving 25 time samples per child, per condition.

During the third term the children were in free play throughout the morning (with the exception of the milk break from 10.15 to 11.00). Both spatial density conditions were given each morning, each condition occupying half a morning (see Table 4.3 and Chapter 6). Because of the extremely crowded conditions, only four weeks of observations were made. In each half-morning, 5 time samples of behaviour were obtained for each child. This gave a total of 20 samples per child, per group size, per spatial density condition.

Methods of analysis

Analyses of variance were used on statistics based on the number of samples in which particular categories of companion choice, activity choice, or behaviour, were recorded.

During Terms One and Two, two-factor designs were used. The first factor (two levels) was group size; the second (five levels) was time, comprising observations for two-week periods within the total of ten weeks. It was considered important to check for possible interactions of time with group size, as the presence of such interaction effects would suggest that the degree of mutual acquaintance between the children, and possible differences between the group sizes in this respect, might be important. Sex was not introduced as a factor with the analyses of variance as the sexes were not so well balanced for age as, for example, in the study in Chapter 5. The leeway in varying group sizes by natural fallout and admissions did not allow for this degree of age-matching across the sexes. However, the computer print-out of results was designed to enable a rapid visual inspection of likely sex differences in relation to group size, and individual categories showing evidence of a sex interaction could then be examined further.

During Term Three, a three-factor design was used. The first factor, group size, had two levels; the second factor, spatial density, also had two levels; the third factor, time, had two levels, corresponding to two successive two-week periods. Analysis of any interaction effects with time were felt to be especially important in this study; outside the four-week observation period, more space and equipment were provided, so the experimental conditions were relatively novel. Only main effects and interactions with group size and time are discussed in this chapter; results for spatial density are presented in Chapter 6.

The significance levels obtained from each individual analysis are an overestimate of the confidence with which results can be generalised to other groups of children, as mentioned in Chapter 2. This is because of the non-independence of behaviour in individual children. However, analyses of variance were carried out separately for both Groups One and Two. When the same effects were found to be significant for both groups, the confidence with which the results could be generalised was thought to be considerable enhanced. It was even stronger of course when similar results were obtained for each of the three different terms in which the series of three studies was carried out.

Analyses of variance were carried out on all the categories of number and nature of companions and choice of equipment item or activity. Also, results for 89 behaviour units, and 16 composite units, were analysed. Definitions are given in Appendix B.

Results

Sociometric analyses

In presenting the results, a diagrammatic portrayal of sociometric relationships is given first. Figures 4.4–4.9 show the friendship networks, based on children observed together in group play with the focal child. These are calculated separately for each term, for Groups One and Two. Each Figure shows the network for Group One or Two (a) by itself or (b) with Group Three.

Strength of friendship is indicated by the number of lines between two children (and, less accurately, by distance on the sociogram). Triple linkage lines indicate that these children were seen playing together in 40 per cent or more of all the sample periods in which they were observed; double linkage lines mean they played together between 20 per cent and 40 per cent of the sample periods; single lines similarly mean between 15 per cent and 20 per cent. Children who did not play with any other particular child for more than 15 per cent of the sample periods are shown as isolates, unconnected with other children. Boys are shown as squares, girls as circles. Children in Group Three are shown as squares or circles surrounded by a hexagon.[1]

Group One, Term One

When by themselves, most of the Group One children formed a close-knit network, especially involving cross-sex friendships between four girls (20, 21, 23, 56) and three boys (17, 49, 51) (Fig. 4.4a). Other cross-sex friendships are noticeable (53 and 66; 65 and 70; 50 and 54 or 71).

When mixed with the Group Three children, the tight central network loosened (Fig. 4.4b). Girls 20 and 56 separated as a same-sex pair. Boy 50 formed a close friendship with boy 84 and has drawn away from the central network. Girl 55 also separated to form loose links with girls 54 and 89. Nevertheless the 'core' group of girls 21 and 23 and boys 17, 49, and 51 remained. The Group Three children were moderately well integrated, but apart from boy 84 (a confident boy who knew 50 beforehand), they were not in central positions.

Boy 85 and girl 86 were a brother and sister who frequently played together.

[1] Friendships between Group Three children and those in Group One or Two can be estimated accurately from the focal samples on the latter. Friendships *between* Group Three children were estimated from additional sociometric scans. During Terms One and Two these were based on only 12 scans, so they are less reliable than the other data.

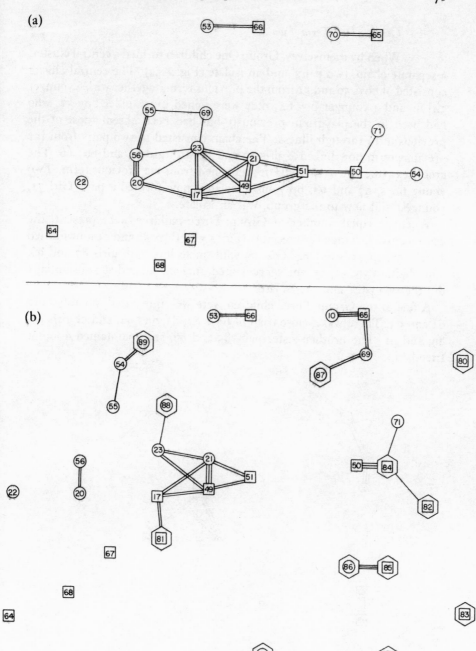

Figure 4.4a, b. Sociometric structure of Group One children by themselves (N = 20), and with Group Three children (N = 32), during the first term

Group One, Term Two

When by themselves, Group One children formed a central cluster, a separate chain, two pairs, and an isolate (Fig. 4.5a). The central cluster consisted of boys 50 and 51 from the previous term, together with a younger girl 69 and a younger boy 64; they were joined by an older boy 52, who had been in the playgroup previously but had been absent most of the previous term through illness. The chain consisted of two pairs from the previous term now linked – girls 56 and 55 with girl 53 and boy 66. The cross-sex pair, boy 65 and girl 70, remained from the previous term. Two young boys, 67 and 68, previously isolates, now formed a pair. Girl 71, youngest and new to the group, was an isolate.

When an equal number of Group Three children were present, the central cluster changed appreciably (Fig. 4.5b). Boys 50 and 51 now formed a tight group with boy 84. Girl 69 split off to link with girls 87 and 96. The chain of 56, 55, 53, and 66 remained unchanged, and so substantially did the two pairs and the isolate.

A few of the Group Three children were well integrated, notably boys 84 and 93. There was a close triad of boys 82, 83, and 94, and of girls 88, 89, and 91. The brother–sister pair, 85 and 86, still maintained a looser friendship.

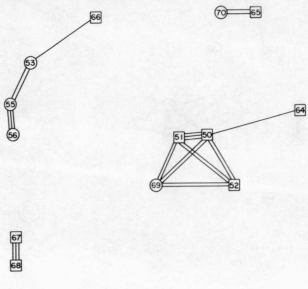

Figure 4.5a. Sociometric structure of Group One children by themselves ($N = 14$), during the second term

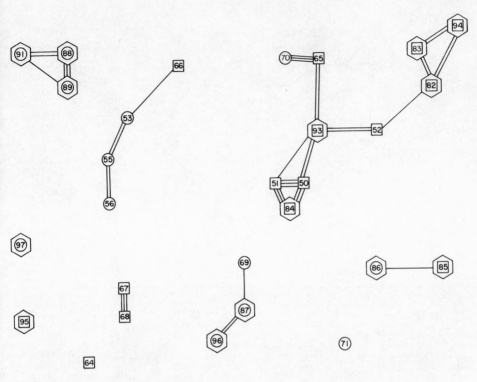

Figure 4.5b. Sociometric structure of Group One children with Group Three children ($N = 28$), during the second term

Group One, Term Three

When by themselves, Group One children formed a large cluster with both strong and weaker links, many of them cross-sex (Fig. 4.6a). The consistent pair, girl 70 and boy 65, was drawn in via 70 to a central core of boys 51 and 52 and girls 56, 69, and 71. The pair of younger boys 67 and 68 remained apart. Boy 66 was an isolate now that girl 53 had left. Girl 98, newest and youngest, was also an isolate.

When a larger number of Group Three children were present, the core cluster of same- and cross-sex links was shattered (Fig. 4.6b). Boys 51 and 52 separated off to join a larger boys' group including 82, 84, and 93, and also a girl 111 who was boy 52's younger sister. Girl 56 separated to form a pair with boy 100. Girl 69 separated to join a same-sex chain link with girls 89 and 104. Girl 71 separated to form a same-sex pair with girl 105.

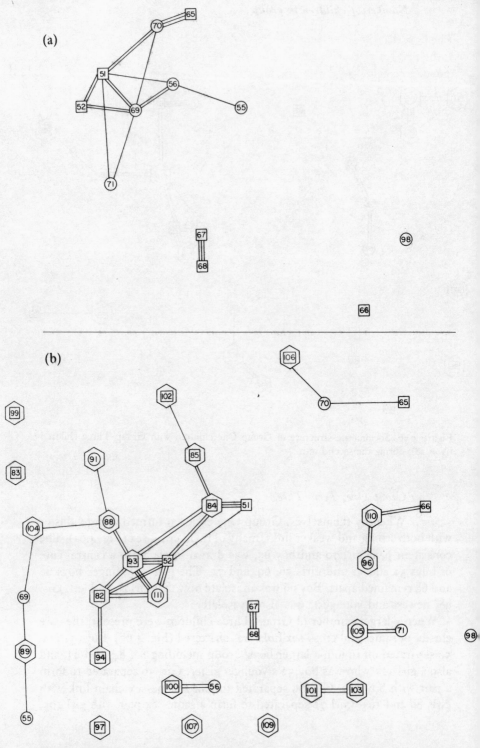

Figure 4.6a, b. Sociometric structure of Group One children by themselves ($N = 12$), and with Group Three children ($N = 35$), during the third term

The pair girl 70 and boy 65 moved away and had a much looser friendship, 70 being also attracted to girl 106. The pair of younger boys 67 and 68 remained unchanged.

The Group Three children were well integrated with the others and the friendship structure of Group One was radically altered in the larger group. There was a large central core of mainly older boys (incorporating only one girl who tagged along as sister of one of the boys), together with a long chain link of girls, and many pairs and isolates.

Group Two, Term One

When by themselves, the Group Two children formed two tight clusters, a chain, and some isolates (Fig. 4.7a). The largest and tightest cluster was of five boys, 38, 40, 42, 58, and 72. There was also a tight cluster of four girls, 45, 46, 48, and 62. There were looser chain-like links between two boys, 57 and 59, and three girls, 47, 63, and 79. It is noticeable that the link between 59 and 63 is the *only* cross-sex link appearing in the sociogram.

There were minor changes with the addition of a smaller number of Group Three children (Fig. 4.7b). The core of five boys remained intact and virtually unchanged. Boys 57 and 59 broke their chain links, and boy 73 also tagged along. Girls 47 and 63 remained linked together, and also loosely with girls 61 and 78. The core of four girls remained together, and with links to girl 60 and to boy 84.

Apart from boy 84, the Group Three children were not well integrated and had little impact on the friendship network. Boy 85 and girl 86 were a brother–sister pair.

Group Two, Term Two

When by themselves, the Group Two children formed one large loose cluster, with several isolates (Fig. 4.8a). This is very different from the previous term's sociogram, owing to the departure for school of all the core children apart from girl 62. There was now a central triad of girls 62 and 63 with boy 92, with several other linkages.

When present with an equal number of Group Three children, the picture changed considerably (Fig. 4.8b). The central triad was broken, with boy 92 linking closely with boys 84 and 93. Girl 62 linked with girl 96, and more loosely with girl 63 who now linked with girl 61.

The Group Three children were well integrated. In particular, there was a strong friendship network between five girls, 87, 88, 89, 91, and 96. Boy 84 was again fairly central.

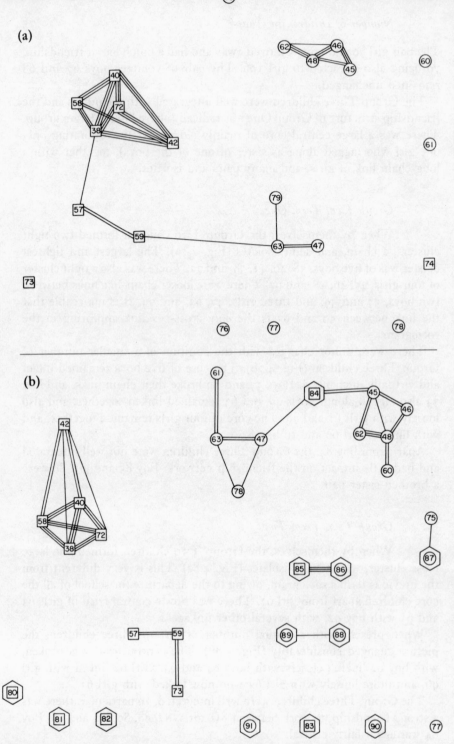

Figure 4.7a, b. Sociometric structure of Group Two children by themselves ($N = 22$), and with Group Three children ($N = 34$), during the first term

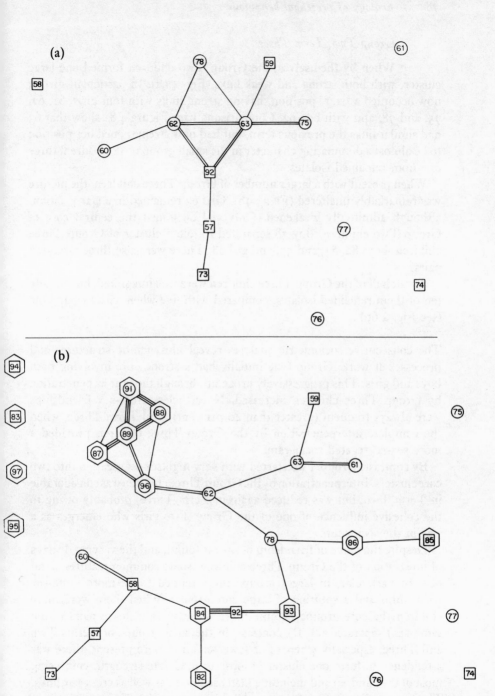

Figure 4.8a, b. Sociometric structure of Group Two children by themselves ($N = 14$), and with Group Three children ($N = 28$), during the second term

Group Two, Term Three

When by themselves, the Group Two children formed one large cluster, with both strong and weak links (Fig. 4.9a). In particular, girl 63 now occupied a 'star' position, having strong links with four girls, 61, 62, 75, and 78, and with boy 92. Comparisons with Figure 4.8a show that 63 had similar links the previous term, but had now strengthened her position to be almost a dominating character in the small group of 11 children, three of whom remained isolates.

When present with a larger number of Group Three children, the picture was remarkably unaltered (Fig. 4.9b). Girl 63 remained in a star position, although admittedly weakened. Only girl 89 joined the central core of Group Two children. Boy 58 separated to join a cluster of Group Three children, boys 82, 84, and 93, and girl 88. There were also three same-sex pairs.

About half of the Group Three children were well integrated, but equally ten of them remained isolates, compared with five when with Group One (see Fig. 4.6b).

The consecutive sociometric analyses reveal idosyncratic structures and processes at work. Group One initially had a strong core involving both boys and girls. This progressively broke up through the year as penetration by Group Three children increased. Nevertheless cross-sex friendships were always frequent (greater than 40 per cent) until Term Three, when the complete interpenetration by the Group Three children provided a more sex-segregated sociogram.

By contrast, Group Two started with very high sex segregation into two core clusters. Interpenetration by the Group Three children was considerable in Term Two, but was reduced again in Term Three, probably owing to the cohesive influence of one of the Group Two girls who emerges as a star in the sociogram.

Despite the range of friendship networks found, and the varying degrees of integration of the Group Three children, some common features stand out. In particular, in larger groups there tended to be more same-sex friendships and a splitting of large core groups. When there were more children the core groups became more unisexual and more pairs (often same-sex) separated off. By contrast, in the small groups of Terms Two and Three, especially when 14 or fewer children were present, there was a tendency to form one cluster of loose to moderate strength, embracing most of the children and including many same-sex as well as cross-sex links. These generalisations are supported by the quantitative data reported next on choice of companions.

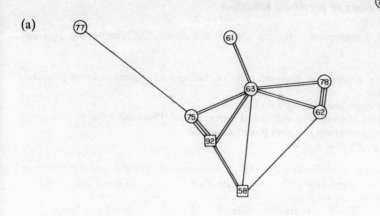

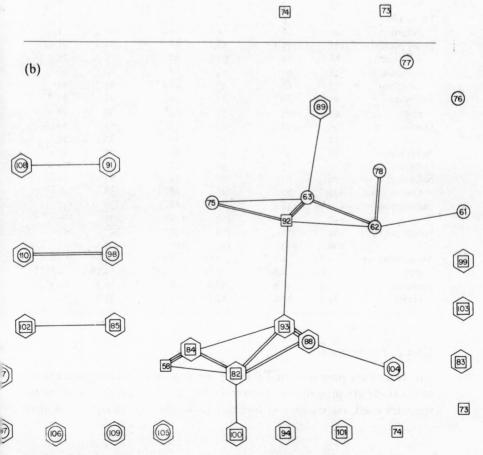

Figure 4.9a, b. Sociometric structure of Group Two children by themselves ($N = 11$), and with Group Three children ($N = 34$), during the third term

Table 4.4. *Companions: results, and significance levels, comparing different group sizes*

Totals for 11 categories of companion choice; means for subgroup size and percentage same-sex choice.
Group One upper line; Group Two lower line.
S   Interaction of group size with spatial density (Term Three only)
T   Interaction of group size with project experience
* $P < 0.05$ ** $P < 0.01$

	Term One		Term Two		Term Three	
	Small ($N = 20$)	Large ($N = 30$)	Small ($N = 12$)	Large ($N = 24$)	Small ($N = 10$)	Large ($N = 30$)
Alone	74	73	63	64	66	67
	78	99	93	65*	69	87
Small adult	17	10	5	6	6	11
subgroup	15	7	4	1	5	2
Large adult	1	0	1	1	3	7
subgroup	2	3	1	2	0	3
Small parallel	101	79 T*	57	68	82	81
subgroup	88	85	60	67	75	76
Large parallel	48	67	25	18	80	66
subgroup	71	68	43	48 T**	64	53
Same-sex	65	86	83	71	60	95**
pair	92	104	53	84*	65	78
Opposite-sex	56	57	49	45	57	52
pair	13	20	32	30	33	30
Subgroup of	59	66	39	47	63	48 S**
three	70	77	38	35	71	73
Subgroup of	79	62	28	30	63	52 T*
four or more	121	87	26	18	58	48 T*
Parallel play	149	146	82	86	162	147
	159	153	103	115	139	129
Group play	259	271	199	193	242	247
	296	288	149	168	227	219
Mean subgroup	3.00	2.78*	2.62	2.57	2.92	2.62*
size	3.09	2.89**	2.70	2.44*	2.78	2.64**
Same-sex	54.3	56.9	58.0	58.8	50.5	66.4*
choice	84.0	87.2*	62.7	69.5	57.0	69.1

Choice of companions

The results are presented in Table 4.4. Results for all three separate terms of the study are presented concurrently. Bearing in mind the nature of the statistics used, consistency of findings across the two groups of children and the three terms is more indicative of a genuine effect than one isolated 'significant' result. The relatively small numbers of focal children during Terms Two and Three mean that only quite strong and pervasive effects are likely to emerge as significant in individual comparisons. However, if all six comparisons show the same trend, this is itself significant at beyond the 5 per cent level on a binomial test, even though each individual comparison might be non-significant at this level.

From Table 4.4 it can be seen that children were very seldom scored as being in a *small adult subgroup* or *large adult subgroup*. As intended, during the free-play conditions interaction between staff and children was infrequent. Also, there were no consistent variations with group size.

Children were quite often scored as being *alone*, but despite one significant comparison (Group Two, Term Two, more *alone* in smaller group), the overall variations with group size were small or inconsistent. This was also true for *small parallel subgroup*, *large parallel subgroup*, and *group play*. The variations in group size clearly did not affect gross levels of social participation as measured by these indices.

Some effects were apparent when more detailed analysis of companions in group play was undertaken. From Table 4.4 it can be seen that there tended to be more *same-sex pairs* with larger group size (five comparisons, two significant). There was no similar trend for *opposite-sex pairs*. Looking at percentage of *same-sex choice* for all sub-group sizes, there was a clear and consistent trend in all comparisons, significant in three of them, for a greater proportion of same-sex companions when the group was larger. This was especially marked in Term Three. In all cases children tended to choose more same-sex than opposite-sex companions, but this tendency was less marked in small groups.

There was also a consistent trend (five out of six comparisons, one significant) for fewer *subgroups of four or more* children in the larger group conditions. This shows up even more clearly in the results for *mean subgroup size*. This refers to the mean number of participants in subgroups engaged in group play, and is an average of the statistic calculated separately for each child. On all comparisons *mean subgroup size* was smaller in the larger groups, and significantly so in five of the six comparisons.

This last finding may seem paradoxical. Superficially one might expect that in a larger overall group, there might be more chance of larger subgroups forming. In fact the reverse was the case. The explanation probably lies in the fact that in the larger overall group children were making more diffuse contacts, that is, more contacts with children with whom they play relatively seldom. This is shown for each term in Table 4.5. Here, summed over children, are presented the number of friendships

Table 4.5. *Number of friendship pairings of different strengths, summed over children*

Small group upper line; large group lower line

	Friendship strengths						
	1	2	3–4	5–8	9–13	14–19	20–5
Term One							
Group One	103	38	39	24	8	1	0
	108	48	28	15	6	3	0
Group Two	91	23	33	13	14	10	2
	108	29	19	24	11	6	0
Term Two							
Group One	44	18	23	12	2	5	0
	56	25	10	9	4	3	1
Group Two	44	21	22	13	1	0	0
	57	24	22	9	1	0	0
Term Three							
Group One	25	16	27	14	12	5	1
	52	21	19	7	10	4	3
Group Two	14	10	27	16	14	5	0
	65	27	17	8	11	3	2

of different strengths (number of samples in which two particular children played together). In a larger overall group, there were many more occasions of children playing with other children whom they seldom played with (weak friendships), fewer cases of medium strength friendships, and perhaps one or two more cases of very strong friendships (where the larger group has provided a child with a real 'buddy').

We can expect that if a child is playing with another child whom it does not know well, the coordination of activities will be correspondingly difficult. Another way of saying this is that inter-personal contingent behaviour, necessary in play (Garvey, 1974), is less easily maintained.

One of the social skills which preschool children acquire is this ability to maintain effective inter-personal contingencies, and we may expect this ability to improve between the ages of 2 and 4. One source of evidence to support this is the increase in mean subgroup size with age in children's playgroups (Parten, 1932; Eifermann, 1970). Table 4.6 documents this for the results from Term One of the present study; to get an appreciable sample size, results for Groups One and Two are summed. The children are grouped into three age levels. It can be seen that the younger children, aged $2\frac{1}{2}$–$3\frac{1}{2}$, are most often in pairs when in group play. Children aged $3\frac{1}{2}$–$4\frac{1}{4}$

Table 4.6. *Percentage occurrence of different size of subgroups, and mean subgroup size*

Term One; data from Groups One and Two combined

Number of children	Age range (years)	Number of instances of group play	Subgroup size: percentage occurrence								Mean subgroup size
			2	3	4	5	6	7	8	9+	
14	$4\frac{1}{4}$–5	528	35	25	19	14	5	2	0.2	0	3.35
15	$3\frac{1}{2}$–$4\frac{1}{4}$	401	50	23	14	9	3	1	0	0	2.96
13	$2\frac{1}{2}$–$3\frac{1}{2}$	188	58	26	13	2	1	0	0	0	2.62

are still as likely to be in pairs as in a large subgroup of three or four children. The older children, aged $4\frac{1}{4}$–5, are more likely to be in a larger subgroup (such as three, four, or five children) than in a pair. Right through this age range, subgroups of six or more are very infrequent.

As inter-personal contingencies are more effectively acquired and retained by older children, play in larger subgroups becomes possible. On a similar basis one could argue that if a child at a given age is in a group where he knows other children less well, his reduced effectiveness at maintaining inter-personal contingencies (relative to better-known companions) will be manifested in his being in a smaller subgroup. That is, the children in larger overall groups play in smaller subgroups to compensate for the fact that they know their play partners less well.

This finding provides quantitative justification for the generalisation made from the sociometric data. Also, there is quantitative support for the generalisation made earlier that same-sex friendships increase in larger groups. This is true even for Group Two in Term One (Fig. 4.7), when same-sex choice was already very high in the smaller group. We know that on average children prefer same-sex companions, despite marked individual differences evident in the sociometric diagrams. It would seem that larger groups provide a wider choice of play companions, so that choices which are, on average, more attractive are more likely to be made. The cohesive power of subgroups of boys is shown in most of the larger group sociograms (Fig. 4.5b–4.9b), and of subgroups of girl clusters or chains in several (Figs. 4.5b, 4.6b, 4.7b, 4.9b). These predominantly unisexual groups may facilitate certain types of play (for example, rough-and-tumble play in boys and certain types of fantasy play in girls) which in turn tend to maintain the unisexual composition of the group.

Table 4.7. *Activities: total occurrences, and significance levels, comparing different group sizes*

Group One upper line; Group Two lower line
S   Interaction of group size with spatial density (Term Three only)
T   Interaction of group size with project experience
* $P < 0.05$ ** $P < 0.01$ *** $P < 0.001$

	Term One		Term Two		Term Three	
	Small ($N = 20$)	Large ($N = 30$)	Small ($N = 12$)	Large ($N = 24$)	Small ($N = 10$)	Large ($N = 30$)
Table play	40	55	32	53	65	96*
	66	51	52	83**	62	66
Sandpit	80	56*	48	46	155	136
	63	79	52	48T*	160	99**
Easel	32	32	19	19	46	30S*T*
	44	25*	18	12	29	29
Wendy house	108	115	64	50	117	63**S*
	63	72	30	40	79	64
Doll	45	34	18	31	34	34
	20	34	20	10	28	42
Dressing-up clothes	24	33	27	22	25	29T**
	16	20	21	11	35	35
Climbing-frame	54	51	53	33*	—	—
	92	73	45	21**	—	—
Rocking-boat	20	12T*	22	27	—	—
	21	27	16	22	—	—
Toy chest	52	67	29	30	35	16*
	22	25	8	13T*	31	50S**T**
Tricycle	50	63	29	43T*	—	—
	53	72	19	22	—	—
Rough-and-tumble play	31	24	22	29	15	26
	48	42	22	18	4	13*
Books	22	23	17	12	37	34T**
	20	19	33	34	22	29
Miscellaneous play	56	59	48	36	44	29
	79	52*	30	18	34	39
Fantasy play	130	117	102	97	151	90***
	106	90	58	50	114	88*
Unusual uses of apparatus	29	18T*	12	15	0	2
	8	14	2	0	0	0
Room fitments	0	2	0	0	0	2
	0	2	0	0	0	0
No activity	26	37	14	16	29	38S*T*
	66	69	37	38	41	57

Choice of activities

The results for 17 categories of activity choice are presented in Table 4.7, together with significance levels from analysis of variance. The category *miscellaneous play* here includes *blocks, doll's house, jigsaws, telephone*, and *musical instruments*, each of which occurred relatively infrequently as single categories.

The majority of the activity choice categories showed small or inconsistent changes with the group size variations. These categories are *Wendy house, toy chest, easel, books, dressing-up clothes, doll, unusual uses of apparatus*, and *miscellaneous play. Room fitments* was hardly ever scored. The results for *rough-and-tumble play* are also variable, although the results for Term Three suggest that it occurs seldom in very small groups.

Three activities tended to be scored more frequently in the larger group conditions. *Table play* shows this tendency in five out of six comparisons, two of which are significant. Use of the *tricycle* was also seen consistently more in the larger groups during Terms One and Two (it was not provided in Term Three). Finally, there was a consistent trend for more scores of *no activity* on all six comparisons, although the differences are small, and none individually reaches significance.

Three activities tended to be scored more frequently in the smaller group conditions. *Fantasy play* was always seen more often in the smaller groups, and this is significant for both comparisons in Term 3. The *climbing-frame* was also seen in use more in the smaller groups during Terms One and Two, significantly for both groups in the latter term (it was not provided in Term Three). Finally, children were seen more often playing with the *sandpit* in five out of the six comparisons, two of which are significant.

Perhaps the most interesting result here (and also the most consistent) is the lower occurrence of fantasy play in the larger groups. This did not seem to be specific to certain types of fantasy play. On the one hand, the Wendy house and dressing-up clothes were often used for domestic fantasy or sociodramatic play, but results for these activities were not the same (although the Wendy house was used appreciably less by the larger groups in Term Three). On the other hand, rough-and-tumble play is often a basis for fantasy play in boys especially (Smith, 1977), but the results for that activity too were somewhat dissimilar. (Of course, both use of the Wendy house and rough-and-tumble play were often scored in non-fantasy contexts). It would seem that fantasy play in general occurred less in the larger groups; this may be because in the larger groups the children were less well acquainted, and further evidence will be brought to support this inference later.

It will also be argued subsequently, in connection with the results presented in Chapter 5, that the findings for use of the tricycle, and climbing-frame and slide, were due to variations in resource (R), rather than to group size (N) as was probably the case with the other activities.

Occurrence of behaviours

The results for the shorter list of 27 behaviour units are presented in Table 4.8, together with significance levels from analysis of variance. Fuller results for 89 behaviour units are in Appendix D.

Ten of the 27 behaviour units showed some consistent effect of the group size variations. In smaller groups, there was a greater occurrence of *watching* (all six comparisons), although the effect was a small one. The effect was specific to watching children (rather than adults). In larger groups, by contrast, there was more *looking around* or *looking in the distance*; this was so in all six comparisons, three of which were significant. It will be argued later that this was due to the larger space available in these conditions.

Although watching children was slightly more frequent in the smaller groups, there was little evidence that the occurrence of social contacts was changed. *Verbal, visual,* and *physical contacts* did not show consistent variations with group size, although *talking to/from an adult* was slightly more frequent in smaller groups (five out of six comparisons). So was *object exchange* (all six comparisons, one of which was significant). *Agonistic behaviour* was also slightly more common in smaller groups (five out of six comparisons). This effect for *agonistic behaviour* was not true for *physical aggression*, but was true for the smaller units of *dispute toy, fail take toy,* and *submit* (five out of six comparisons, one or two significant for each category). Thus it was conflicts over objects which were more common in the smaller groups, rather than fighting or aggression for other reasons.

Climbing and sliding were seen more often in the smaller groups (five out of six comparisons, one significant), while in larger groups *pedalling and propelling* were more frequent (four out of four comparisons, two of them significant). *Gross manipulation* of objects generally showed the same effect (all six comparisons, two of them significant), but there was no consistent variation in *fine manipulation* of objects.

Open smile was seen more often in the large group conditions (five out of six comparisons). *Walk, run,* and *chase/flee/group run* showed little variation in Terms One and Two, but in Term Three it is fairly clear that these behaviours occurred more in the larger groups.

There was no consistent variation in automanipulative behaviour. There was a significant effect in Term Three for Group Two, when there was

Table 4.8. *Behaviours: total occurrences, and significance levels, comparing different group sizes*

Shorter list of 27 behaviour units; Group One upper line; Group Two lower line
S   Interaction of group size with spatial density (Term Three only)
T   Interaction of group size with project experience
* $P < 0.05$ ** $P < 0.01$ *** $P < 0.001$

	Term One		Term Two		Term Three	
	Small $(N = 20)$	Large $(N = 30)$	Small $(N = 12)$	Large $(N = 24)$	Small $(N = 10)$	Large $(N = 30)$
Upper smile	151	147	117	106	88	89
	153	186	94	93	80	77
Open smile	59	65	34	45	40	38
	58	77	31	36	20	32 S*
Play noise	68	62	53	45	51	35
	79	94	26	34	29	19
Talking between children	320	334	245	234	289	281
	362	366	205	221	272	245
Talking to/from adult	53	48	32	37	47	46
	52	38	25	17	33	21 S**T**
Look around/ distance	17	25	8	16	6	15*
	22	27	7	20*	1	19***
Watch	95	94	54	40	63	56
	139	128	76	61	71	69
Visual contact child	350	346	239	211	259	276
	382	409	211	242*	247	247
Visual contact adult	61	67	38	35	39	41 T**
	77	59	34	28	35	33 T*
Contact apparatus	258	271	178	173	243	241
	246	239	188	181	270	234
Physical contact between children	157	167	127	136	186	162
	218	182	121	114	154	149
Physical contact with adult	12	13	6	9	9	10
	22	9**	6	5	6	2
Walk	253	268	192	182	188	212
	314	285	177	173	138	188**

Table 4.8. (*cont.*)

	Term One		Term Two		Term Three	
	Small (N = 20)	Large (N = 30)	Small (N = 12)	Large (N = 24)	Small (N = 10)	Large (N = 30)
Run	101	103	85	98	32	52*
	112	100	79	60	23	58***S***
Climb/slide	59	58	50	34	12	11
	78	67	48	24*	12	12
Chase/flee/ group run	18	16	6	20*	6	14*
	24	20	18	15	3	10
Object exchange	56	46	49	47	88	85
	64	57	41	37	84	51**
Push/pull	58	67	29	53*	23	28
	50	53	20	19	23	37*
Kick/throw/ hit	23	20	21	16	35	36
	27	36	17	13	17	14T*
Pedal/propel	38	51	23	29	0	0
	44	68*	16	18	1	2
Fine manipulation	251	251	188	177	351	335S*
	246	235	191	204	320	279*
Gross manipulation	70	77	41	66*	19	31
	62	78	27	32	20	45**
Physical aggression	26	22	14	18	25	15
	16	16	13	7	12	16
Agonistic behaviour	66	50	36	32	52	53
	50	45	41	28	46	42
Suck	32	29	23	17	28	26
	47	56	32	34	31	21
Face contact	84	72	59	62	47	45
	85	99	68	65	49	56
Auto- manipulation	190	175	136	132	145	148
	245	258	151	154	130	176**

more *automanipulation* in the larger group, and also less *fine manipulation* of objects. Other evidence (Chapter 6) suggests that these two behaviours are antagonistically related; however, this significant finding on one comparison is not reliably supported by the others.

Overall, the effects of the group size variation on the occurrence of behaviour units were fairly small. The most obvious relate to different activity choices (see Table 4.7). The slightly increased rates of object exchange and disputes over objects in the smaller group sizes may be related to the increased use of the sandpit in these conditions; the sandpits contained many small cartons and objects which were often squabbled over or exchanged. The climbing-frame was also used more, so there was more climbing and sliding. Conversely, there was less pedalling, propelling, pushing, and pulling with decreased use of the tricycle (and also perhaps of the toy chest), in the smaller groups. There was less gross motor activity and rough-and-tumble play only in the Term Three comparisons, where the smaller groups were of 12 or fewer children, and in a correspondingly small area.

Thus the effects seen with respect to behaviour units can, by and large, be explained in terms of differential activity choice. Changes in occurrence of social contacts in the differing group size conditions were small or non-existent, and this corresponds to the lack of effect for overall parallel or group activity noted in the companions analyses.

Behavioural contacts

In the course of the sampling procedure, each child contacted by the focal child was noted individually (see Chapter 2). This was done for verbal, visual, and physical contacts, contacts via object exchange, and agonistic encounters. As well as counting up the number of samples in which each kind of contact occurred, it was also possible to count the average number of children per sample to whom contacts were made by each child. This was done for the kinds of contact mentioned above, and also for group and parallel companions. The results are tabulated in two ways. First, how many children were contacted in large compared with small group sizes; second, within the large groups, the proportion of children contacted within Group Three, compared with those in Group One or Group Two.

The proportion of children contacted in the large group relative to the small group is shown in the first part of Table 4.9. The proportions do not diverge far from unity; thus a particular child made contacts with a similar number of other children in the two conditions. Close friendly contacts – *group*, *verbal*, *physical*, and *object exchange* – were slightly fewer in the large groups. From the earlier data reported on companion choice we know that this is due to smaller subgroup sizes, rather than less group play, in these conditions. *Visual contacts*, and especially *parallel companions*, were slightly more numerous in the large groups. Conversely, *agonistic contacts* were relatively fewer. This seems to be related to the lower frequency of sample occurrence, as noted earlier.

The proportion of children contacted in Group Three (the less familiar children), compared with those in Group One or Group Two is shown in

Table 4.9. *Average number of children with whom different kinds of contact were made by focal child*

(a) Proportion of contacts in large compared with small groups; (b) proportion of contacts to Group Three children compared with Group One or Group Two children, relative to expected contacts based on mean attendance

	Overall mean	Group One mean	Group Two mean	Group One			Group Two		
				Term One	Term Two	Term Three	Term One	Term Two	Term Three
a									
Parallel	1.07	1.09	1.05	1.06	1.25	0.97	1.10	1.23	0.82
Visual	1.01	0.98	1.07	0.99	0.90	1.04	1.09	1.10	1.01
Verbal	0.98	1.00	0.95	1.03	0.99	0.98	0.95	0.96	0.94
Physical	0.98	1.02	0.93	1.08	1.08	0.89	0.79	0.88	1.13
Group	0.92	0.93	0.91	0.93	0.91	0.96	0.86	0.98	0.90
Object exchange	0.91	0.95	0.87	0.84	1.05	0.95	1.05	0.95	0.62
Agonistic	0.88	0.90	0.86	0.81	0.82	1.08	0.98	0.59	1.00
b									
Parallel	1.05	1.07	1.03	1.00	0.89	1.33	0.99	0.79	1.32
Agonistic	0.90	0.96	0.84	0.78	1.15	0.94	0.84	1.02	0.67
Visual	0.73	0.89	0.57	0.55	0.85	1.28	0.59	0.54	0.59
Object exchange	0.68	0.88	0.48	0.69	0.89	1.05	0.58	0.35	0.51
Group	0.61	0.83	0.39	0.46	0.64	1.39	0.29	0.56	0.33
Physical	0.59	0.72	0.46	0.39	0.70	1.08	0.36	0.56	0.46
Verbal	0.58	0.74	0.43	0.46	0.68	1.07	0.39	0.48	0.41

the second part of Table 4.9. The proportions for *parallel contacts* are near unity. This would be expected if the children mixed fairly randomly with regard to spatial distribution and activity choice. However, as regards close friendly contacts, it can be seen that *group*, *verbal*, *physical*, and *object exchange* contacts were much less frequent overall to Group Three. *Visual contacts* and *agonistic contacts* were intermediate.

This finding is consistent with the sociometric data reported previously. By and large, the Group Three children were not as fully integrated with the Group One or Group Two children as the latter were amongst themselves. The clear exception to this generalisation is Group One in Term Three (Fig. 4.6a, b). Here there was a high degree of interpenetration, and the data in the second part of Table 4.9 show that in this case the pattern is largely reversed, with all kinds of contacts (except agonistic) being more frequent to Group Three children.

Examination of the data for agonistic contacts provides the most intriguing finding. In Group One, Term Three, there were many group contacts with Group Three children, but agonistic contacts remained at the average level. This was also the only comparison for which there were as many incidents of agonistic encounters in the large as in the small group size (Table 4.8). Usually there were fewer incidents in the large group conditions (Tables 4.8, and first part of 4.9), although the proportion of agonistic contacts with Group Three children approached unity and was appreciably greater than the proportion of close friendly contacts (second part of Table 4.9). This would suggest that there were fewer agonistic incidents per group play incident among Group One or Group Two children when they were in a larger overall group. Perhaps the greater freedom of choice in a larger group (see Table 4.5) means that a child can more readily play with another child whom he or she is less likely to quarrel with; or that a potential agonistic situation is more readily resolved by a child's going off to play with a different companion. Conversely, in a small, intimate group, a child may be 'trapped' into playing with a particular companion, even if they quarrel. This would tend to make agonistic encounters more frequent (per child) in a smaller group. This effect is probably partially offset by the relative strangeness of children in a larger group, and therefore the relatively greater probability of an agonistic conflict *if* contact is made. This offsetting factor would be particularly great for Group One in Term Three when many contacts with Group Three children were being made during the term.

Table 4.10. *Number of main effects and interactions significant at 5 per cent level for main effects of group size and project experience*

Results from analyses of variance, compared with number of results expected by chance; separate totals for Groups One and Two in brackets; figures for analyses from all three terms combined

	Main effects		Interaction effects group size × project experience	Expected by chance (approx.)
	Group size	Project experience		
Choice of companions	10	5	5	4
(13 categories)	(4, 6)	(3, 2)	(2, 3)	
Choice of activities	13	15	8	5
(17 categories)	(6, 7)	(8, 7)	(5, 3)	
Behaviour units	19	23	7	8
(27 categories)	(6, 13)	(14, 9)	(3, 4)	
Behaviour units	43	53	17	27
(89 categories)	(20, 23)	(31, 18)	(9, 8)	

Project experience

Apart from group size, the other main factor in the analyses of variance carried out on the data was project experience, defined as time elapsed through each term. Any effects of this factor could be due to age and/or experience of the children.

About the same number of comparisons emerged as significant for project experience as for group size (see Table 4.10). As the former was not a primary factor of interest in the investigation, it seemed appropriate to take a more stringent condition for consistency and significance of results than was done for the group size results. This is because it is less important to avoid a Type 1 error (rejection of a true result). In first examining the results for project experience, only categories for which two comparisons were significant and consistent (effects in the same direction) were considered further.

By this criterion, none of the categories of choice of companions showed effects of project experience, while two of the categories of activity choice did, and were examined further. These were *Wendy house* and *creative uses of apparatus*. Two other categories – *toy chest* and *miscellaneous play* – showed markedly irregular variation with time.

Detailed results for the *Wendy house* and *creative uses of apparatus* are shown in Table 4.11. Use of the *Wendy house* showed a significant decline in both Groups One and Two during Term One; after that its use was fairly

Table 4.11. *Project experience for selected categories*

See p. 92. Terms One and Two divided into five blocks each; results presented for first two and last two blocks; Term Three divided into two blocks, results shown directly
* $P < 0.05$ ** $P < 0.01$ *** $P < 0.001$

See p. 92.

	Term One		Term Two		Term Three	
	Group One	Group Two	Group One	Group Two	Group One	Group Two
Wendy house	113 76*	72 38**	41 46	31 26	86 94	85 58
Creative uses of apparatus	18 26	1 17**	0 14**	2 0	2 0	0 0
Talking between children	245 289*	292 299	184 194	158 184	254 316***	270 247
Look at observer	48 22*	34 17**	12 9	13 10	21 10	7 5
Stare at observer	11 1**	15 3**	6 2	5 5	8 1*	5 5

constant. It seemed that this piece of apparatus was initially very attractive; the amount of usage subsequently became more stable.

Creative uses of apparatus was scored a number of times during Term One, but by Term Three was virtually absent. The decrease across terms contrasts with the increase within terms, significant on two comparisons. The explanation for this strange result may lie in the earlier experiences of some of the older children. The category was scored for very unusual uses of apparatus such as improvising chair-trains, or spinning rocking-boats upside-down. These had been largely 'discovered' and utilised during an earlier short experiment when only the large apparatus had been presented to the children (see Chapter 6 and Table 2.1). This experiment had taken place more than a year earlier, and only a few of the remaining older children in Term One of the present study had experienced it. All these children had left by Term Two. It would seem that the 'tradition' of these kinds of apparatus use was dying out as the children who had originally experienced optimal conditions for facilitating the behaviour left the playgroup.

Only a few of the behaviour units showed consistent effects of project experience. These were *talking to child* and *talk from child*, and the composite category *talking between children*; and *look at observer* and *stare at observer*. In addition some markedly irregular time variations were noted for *glance at child, throw, receive physical contact adult, contact apparatus, mouth fumble*, and *automanipulation*. Several of these latter categories had low inter-observer agreement (Appendix B), which may have been responsible.

Effects of project experience for *talking between children* are shown in Table 4.11. Five of the six comparisons showed an increase with time, two of them being significant. This could well be an effect of increased age of the children (Smith and Connolly, 1974) and is not a surprising finding.

Results for *look at observer* and *stare at observer* are also given in Table 4.11. There was a consistent decline within each term, most pronounced in Term One when the overall rate of occurrence was also higher. By Terms Two and Three the occurrence of these behaviours was fairly stable, at about one sample in eighty for *stare*, and about one sample in forty for *look*. The occurrence of *talking to observer* was even rarer – only four samples during the whole year (three during Term One). These findings serve to support the claim that observer presence did not appreciably disturb the children's behaviour.

Interactions of group size with project experience

The number of significant interactions found between the two main factors of group size and project experience are shown in Table 4.10. They did not differ greatly from the number that would be expected purely by chance. Furthermore, no categories gave consistent results by the criteria outlined earlier. We therefore conclude that age and experience in the playgroup are not important with regard to the effects of the group size variations.

Sex differences in relation to group size effects

Boys and girls were not equally balanced for number and age within each group, so taking account of sex as a factor in the analysis of variance would have been difficult. However, a computer print-out of separate data for boys and girls in both the small and large group conditions did enable a rapid visual scan of likely interactions with sex. Overall differences between the sexes are not discussed here, but only possible interactions of sex with group size.

Scanning the results suggested that by and large the group size effects held true for both boys and girls, and that interaction effects were few and not consistent across the six possible comparisons. It was concluded that sex could be disregarded as an important factor so far as the group size effects were concerned. Evidence for this is presented in Table 4.12, which

Table 4.12. *Percentage difference in occurrence from small to large group size*

Results average over both groups and all three terms

	Boys	Girls		Boys	Girls
Companions			Behaviour units		
Mean subgroup size	−4.1	−9.1	Open smile	+12.5	+28.8
			Talking to/from adult	0.0	−22.7
Same-sex choice	+23.4	+3.3	Look around/distance	+102.6	+100.9
Activities			Watch	−7.6	−15.4
Table play	+47.5	+21.8	Object exchange	−20.5	−9.1
Sandpit	−6.0	−9.3			
Climbing-frame	−17.3	−33.0	Gross manipulation	+71.4	+40.6
Tricycle	+76.0	+7.2			
Fantasy play	−18.8	−8.1	Agonistic behaviour	−3.4	−22.8
No activity	+20.6	+20.2			

gives separate results for boys and girls for the companion categories, activity categories, and main behaviour units for which significant group size effects were found. Results are presented in terms of the percentage difference in occurrence between small and large group sizes, averaged over the six comparisons. In all cases but one, boys and girls showed changes in the same direction and generally of the same order of magnitude. This conclusion is confirmed by a separate consideration of results for each group in each term. The one exception is for *talking to/from an adult*, where the decrease in the larger group conditions was found consistently only for girls, the overall effect being absent for boys.

Staff comments on the group size variations

Towards the end of the third term each of the three staff at the playgroup was given an open-ended questionnaire sheet to fill in. This asked the following questions:

What effect do you think it has on the children's behaviour having large (25–35) or small (10–14) groups of children at playgroup?
   (a) generally?
   (b) any special effects on particular children?
   (c) how does it affect you?

The answers to part (a) of the questionnaire are reproduced verbatim below:

Miss C (supervisor):

The children seem more ready to settle and play in the small group. Behaviour is better generally and less aggressive, though there is less fighting in the large group over popular toys like tricycles.

The large group seems to frighten some children, causing them to retire, and brings out leadership and cooperation (and more aggression in some children) in other children.

Mrs Y (assistant):

Small group seems to encourage table play and Wendy house play. The children seem to be more aware of each other's names. In the large group the children seem to push and shove and grab to a larger extent, and the speed of play seems faster and less coordinated. More toys seem to be thrown around and more children seem to have bumps and knocks than in the small group. This is because it is difficult for the staff to see them at a glance when they are playing in a group.

Mrs Z (assistant):

Less aggression with the smaller group, but more isolated play as children can play on their own more easily. Children don't fight over apparatus as much as there is less competition.

These comments are more valid as personal impressions than as reliable guides to changes in the children's behaviour. Regarding social participation, Miss C and Mrs Z have opposite views of the effects of solitary play, but in fact no overall effect was observed. Mrs Y's comments on table play and Wendy house play are also not borne out by the observational data; indeed table play was rather *less* frequent in the smaller groups.

All three staff report more aggression in the larger group, although Miss C qualifies this. In a sense there was of course more aggression in the larger group, because there were more children, and therefore the number of conspicuous incidents noticed by staff was likely to be greater. However, the observational data show that in terms of aggression frequency *per child*, this was if anything reduced in the larger groups.

Similarly, Miss C's comments on leadership may be correct in that she could observe more instances of it in a larger group, but the incidence per child was probably less; certainly subgroups were smaller in the larger group conditions.

Only Miss C answered part (b) of the questionnaire. Her answer was to the effect that some new children found it easier to settle in a smaller group. She also remarked that one or two well-established children were much more noisy and boisterous in the larger groups.

The answers to part (c) are reproduced verbatim below:

Miss C (supervisor):

The very small groups of children (10) soon became boring, as the group is not only small but also instant: projects cannot be worked on over a period of time – stimulating a subject of conversation that can be added to. Each small group starts afresh and topics can become over-used.

The largest groups (30–35) create difficulties as organisation becomes difficult and time-consuming, leaving little personal contact, and detachment through frustration.

Mrs Y (assistant):

The small group is very boring to watch after a while, because the staff are not so constantly involved. There are fewer paintings to take down, aprons to put on, hands to wipe and less toilet-taking. This kind of involvement leads to conversation, therefore there seems less adult–child relationship in the small group during free play. The less involved we become the less we make the effort of being involved and aware of what the children are doing. During the structured part it is easier and more satisfying with a smaller group. The noise level can be more irritating in a large group and the atmosphere seems more hectic.

Mrs Z (assistant):

I find the larger group more interesting as there are more demands on me and I am therefore more involved – even if it's only taking them to the loo! The small group can be very boring as there is so much less to be involved with.

In part, these comments reflect thoughts on the more structured half of the morning, in which activities were organised and staff–child interaction was encouraged (see Chapter 10). This is especially the case with the comments of Miss C, the supervisor. So far as the comments on the free-play sessions are concerned, the consensus seems to be that very small groups can be boring and uninvolving, even at a routine level, but conversely that really large groups can be difficult to organise and create a noisy, hectic environment.

It should be noted again that perceptions of staff need not necessarily be congruent with perceptions or experience of children. Mrs Y comments that there was less adult–child relationship in the small group during free play. This was true from her viewpoint, as there were fewer children for her to interact with. From the children's point of view, however, there may have been as much or more interaction with an adult in the smaller group conditions. Indeed there were more observations of *talking to/from an adult* by children when in the smaller groups.

Pointing out that staff perceptions are not necessarily congruent with children's experience is not intended to denigrate the former. The comments are obviously valid, and therefore valuable, as indications of how the staff perceived the situation. It is clear that they preferred group sizes between the extremes, neither too boring nor too difficult. Also, they were more likely to notice and experience certain salient types of behaviour in the large groups, such as aggressive behaviour, leadership, and withdrawal. However, from the viewpoint of an individual child these are no more likely in a large group than a small one. The data from the staff should not be used as a substitute for data from direct observations on child behaviour, any more than one would use observations of child behaviour to infer staff perceptions.

Summary

Using the terminology of Chapter 3, this was an *NR* type study, carried out on two groups for three separate terms (six comparisons). Sociometric plots based on observational data revealed the social structure of each group in each term. These varied considerably in characteristics such as the amount of sex segregation in friendships. In most cases, there was a tendency in the larger group conditions for there to be some segregation between Group One (or Two) and Group Three, in the sense that there were fewer friendships between these two sets of children than would be expected on a purely random basis. This was to be expected, as the Group One (or Group Two) children would know each other better than the Group Three children, whom they only met half as often. However, the extent of this also varied, and indeed in Term Three the Group One and Group Three children were fully integrated.

Despite variations in sociometric structure, the effects of the group size variations showed some common features in all the separate comparisons. In the main, these seem to be changes in activity choices occurring with changes in structure of companion preferences for group play. Children knew each other better in the small groups and probably because of this mean subgroups were larger and subgroups of four or more children especially were facilitated. There was more fantasy and sociodramatic play in these circumstances.

In the larger groups children knew each other less well, but had a wider potential choice of playmates. This produced smaller subgroups and also an increase in same-sex companions, thus same-sex pairs of children in group play were more frequent. There was more table play in these conditions, and also perhaps more records of no activity.

As resources were also varied with number of children, some results may primarily be due to amounts of space and play equipment available. In the larger groups there was more use of tricycles (more space, and more tricycles available), in the smaller groups more use of the climbing-frame and slide, and sandpit (less space available). Perhaps because of more sandpit activity, there were slightly more records of object exchange, and also of agonistic (aggressive and submissive) behaviour in the smaller group conditions. Also there was more visual watching of other children's activities. In very small groups (around ten children) there was less rough-and-tumble play and less motor activity generally (apart from climbing and sliding) in the smaller space available.

The results obtained in this investigation held fairly generally for all the children. The effects were very similar for both boys and girls. It was particularly relevant to find that the group size effects did not change with time. Interactions between group size and project experience did not occur at above a chance level. There were of course some changes in behaviour over time, notably an increase of talking between children, a decrease in responses to the observer, and some changes in activity choice; however, these held true for both large and small groups.

Comments of playgroup staff on the different group size conditions revealed that they personally tended to prefer medium sized groups, neither so small as to be boring nor so large as to be noisy and uncontrollable. Medium sized here would probably mean about 15–25 children, with three staff present. Staff comments also revealed that certain behaviours of the children were more salient to them in different conditions – table play and Wendy house play in small groups, perhaps, and aggressive encounters, leadership, and withdrawal in larger groups. These differential perceptions may reflect the absolute occurrence of these behaviours and the ease of perception in different conditions. However, they did not accurately reflect the likelihood of behaviours or activity choices from the point of view of an individual child.

In Chapter 7 these results will be integrated with those from other experiments (Chapters 5 and 6), and compared with previous findings (Chapter 3).

5   Amounts of space and play equipment

This chapter describes one extensive study carried out over two and a half consecutive terms in the first year of the research programme. It examined simultaneously the effects of both the amount of space and the amount of play equipment on friendships, activities, and behaviours of children engaged in free play. Age and sex differences, and time factors both within a morning and through the project, were also controlled and their effects documented.

Population sample

The variations of space and play equipment were carried out independently on the children in Groups One and Two. Each group contained 24 children. As these groups were formed at the start of the project, it was possible to select the intake of children so as to balance age and sex subgroups within each group, and to equate the two groups closely. In each group the 24 children consisted of 12 boys and 12 girls, each sex subdividing into 6 older and 6 younger children. The mean age of each group was about 3 years on entry. Full details of group composition and attendance are given in Tables 5.1 and 5.2. Background details for each child are available in Appendix A.

There was an initial three-week settling-in period, during which only pilot observations were made. Towards the end of the main project, two children – number 12 in Group One, and number 39 in Group Two (see Appendix A) – left the playgroup before the termination of the study. Fortunately, sufficient advance notice was given to enable enough extra samples to be made on these children to reach the requisite total.

Resource variations

This was a *DR* type study, designed to separate the effects of *N*, *D*, and *R*, and complementing the series of *NR* studies described in Chapter Four. Resources were varied, while the number of children in the group was kept

Table 5.1. *Age and sex composition of groups, and mean attendance*

	Number of children	Boys	Girls	Mean age at start of project (months)	Age range (months)	Attendance (percentage)
Group One	24	12	12	35	28–47	91
Group Two	24	12	12	36	28–48	90

Table 5.2. *Age structure of subgroups*

	No. of children	Mean age (months)
Group One		
Older boys	6	39
Younger boys	6	32
Older girls	6	40
Younger girls	6	31
Group Two		
Older	6	40
Younger boys	6	31
Older girls	6	40
Younger girls	6	31

constant. The important resources were taken to be amount of space and amount of play equipment.

The total floor space available in the hall in which the playgroup met was just under 2,000 sq. ft, or nearly 80 sq. ft per child. In order to provide a clear indication of any trends in the behavioural effects of varied spatial density, three different density conditions were investigated. The Local Authority regulations for playgroups recommended a minimum floor space of 25 sq. ft per child. Taking this as our lowest figure, it was feasible to have three different spatial densities of 25, 50, and 75 sq. ft per child. These are subsequently referred to as the one-, two-, and three-space conditions.

The space manipulations were achieved by means of movable screen and curtain barriers (Fig. 5.1). Three movable screens, painted green, were linked by green curtains, the whole presenting a fairly uniform appearance, and reaching from the floor to a height of about 7 feet. The use of the screens did not seem to bother the children. There were very few instances of children looking or going behind them.

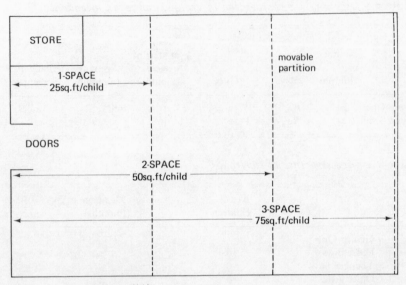

Figure 5.1. Plan of the hall

Some chairs and folding tables were stacked along the two long walls of the hall. Calculations of spatial densities made allowance for this 'unusable' space and for the store for toys which children were not normally allowed to enter. Also, an adjustment was made for space occupied by apparatus such as tables, toy chests, and climbing-frames. The screen/curtain positions were then fixed to give the requisite spatial densities, relative to anticipated mean attendance.

In manipulating the amount of play equipment available, care was taken not to confuse the quantity of equipment with the kinds of item available. This was achieved by taking a basic set of toys and apparatus, and duplicating or triplicating it to provide three conditions of equipment density. In this way the relative amounts of each kind of equipment remained constant, and there were no novel items on certain days.

The basic set of equipment was chosen such that it would be highly probable that many items would be shared by several children at the same time, unless many children did not use the equipment at all (for example, by doing nothing, playing with room fitments, or rough-and-tumbling). The toys were of the kind typically found in nursery institutions, and the basic set was as on p. 64, except that there was only one pair of nursery tables, with four chairs; the Wendy house set included an ironing board; the bowl had sand and small objects, never water; each jigsaw was on a chair, and there was a clothes-horse with assorted dressing-up clothes.

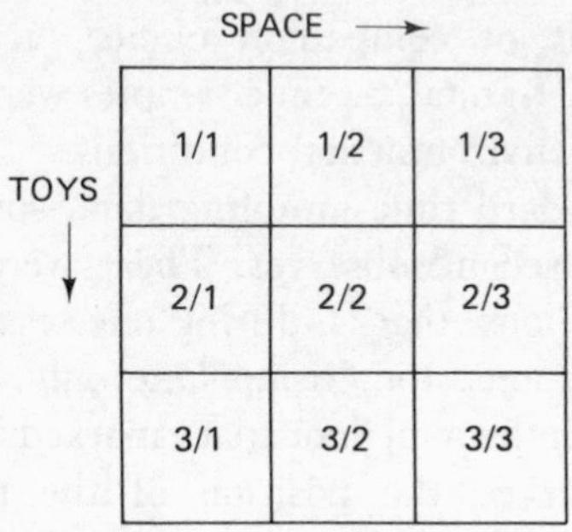

SPACE ⟶

TOYS			
	1/1	1/2	1/3
↓	2/1	2/2	2/3
	3/1	3/2	3/3

Figure 5.2. The nine environments used in the investigation

The condition in which this single basic set of play equipment was provided is subsequently referred to as a one-toy condition. In the alternative conditions two or three of each item in the basic set were available (two-or three-toy conditions).

The three space and three toy conditions were covaried, giving nine possible environments (Figs. 5.2 and 5.5–5.13). On any particular morning only one of these nine environmental conditions was presented to the children. The median condition (two-space, two-toy) was used for the three-week settling-in period at the beginning. When the observations commenced, all the conditions were given in sequence. A sequence commenced with a median condition, was followed by the remaining eight conditions in random order, and concluded with another median condition. (Alternate observations from these two median conditions were used in analysis; this was to avoid a systematic bias towards early or late occurrence for this condition.) Six such sequences were presented to each group of children. The random order of conditions varied each time, being determined by a partial latin square design. These sixty experimental sessions, presented to each group at the rate of two a week, lasted from October to June. (The playgroup was closed during school holidays at Christmas and Easter.)

Observational methods

The observer moved around quietly in the playroom so that he could easily watch the behaviour of the target child. The children became used to the observer's presence during the initial three-week settling-in period and thereafter paid little attention to him.

Data were gathered by using the standard 40-second time-sampling technique described in Chapter 2. On each morning session four samples were obtained for each child, two between 9.30 and 10.15, and two between 11.00 and 11.45. Details of companion choice, activity choice, and behaviours were recorded. In total, 24 time samples were obtained for each child in each of the nine environmental conditions.

In addition to the standard time-sampling data, some spatial plots of location were made by a second observer. These were made during the second sequence of conditions, that is, during one session for each of the nine environmental conditions, for Group One only. The observer had plans of the playroom, with the total floor space marked into six equal areas, and each session he marked the position of the principal items of equipment. Throughout the first half of the session, lasting 45 minutes, he plotted the position of each child at regular 5-minute intervals. This gave a total of ten spatial plots, showing positions of children, for a particular session.

Methods of analysis

The main analyses were of the time-sampled data. Analyses of variance were used on statistics based on the number of samples in which particular categories of companion choice, activity choice, or behaviour were recorded.

The balanced nature of the group compositions and the observational procedures meant that altogether six factors could be taken account of in the analyses of results. Two of these – amount of space and amount of play equipment – were the principal factors of interest in the study. However, it was possible to take both age and sex into account as two further factors. Finally, the time-sample observations for a particular child were made at different times, both in a morning's session and through the year. These potential sources of error variance could also be treated instead as independent factors. Since four series of time samples were made each session, time of day could be categorised into one of four levels. Since six sequences of environmental conditions were presented to each group, project experience, defined as time through the year, could be categorised into one of six levels.

A six-way analysis of variance was therefore set up, comprising the following factors:

(1) age – two levels
(2) sex – two levels

Factors (1) and (2) are nested, with six individuals in each cell.

(3) time of day – four levels
(4) project experience – six levels

(5) amount of space – three levels
(6) amount of equipment – three levels

Variance between individual children was taken as the source of error variance in computing F ratios. These were used in the calculation of significance levels quoted in Tables 5.3–5.5.

These significance levels overestimate the confidence with which the results can be generalised to other groups of children (see Chapter 2). However, analyses of variance were carried out separately for Groups One and Two. When the same effects were found significant for both groups, then the confidence with which the results may be generalised is greatly enhanced.

Analyses of variance were carried out on all the categories of number and nature of companions and choice of equipment item or activity. Also, results for 89 behaviour units and 16 composite units were analysed. Definitions are given in Appendix B.

Results

The presentation of results is divided into seven main sections. First, an overall sociometric analysis of group structure for Groups One and Two is presented. This is followed by the data from spatial location plotting for Group One, which gives a good impression of the layout of equipment in the different conditions and the distribution of children's activities. Third comes a quantitative analysis of the effects of the spatial variations on the measures of companion choice, activity choice, and occurrence of behaviour units. Fourth, a similar quantitative analysis is presented for the effects of amount of play equipment. Age and sex differences in the two groups are then considered, together with their interactions with the spatial and play equipment variables. This is followed by an analysis of time effects, both within sessions and across the duration of the project. The development and stability of friendships over the nine-month period is examined sociometrically. Again, interactions with the spatial and play equipment variables are considered. Finally, staff comments on the varying conditions are documented.

Overall sociometric structure of the two groups

Figures 5.3 and 5.4 show the friendship network for Groups One and Two respectively over the nine months of the study. These are based on the time-sampled data, being compiled on the basis of children observed in group play with the focal child. The sociograms were constructed as

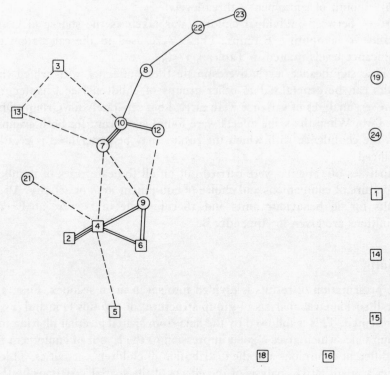

Figure 5.3. Sociometric structure of Group One children

described on p. 70; in addition, children seen playing together between 10 and 15 per cent of sample periods are indicated by broken lines.

Group One

There were two very strong friendships in this group, each associated with looser relationships. Older boys 2 and 4 had a very strong friendship and also played a lot with boy 6 and girl 9 (also older children). Older girls 7 and 10 were similarly very close, 10 having links also with older girls 8 and 12. Thus eight of the twelve older children were strongly situated in the sociogram, predominantly but not entirely sex-segregated. The younger children were generally more peripheral, or isolates. Younger girls 22 and 23 formed a chain linkage with the older girls' group.

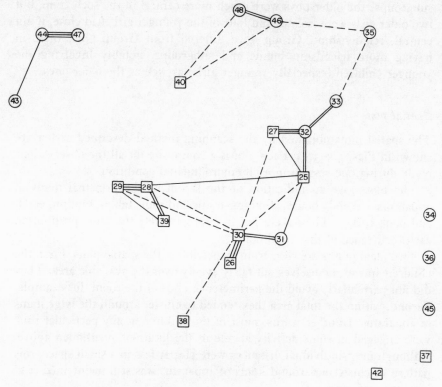

Figure 5.4. Sociometric structure of Group Two children

Group Two

There were four very strong friendships in this group, and altogether some five friendship groups. Older boy 30 had a close tie with older boy 26; he also was a friend of older girl 31, and had loose ties with five other boys. Another subgroup involved older boys 28 and 29, loosely involving a younger boy, 39. A third subgroup consisted of an older boy, 27, and an older girl, 32. There were other ties with another older boy, 25 (who linked also with the previous two subgroups), and with an older girl, 33. Two additional subgroups involved most of the younger girls. 44 and 47 were close friends, with 43 loosely linked. 46 and 48 similarly formed a fairly strong pair.

In both groups there was a tendency, not complete, for same-sex rather than cross-sex friendships. In Group One there were two main subgroups, mostly involving older children. In Group Two there were five main subgroups; the older boys were much more central in the sociogram, but two older girls were isolates and four of the younger girls had close, if not central, relationships. Group Two differed from Group One, then, in having more friendship bonds and subgroups, notably involving the younger children (especially younger girls) as well as the older ones.

Spatial plots

The spatial plots obtained by the scanning method described earlier are shown in Figs. 5.5–5.13. Each plot is a composite for all the observations made during one session in each environmental condition.

The plots give an indication of the layout of the principal items of apparatus – Wendy house, climbing-frame and slide, tables, sandpit, easel, and book corner. These were put in approximately the same position on each recurrence of that condition.

Two main points are clear from inspection of the spatial plots. First, the children spread themselves out fairly evenly over the available area. They did not particularly avoid the perimeter or ends of the room, for example. Second, within the total area they tended to cluster around the large items of apparatus. In other words, most of the children at any particular time were engaged in some activity at one of the locations mentioned above. Although inter-individual distances were clearly less in a small space, this pattern of clustering around items of apparatus was still maintained (e.g. Figs. 5.5, 5.6, and 5.7).

Results for amount of space and amount of play equipment

The analyses of variance carried out on categories of companion choice, activity choice, and behaviour units, yielded main effects of amount of space and amount of play equipment, and also interactive effects between these two factors.

The number of significant such interactions is shown in Table 5.9. They are very few, and are approximately equivalent to what would be expected by chance. Consequently, the results for the two principal factors – amount of space and amount of play equipment – are presented separately. The totals for categories under different conditions of one factor are given, summed over conditions of the other factor. For example, the number of occurrences of a category in the one-space condition is the sum of the one-space–one-toy, the one-space–two-toy, and the one-space–three-toy totals. These numbers are given in Table 5.3 for categories of companion

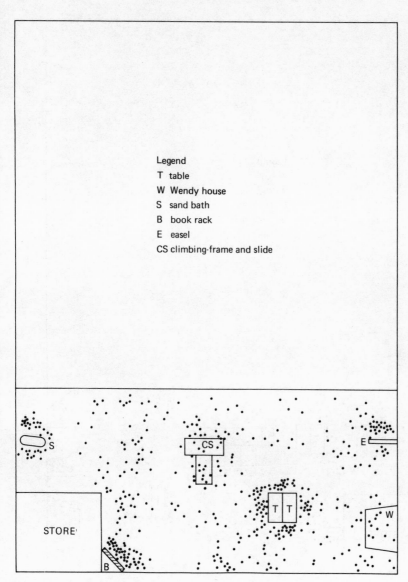

Figure 5.5. Spatial plot of the one-space–one-toy condition

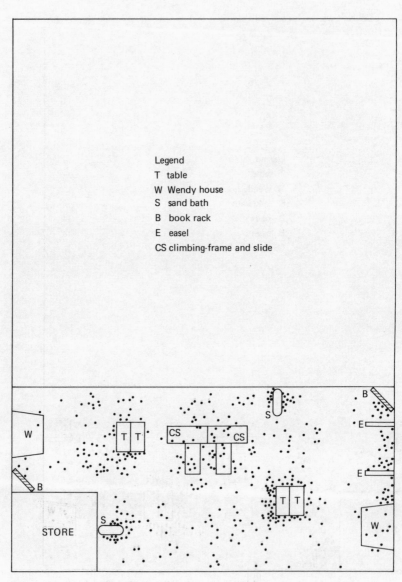

Figure 5.6. Spatial plot of one-space–two-toy condition

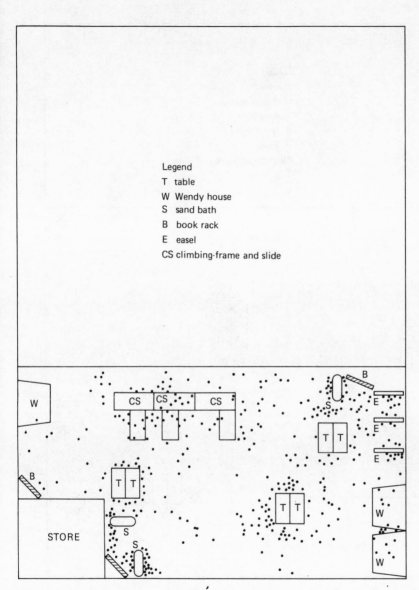

Figure 5.7. Spatial plot of one-space–three-toy condition

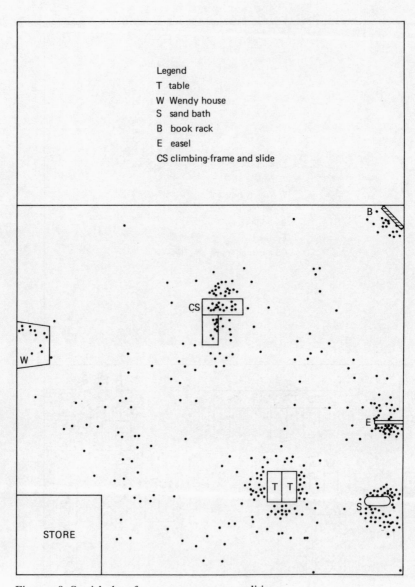

Legend
T table
W Wendy house
S sand bath
B book rack
E easel
CS climbing-frame and slide

Figure 5.8. Spatial plot of two-space–one-toy condition

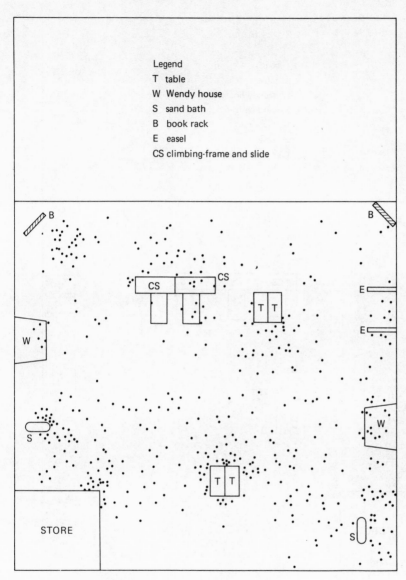

Figure 5.9. Spatial plot of two-space–two-toy condition

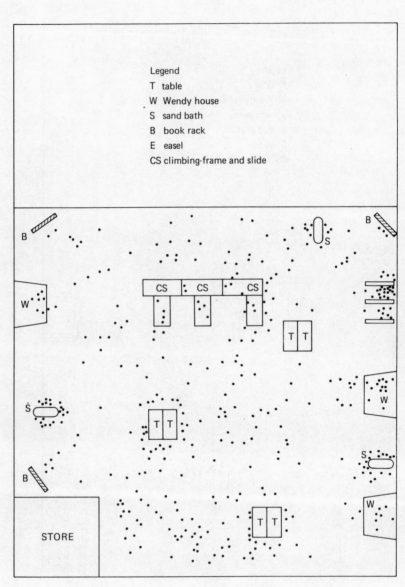

Figure 5.10. Spatial plot of two-space–three-toy condition

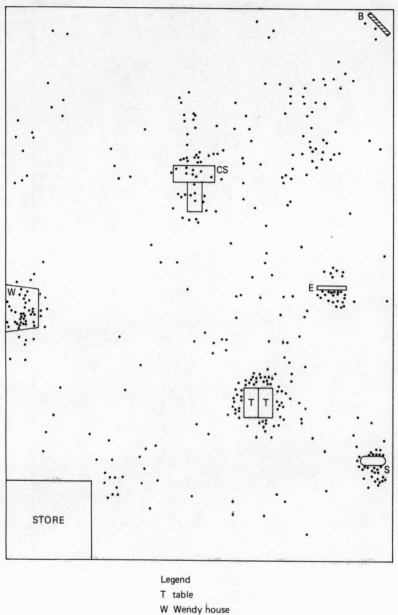

Legend
T table
W Wendy house
S sand bath
B book rack
E easel
CS climbing-frame and slide

Figure 5.11. Spatial plot of three-space–one-toy condition

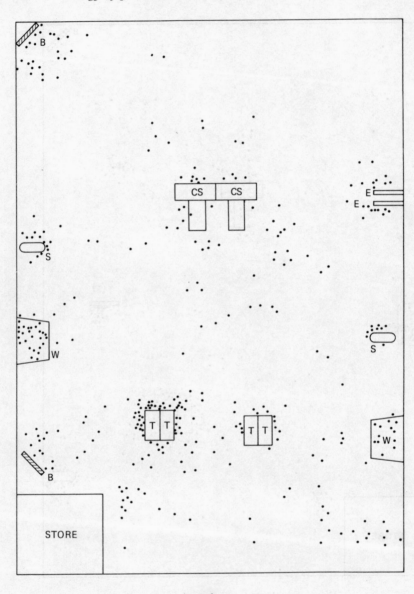

Legend
T table
W Wendy house
S sand bath
B book rack
E easel
CS climbing-frame and slide

Figure 5.12. Spatial plot of the three-space–two-toy condition

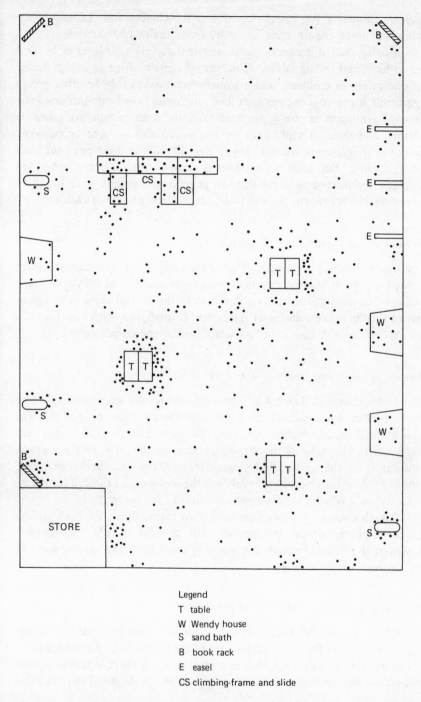

Legend
T table
W Wendy house
S sand bath
B book rack
E easel
CS climbing-frame and slide

Figure 5.13. Spatial plot of the three-space–three-toy condition

choice, Table 5.4 for categories of activity choice, and Table 5.5 for behaviour units. Significance levels are from analysis of variance.

Normally, only differences significant at the 5 per cent level or beyond are so indicated in the tables. However, *if* a main effect is so significant for one group of children, and a similar trend exists for the other group significant at the 10 or 25 per cent level, the latter is indicated in brackets. Results significant at the 5 per cent level for both groups are taken as reliable, and those at 5 per cent for one group and at 10 or 25 per cent for the other group as strongly suggestive. Results at the 5 per cent level for one group but with no significant similar trend for the other are generally discounted as unreliable. In general, the results were found to be reasonably consistent for the two independent groups of children.

Amount of space and choice of companions

Results are shown in Table 5.3. None of the categories of companion choice showed any reliable main effects of amount of space. The only consistent trend worth noting is towards a decrease in the overall amount of group play in smaller space conditions. The effect is small, but consistent for both groups and in each case is in fact significant at the 10 per cent level.

Amount of space and choice of activities

Results are shown in Table 5.4. Three reliable results were obtained. The *climbing-frame* was used more in the smaller space conditions, and this was a substantial result, highy significant for both groups. There was less *rough-and-tumble play* in the one-space than in the two- or three-space conditions, and there were also less *unusual uses of apparatus* in the one-space condition. Another suggestive result was the lesser use of the *doll* (or pram, or teddy) in a smaller space, more significant for Group Two.

Although *table play* showed no significant main effects, for both groups there was a significant interaction with amount of play equipment. However, the detailed results are not very consistent, and do not seem to link up with other findings.

Amount of space and occurrence of behaviours

Results for the shorter list of 27 behaviour units are presented in Table 5.5. Fuller results for 89 behaviour units are available in Appendix D.

The reliable results were that in a smaller space there was less *looking around/distance*, and there was also less *gross manipulation* of objects. The

Table 5.3. *Companions: results, and significance levels, comparing different space and equipment conditions*

Totals for 11 categories of companion choice; means for subgroup size and percentage same-sex choice. Group One upper line; Group Two lower line

A Interaction with age
D Interaction with time of day
E Interaction with amount of play equipment
S Interaction with amount of space
T Interaction with project experience
X Interaction with sex
[*] $P < 0.25$ * $P < 0.05$ ** $P < 0.01$ *** $P < 0.001$

	Space condition			Equipment condition		
	One	Two	Three	One	Two	Three
Alone	550	560	564	481	550	643***
	511	508	514	487	517	529[*]
Small adult subgroup	163	142	142	149	139	159
	130	113	147	111	128	151*
Large adult subgroup	170	157	127*	183	148	123***
	157	142	160	164	159	136[*]
Small parallel subgroup	278	264	265	268	306	233***
	332	326	270**	305	308	315
Large parallel subgroup	58	73	67	96	59	43***
	72	94	85	115	80	56***
Same-sex pair	256	220	261	233	243	261
	275	260	276	242	287	282*
Opposite-sex pair	120	134	151	142	126	137
	108	106	102	102	104	110
Subgroup of three	103	126	102	113	112	106
	98	138	126	143	109	110*X*
Subgroup of four or more	26	53	41T*E*	56	45	19***S*
	45	43	49X*	59	38	39*A*
Parallel play	336	337	332	364	365	276***
	404	420	355	420	388	371
Group play	505	533	555	544	526	523
	526	546	552	546	537	541
Mean subgroup size	2.32	2.48	2.35	2.45	2.42	2.29*
	2.40	2.44	2.40	2.51	2.38	2.37**
Same-sex choice	59.1	56.4	57.3	54.5	59.0	59.2
	64.7	66.9	65.0	61.2	67.9	67.5

Table 5.4. *Activities: total occurrences, and significance levels, comparing different space and equipment conditions*

Group One (upper line) and Group Two (lower line) separately for each category
A   Interaction with age
D   Interaction with time of day
E   Interaction with amount of play equipment
S   Interaction with amount of space
T   Interaction with project experience
X   Interaction with sex
[*] $P < 0.25$ * $P < 0.05$ ** $P < 0.01$ *** $P < 0.001$

	Space condition			Equipment condition		
	One	Two	Three	One	Two	Three
Table play	241	226	231E*	245	231	222S*
	235	241	226E**	236	237	229S**
Sandpit	152	160	165	142	167	168[*]
	160	192	160	143	170	199**X**
Easel	116	117	121	129	127	98A**
	138	139	113E*	146	117	127S*
Wendy house	218	205	193	174	195	247***X*
	162	143	155X*	126	160	174*
Doll	84	102	107[*]	72	103	118**
	83	108	135***	83	111	132**X**
Dressing-up	36	49	45	39	50	43
clothes	27	42	35	23	31	50**
Climbing-	180	143	121**	142	169	133
frame	208	161	137***	154	187	165
Rocking-	84	121	90*D*	95	107	93
boat	93	79	80E*	71	100	81*S*
Toy chest	106	108	91	109	91	105
	71	76	88A**	94	74	67
Tricycle	146	160	177	105	164	214***X*
	178	170	164	110	169	233***X*
Rough-and-	23	44	46*	40	34	39
tumble play	46	73	67*	77	56	53*A**
Books	109	104	96	113	102	94X*
	96	91	101X**	109	95	84
Blocks	36	39	38	48	37	28*D*X*
	42	39	46	59	31	37**
Doll's	27	17	32	33	23	20
house	22	16	15	18	18	17
Jigsaws	67	61	52	54	58	68
	40	44	39E*	41	36	46S*
Telephone	30	31	29	33	31	26
	16	21	30	21	30	16*

Table 5.4. (*cont.*)

	Space condition			Equipment condition		
	One	Two	Three	One	Two	Three
Musical	63	56	55	43	76	55**
instruments	62	69	78	67	69	73
Miscellaneous	99	84	96	103	79	97
play	105	88	94	90	94	103
Fantasy	76	68	98*A*	60	97	85*A*
play	72	75	69	72	77	67X*
Unusual	30	53	43*D*	39	50	37[*]
uses of	28	40	51*	58	36	25***D**
apparatus						
Room	10	7	6X*	10	9	4[*]
fitments	10	5	17*E*	19	9	4**S*
No activity	221	199	211	230	198	203[*]
	235	197	223	249	231	175***

occurrence of *running* was greatly reduced, and also of *chase/flee/group run*. There was more *climbing* and *sliding* (significant for separate and composite categories), and more *contact apparatus*. Suggestive results were an increase in *physical contact between children* and *physical contact with adult* with smaller space provided.

There were consistent trends in both groups for less *visual contact with children* but more *visual contact with adult* in smaller space conditions, but in neither case does the trend exceed significance at the 25 per cent level.

Amount of space and behavioural contacts

In the course of the sampling procedure, each child contacted by the focal child was noted individually (see Chapter 2). As well as counting up the number of samples in which each kind of contact occurred, it was also possible to count the average number of children per sample with whom contacts were made by each child. The results for *verbal*, *visual*, and *physical contacts* are shown in Table 5.6, with significance levels from analysis of variance.

The number of verbal contacts did not vary significantly with the amount of space. The number of physical contacts tended to increase with smaller space, only significant at the 10 per cent level for Group One and the 25 per cent level for Group Two. Conversely, the number of visual contacts

Table 5.5. *Behaviours: total occurrences, and significance levels, comparing different space and equipment conditions*

Shorter list of 27 behaviour units; Group One upper line; Group Two lower line
A   Interaction with age
D   Interaction with time of play
E   Interaction with amount of play equipment
S   Interaction with amount of space
T   Interaction with project experience
X   Interaction with sex
(*) $P < 0.1$ * $P < 0.05$ ** $P < 0.001$ *** $P < 0.0001$

	Space condition			Equipment condition		
	One	Two	Three	One	Two	Three
Upper	241	226	237	234	248	222
smile	295	286	294	305	283	287
Open smile	207	207	235	225	240	184
	191	188	213	212	203	177
Play noise	188	184	187	180	176	203
	199	210	170E*	180	196	209S*
Talking	753	744	783	787	729	764
between	691	721	718	713	724	693
children						
Talking	492	474	473	488	476	475
to/from	421	396	419	414	416	406
adult						
Look	195	247	259**	217	221	263X*
around/	233	251	284*	258	274	236
distance						
Watch	526	512	498	553	495	488*
	568	578	575	614	559	548*
Visual	946	981	1002	1020	968	941*
contact	944	991	1000A*	991	984	960
child						
Visual	433	403	388X*	408	418	398
contact	435	397	386	420	411	387
adult						
Contact	844	809	756*	802	806	783
apparatus	831	785	715**	759	812	760A*
Physical	260	197	168*	271	190	164**
contact	228	206	191(*)A*	263	201	161***
between						
children						
Physical	136	117	107(*)	131	113	116
contact	107	81	68**	104	84	68*
with						
adult						

Table 5.5. (*cont.*)

	Space condition			Equipment condition		
	One	Two	Three	One	Two	Three
Walk	815	838	885*	852	847	839
	816	849	841	866	829	811
Run	220	346	399***	358	315	292*
	192	303	352***	324	283	241***
Climb/slide	163	129	115**	129	146	132
	168	140	126*	138	158	138
Chase/flee/	7	18	26**	25	14	12*
group run	9	27	38***D*	38	17	19**A*
Object	209	161	180	183	195	172
exchange	120	131	136	127	131	129
Push/pull	265	272	263	228	262	310***
	190	213	264***	226	227	214A*
Kick/throw/	85	106	87	83	102	93
hit	93	104	132*	114	118	97X**
Pedal/	121	138	140	83	135	181***
propel	135	141	139	78	141	196***A*X*
Fine	784	777	802	773	795	795
manipu-	767	807	717*	754	717	820***
lation						
Gross	261	311	302*	232	319	323***
manipu-	250	287	302*A*	232	285	322***A**
lation						
Physical	45	56	55	68	46	42*X**
aggression	21	25	27	33	21	19(*)
Agonistic	164	146	154X**	179	146	140*
behaviour	104	108	100	122	103	87*X*
Suck	159	170	144	188	145	140*
	172	147	154	180	161	132*
Face	284	249	283	279	262	275
contact	256	261	283	272	267	261
Auto-	529	526	546	551	515	535
manipu-	546	613	606	606	577	582
lation						

Table 5.6. *Average number of children with whom different kinds of contact were made by focal child, in different space and equipment conditions*

Group One upper line; Group Two lower line (*) P < 0.1   * P < 0.05   ** P < 0.01
*** P < 0.001

	Space condition			Equipment condition		
	One	Two	Three	One	Two	Three
Verbal	0.53	0.55	0.57	0.56	0.54	0.55
contacts	0.48	0.53	0.51	0.52	0.52	0.49
Visual	0.74	0.78	0.80(*)	0.79	0.78	0.74*
contacts	0.73	0.81	0.80**	0.83	0.77	0.75**
Physical	0.20	0.18	0.16	0.22	0.16	0.15***
contacts	0.19	0.19	0.16	0.23	0.18	0.14***

tended to decrease with smaller space, only strongly significant for Group Two. This effect, even if reliable, is a fairly small one.

Amount of space – discussion and summary

(Overall, the effects of the amount of space provided were not very great. The effects which did occur consistently were mainly related to the facilitation of different activity choices, probably without much bearing on the social nature of the behaviour.) As already noted, no significant effects for companion choice were found, and there were no significant changes in the occurrence of talking between children. The most relevant finding here is the increase in physical contacts between children, and between child and adult, when less space was provided. In scoring physical contacts, the intentionality of the contact was not invoked as a criterion. Some were obviously not intentional – for example, one child brushing against another in passing. Others clearly were – holding hands, for example. In yet other cases – such as a child touching another in passing on the climbing-frame – the contact was not completely accidental, but may still occur in a situation where social contact is minimal and the physical contact was an unintended feature of the child's purposive behaviour.

For several reasons it seems likely that the increased physical contacts in a smaller space were mainly of a non-intentional kind. Neither group play nor parallel play increased correspondingly, nor did smiling or object exchange. Holding hands with another child did not increase. It may well be that the increased physical contacts with children were brought about by increased use of the climbing-frame (where many such contacts were scored), and by a general increase in chance encounters with other children, as with apparatus, when less space was provided for moving around. The large increase in contacts with apparatus could not be due only to the increase in the use of the climbing-frame, and incidental effects such as leaning against the tables or Wendy house would also be partly responsible. Use of these items did not vary with amount of space, but this would not preclude changes in incidental contacts.

(The increase in climbing and sliding in small space conditions suggests that the climbing-frame provided an outlet for gross motor activity when other forms were inhibited by the reduced space available for free movement.)In the one-space condition especially, there was less chasing, fleeing, and group running, this being sufficient to explain the decrease in general rough-and-tumble play. Many unusual uses of apparatus, such as spinning an upside-down rocking-boat, or making a line or circle of chairs, would also have been less feasible in these conditions. Running was greatly reduced; there was also a slight decrease in walking, only significant for Group One. There was generally less gross manipulation of objects. This category was scored for repeated occurrences of kicking, throwing, hitting, pedalling, propelling, pushing, pulling, or gross limb movements generally which involved moving objects, such as picking up and putting down chairs. For Group Two, the decrease in gross object manipulation can be linked to a decrease in pushing and pulling, which was often scored for pushing the pram and probably explains the decrease in use of doll and pram in this group of children; kicking, throwing, and hitting also decreased. However, these results were not separately significant for Group One, where the decrease in gross object manipulation must have been manifested somewhat differently; there was a suggestion of less pedalling and propelling in this group, and less use of the tricycle, although not statistically significant. For Group One the highest score for gross object manipulation was in fact in the two-space condition. These inconsistencies of detail between the two groups must lead to caution in generalising this result.

It is incidentally surprising that use of the tricycle did not decrease more in the smaller space conditions; indeed there is a slight (non-significant) increase for Group Two. This is despite the fact that use of the tricycle generally involves a lot of rapid movement around the floor space. The explanation is that the tricycle was the most popular item of play equipment, being constantly in demand and almost invariably occupied. Even in the one-space condition, the tricycle was as much in use, although it had to be pedalled around more carefully so as to negotiate easels, tables, and so on. Thus there is a 'ceiling' effect with the use of this item which the spatial variations did not affect. This illustrates the general point that the effects of the spatial variations in facilitating or inhibiting certain activities interacted with the motivations of the children in pursuing them.

Amount of play equipment and choice of companions

Results are shown in Table 5.3. Several consistent effects of the amount of play equipment on social activity and choice of companions were obtained. Although there was no change in the overall frequency of *group play*, the *mean subgroup size* of children playing together consistently and significantly increased when there was less play equipment provided. Whereas in the three-toy condition children usually played together in pairs, sometimes in threes, there was a large increase in the number of children playing in *subgroups of four or more* in the one-toy conditions. With children engaged in parallel play a similar result was found; the frequency of *large parallel subgroups* (four or more children) greatly increased when less equipment was available. There were also more children in a *large adult subgroup*, and fewer children who were playing *alone* (these last two results being highly significant for Group One, but only suggestive for Group Two).

Amount of play equipment and choice of activities

Results are shown in Table 5.4. The use of certain items decreased considerably when less equipment was provided. These were the *tricycle*, *doll* (and pram), and *Wendy house*, especially. The use of the *sandpit* also decreased, significantly for Group Two but only marginally for Group One. These items were presumably the most popular, in the sense that their use was most limited by availability. The item most frequently chosen was *table play*, where many children could play and share together; however, this did not vary with the number of tables provided.

Whereas the use of more popular items decreased with less equipment, other presumably less popular activities increased. Use of the wooden *blocks* increased significantly for both groups. Use of other items, such as *books* and *easel*, also increased, although not significantly. There was more manipulation of *room fitments* (very rare anyway), and a greater occurrence of *no activity*, these last two results being highly significant for Group Two, marginal for Group One.

Amount of play equipment and occurrence of behaviours

Results are shown in Table 5.5 and Appendix D. When less play equipment was provided, there was less *gross manipulation* of objects, mainly because there less *pedalling* and *propelling* of the tricycle. *Fine manipulation* of objects decreased only for Group Two; however, there were decreases in both groups of *picking up objects*, *putting down objects*, and *carrying objects*. *Watching other children* in their activities was more frequent, and so was thumb- or finger-*sucking*. *Physical contacts between children* considerably increased. There were more occurrences of *running*, also of *jumping* and *skipping*, these last two results being only marginal for Group One. There were more occurrences of *chase/flee/group run* in both groups.

Also with less equipment there was more *physical aggression*, and more *agonistic behaviour* generally, this being a consistent and significant trend for both groups.

Amount of play equipment and behavioural contacts

The average number of *verbal*, *visual*, and *physical contacts* per sample, per child are shown in Table 5.6. There was no change in the number of *verbal contacts* as the play equipment was varied. Decrease in the amount of play equipment led to some increase in the number of *visual contacts*, and a substantial increase in the number of *physical contacts*, with other children.

Amount of play equipment: discussion and summary

In coping with situations where differing amounts of play equipment were presented, the children had a number of possible strategies. Sharing might increase with few toys and decrease with many toys, implying changes in mean subgroup size. Alternatively, sharing might have stayed fairly constant, but with a switch to less or more popular items depending on availability. Or again, competition over popular items might increase or decrease as availability varied. All of these strategies were observed to some extent, and the different ways of dealing with item availability seem to provide an explanation for most of the results obtained.

The evidence for increased sharing of fewer toys is particularly strong. For example, the most used single item of equipment was the table and table toys. It is clear from Table 5.4 that there was no appreciable or significant change in the use of the table toys in the different equipment conditions. The results show that, on average, about three children were using the table toys at any one time. These children would be sharing one table in the one-toy condition, but would have had three tables available in the three-toy condition.

Several other play items – the climbing-frame and slide, toy chest, jigsaws, and (less clearly) the rocking-boat and doll's house – also showed little variation in usage in the different conditions. As with the table toys, this suggests that there was more sharing of these items when fewer were available. The data so far are not conclusive, as it is possible that extra items of equipment in the two- and three-toy conditions were simply not used. The data on choice of companions confirm that this was not the case, and that there was indeed more sharing with fewer toys available. It is clear that children played in larger subgroups when there was less equipment, and this is true of cooperative subgroups, parallel subgroups, and subgroups with adults; and fewer children played alone. Conversely, groups were smaller, and more children played alone, when there was more equipment available.

The second possibility, of switching to more popular items when more were available, is particularly in evidence for the tricycle. The tricycles were very popular and almost always in use; they showed the most increase in use as their number was increased. Nevertheless, even for this item there was not a threefold increase in amount of use when three tricycles were available instead of one (it was rather a twofold increase). Although the tricycles were designed for use by one child, when only one tricycle was available it was quite common to see two children, sometimes even three, using it at the same time (two sitting, the third standing on the back). This happened to a much lesser extent when two or three tricycles were available. Thus even the tricycle was shared more in the one-toy condition. Other items also showing an appreciable increase in use when more toys were available were the pram and doll, Wendy house, and sandpit.

Corresponding to the increase in use of these popular items, there was a decrease in use of the wooden blocks, easel, and book corner. The decrease in sharing when more equipment was provided might be expected to be particularly marked for these items.

Although there was more sharing of toys and apparatus when fewer items were available, this does not seem to have had such a marked effect on the overall level of social interaction as might have been expected. Fewer children played alone, and more children played in parallel groups, often in larger clusters. However, the overall frequency of cooperative group play did not show any increase.

It was the older children who more often played together in cooperative groups of two or more – for example, in a Wendy house or toy chest, rough-and-tumbling, with building blocks, dressing-up, and so on. Although pairs of children were always the most frequent combination, groups of three or more children in cooperative play were much more frequent with fewer toys. However, there were no increases in the frequency of smiling (of any kind), talking between children, or giving, receiving, holding out, or showing objects. This is consistent with the finding that the probability of a child being involved in group play did not increase when fewer toys were provided; the effect is limited to increasing the mean size of the small cooperative groups in which children play, rather than whether they played in them.

There were, however, appreciably and significantly more physical contacts between children in the conditions where fewer toys were available. Again, it is not possible to say what proportion of these were incidental, or intentional. It is likely that much of the increase was due to incidental contacts between children playing parallel to one another, for example at the table, sandpit, or climbing-frame. However, there may also be an increase in more intentional contacts, such as in group play with a tricycle or in the Wendy house. In the case of holding hands with other children the evidence is contradictory; there is an increase for Group Two, but no effect for Group One.

There was little evidence to suggest that less equipment caused the children to make more contact with the playgroup staff. There was no consistent or significant increase in the probability of a child being in a small adult subgroup, and no increase in talking to/from an adult, or approaching an adult. Slight increases in making physical contact with an adult, visual contact with an adult, or watching an adult's activities, were small and not significant.

Another option open to the children when less equipment was available was to engage in more free motor activity. Running, jumping, and skipping all increased considerably, as did chase/flee/group run. This increase in free motor activity is similar to that found when more space was available. Although the amount of space provided was held approximately constant in the different equipment conditions, it was impossible to do this exactly, since the equipment also occupied space. This was partially allowed for by moving the screen back to give an extra 100 or 200 sq. ft when two or three sets of equipment were put out. This was based on an estimate of 100 sq. ft for the amount of space occupied and unusable owing to the presence of equipment. It was almost certainly an underestimate, since it did not include the space under tables or climbing-frames, nor the area occupied by Wendy houses. It remains a possibility that the increase in free motor activity with fewer toys is at least partly due to some increase in available space in these conditions. However, the size of the effect suggests that this is at most only a contributory factor.

The decrease in pedalling and propelling with less play equipment was of course due to the decreased use of tricycles when only one was available. This was responsible for the decrease in gross manipulation of objects (together with some decrease in pushing and pulling, for Group One only).

Although there were moderate decreases in picking up, putting down, and carrying objects when there were fewer toys, it is surprising that the results for manipulating objects showed such a small effect. Indeed for Group One there is no reliable effect at all. The decrease for Group Two is highly significant, but the trend is non-linear, and there is only about an 8 per cent decrease in the frequency of object manipulation between the three- and one-toy conditions.

There is evidence, however, that the greater crowding of children relative to the equipment available did lead to greater levels of social discord and stress. For instance, the frequency of aggressive encounters can be considered. There was a significant increase in physical aggression – fighting, hitting, and pushing – and similar trends for most of the categories of object conflict. The overall category of agonistic behaviour showed appreciable and significant increases for both groups of children. There was also rather more crying and screaming in these conditions. Most of the fights were over possessions, and these findings are probably due to increased competition over the relatively fewer items of equipment available.

Further, there were appreciable and significant increases in the amount of finger- and thumb-sucking. As with younger infants, digit-sucking in preschool children may be taken as an indicator of over-arousal or discomfort, and this is good evidence of greater stress where fewer toys were available. There were also more instances of children watching other children, playing with room fitments, or not engaged in an activity.

None of the many categories of automanipulative or stereotypic behaviours recorded showed reliable effects due to amount of equipment available. The composite category of automanipulation showed no appreciable or significant effects for either group.

Age of children and interactions with resource factors

The number of significant main effects for age is shown in Table 5.7. Although clearly above the chance level, they are not especially numerous except for categories of companion choice.

As age was not a primary factor of interest, only results found significant at the 5 per cent level for both groups are considered. These are shown in Table 5.10. By this criterion, only three of the companion choice categories are consistently significant. Younger children engaged in more *parallel play*, especially in *small parallel subgroups*; and other children engaged in more *group play*.

Table 5.7. *Number of main effects significant at 5 per cent level*

Result from analyses of variance compared with number of results expected by chance; separate subtotals for Groups One and Two in brackets

	Age	Sex	Time of day	Project experience	Amount of space	Amount of equipment	Expected by chance (approx.)
Choice of companions (13 categories)	12 (8, 4)	1 (0, 1)	8 (3, 5)	20 (9, 11)	2 (1, 1)	13 (6, 7)	1
Choice of activities (17 categories)	8 (6, 2)	17 (7, 10)	20 (10, 10)	26 (12, 14)	10 (5, 5)	18 (6, 12)	2
Behaviour units (27 categories)	10 (6, 4)	9 (2, 7)	17 (7, 10)	38 (18, 20)	19 (8, 11)	21 (11, 10)	3
Behaviour units (89 categories)	33 (23, 10)	26 (5, 21)	35 (14, 21)	108 (55, 53)	33 (15, 18)	44 (20, 24)	9

Table 5.8. *Number of interactions with main variables significant at 5 per cent level*

Results from analyses of variance compared with number of results expected by chance; separate subtotals for Groups One and Two in brackets

	Interactions with amount of space				Interactions with amount of play equipment				Expected by chance (approx.)
	Age	Sex	Time of day	Project experience	Age	Sex	Time of day	Project experience	
Choice of companions (13 categories)	0	1 (0, 1)	0	0	1 (0, 1)	1 (0, 1)	0	0	1
Choice of activities (17 categories)	2 (1, 1)	3 (1, 2)	2 (2, 0)	0	3 (2, 1)	8 (4, 4)	2 (1, 1)	0	2
Behaviour units (27 categories)	3 (0, 3)	2 (2, 0)	1 (0, 1)	0	5 (0, 5)	5 (2, 3)	0	0	3
Behaviour units (89 categories)	10 (1, 9)	12 (8, 4)	1 (0, 1)	1 (0, 1)	12 (5, 7)	11 (5, 6)	1 (0, 1)	1 (1, 0)	9

Table 5.9. *Number of space × equipment interactions and higher-order interactions significant at 5 per cent level*

Results from analyses of variance compared with number of results expected by chance; separate subtotals for Groups One and Two in brackets

	Space × play equipment interactions	Expected by chance (approx.)	Third- or higher-order interactions	Expected by chance (approx.)
Choice of companions	1	1	8	23
(13 categories)	(1, 0)		(5, 3)	
Choice of activities	6	2	16	40
(17 categories)	(1, 5)		(8, 8)	
Behaviour units	1	3	9	49
(27 categories)	(0, 1)		(2, 7)	
Behaviour units	4	9	35	160
(89 categories)	(2, 2)		(18, 17)	

Table 5.10. *Significant and consistent effects for age of child*

Group One upper line; Group Two lower line
* $P < 0.05$ ** $P < 0.01$

Choice of companions	Younger	Older
Small parallel subgroup	468	339**
	575	353**
Parallel play	583	422**
	732	447**
Group play	516	1077**
	682	942*

As noted above, the two groups differed in their sociometric structure (Figs. 5.3 and 5.4). Group One's sociogram was probably more age- and sex-typical, older children of both sexes having more friends than the younger children. Group Two, in contrast, contained a number of highly sociable younger girls, and two older girls who were rather isolated. This asymmetry in Group Two is illustrated also by Table 5.11, which presents data for *same-sex* and *opposite-sex* pair.

The difference between the two groups meant that Group Two showed many significant age–sex interactions, but rather fewer main effects for age than did Group One. For example, in Group One younger children more often played *alone*, but for Group Two only the interaction with sex was significant, younger boys playing more *alone*, but not younger girls.

Table 5.11. *Totals for same-sex pair and opposite-sex pair companions*

	Boys with		Girls with	
	Boys	Girls	Boys	Girls
Group One				
Older	228	121	126	275
Younger	116	81	77	118
Group Two				
Older	321	87	111	138
Younger	124	57	61	228

The lack of consistently significant age differences contrasts with the large number of significant effects of project experience, to be discussed shortly.

The number of significant interactions of age with amount of space and amount of play equipment is shown in Table 5.8. These are at about the expected chance level, and none was consistent and significant for both groups. It is therefore concluded that the age of the child was not important with respect to the effects of the resource variables.

Sex of children and interactions with resource factors

The number of significant main effects for sex is shown in Table 5.7. These are above the chance level for choice of activities and occurrence of behaviour units, being particularly numerous for the former.

Again, only results significant at the 5 per cent level for both groups are shown, in Table 5.12. Girls made consistently more use of the *doll* and the *rocking-boat*. The greater use of dolls and prams by girls is well known (e.g. Clark *et al.*, 1969). In both groups girls also used the rocking-boats a great deal, singing songs while rocking in them; however, we do not know of any earlier reports of this sex difference. Girls had a higher incidence of *look distance* and of *clothes hitch*.

Boys had a higher incidence of *play noise* and *kick/throw/hit* (Table 5.12), and also of *propel*. This is consistent with a general preference of boys for more vigorous physical activity and gross limb movements (Clark *et al.*, 1969; Goldberg and Lewis, 1969; Smith and Connolly, 1972). The sex difference in play noise (also found by Smith and Connolly, 1972) is probably associated with vigorous physical activity in combination with particular kinds of fantasy play – pretending to be aeroplanes, cars, or monsters, for example.

Table 5.12. *Significant and consistent effects for sex of child*
Group One upper line; Group Two lower line
* $P < 0.05$ ** $P < 0.01$ *** $P < 0.001$

	Girls	Boys
Choice of activities		
Doll	211	82**
	259	67**
Rocking-boat	201	94*
	167	85*
Occurrence of behaviour units (from list of 27)		
Play noise	168	391**
	88	497***
Kick/throw/hit	103	175*
	99	230***

Table 5.13. *Interactions of sex of child with amount of play equipment*
* $P < 0.05$ ** $P < 0.01$

		Group One			Group Two		
		One-toy	Two-toy	Three-toy	One-toy	Two-toy	Three-toy
Sandpit	Boys	60	82	87	76	96	130
	Girls	82	85	81	67	74	69**
Wendy	Boys	104	94	113	92	101	97
house	Girls	70	96	134*	34	61	77*
Doll	Boys	17	35	30	18	29	20
	Girls	55	68	88	65	82	112**
Tricycle	Boys	66	92	138	79	125	165
	Girls	39	74	76	31	44	68

Overall, the number of consistently significant sex differences was smaller than might have been expected. Thus although there were seven significant activity differences for Group One and ten for Group Two, only two of these were significant for both groups. The difference in age–sex character of the two groups may have been be partly responsible for this. The general point to be drawn here is that age and sex differences depend considerably on the individual 'character' of a group of children. As noted in Chapter 2, supposedly significant age and sex differences drawn from just one group may not be generalisable.

The number of significant interactions of sex with amount of space and amount of play equipment are shown in Table 5.8. These are at about the expected chance level, except for interactions between sex and amount of play equipment for activity categories. The only one of these consistent for both groups was for the *Wendy house*, significant at the 5 per cent level in each case. Table 5.13 shows interactions between sex and amount of play equipment for the *Wendy house* and for the other three items of equipment which showed main effects of amount of play equipment – the *sandpit*, *doll*, and *tricycle*. It can be seen that the increase in use of the Wendy house when more were available holds true mainly for the girls. By contrast, only the boys made more use of the sandpit (interaction only significant for Group Two). Both boys and girls increased their usage of the *doll* and the *tricycle*, despite the overall sex difference in preference for these two items.

For the behaviour units, the only consistent interaction was between sex and amount of space, for *simple smile*. This result is difficult to account for and does not fit into any overall pattern.

It is concluded that sex of child was of little importance with respect to the effects of the resource variables. The main proviso is that boys and girls did show some differential switching of activities as the amount of play equipment was varied.

Time of day and interactions with resource factors

The number of significant main effects for time of day is shown in Table 5.7. There are a considerable number, well above chance level. Results significant at the 5 per cent level for both groups are shown in Table 5.14.

In two cases – for *small parallel subgroup* and *play noise* – the trends were inconsistent between the two groups, although separately significant. There was a general decrease in *no activity* through the morning, and of *look around/distance* and *visual contact adult* (Table 5.14), and also of *watch group*. There were corresponding increases in use of the *sandpit*, *Wendy house*, *dressing-up clothes*, and *toy chest*, and – especially in the last period of the morning – of *unusual uses of apparatus*. *Pushing/pulling* objects became more frequent (Table 5.14), and there were also increases in *kneeling* and *picking up* and *putting down objects*.

These results are indicative of a general settling-in of the children at the beginning of the playgroup session, and are in agreement with similar findings by McGrew (1972). However, it is also noticeable that there is a curvilinear tendency in much of these data, with a tendency for behaviours in the last period of the morning to revert somewhat to those of the initial period. In this last period there was a slight pick-up in *no activity*, *looking*

Table 5.14. *Significant and consistent effects for time of day*
Group One upper line; Group Two lower line
* $P < 0.05$ ** $P < 0.01$ *** $P < 0.001$

	Sample period			
	1	2	3	4
Choice of companions				
Small parallel subgroup	180	202	225	200**
	259	239	239	191***
Choice of activities				
Sandpit	74	138	126	139**
	112	117	137	146*
Wendy house	110	158	170	178***
	72	110	112	166***
Dressing-up clothes	18	30	39	45***
	9	21	31	43***
Toy chest	77	65	70	93*
	31	58	74	72***
Unusual uses of apparatus	17	36	17	56***
	6	33	24	56***
No activity	199	206	98	128***
	207	201	111	136***
Occurrence of behaviour units (from list of 27)				
Play noise	167	133	128	131*
	132	147	172	134*
Look around/distance	211	168	156	166**
	218	199	171	180*
Visual contact adult	332	323	278	291*
	330	285	278	325*
Push/pull	179	172	218	231**
	142	146	183	196***

around/distance, visual contact adult (Table 5.14), and *watch group*. This could be because the children were becoming tired, or were aware that the morning was nearly over and that soon they would be collected and taken home.

An alternative interpretation could be that time trends were due to the effects of observer fatigue. Curvilinear time trends could reflect a decline in vigilance, followed by a pick-up towards the end of the observation period. However, vigilance variations would be expected to affect only behaviour unit frequencies, and these fairly generally; they would be unlikely to affect companion or activity categories. The observed pattern of results, showing many significant effects on activities, and only selected effects for behaviour units, argues against this explanation.

The number of significant interactions of time of day with amount of space and amount of play equipment are shown in Table 5.8. These are generally less than what would be expected at chance level. There were no significant interactions consistent for both groups. It is concluded that the time during the morning session was not important with respect to the effects of the resource variables.

Project experience and interactions with resource factors

The number of main effects of project experience are shown in Table 5.7. The majority of the categories show significant effects of this variable. Results significant at the 5 per cent level for both groups are shown in Table 5.15. In examining these results, three possible explanations should be borne in mind. First, the children are getting older. Second, they are getting more specific social experience in the playgroup; few of the children were acquainted with one another before the playgroup was opened, although some friendships made there were continued outside. Third, observer criteria for vigilance for scoring categories may have gradually shifted; again, vigilance shifts or practice effects would be most likely for certain behaviour units, especially those with low inter-observer agreement. A final explanation might be in terms of seasonal effects. However, as the children were always indoors in the playgroup, the immediate impact of seasonal changes at least was very small.

There were clear and consistent trends towards an increase in *group play*, *mean subgroup size*, and *same-sex choice*. This is consistent with the expected effects of both age and playgroup experience. Similarly, *talking between children* increased, as did *visual* and *physical contacts* with children. *Upper smile*, *open smile*, *play noise*, and *chuckle* also increased.

Parallel play did not vary much, but being *alone* showed a steady decline; so did *look around/distance*, *suck*, and *no activity*. Results for *watch* and for *small adult subgroup* and *large adult subgroup* were rather variable, though also tending to decline.

As fewer children were unoccupied with increased age and playgroup experience, so the use of certain items or the occurrence of certain activities noticeably increased. This was consistent and significant for the *sandpit*, *easel*, *dressing-up clothes*, *tricycle*, *fantasy play*, and *unusual uses of apparatus*. *Push/pull* and *pedal* also increased. The results for the *climbing-frame* showed some decline in use at first, when the children used it only for climbing and sliding. Subsequently its use increased, probably because it

Table 5.15. *Significant and consistent effects for project experience*
Group One upper line; Group Two lower line
* $P < 0.05$ ** $P < 0.01$ *** $P < 0.001$

	Sample period					
	1	2	3	4	5	6
Choice of companions						
Alone	318	305	278	282	282	209***
	328	340	260	220	185	200***
Small adult subgroup	67	70	87	91	72	60*
	73	65	84	71	41	56**
Large adult subgroup	122	78	63	63	54	74***
	96	97	81	52	49	84***
Same-sex pair	75	114	118	141	134	155***
	76	90	139	156	171	179***
Subgroup of four or more	5	15	16	20	27	36***
	5	6	21	27	47	30***
Group play	171	234	262	282	287	347***
	143	164	260	329	388	340***
Mean subgroup size	2.31	2.35	2.39	2.36	2.41	2.48**
	2.28	2.25	2.39	2.43	2.57	2.47**
Same-sex choice	57.9	60.7	57.3	63.0	64.5	64.0**
	68.2	74.2	73.0	71.6	64.8	70.2**
Choice of activities						
Sandpit	58	49	107	76	99	88***
	55	39	103	96	115	104***
Easel	46	48	58	68	71	63*
	53	78	73	61	57	68*
Dressing-up clothes	9	14	19	30	36	24***
	12	10	16	17	17	32**
Climbing-frame	81	57	64	72	76	94*
	73	63	53	105	107	105***
Tricycle	66	85	69	78	90	95*
	66	65	90	101	87	103**
Fantasy play	11	32	31	52	56	60***
	12	19	30	51	63	41***
Unusual uses of apparatus	9	12	20	23	27	35***
	13	14	10	28	29	25***
No activity	167	137	78	86	98	65***
	187	165	87	75	74	67***

Table 5.15. (*cont.*)

	Sample period					
	1	2	3	4	5	6
Occurrence of behaviour units (from list of 27)						
Upper smile	82	94	105	99	139	185***
	71	99	124	165	229	187***
Open smile	127	90	94	90	116	132**
	90	67	84	112	125	114***
Play noise	89	86	71	80	99	132***
	59	65	87	110	131	133***
Talking between	250	324	378	402	437	489***
children	226	257	335	417	467	428***
Look around/distance	227	169	99	98	61	47***
	237	190	111	108	73	49***
Watch	235	273	225	239	304	260***
	322	309	249	264	283	294***
Visual contact child	468	493	460	471	501	536***
	445	454	435	499	562	540***
Visual contact adult	238	176	176	213	186	235***
	245	210	193	182	166	222***
Physical contact	55	57	86	120	131	176***
between children	45	59	87	100	167	167***
Push/pull	103	128	135	150	141	143*
	96	89	103	124	123	132*
Suck	91	92	58	73	81	78*
	111	104	54	54	89	61***
Automanipulation	202	263	235	292	297	312***
	245	290	242	290	342	356***

was used in fantasy play, for example as a 'den' or a 'space rocket'.

Overall, the results formed a not unexpected pattern, consistent with an increase in social competence and maturity of the children both with regard to each other and to using the toys and apparatus provided. Increased age and playgroup experience were probably jointly responsible. The effects were much more marked than the single age differences noted earlier, so certainly playgroup experience was important. The increase in social contacts and decrease in solitary or staff-orientated behaviour are in agreement with the findings of much earlier work in relation to both these factors (e.g. Arrington, 1943; Hartup, 1970).

It is unlikely that changes in observer criteria or vigilance were responsible for these findings. Inter-observer agreement remained much the same from the beginning to the middle of the study, and was high for companion and activity categories. However, a change in observer vigilance was probably responsible for the apparent increase in *automanipulation*; also, inter-observer agreement for this category (and many of its component categories) was very low. This increase is contrary to naive expectation and the general pattern of results. The observer was also aware of a practice effect, in becoming better at noticing units such as hand- and mouth-fumbling and clothes-hitching as the project progressed.

The number of significant interactions of project experience with amount of space and amount of play equipment are shown in Table 5.8. Virtually no significant interactions were obtained. It is concluded that the effects of the resource factors did not change as the children gained more experience in the playgroup.

Project experience and changes in sociometric composition

The data on choice of companions in group play could be analysed to give the sociometric structure of each group of children, as was presented earlier in Figures 5.3 and 5.4. In addition, it was possible to examine the changes in sociometric structure with project experience. In part this could be expected to confirm the increases in *group play, mean group size*, and *same-sex choice* noted earlier. However, it would also reveal whether friendships were fairly stable over the nine months.

The six blocks of sample periods for each group were paired into three larger blocks, to give sufficient sociometric data for each. Each of these three blocks – early, middle and late – was analysed as before. The results are shown in Figures 5.14–5.16 for Group One, 5.17–5.19 for Group Two. The sociograms are constructed as described on p. 70.

Group One

Figures 5.14–5.16 show a steady increase in the number of friendships and a reduction in the number of isolates as the project progressed. However, the skeletal form of the social structure present early on (Fig. 5.14) was largely maintained throughout. The key elements of this were three older boys, 2, 4, and 6, of whom 4 approached a star position in the sociogram; a strong friendship between two older girls, 7 and 10; and an intermediate position of another older girl, 9, who had links with both these subgroups. Girl 9 eventually strengthened her position with the boys' subgroup at the expense of her links with the other girls.

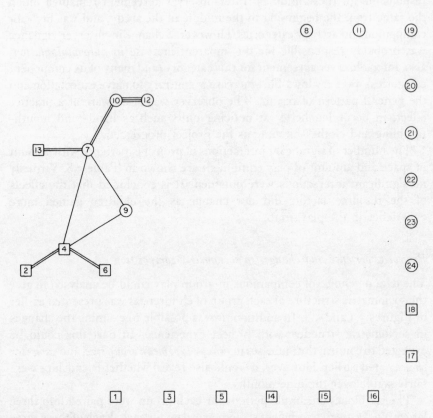

Figure 5.14. Sociometric structure of Group One children, early in project

The sex segregation increased, being nearly complete, apart from girl 9, by the final period. Amongst other points to note are the gradual incorporation of girls 8, 22, and 23 in a 'chain' link with the older girls' subgroup; and the shifting positions of boys 3 and 13, moving from the girls' subgroups, through an 'isolate' stage to join the boys' subgroup. Girl 12 lost her initial strong position in the sociogram; in Figure 5.16 this is, to some extent, an artefact of her early departure (see p. 100).

Group Two

Figures 5.17–5.19 show a steady increase in the number of friendships and a reduction in the number of isolates. The main friendships seen early on (Fig. 5.17) were maintained throughout. These were the bond

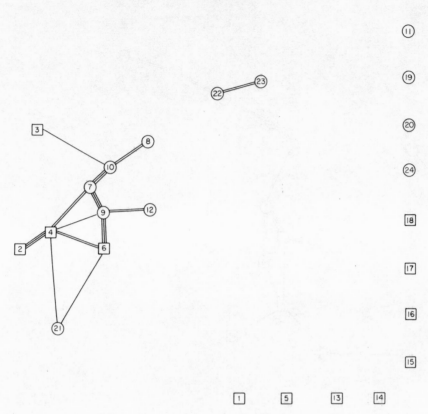

Figure 5.15. Sociometric structure of Group One children, middle of project

between two older boys, 30 and 26; the triangle involving two more older boys, 28 and 29, with a younger boy 39 tagging on; and a quite separate friendship between two young girls, 44 and 47.

By the middle period, two distinct new subgroups had become evident. Older girl 32 had more, but separate, links with another older girl, 33, and an older boy, 27. There was also the relationship between younger girls 46 and 48 which strengthened with time. By the final period the 27–32–33 triangle had strengthened, and also attracted older boy 25; in consequence older girl 31 lost her link with 25 and became an isolate. The effect of 25's shift also seemed to change and loosen the previously quite tight boys' group seen in the middle period.

The increase in sex segregation in Group Two was not so marked, having been greater than in Group One to start with. It is again noticeable how

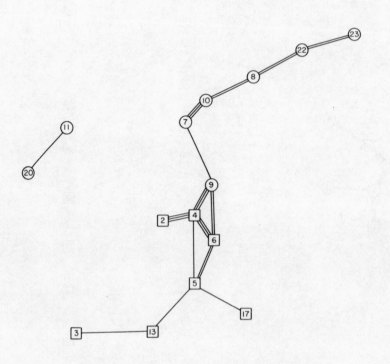

Figure 5.16. Sociometric structure of Group One children, late in project

certain younger boys, notably 38 and 40, shifted their friendships quite substantially during the period.

Some of the quantitative results from the sociograms are presented in Table 5.16. This shows the increase in number of friendship bonds and decrease in number of isolates through the period of the project. It should be noted that 'isolates' are not necessarily playing alone, but they do not engage in group play with any particular other child for more than 15 per cent of sample periods. However, most of them would be engaged in rather little group play, as the data presented in Table 5.15 would suggest.

Table 5.16 also indicates in quantitative terms a fair degree of stability in the core friendships of the group, also visible in the figures. On average, about two-thirds of friendship bonds persisted from one period into the next (each period being about three months), and between one-third and

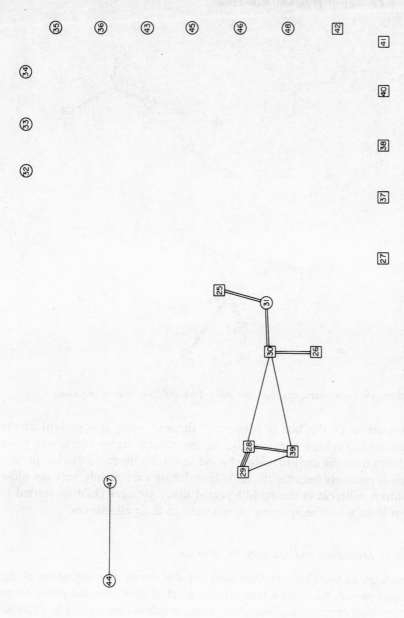

Figure 5.17. Sociometric structure of Group Two children, early in project

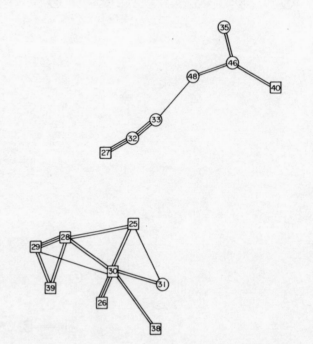

Figure 5.18. Sociometric structure of Group Two children, middle of project

one-quarter of the bonds present at the end were also present at the beginning. Perhaps surprisingly, in percentage terms there was more stability from the early to middle period than from the middle to late period. This is probably because the early friendships were mainly between older children, whereas in the middle period many younger children started to form links while being more inconsistent in their allegiances.

Project experience and reactions to observer

Reactions to the observer decreased rapidly during the beginning of the project period, reaching a fairly steady level of about one sample in seven for any kind of reaction (*glance, look, stare,* or *talk to* observer). The decrease in reactions to observer during the project is shown in Table 5.17. *Glance* and *look* at the observer formed the bulk of these. *Talk* to observer was rare, occurring only 41 times in Group One and 28 times in Group Two out of 5,184 samples in each case.

The occurrences of reactions to the observer were relatively more

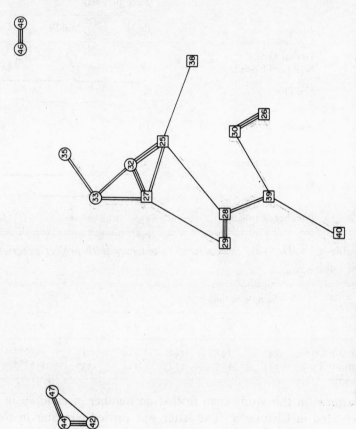

Figure 5.19. Sociometric structure of Group Two children, late in project

Table 5.16. *Changes in sociometric structure with project experience*

Number of strong friendship bonds (greater than 15 per cent of sample periods); number of bonds constant from early to middle, middle to late, and continuously through the project; number of isolate children (no strong friendship bonds)

	Time period		
	Early	Middle	Late
Group One			
Number of bonds	8	13	15
Stability		6 8	
		5	
Number of isolates	16	12	9
Group Two			
Number of bonds	9	18	19
Stability		8 8	
		5	
Number of isolates	15	7	6

Table 5.17. *Decrease in reactions to observer with project experience*
*** $P < 0.001$

	Sample period					
	1	2	3	4	5	6
Group One	243	141	140	114	115	121***
Group Two	251	155	172	141	137	116***

frequent in this study than in that on number of children in the group reported in Chapter 4. The latter was carried out later in the research programme than the present study (Table 2.1); the children were therefore not quite so acclimatised to observation in this study as they were in the later one. Nevertheless most of the reactions – a glance or a look – were minor, and it was not felt that the child's overall behaviour was substantially altered except in a very few instances.

Staff comments on the resource variations

The three staff at the playgroup were asked to give written open-ended comments on 'differences in the children's behaviour – or your behaviour to them – which you feel you have noticed in the different space and toy conditions'. They were asked to do this at the end of each term. One of the assistants, Mrs X, was ill at the end of the third term, and only the first two reports were obtained from her.

The relevant parts of the comments are reproduced below.

Mrs A (supervisor):

Term One: I personally find a big difference in the behaviour of the children when the space and toys are altered. In the cramped conditions of one-space–three toys, everyone seems to get in each others' way. I think it is worse, however, with one-space–one toy, as the more aggressive children do not seem to find an outlet for their feelings. Particularly as far as the tricycles are concerned, there is more fighting over the toys. I feel more tired in these conditions, but I hope I don't behave any differently towards the children.

With the three-space–three-toy condition the children seem very satisfied. Plenty of room, combined with lots of toys, means the aggressive children are occupied, leaving the normally quiet children to do what they wish without interruption.

The differences due to space and toys do not seem so noticeable in Group Two.

Term Two: I least prefer the one-space condition, especially with one toy, although three-toy days feel very crowded. Group One particularly behave rather worse on the one-space days. I feel rather tired at the end of these sessions.

I consider the three-space and three-toy days are the best conditions. The children are on the whole quieter and more content.

Term Three: I think the children were very adaptable to the completely different situations they have encountered, but that they play in a completely different way in each new situation. The atmosphere seems more restful with a good variety of toys, plenty of them, and enough space. Group One appeared to be much more noisy and aggressive with fewer toys.

Mrs X (assistant):

Term One: The one-space–three-toy condition is obviously the most difficult because it is so crowded. The more aggressive children, particularly in Group One, miss the space of a two- or three-space condition. But there doesn't appear to be any more aggression than on a three-space day. I haven't been aware of any consistent reaction of aggression according to space – more so when it's only a one-toy day, particularly over tricycles and dolls' prams.

I find it very difficult to assess differences in the children's behaviour, or mine to them, according to the space–toy conditions. To work this out, I feel I should have to write a comment after each morning's work to use as reference now. Each morning the children all vary in moods and situations, and I find it difficult to be objective now and remember or sum up many situations.

It still being a relatively new environment, I think the children are still basically involved with socially integrating and forming relationships with one another. I don't think that changing the conditions daily has upset any child. In a small-space condition more table play and painting are done, or space beneath a slide, for example, is utilised.

Of all conditions I enjoy most a two- or three-toy in a two-space.

Term Two: The one-space condition is the most difficult, better I think with one-toy condition than when crowded with three sets of toys.

A three-space–one-toy condition works well; there isn't the friction that there is in a one-space–three-toy condition; therefore I feel space is the factor for a happier playgroup. Tricycles are still the most coveted of all the toys even when three are available.

Mrs Y (assistant):

Term One: In the one-space–three-toy conditions I tend to stay put, and encourage creative play amongst the children. Play in these conditions tends to make me more tense and more aware of noise. The aggressive children appear to be more aggressive, probably because they are closer at hand.

One-toy conditions seem to cause tension amongst the dominant children and unhappiness amongst the shy children, who seem to get rather bullied. The children seem to improvise with the toys more when there are a lot in a large space by making tunnels from the slides, forming bands with the musical instruments and such like, and they seem to improvise with the chairs more when there are few toys and plenty of space.

Term Two: One-toy conditions seem to make the children more aggressive, particularly in a small space. With the opportunity to run around this seems to diminish. A small amount of space, no matter how many toys, seems to make both staff and children irritable. Boredom seems to set in and with this comes friction. If there is sufficient space, Group Two seem more able to substitute toys with imaginative play than Group One. I myself feel less energetic when there is very little space.

The children with a short attention span, usually the young ones, seem to be most affected by lack of space or toys, probably because they haven't developed the ability to invent as fully as the older ones.

Certain group play is brought about by duplication of toys. For instance, interplay on the slide, toy chests, Wendy houses is impossible during a one-toy day. The social aspect of playgroup seems to be increased by the fact that children can do the same thing at the same time as their companions. This shows itself in the wearing of dressing-up clothes, pushing prams, and playing musical instruments together.

Term Three: More active, noisy games take place when there are fewer toys, and aggressive behaviour seem to be triggered off, though less by the amount of toys available than by the presence or absence of certain key children. When there are more space and more toys, the tempo of the games and the noise seems to increase after the routine of the milk break. I think this happens when we are very confined amongst a lot of toys, too.

It is clear from the reports that the playgroup staff generally found one-space conditions unpleasant, and the one-space–three-toy condition very crowded. It was indeed relatively more difficult to move around easily in this condition (Fig. 5.7). Overall, more plentiful conditions of space and equipment were preferred.

Mrs X (Term One) clearly made very cogent qualifications as to the extent to which the questionnaires, only given at the end of each term, can expect to elicit accurate accounts of the children's behaviour in the different conditions. One aspect very salient to the staff was children's aggressiveness. There was some disagreement or uncertainty amongst all the staff as to the relative importance of space or toys for aggressive behaviour. Mrs X's (Term One) comments are in fact closely congruent to the observational results, but she reverses her conclusions later (Term Two). Both she and Mrs A mentioned the tricycle as being a popular toy which often prompted struggles over possession. Mrs Y (Term One) sensibly qualified her conclusion as to the relation between space and aggression by pointing out that an apparent connection may be a misleading perception of what the children actually experience. Indeed she was probably correct here, as the observational data revealed no systematic connection of aggression with amount of space available.

As Mrs A (Term Two) and Mrs X (Term One) pointed out, Group One did show an overall higher level of aggression (Table 5.5) and were generally felt to be a more difficult group. Mrs Y (Term Three) was also probably accurate in pinpointing the presence of certain children as important in this respect. Nevertheless observational results showed that the equipment variations did have systematic effects on aggression, common to most children in each group.

Summary

The independent character of the two groups is revealed in part by the sociometric analyses. Group One had two main friendship groups, mainly involving older boys and older girls respectively, but with links between them. Group Two showed more sex segregation and some five separate friendship groups; two of these involved younger girls especially, whereas older girls were not quite so sociable. Friendships became more numerous during the project, but the sociometric structure showed appreciable stability, although few of the children knew each other before the playgroup was started.

Generally, the older children engaged in more group play and less parallel play. Girls played with the doll and pram and the rocking-boat more than boys. However, few age and sex differences were found significantly for both groups, probably because of the differences in group characteristics just mentioned. Common to both groups, however, was a steady increase in social maturity and use of the items of equipment as the project progressed. There was also evidence of settling-in effects during each morning when the playgroup met.

Throughout all these changes, and superimposed on them, are the effects found to be attributable to the resource factors. To a considerable extent these results seem to be due to differing activity choices, constrained by the amount of space needed for certain activities, and/or by differing availability and popularity of certain items. The effects of the two resource variables were largely independent of each other and are summarised separately.

The most substantial and reliable effect found in manipulating the amount of space available was on the level and kind of physical, especially motor, activity. The children utilised the potential available in a larger space with increased running, more group running, chasing, and fleeing, and more unusual uses of apparatus such as spinning the rocking-boats around or making 'chair-trains'. They seem to have increased the amount of object manipulation by gross limb movements, such as pushing prams in Group Two. Use of the tricycle did not increase, because it was already popular. When less space was available the decrease in free motor activity seems to have been partly compensated for by a greater incidence of vigorous activity (climbing and sliding) on the climbing-frame and slide. There were more, probably incidental, contacts with other immovable apparatus. The evidence for greater physical contacts between children in the smaller space conditions is compatible with the suggestion that the increase in these, too, was mainly incidental in character. There was little evidence for any substantial changes in overall level of social contacts, choice of companions, or amounts of aggressive or automanipulative behaviour brought about by the changes in activity preference consequent upon the spatial variations.

In contrast, the variations in the amount of toys and apparatus available to the children produced reliable and appreciable effects on the choices of play activity, the size of groups, the amount of free motor activity, and the frequency of agonistic and stress-indicative behaviours. However, the levels of social contact and object manipulation were not greatly affected.

Providing more play equipment meant that more children played alone, fewer in parallel groups. Also, parallel and cooperative groups tended to be smaller. There was less sharing of particular items, and popular toys such as the tricycle, Wendy house, pram and doll, and sandpit were used more extensively.

Conversely, when there was less play equipment available, there was more sharing of toys and apparatus, and also some switch to the less popular items such as easel, blocks, book corner, and even occasionally to playing with room fitments. There was also more group running and chasing, and more free motor activity generally such as running, jumping, and skipping. (This increase in free motor activity may in part be due to the incidental increase in space when less equipment was provided.) Increased sharing of equipment could have precipitated much increased social interaction, but in fact this occurred only to a very limited extent. Children who might otherwise have played alone were more likely to be near other children, for example at the same table, book corner, or sandpit, and there was some increase in the number of visual and physical contacts. The more sociable children who played together, usually in pairs, were more likely to form into threes and fours, for example sharing in cooperative play a Wendy house, toy chest, or rocking-boat. However, the overall likelihood of a child being in cooperative play, or smiling, talking, or exchanging objects with another child, did not increase.

In addition to increased sharing and a switch to less popular items when fewer toys were available, there was also more competition, especially over popular items such as tricycles and prams. More aggressive behaviour was noted in these conditions, and more crying and sucking. This, together with the observations that more children were seen doing nothing, or perhaps just watching others' activities, suggests that an environment with relatively little play equipment was in some ways more stressful for the children. However, contacts with playgroup staff did not greatly increase, perhaps because of the largely non-interactive way in which they had been asked to behave.

The separate effects of D (density of resources) and R (amount of resources) are discussed in Chapter 7; they are integrated with results from the NR studies of Chapter 4 and the further studies of Chapter 6 and compared with previous findings (Chapter 3).

The results for amount of resources found in this study held fairly generally for all the children, and largely irrespective of the time of day or the project experience when data were collected. Interactions of resource factors with these other factors were generally at or below a chance level. The main exception here was that some of the effects of amount of play equipment did depend on sex of child. Items of equipment differed somewhat in popularity for boys and girls; therefore their differing availability showed some variation with sex. With more equipment, only girls increased their use of the Wendy house, whereas boys mainly increased the use of the sandpit. The most popular items – tricycle and doll and pram – increased in usage with both sexes, despite an overall sex difference in preference being maintained.

Comments of the playgroup staff on the differing resource conditions indicated that they preferred the more plentiful environments, and particularly disliked the one-space–three-toy condition which made movement difficult, and any noise and aggression very salient.

6 Subsidiary studies on physical resources

This chapter describes three smaller studies, two of which directly follow on from the research and results described in Chapter 5.

The first study examines a wider range of spatial density parameters than was used in the study reported in Chapter 5. This was considered especially important, given that the earlier investigation revealed so few effects of this factor. Could this be generalised to a wider range of spatial densities, or would a 'threshold' effect be found, beyond which high densities had more noticeable consequences? Spatial densities of 60 and 15 sq. ft per child were compared in an attempt to answer this question.

The second study similarly extended the range of variation in the amount of play equipment provided. On certain sessions the amount of equipment was reduced to half a basic set, and the results were compared with those for sessions with one basic set. Some less systematic observations were also made of short periods when no equipment was provided.

The third study examined how variations in the *kind* of play equipment provided affected the children's behaviour. Specifically, sessions with only large apparatus available were compared with those when only small toys were available, and with the more usual sessions when both kinds of equipment were provided.

Further study of spatial variation

The results of the main study on variation of the amount of space (and spatial density) described in Chapter 5 indicated that within a range of 25–75 sq. ft per child, spatial density had little impact on social or aggressive behaviour, although it did affect gross motor activity. Overall, the effects of spatial density seemed very limited (see Table 5.7).

These findings are consistent with much previous work, as will be discussed in Chapter 7. However, two studies by Price (1971) and Loo (1972) reported less social play in very restricted spatial conditions; in addition, Loo, surprisingly perhaps, reported less aggression. These studies differed from our own and other previous $D_s R_s$ type studies (Table 3.1), in that both utilised very crowded conditions, below the limit of 25 sq. ft per child we had utilised previously. Perhaps this was the reason for the discrepancy in findings.

There are drawbacks to both these studies. In the case of Price's research, the crowded conditions were novel compared with the normal uncrowded conditions; thus spatial crowding was confused with novelty. In Loo's study, both conditions were novel to the children, but the situation was rather unnatural with apparently unacquainted children being put together for the experimental sessions. Also, the definitions of some behaviour categories are unclear, notably for aggressive behaviour which apparently also included rough-and-tumble play in both studies (Price, 1971; Loo, personal communication). However, both investigations employed a large number of groups of children (22 in Price's research, 10 in Loo's), and their consensus in finding some important effects of spatial crowding, compared with other studies using less severe crowding conditions, clearly merited further investigation.

The study by Loo, which was carried out exclusively on 4- and 5-year-olds, linked up most closely with our own research programme. We decided to make a constructive replication (Lykken, 1968) of Loo's results. We used similar spatial densities to those in her experiment, and the children were of similar age. However, our group sizes were larger than Loo's groups of six. In addition, our children, unlike hers, were in a pre-existing playgroup and therefore well acquainted. Our intention was to see if Loo's results would be replicated under these slightly different conditions. If so, then taken in conjunction with our previous results this would provide evidence for a 'threshold' effect of spatial density on behaviour – an indication of a lower limit below which noticeable behavioural changes would begin to occur.

The study was carried out in the third term of the third year. During this term spatial density was covaried with group size. The main results of the group size variations were discussed in Chapter 4, which also contains further details of group composition and methodology, presented more briefly here.

Population sample and resource variations

The composition of the playgroup varied on the four days the playgroup met. Details of the children are given in Table 4.1 and Appendix A.

Covaried with these group sizes were two spatial densities of 15 and 60 sq. ft per child (see Fig. 4.3). On Wednesdays and Thursdays about 30 children were expected; the large space then corresponded to all the hall,

Table 6.1. *Number of children, attendance, and spatial and equipment densities (further study of spatial density)*

	Number of children	Attendance percentage	Spatial densities (sq. ft/child)	Equipment densities (approx.)
Group One	12	85	61 and 15	1 reduced set/ 10 children
Group Two	11	88	63 and 15	1 reduced set/ 10 children
Group Three	23	86	61 and 15	1 reduced set/ 10 children

or 1,824 sq. ft, and the small space to about one-third of the hall. On Tuesdays and Fridays about 10 children were expected; the large space corresponded to one-third of the hall, or 628 sq. ft, and the small space to about one-third of this. The large space conditions gave densities of approximately 60 sq. ft per child, depending of course on attendance at each session. Our previous research (Chapter 4) suggested that slight variations around 60 sq. ft per child would not be important. However, for the small space conditions (for both groups sizes) the position of the curtain screen was adjusted at the beginning of each session to give *exactly* 15 sq. ft per child (on the basis of the actual attendance that morning). Spatial densities and other project details are summarised in Table 6.1.

In the very crowded conditions of 15 sq. ft per child it was not possible to use all the usual equipment. Instead a smaller basic set of equipment was used, comprising: Wendy house with tea set, ironing board, dressing-up clothes, and telephone; toy chest; pram and doll; easel; bookcase and three chairs; one table, four chairs, and crayons and paper, or jigsaws, and Lego or plastic Meccano; one table with sand, water, or dough; and a bucket of wooden blocks. The small groups had one set of this equipment, the large groups had three sets, so that the amount of play equipment per child was held constant (Table 6.1).

Observational methods and methods of analysis

During most of this term and all the experimental sessions, the children were engaged in free play throughout the morning. Both spatial density conditions were used each morning, each condition occupying a half-session (9.30–10.15, or 11.00–11.45). The order of the conditions was alternated. Altogether four half-sessions of observation were made of each spatial density condition for each group size condition. In each half-session, five samples of behaviour were obtained for each child. These were the standard observational samples of companions, activities, and behaviours described in Chapter 2. However, the sample length was reduced to 30 seconds so as to get more independent samples per child in the restricted time available. Altogether 20 samples were obtained per child, per space condition, per group size condition.

The time samples were obtained only for the children in Groups One and Two. That is, during the large group sessions, only the 12 or 11 children present also in the small groups were observed. This was so that the behaviour of the same children could be compared in the different group size conditions.

In addition it seemed worthwhile to collect some data on the behaviour of the Group Three children in the different space conditions. However, time considerations ruled out the standard technique of sampling individual children. Instead, it was found feasible to use a rapid scan technique to obtain data only on the social nature of the children's activity, and their companions. By this method, the whole group was scanned rapidly but systematically, recording whether children were alone, or in parallel or group activity, and with whom. This only took about a minute or so to complete, and could be carried out after each round of time samples on the Group One and Group Two children; it provided data for Group Three equivalent to the companions data for Groups One and Two. However, it must be borne in mind that as the scans were made within short intervals, the scores for individual children will exhibit a considerable degree of non-independence. As a result, significance levels are likely to overestimate the degree to which the results may be generalised.

Only eight half-mornings of observation per spatial density condition (or four weeks in total) were carried out, because we judged it important to have regard to ethical implications and possible adverse effects on the children of the very high density conditions. This also was the reason for limiting the small space sessions to 45 minutes. We proceeded after consultation with the playgroup staff, and after a trial of the small space conditions on each group. The parents were informed prior to the experiment that we intended to do further space variations. In fact little apparent disturbance was seen in the children, although one or two were slightly distressed, possibly as much at the absence of favourite toys such as the climbing-frame or tricycle. Nevertheless the conditions were rather stressful for staff, who found it difficult to move around easily, and the conditions did not seem so congenial as those where more space and equipment were available. The experiment was therefore kept as short as possible, consistent with collecting sufficient observational data. On other days during the term, when no observations were made, more space and equipment were provided, so the experimental conditions were somewhat novel. This made the analysis of time effects especially important, as, if any novelty of the conditions were an important factor, significant time effects would be expected.

Analyses of variance were used on statistics based on the number of samples in which particular categories of companion choice, activity choice, and behaviour were recorded. A three-factor design of group size (two levels), spatial density (two levels), and time (two levels) was used. Variance between children was taken as the source of error variance in computing F ratios. Sex was not introduced as a factor, as the groups were not exactly balanced; however, individual results were examined for possible sex differences or interactions where appropriate.

The analyses were carried out separately for Groups One and Two. Only main effects of spatial density, and its interactions with group size or time, are considered here. The results are presented in Tables 6.2–6.4; other results are presented in Chapter 4. Table 6.2 also includes the additional sociometric scan data obtained for Group Three, analysed for spatial density effects only by the Wilcoxon matched-pairs signed-ranks tests. For all the analyses, and especially the sociometric data on Group Three, non-independence of behaviour in individual children means that significance levels are likely to be an overestimate as regards the generalisation of results to other groups of children. Thus the pattern of results is more important than any individual findings.

Definition of the categories used as provided in Appendix B.

Results

The sociometric structure of the two groups was as presented in Figures 4.6 and 4.9.

Choice of companions

Results are given in Table 6.2. There was a consistent finding of more *parallel play* in the spatially crowded conditions, significant for two of the four comparisons. In the main, this increase was in *large parallel subgroups*. There was a tendency for less *group play*, though only significant on one comparison, and for fewer *subgroups of four or more*, significant on two comparisons. The *mean subgroup size* was smaller, significant on three comparisons. There was some tendency for more *same-sex choices*, only significant on one comparison.

Table 6.2. *Companions: results, and significance levels, comparing different spatial density conditions*

Totals for 11 categories of companion choice; means for subgroup size and percentage same-sex choice
G = Interaction of spatial density with group size
T = Interaction of spatial density with project experience
* $P < 0.05$ ** $P < 0.01$ *** $P < 0.001$

	Group One (upper line) Group Two (lower line)		Group Three with Group One (upper line), Group Two (lower line)	
	15 sq. ft/child	60 sq. ft/child	15 sq. ft/child	60 sq. ft/child
Alone	57	76	103	121
	83	73	121	143
Small adult	8	9	5	3
subgroup	2	5	0	1
Large adult	4	6	6	13
subgroup	2	1	13	15
Small parallel	79	84	93	61**
subgroup	84	67	78	75
Large parallel	95	51**	82	49*
subgroup	62	55	79	59
Same-sex	74	81	57	82
pair	68	75	81	48*
Opposite-	52	57	22	35
sex pair	26	37	25	27
Subgroup	55	56 G**	35	45
of three	76	58	34	40
Subgroup of	56	59	57	57
four or more	37	69**	17	52***
Parallel	174	135*	175	110***
play	146	122	157	134
Group	236	253	171	213*
play	207	239	169	167
Mean	2.67	2.87*	2.88	2.94
subgroup size	2.60	2.84*	2.43	2.74***
Same-sex	56.7	60.2	73.0	64.7
choice	65.9	60.2 G*	72.0	57.0*

Choice of activities

Results for the 14 relevant categories are given in Table 6.3. The *climbing-frame*, *rocking-boat*, and *tricycle* were not present in this study.

The two consistently significant results were that there was less *rough-*

Table 6.3. *Activities: total occurrences, and significance levels, comparing different spatial density conditions*

Group One upper line; Group Two lower line
G   Interaction of spatial density with group size
T   Interaction of spatial density with project experience
(*) $P < 0.1$ * $P < 0.05$ * $P < 0.01$ *** $P < 0.001$

	15 sq. ft/child	60 sq. ft/child
Table	89	72 T**
	54	74
Sandpit	181	110***
	141	118
Easel	24	52**
	41	17*
Wendy house	107	73*G*
	85	58(*)
Doll	40	28
	32	38
Dressing-up clothes	29	25
	37	33
Toy chest	28	26
	29	52 G**T*
Rough-and-tumble play	6	35***
	3	14*T*
Books	29	42(*)
	18	33*
Miscellaneous play	26	47*T**
	26	47*
Fantasy play	119	122
	86	116*
Unusual uses of apparatus	0	2
	0	0
Room fitments	0	2
	0	0
No activity	36	31
	59	39

and-tumble play in the spatially crowded conditions, and also less *miscellaneous play*. The findings of more use of the *Wendy house*, and use of *books*, were also fairly reliable.

Consistent trends, only significant for one group, were for more use of the *sandpit* (this category also included play with water or clay), and less *fantasy play*. Results for the *easel* were clearly inconsistent.

Table 6.4. *Behaviours: total occurrences, and significance levels, comparing different spatial density conditions*

Shorter list of 27 behaviour units; Group One upper line; Group Two lower line
G   Interaction of spatial density with group size
T   Interaction of spatial density with project experience
(*) $P < 0.1$ * $P < 0.05$ ** $P < 0.01$ *** $P < 0.001$

	15 sq. ft/child	60 sq. ft/child
Upper smile	89	88
	62	95**
Open smile	32	46(*)
	18	34*G*
Play noise	43	43T*
	17	31
Talking between	284	286
children	242	275*
Talking to/from	37	56
adult	28	26G*
Look around/	6	15*
distance	9	11
Watch	75	44**
	78	65
Visual	272	263
contact child	238	256
Visual	36	44
contact adult	41	27
Contact	267	217**
apparatus	258	246
Physical contact	194	154*
between children	143	160
Physical contact	8	11
with adult	5	3
Walk	169	231***
	149	177(*)
Run	14	70***
	12	69***G**T*
Climb/slide	15	8
	12	12
Chase/flee/	2	18***
group run	1	12*
Object	108	65***
exchange	72	63
Push/pull	23	28
	21	39*T*

Table 6.4. (*cont.*)

	15 sq. ft/child	60 sq. ft/child
Kick/throw/hit	42	29
	12	19
Pedal/propel	0	1
	2	1
Fine manipulation	359	327*G*
	297	302
Gross manipulation	20	30
	23	42*
Physical	25	15
aggression	16	12
Agonistic	67	38**
behaviour	47	41
Suck	24	30
	33	19
Face contact	35	57*
	51	54
Auto-manipulation	129	164*
	156	156T*

Occurrence of behaviours

Results for the shorter list of 27 behaviour units are given in Table 6.4. (For results for the full list of 89 behaviour units, see Appendix D.) There were four consistently significant results, and nine consistent trends.

There was clearly much less *running* and *chasing/fleeing* in the spatially crowded conditions, also less *walking* and fewer *open smiles*. There were trends for less *talking between children, looking around/distance, pushing/pulling*, and *gross manipulation* of objects, for increases in *watching, contact with apparatus, object exchange*, and *agonistic behaviour*.

The trend for less *face contact* did not seem very substantial, especially given the inconsistent results for *automanipulation* generally, and the rather low observer reliability of these categories.

Interactions of spatial density with group size

The number of significant interactions of group size with spatial density is shown in Table 6.5. They are at about the level expected by chance, and none is consistent for both Groups One and Two. It is therefore concluded that the size of group did not materially affect the impact of the spatial density variations.

Table 6.5. *Number of significant main effects and interactions at 5 per cent level*

Results from analyses of variance compared with number of results expected by chance; separate results for Groups One and Two in brackets

	Main effects		Interaction effects		Expected by chance (approx.)
	Spatial density	Time	Spatial density × project experience	Spatial density × group size	
Choice of companions	2	4	0	2	1
(13 categories)	(1, 1)	(2, 2)	(0, 0)	(1, 1)	
Choice of activities	10	3	4	2	1
(14 categories)	(5, 5)	(2, 1)	(2, 2)	(1, 1)	
Behaviour units	19	13	4	4	3
(27 categories)	(12, 7)	(7, 6)	(1, 3)	(1, 3)	
Behaviour units	31	21	6	6	9
(89 categories)	(19, 12)	(12, 9)	(1, 5)	(3, 3)	

Interactions of spatial density and project experience

Two levels for the time factor were introduced into the analyses of variance. These corresponded to the data from the first two weeks and second two weeks of the study.

The number of significant interactions of project experience with spatial density is shown in Table 6.5. They are at about the level expected by chance, apart perhaps from the activities categories. No interaction was significant for both Groups One and Two. Overall, it is concluded that project experience did not affect the impact of the spatial density variations. This conclusion is qualified by the short duration of the experiment, and possibly by idiosyncratic changes of impact of spatial density on activity choice in the two groups of children.

Sex of children and spatial density factor

As boys and girls were not equally balanced within each group, taking account of sex as a factor in the analyses of variance would have been difficult. However, a computer print-out of separate data for boys and girls in both the high and low spatial density conditions enabled a visual scan of likely interactions with sex.

This scanning procedure did not suggest any consistent differences between boys and girls in their reactions to the different spatial density

Table 6.6. *Percentage change in sampled occurrence from less to more spatially crowded conditions*

Separate results for boys and girls, averaged over both groups, for categories showing consistently significant overall spatial density effects

	Boys	Girls
Companions		
Large parallel subgroup	+70.7	+33.8
Parallel play	+16.2	+31.4
Group play	−2.4	−15.5
Mean subgroup size	−4.4	−18.4
Activities		
Rough-and-tumble play	−77.8	−86.4
Miscellaneous play	−50.0	−39.6
Wendy house	+65.2	+36.5
Behaviour units		
Open smile	−41.4	−35.3
Walk	−25.5	−19.2
Run	−81.7	−80.9
Chase/flee group run	−91.7	−88.9

conditions. Further evidence for this is given in Table 6.6. This presents separate results for boys and girls, for those categories for which consistent significant main effects were found (*group play* is also included). Results are averaged for Groups One and Two because of the relatively low numbers of children involved. They are presented in terms of the percentage change of sample occurrence from the less spatially crowded to the more spatially crowded conditions. In every case, boys and girls show changes in the same direction, and generally of the same order of magnitude.

It is concluded that the sex of a child is not an important factor in relation to the effects of spatial density.

Staff comments on spatial density variations

At the end of the study, each of the three staff at the playgroup were given an open-ended questionnaire to fill in. This asked the following questions:

What effect do you think it has on the children's behaviour when the space is reduced to about one-third the usual amount?
  (a) generally?
  (b) any special effects on particular children?
  (c) how does it affect you?

The answers to part (a) are reproduced below.

Miss C (supervisor):

Reduced playing area affects practically all the children. They become bored very quickly with the toys they have and become frustrated with the lack of space and climbing equipment. Aggression is much more noticeable, and leadership in the organisation of play becomes prevalent. A lot of the children need to go to the toilet much more than usual.

Mrs Y (assistant):

When the space is reduced a 'family' feeling seems to evolve. Children seem more aware of the presence of other children they don't usually notice in the group. There seems to be more table and Wendy house play, and less running games. There seem to be more toilet sessions when space is reduced. More dominant children seem to spread their influence over a larger group of children in the smaller space. Creativity seems to increase in the smaller space.

Miss Z (assistant):

They get bored and restless much quicker (this could also link up with limited choice of activities, i.e. no tricycles, slides etc.). They seem to be much more destructive with apparatus, no doubt because with a smaller space anything on the floor is more likely to be trodden on. There seems to be a greater need for trips to the toilet. They ask more frequently if it's time to finish. Some children obviously benefit and feel more secure in a smaller space, take more part in table activities, are drawn more into group play.

Several of the staff's impressions are validated by the observational data – Miss C's comments on aggression, Mrs Y's on Wendy house play and running games. Other remarks – on boredom or activity span, leadership, and creativity, could not be checked in this way. All three staff remarked on more frequent visits to the toilet by the children when in the smaller space. This could be taken as a sign of increased anxiety, or perhaps of a wish to feel more spatial freedom. However, it is also possible that this activity was simply more noticeable to the staff. In the large space conditions, children could often go to the toilet in the foyer themselves, or at most one member of staff would watch them. In the small space conditions – especially the small group–small space condition – the three staff were grouped up together in close contact, usually stayed together, and all three would be aware of any toilet request. Also, any such request entailed more difficulty in letting a child through the screens and back again. Thus while it is certainly possible that toilet visits increased, it is difficult to be certain about this.

Mrs Y and Mrs Z both answered part (b) of the questionnaire. Both saw some children as benefiting from the small space, others as not. Mrs Y named two boys and three girls as being more sociable, and two boys and two girls as being more restless or destructive. Mrs Z similarly named two boys and one girl as settling better, and three boys as being more bored, restless, or destructive. (Only two children were named in common by Mrs Y and Mrs Z.)

The answers to part (c) are reproduced below.

Miss C (supervisor):

The lack of equipment as well as the lack of space tends to make this way of working unrewarding and frustrating.

Mrs Y (assistant):

The small space feels cramped and too close for actual contact. Reaching children quickly is difficult because of the litter of toys in the floor area. The noise level seems to increase. Bending down or sitting down to be at their level is difficult without being pushed over. Talking quietly to aggressive children seems impossible, without all the others overhearing.

Mrs Z (assistant):

Adversely! Restlessness of children is transmitted, also everything seems much more messy and disordered. Don't feel as much a part of the group because there is nowhere to stand or sit!

It is clear that all three of the staff disliked the small space conditions. It was indeed difficult to move around freely, and therefore difficult for the staff to carry out their normal duties – comforting a distressed child, recovering toys, replenishing easel materials, and so on – with ease and efficiency.

Discussion and summary

The general finding was that spatial density changes to 15 sq. ft per child probably did have somewhat more impact than the variations reported earlier (Table 6.5; cf. Table 5.7). The findings for spatial variations in Chapter 4 were generally replicated, and there was some evidence for additional effects not found in the previous study.

Some findings, significant for both Groups One and Two, are reasonably firm. It seems clear that the very small space condition severely inhibited gross motor activity. Running, chasing and fleeing, and rough-and-tumble play were reduced to an almost insignificant level, and laughing (open smiling) was also reduced. Even walking was observed substantially less often. This is an intensification of the general finding obtained in the previous study.

In line with the previous study, there were also trends for less gross manipulation of objects (especially pushing and pulling) in the smaller space, less looking around or in the distance, and more contact with immovable apparatus such as tables and Wendy houses.

Other findings seem to indicate some effects of the space variations which go beyond those of the previous study. A common factor may well be that the space variations have their effects through changes in activity choices constrained by spatial variations. However, if that is the case, the changes consequent on a reduction to 15 sq. ft per child are probably more far-reaching than on a reduction to 25 sq. ft.

In the previous study the main changes were an increase in use of the climbing apparatus and a decrease in free motor activity, use of tricycles, and pram pushing. In this study no climbing apparatus was available, and the spatial constraints were more extreme. Even walking was reduced, and running almost impossible. One consequence seems to have been an increase in use of the Wendy house. However, this did not lead to an increase in fantasy play. The Wendy house was used for other purposes, such as conversation, taking objects for manipulation, and even climbing on. Indeed this use of the Wendy house space for other purposes may be responsible for a possible reduction in fantasy play.

There was also more play with sand, water, or clay in bowls or at tables when space was reduced. These activities involved little movement, and so were favoured. Surprisingly, there seemed to be less use of books, possibly because the book corner – a bookcase with chair nearby – was more disrupted by the movements of other children.

Inter-personal distance was obviously reduced in the small space. However, it is not clear whether physical contacts between children increased as a consequence. There seemed to be more watching of other children. There was clearly more parallel play, often in large groups. This is probably connected with the increase in play with sand, water, and clay – often parallel activities.

There were trends for more object exchange, and for more agonistic behaviour, perhaps as a consequence either of the object exchanges or of difficulty in getting to desired resources or avoiding other children.

Although parallel groups were more frequent and larger, the trend was for group play to be less frequent, and for such groups to be smaller. The result for group play was significant only for Group One, but Group Two showed a significant reduction in talking amongst children. It may well be that the kinds of activities which encouraged group play – such as fantasy play in the Wendy house, or group chasing games – were inhibited by the spatial restrictions, and in addition that coordinated group activity by several children was more difficult, resulting in a smaller mean subgroup size. Subgroups of four or more children especially were less frequent.

The results of the study held fairly generally for all the children and the effects were very similar for both boys and girls. However, the staff commented that the changes affected some children beneficially and others adversely. There were not sufficient observational data to validate this.

Interaction with project experience did not occur at above a chance level, except perhaps for idiosyncratic changes in activity choice in the two groups. This suggests that although the spatially crowded conditions were relatively novel, this may not be too important a qualification in considering the extent to which the findings can be generalised.

Interactions with group size were at or below a chance level. Actual amount of space, R_s, varied with group size; this suggests that the results (common for both N and R levels) are attributable to D_s, or spatial density, rather than R_s.

The comments made by the staff showed that they found the small space conditions difficult and unrewarding to work in. They also remarked on increased boredom and restlessness in the children and the increase in visits to the toilet. These comments could not be checked against observational data.

Overall, the extent to which the results can be generalised is limited by the small size of the groups and the small number of observational sessions, as well as the relative novelty of the more spatially crowded conditions. Nevertheless there is a strong suggestion that reducing available space from 25 to 15 sq. ft per child begins to have quite noticeable effects on social behaviour. The inhibition of gross motor activity is increased, and even walking is reduced. There is more parallel play in large subgroups, often with sand, water, or clay where little movement is required. Group play seems to be less frequent, and to be in smaller subgroups. There may be less fantasy play, more object exchange, and more agonistic encounters. The results will be discussed further in Chapter 7.

Further study of equipment variations

The findings from the main study on the variation of the amount of play equipment, described in Chapter 5, indicated that the most noticeable effects were on the children's choice of toys and activities. With less equipment, there was some shift of attention to less popular items, and there was more sharing of popular items. There was more free motor activity. Fewer children played alone, more in parallel subgroups, and there were more subgroups of three or four children in cooperative group play. Levels of aggressive behaviour and stress behaviours also increased.

The study was carried out using either one, two, or three basic sets of play equipment, chosen from typical playgroup items; it was intended to provide a reasonable minimum of equipment, while making it probable that some appreciable sharing of items among children would occur. With two or three sets, the sharing of items would not be necessary (though it might, and to some extent did, still occur).

As with the studies on spatial variation, it is possible that a wider range of parameter variation might produce different results. However, amount of play equipment is a more difficult variable to quantify than amount of space; inevitably the kinds of play equipment available are a very important consideration. In the main study this difficulty was overcome by varying the amount independent of the variety of equipment.

It would have been possible to extend the range of parameter variation for play equipment by having four or more sets of equipment, but this seemed pointless. Three basic sets seemed plentiful – much more so than in most playgroups. The variety of equipment was not exceptional; but any increase in variety would have increased the size of the basic set, and then even the one-toy condition would have been a rich one.

It seemed more worthwhile to investigate the effects of having even fewer toys present than in the basic or one-toy condition. This condition, while it would certainly not be described as a rich one, was nevertheless probably well within the usual range to be found in registered playgroups. Some playgroups, especially ones just starting, have very little equipment, and it seemed important to us to try to assess the likely behavioural effects of such circumstances. Would the behavioural trends found earlier continue to be manifest?

To investigate this, an experiment was carried out using sessions in which only half a basic toy set was available. This inevitably affected the variety of equipment available as well, but by having the two different halves of the basic set available on different sessions this factor was minimised. A second, much briefer study was made of two short periods when the children were in the hall and no toys or apparatus were available. This is described subsequently.

Population sample and resource variations

The study using the reduced equipment conditions was carried out in the third term of the first year, following the main study on amounts of space and play equipment, described in Chapter 5. The composition of the playgroup is given in Appendix A, except that one child had left each group (child 12 from Group One, and child 39 from Group Two). Also two children (25 and 26) were absent from Group Two during the experiment. Thus there were 23 children in Group One and 21 in Group Two. For six children in Group One, and two in Group Two, complete data were obtained only for one session in each condition.

Each group experienced identical environmental variations lasting for four whole-morning sessions. On the first session, one-half of the basic set of equipment was present in the two-space condition (Fig. 5.1). For the next two morning sessions, two extra one-toy–two-space conditions were used as a control. On the fourth session, the other half of the basic set was available, again in the two-space condition.

The two halves of the basic equipment set used were: (1) one table with two chairs and small table toys; climbing-frame and slide; rocking-boat; pram and doll; bookcase with two chairs; easel; jigsaw; four toy cars; drum and bells; toy telephone; clothes-horse and dressing-up clothes; (2) one table with two chairs and (different) small table toys; toy chest; tricycle; jigsaw; Wendy house and small table and two stools, tea set and iron; teddy, sandpit; doll's house and chair; bowl of wooden blocks; musical roller; cymbals.

Observational methods and methods of analysis

The children were in free play from 9.30 to 10.15, and from 11.00 to 11.45. The standard 40-second time-sampling procedure was used to obtain records of children's companions, choice of activities, and occurence of behaviour units. Four samples were obtained for each child on each session; thus there were eight samples per child in the control condition. The experimental conditions were novel, although they had been tried out about four months earlier for one session. It is thus possible that effects were due to novelty of the condition, although the children had about 30 minutes (9.00–9.30) to get used to the condition before observations commenced.

Analyses were carried out on individual child totals for the half-toy condition (H) compared with the control condition (O). The Wilcoxon matched-pairs signed-ranks test was used to assess significance of differences in occurrence between the two conditions. As usual, reliance was placed only on results found to be significant for both groups of children. Definition of the categories used are provided in Appendix B.

Table 6.7. *Companions: total occurrences for different play equipment conditions*

Group One upper line; Group Two lower line; significance levels from Wilcoxon matched-pairs signed-ranks test
A   Apparatus only
C   Control
H   Half-toy set
O   One-toy set
T   Toys only
(*) $P < 0.1$ * $P < 0.05$ ** $P < 0.01$

	H	O	H vs O	A	C	T	A vs C	C vs T	A vs T
Alone	45	36		38	42	42			
	28	29		42	38	32			
Small adult	6	3		10	10	12			
subgroup	6	10		9	11	14			
Large adult	7	22	*	6	12	17			(*)
subgroup	16	22		4	15	27	*		**
Small parallel	17	28		11	29	32	*		**
subgroup	15	26		16	24	20			
Large parallel	11	7		11	5	5			
subgroup	23	7	**	11	4	4			
Same-sex	31	31		37	28	25			
pair	35	26		32	42	29			
Opposite-sex	14	15		16	7	9			
pair	9	7		9	8	15			
Subgroup	16	13		20	18	13			
of three	21	21		19	12	14			
Subgroup of	13	5		11	9	5			
four or more	7	12		18	6	5			**
Parallel	28	35		22	34	37			
play	38	33		27	28	24			
Group	74	64		84	62	52	*		**
play	72	66		78	68	63	(*)		*
Mean subgroup	2.76	2.35	*	2.46	2.67	2.41			
size	2.54	2.94		2.89	2.44	2.41			**
Same-sex	61.4	65.3		64.5	64.7	72.9			
choice	67.9	59.6		64.6	65.2	56.4			

Results

The results are presented for choice of companions, activities, and occurrence of behaviour units (shorter list of 27 units) in Tables 6.7–6.9.

Few reliable significant results were obtained. In the further reduced toy conditions, there was less use of the *tricycle* in both groups. There was more

Table 6.8. *Activities: total occurrences for different play equipment conditions*

Group One upper line; Group Two lower line; significance levels from Wilcoxon matched-pairs signed-ranks test
A Apparatus only
C Control
H Half-toy set
O One-toy set
T Toys only
(*) $P < 0.1$ * $P < 0.05$ ** $P < 0.01$

	H	O	H vs O	A	C	T	A vs C	C vs T	A vs T
Table play	24	16		5	19	37	**	*	**
	32	25		0	19	36	**	*	**
Sandpit	7	15		0	13	17	**		**
	7	13		0	15	15	**		**
Easel	11	16		0	8	15	**		**
	14	14		0	12	21	**		**
Wendy house	12	10		31	16	13	*		*
	7	7		27	12	3	*	*	**
Doll	5	7		18	18	8			
	12	7		13	10	3			*
Dressing-up clothes	2	3		0	11	3	**	*	
	2	11		1	13	4	**		
Climbing-frame	12	17		19	18	0		**	**
	20	15		29	17	0		**	**
Rocking-boat	12	11		17	16	0		**	**
	7	9		10	13	0		**	**
Toy chest	10	16		31	8	0	**		**
	12	14		39	8	0	**		**
Tricycle	3	13	*	20	21	0		**	**
	4	11	(*)	28	16	0		**	**
Rough-and-tumble play	9	7		7	3	10			
	19	9	*	6	1	10		*	
Books	14	20		0	11	23	**		**
	11	11		0	8	16	**		**
Blocks	11	4		0	8	5	**		
	8	5		0	2	5			
Doll's house	4	0		0	2	0			
	1	1		0	0	2			
Jigsaws	4	1		0	1	2			
	2	1		0	3	4			
Telephone	3	0		0	2	5			
	0	0		0	1	2			
Musical instruments	9	12		0	12	14	**		*
	3	5		0	11	17	**		**

Table 6.8. (*cont.*)

	H	O	H vs O	A	C	T	A vs C	C vs T	A vs T
Miscellaneous	12	12		4	5	12			
play	12	14		4	9	18			*
Fantasy	15	11		21	18	15			
play	12	15		12	7	9			
Unusual uses	8	9		64	6	6	**		**
of apparatus	8	12		44	8	4	**		**
Room	5	5		3	1	2			
fitments	2	0		3	0	3			
No activity	22	16		12	11	15			
	6	10		5	15	10	*		

Table 6.9. *Behaviour units: total occurrences for different play equipment conditions*

Group One upper line; Group Two lower line; significance levels from Wilcoxon matched-pairs signed-ranks tests
A   Apparatus only
C   Control
H   Half-toy set
O   One-toy set
T   Toys only
(*) $P < 0.1$ * $P < 0.05$ ** $P < 0.01$

	H	O	H vs O	A	C	T	A vs C	C vs T	A vs T
Upper smile	59	38	*	44	31	27			*
	43	43		56	30	51	*	*	
Open smile	28	14	*	30	24	11			*
	29	26		33	20	17			*
Play noise	14	19		25	23	22			
	33	20	*	22	23	16			
Talking between	99	87		103	82	75	*		**
children	90	76		95	77	76	*		*
Talking to/	20	33	*	28	44	38			
from adult	26	31		21	31	35			
Look around/	4	9		8	9	8			
distance	4	7		9	8	8			
Watch	66	68		53	51	63			
	52	53		56	61	53			
Visual	110	98		119	96	85	*		**
contact child	106	97		112	104	107			
Visual	39	54	*	35	57	40	*	*	
contact adult	37	45		33	43	39	*		

Table 6.9. (*cont.*)

	H	O	H vs O	A	C	T	A vs C	C vs T	A vs T
Contact	68	78		96	76	85	*		
apparatus	70	73		91	80	72			
Physical contact	62	49	*	66	32	22	**		**
between children	41	33	(*)	62	37	34	*		**
Physical contact	10	11		12	14	16			
with adult	12	11		9	11	10			
Walk	105	74	*	100	81	69			**
	80	61	*	93	78	66	*		*
Run	43	34		47	34	18			**
	46	23	**	33	38	24			(*)
Climb/slide	10	13		23	13	0		**	**
	11	9		33	13	0	*	**	**
Chase/flee/	7	7		7	1	6			
group run	13	5	*	5	3	11			
Object	13	14		6	21	28	*		**
exchange	22	21		3	23	31	**		**
Push/pull	18	21		53	35	16	*	*	**
	26	19		52	27	15	*	*	**
Kick/throw	13	16		2	11	17			*
hit	10	10		6	17	19			*
Pedal/propel	2	9		21	19	0		**	**
	3	9		29	13	0		**	**
Fine	62	67		3	68	106	**	**	**
manipulation	65	70		3	61	98	**	**	**
Gross	15	27	*	53	36	9	*	**	**
manipulation	21	21		50	31	17	*	*	**
Physical	6	7		8	3	6			
aggression	3	6		7	3	4			
Agonistic	15	19		17	8	13			
behaviour	13	20		14	5	12			
Suck	16	19		21	12	17			
	23	12	*	19	9	13			
Face contact	33	28		39	24	18	*		*
	28	27		20	31	14		*	
Automanipulation	74	81		84	75	48		*	**
	65	69		77	73	50		*	**

walking in both groups, and more *running* and *rough-and-tumble play* in Group Two, more *upper smile* and *open smile* in Group One.

Group One children showed significantly less play in *large adult subgroups*, *talking to/from adult*, or *visual contact adult*, these all being non-significant trends in Group Two. Group Two showed significantly more play in *large parallel subgroups*.

Discussion and summary

The relative paucity of reliable and significant results probably reflects the rather inadequate data base in this subsidiary study. In addition, the reduced equipment condition was relatively novel compared with the one-toy condition.

The previous study (Chapter 5) found a number of effects consequent on decreased play equipment. Only one of these is fairly clearly extended in this study – the increase in free motor activity, represented by running, walking, and rough-and-tumble play. The other trends which might have been expected to continue – more parallel play, larger subgroup size, more aggression, more thumb-sucking, more records of no activity – were not found, or were found only for one group of children.

One finding does stand out from this study. With so few toys available one might expect that the children would divert more attention to the playgroup staff, and cluster around them for activities. This quite clearly did not happen; if anything, the opposite occurred. The children seemed able to occupy themselves about as adequately as when the full set of toys was available, perhaps making rather more use of less popular items such as the wooden blocks or musical instruments.

It must be emphasised that the study was a short one – only two sessions for each group in the reduced toy conditions – and it might well be the case that other results would be obtained if such circumstances were maintained over a longer period.

Observations for short periods with no equipment present

It was not considered feasible or ethical to have many or lengthy sessions in which no equipment was provided. However, one short experiment was carried out with each group, towards the end of the second term in the first year. This was clearly very much in the nature of a pilot study, and the results must be treated as such.

These short periods lasted 10 minutes, and were held from 10.45 to 10.55; the children returned from milk break and toilets to a two-space condition from which all the usual toys and apparatus had been removed. The staff told the children that the toys would not be out for 10 minutes, and were instructed not to structure the children's activities but to be available if children needed them. The space available to the children was completely bare apart from a few items, namely, a weighing machine in the corner of the room, a lectern, a few folded trestle tables stacked against a wall, and a fire extinguisher near the door. In addition, the curtain screen blocked off one side of the available space, and there were radiators and windows on two other sides.

All 24 children were present when Group One experienced this condition; but two children (29 and 40) were absent when Group Two experienced it, leaving 22 children.

As time sampling was not feasible during the 10 minutes available, one observer dictated a continuous running commentary of the children's main activities on to a cassette-recorder, while a second observer filmed continuously on videotape, scanning across the room. Together these data sources enabled a categorisation of each child's main activities through the period, broken down into half-minute intervals. The main categories of activity observed were:

(1) Gross motor activity: this started very soon after the children entered, and consisted mainly of running in a circle, often with open smiles and squealing, sometimes collisions. Jumping and skipping around were also frequent. This seemed to be a socially facilitating behaviour, children being attracted to join in, while others dropped out for a time and perhaps rejoined later. There was relatively little contact rough-and-tumble play. This category was observed for 46 per cent of the intervals in Group One and 41 per cent in Group Two.

(2) Standing or walking around: usually doing nothing except watching other children. This category occupied 22 per cent of the intervals in Group One and 24 per cent in Group Two. In addition, standing near an adult occupied 10 per cent of intervals in Group One and 8 per cent in Group Two.

(3) Sitting or lying on the ground: this was usually at the periphery of the room, sometimes while watching other children, sometimes in conversation. This occupied 15 per cent of the intervals in Group One and 19 per cent in Group Two.

(4) Exploring or playing with room fitments, such as the weighing machine, curtains, windows or radiators: this occupied 8 per cent of the intervals in both Groups One and Two.

In summary, nearly half the time the children were observed in gross motor activity. About a third of the time they were observed walking or wandering around. The remainder of the time they were generally observed in conversation, or exploring room fitments.

Study of effects of different kinds of play equipment

The studies of the effects of varying the amount of play equipment did not consider differences in the kinds or variety of equipment available. The amount was varied while keeping variety constant by having multiples of a particular basic set of equipment. However, it was apparent from our own observations, as well as from previous research and experience with preschool children, that different kinds of equipment encourage different kinds of behaviour (see Chapter 3). A full and systematic study of the potentials of different kinds of toys and equipment for eliciting different kinds of response from the children was beyond the scope of our enquiry. However, we carried out one small project which is reported here. Perhaps the most obvious difference in the kinds of equipment we had provided was between apparatus which encouraged mainly gross motor activity, such as climbing-frame, rocking-boat, tricycle, and toys which encouraged fine manipulative activity, such as the small table toys, dressing-up clothes, tea sets, and musical instruments. In some nurseries the larger equipment is reserved for outdoor play, while mainly smaller toys are provided indoors. Our playgroup, like most playgroups, did not have an outdoor area, so both large apparatus and small toys were found together. In this study we compared the children's behaviour when only large apparatus was available, and when only small toys were available. We also used a control condition with both apparatus and small toys present.

Population sample and resource variations

Subject details are identical to those for the study of reduced equipment conditions, given on p. 170.

Each group experienced identical environmental variations, lasting six morning sessions. The sequence of variations was: apparatus only (A); toys only (T); control (C); control; toys only; apparatus only.

In condition A there were thirty chairs, three pairs of tables, and three each of toy chest and lid, climbing-frame and slide, Wendy house with table and two stools, pram, tricycle, and rocking-boat. In condition T there were twenty chairs, three pairs of tables, and three each of large jigsaws, small jigsaws, plastic links, beads and string, doll, teddy, dressing-up clothes, tea set, drum, cymbals, bells, musical roller, doll's house, sandpit and toys, easel and paints, bookcase and books, wooden blocks, telephone. In condition C there were twenty chairs, two pairs of tables, and two each of all the items of apparatus and toys mentioned above. All the conditions used two-thirds of the total available floor space (see Chapter 5 and Fig. 5.1).

Observational methods and methods of analysis

The children were in free play from 9.30 to 10.15, and from 11.00 to 11.45. The standard time-sampling procedure was used to obtain records of children's companions and choice of activities, and occurrence of behaviour units. Four samples were obtained for each child on each session; thus there were eight samples per child in each of the three conditions. Condition C was familiar to children from the previous project, but conditions A and T were novel. It is thus possible that differences between the experimental and the control conditions can be ascribed to this factor. However, the children had about thirty minutes (9.00–9.30) to get used to the condition before observations began. The largest differences were between conditions A and T – both novel – and these differences were noted again when the experimental conditions were repeated.

Analyses were carried out on individual child totals for each condition, making the comparisons A versus C, C versus T, and A versus T. The Wilcoxon matched-pair signed-rank test was used to assess significance of differences in occurrence. As before, reliance was placed only on results found to be significant for both groups of children. Definitions of the categories used are available in Appendix B.

Results

The results are presented for choice of companions in Table 6.7, for choice of activities in Table 6.8, and for occurrence of behaviour units (shorter list of 27 units) in Table 6.9. The pattern of results will be considered first in relation to the effects of condition A compared with C and T, and second in relation to the effects of condition T compared with C and A.

Apparatus only condition

For some categories the number of occurrences was less in condition A than in either C or T, without any significant difference between C or T. This is true for use of the *sandpit, easel, books, musical instruments*, and for *object exchange*. These are obvious findings, as these activities (and small objects for exchange) were absent in condition A. Similarly, there was less *table play*, and less *fine manipulation* of objects in condition A compared with C.

Other categories were more frequent in condition A than in C. These were *group play, talking between children, physical contact between children*, use of the *Wendy house*, the *toy chest*, and *unusual uses of apparatus*, and also *pushing/pulling* and *gross manipulation* of objects.

Finally, some categories showed a consistent trend in frequency of occurrence from condition A through C to T, although only the difference between the A and T is significant. In condition A there tended to be more occurrences of *open smile, walk, run,* and *kick/throw/hit,* and fewer occurrences of *large adult subgroup.*

This bald statement of significant findings reflects, but does not do full justice to, the impact this condition obviously had on the children. At first, we felt some trepidation at putting out bare tables and empty Wendy houses, leaving all the small toys in the store-room. The children seemed surprised on arrival, and the staff explained that only the large apparatus was out for that morning. From a slow start, activities then gained momentum over the next twenty minutes or so. As the findings indicate, the sessions became very active and sociable, with every indication that most of the children were fully enjoying themselves. One or two children seemed to need some extra staff reassurance, but as the data indicate, this was certainly not a general trend.

All of the items of apparatus available were put to use. However, the climbing-frame, rocking-boat, tricycle, and pram were not used significantly more than in the control condition. The main increases in activity were in the use of the Wendy house and the toy chest. Most noticeable is a very startling increase in *unusual uses of apparatus*; this was scored for something like one-third of all samples (Table 6.8). Most of these uses had seldom or never been observed previously. Some examples recorded were:

lying on the toy chests put on their side, as houses or hiding places;
using upside-down toy chests, with tables, as dancing platforms;
sitting on upside-down tricycles, in a toy chest, or on the ground;
sitting on an upside-down rocking-boat and spinning it round;
walking along the tops of a line of chairs;
sitting on a line of chairs, as a pretend train;
putting chairs in lines in Wendy house as a pretend theatre, and dancing in front of it;
sitting on chairs on tops of tables, as a pretend bus;
putting tables and chairs next to climbing-frame for a pretend picnic;
lying on tables put end to end, and sliding along;
sitting in prams, propelling them under the climbing-frame;
walking prams along tops of tables put end to end.

Some of these activities in particular involved the use of familiar objects (e.g. chairs, tables) in unexpected ways and combinations, so as to further the aims of imaginative social play. The situation was probably more like that of an adventure playground than the usual outdoor play areas where equipment is often large and immovable. An advantage of movable items over fixed structures is that they have greater potential for promoting new uses and experiences, and children can make use of them in a way and at a level appropriate to their stage of development. The results from this condition suggest that small wooden chairs, tables, and toy chests can be used in various such ways when freed from their normal function.

Many of these activities involved fantasy or sociodramatic play. The incidence of fantasy play was in fact highest in condition A, although non-significantly so. What clearly was significant, however, was the increase in social behaviour probably consequent on these activities. The frequency of group play noticeably increased, as did verbal and physical contacts between children. This is particularly striking because this was the only environmental manipulation in the entire project to have this result. Several children who usually played alone or in parallel groups seemed to be drawn into cooperative play in the noisy and exciting activities which started up. Many of the activities clearly involved moving apparatus around (hence the increases in pushing, pulling, and gross manipulation), and these would indeed have been easier with several children cooperating.

There was no increase in children being unoccupied in condition A, and no significant increase in measures of agonistic or stress behaviours. On the whole, the removal of the small toys seems to have prompted the children into unusual and exciting uses of the remaining apparatus, which in turn increased the level of motor activity and the amount of social contact and group play.

Toys only condition

For some categories the number of occurrences was smaller in condition T than in C or A. This is true for the *rocking-boat*, *climbing-frame*, and *tricycle*, and for *climbing/sliding* and *pedalling/propelling*. These are obvious findings, as these activity choices were absent in condition T. It is also not surprising that there was less *pushing/pulling*, and general *gross manipulation* of objects. An unexpected result was the lesser occurrence of *automanipulation* in condition T, compared with either A or C.

Both *table play* and *fine manipulation* of objects were more frequent in condition T than in C or A. Finally, some categories showed a consistent trend in frequency of occurrence from condition T through C to A, although only the difference between conditions T and A is significant. In condition T there were more occurrences of *large adult subgroup*, and fewer occurrences of *open smile*, *walk*, *run*, and *kick/throw/hit*.

The impact of this condition, while appreciable, was not nearly so startling as that of the apparatus only conditions. Many of the small items, such as the books, telephone, musical instruments, and easel, tended to show an increase in usage, but these trends were non-significant. The only significant increase was in the use of table toys, approximately double that of condition C. Often a member of the playgroup staff was at a table, and this probably explains the increase in large adult subgroups. Verbal, visual, and physical contacts with adults did not increase.

The shift in activities resulted in a significant increase in fine manipulation of objects, and a trend towards an increase in object exchange. There was also a decrease in automanipulation. These two findings are probably related; object manipulation directly interferes with automanipulative and stereotypic behaviours such as eye-rubbing, nose-picking, hair-brushing, and clothes-fumbling. Other studies have found a similar inverse relationship between object manipulation and self manipulation (Hollis, 1965; Berkson, 1967).

There was no appreciable or significant difference in the social activity of the children, although there was some trend towards less group play and fewer contacts between children. On the whole, table play is probably more conducive to parallel than group activity. Although there was less general motor activity, levels of rough-and-tumble play were if anything higher. Probably a few children, who typically played more with apparatus when it was available, switched to chasing games rather than quieter play at the tables, sandpit, easel, or book corner.

Occurrences of no activity did not increase in condition T, and there were no significant increases in measures of agonistic or stress behaviours. Overall, the removal of the large apparatus seems to have prompted most children into more activities involving fine object manipulation, for example with the plastic links, beakers, beads, and crayons on the tables. A few children probably increased their levels of chasing and rough-and-tumble play, although overall the level of gross motor activity fell. There was little impact on levels of social contacts, though if anything they declined, with an increase in large groups clustered around an adult at table activities.

Discussion and summary

The extent to which the results may be generalised is limited by the small number of observational sessions. It must also be borne in mind that conditions A and T were both novel, unlike condition C. Any effects of environmental novelty, however, were probably outweighed by the direct effects of the environments themselves. Most categories showed linear trends in occurrence from condition A through C to T. Very few showed a similar difference between conditions A and T, and condition C, which would be expected if environmental novelty were a primary factor. It still remains true of course that the effects found might change if conditions A or T were repeated over more or longer sessions.

Removal of the small toys produced what appeared to be a challenging environment to the children, with quite dramatic effects. The children were more sociable, more physically active, and – by adult standards at least – more creative in terms of unusual uses of the items of apparatus available to them. The increases in group play and social contacts cannot be ascribed to any change in the amount of equipment available (Chapter 3), but rather seemed to be due to the socially facilitating nature of the activities engaged in. Children who might usually have played alone or in parallel, for example at a sandpit or with table toys or a jigsaw, engaged more in social interaction with other children in physically active and unusual play activities with chairs, tables, toy chests, Wendy houses, rocking-boats, prams, and tricycles. Use of the toy chests and Wendy houses noticeably increased. Both groups of children reacted in a very similar way in all these respects.

Thus the removal of the small toys and the consequent reduction in the children's freedom of choice seem to have had what would generally be considered beneficial effects. The children were stimulated to greater versatility in using the remaining potential in the environmental resources. In this respect it is probably relevant that the study was done at the end of the first year, when the children were well acquainted with each other and the playgroup setting.

The removal of the large apparatus, leaving only small toys, showed some analogous effects, but much less dramatically. There was a switch from gross motor activities to fine object manipulation, particularly with the small table toys. The increase in fine object manipulation cannot plausibly be ascribed to the difference in the quantity of small toys available (Chapter 5) but rather to the absence of items promoting alternative activities. Thus many children who would normally have engaged in much gross motor activity were encouraged to participate in activities centred upon object manipulation, often at a table with an adult. Probably as a consequence, automanipulative behaviours were less frequent. There were non-significant trends for less group play and fewer social contacts with other children. A few children probably switched to rough-and-tumble play and chasing, rather than to more sedentary object manipulation activities.

7 Preschool behaviour and the physical environment: comparison of the separate studies with each other and with previous research

This chapter compares the results of the investigations reported in Chapters 4, 5, and 6, in order to separate out the effects of number of children (N), spatial and play equipment densities (D_s and D_p), and amounts of space and play equipment (R_s and R_p). These integrated findings are then considered alongside previous studies.

In general, the results found in the studies we carried out were reasonably consistent for the two groups observed, and for the majority of the individual children, age or sex interactions being of little or no importance. This gives us some confidence in generalising the results to similar groups in similar conditions. Some provisos must nevertheless be made about the extent to which the results can be generalised to other playgroups or preschool institutions, possibly functioning in quite different circumstances. First, the children in our groups were from varied socio-economic backgrounds; they could not be described as suffering from physical or social deprivation. Some of our findings (for example, on aggression or imaginative play) might well not apply to children from areas of multiple deprivation.

Second, the particular conditions of the project – the number of staff, the usual free-play setting, the kinds of equipment provided – may limit generalisability to playgroups run in a quite different fashion. Our exploration of certain of these variables clearly goes only a little way in investigating the range of possible variations on these conditions.

Third, the results for the closely controlled and quantified variables – size of group, amount of space, amount of equipment – clearly hold only over the range of variations studied. The study reported in Chapter 6, in which a spatial density condition outside the range of the previous study was observed and more wide-ranging effects were obtained, illustrates the danger of extrapolating results beyond the established range of validity.

Finally, a most important reservation is that children's experiences of the conditions were essentially short-term. Although cumulative effects or time interactions were not generally observed during the investigation, it is possible that long-term effects might be more significant than, or possible different from, those reported. This reservation would clearly apply more to nursery school classes, or reception classes in first schools, where children attend for many hours a week, than to most playgroups, such as our own, which children attend for a smaller proportion of their time.

Effects of spatial density and amount of space

Results found both in the *NR* studies of Chapter 4 and in the *DR* studies of Chapter 5 can be attributed to the common resource (*R*) parameter. Results found in the *DR* studies but absent in the *NR* studies can be attributed to the density (*D*) parameter.

By this criterion, many of the results from the spatial study of Chapter 5, in which both D_s and R_s were varied, can be attributed to D_s, or spatial density. In particular, when there is less space per child there is less free motor activity – less running, chasing, and rough-and-tumble play. Active play of this kind decreases slightly from 75 to 50 sq. ft per child, and much more appreciably at 25 sq. ft per child. By 15 sq. ft per child, chasing play is virtually absent, and even the frequency of occurrence of walking is reduced. At 25 and 15 sq. ft per child there are also fewer occurrences of unusual uses of apparatus, such as spinning upside-down rocking-boats, or turning toy chests over, both of which require some free space. There is less pushing and pulling of large objects.

Again, when there is less space per child, children make more physical contacts with each other, with adults, and also with immovable apparatus such as tables and climbing-frames. On the whole, the evidence is that these are incidental rather than purposeful contacts – the increase is in children in bodily contact on a piece of apparatus, or standing by a table, for example, rather than in some deliberate action such as holding hands.

The study of the 15 sq. ft per child condition suggested certain behavioural effects which became apparent only in these very crowded circumstances, a threshold effect of spatial parameters. As these effects occurred at levels of both group size and amount of space, the threshold effect is presumably one of spatial density. The threshold effects appear to be first, a decrease in group play and mean subgroup size of cooperative groups, with an increase in large parallel groups and in watching other children; and second, a probable increase in aggressive behaviour. Certain changes in activity choice – an increase in use of the Wendy house and sandpits, decrease in the use of books and perhaps of fantasy play – were also found. Staff found this degree of crowding uncomfortable, and less pleasant than the other conditions.

A few results can be attributed to the amount of space, R_s, largely irrespective of the number of children present. In particular, less space implied more use of the climbing-frame and slide. It also seems to be the main parameter affecting gross object manipulation, although amount of equipment may also have some effect on this. Finally, in a larger space children were more often observed looking around the room or into the distance.

Overall, the effects of spatial parameters are not very marked. Provided spatial density is not more crowded than 25 sq. ft per child, and a space of at least 600 sq. ft is available, further increases of the amount of space for a given group of children will not have very marked effects. There is no reason to expect any impact on social or aggressive behaviour. The main impact of increasing space will be to allow more opportunity for free motor activity, which leads to running and chasing games. If space cannot be increased, then the reduced opportunity for free motor activity can partially be compensated for by providing suitable climbing equipment.

The present recommendation of a minimum of 25 sq. ft per child for playgroups seems realistic. In more crowded conditions it was impossible to make a full range of equipment (including climbing-frames) available. There is evidence of effects on the children which would generally be considered detrimental – a lower level of social participation, and a tendency for more aggressive behaviour.

Effects of equipment density and amount of play equipment

By the same criteria applied in the previous section, many of the results of the play equipment study of Chapter 5, in which both D_p and R_p were varied, can be attributed to equipment density, D_p.

When there is more play equipment per child, more children play alone, fewer in parallel groups. There are fewer physical and visual contacts with other children. There is a switch to more popular items, such as tricycles, Wendy house, pram and dolls, and sandpits, at the expense of less popular items such as easel, blocks, book corner, or room fitments. There also tends to be less running and chasing, or free motor activity. This last effect is not so marked as the one induced by spatial variations of equivalent magnitude; however, neither is it so small as to make it likely to be due only to the reduction in space physically occupied by the equipment.

More play equipment per child also means more picking up, putting down, and carrying of objects, though not much change in fine object manipulation. There is less aggressive behaviour, and fewer signs of stress such as crying or thumb-sucking. Conversely, less play equipment per child would have the opposite effects.

A few results can be attributed to the amount of play equipment, R_p, largely irrespective of the number of children present. The most significant of these is the mean subgroup size of children in cooperative group play. The studies reported in Chapters 4 and 5 both affected this variable. It was suggested that an increase in the number of children implied a smaller mean subgroup size, owing to the degree of mutual acquaintance between children. It was also suggested that a decrease in the amount of play equipment per child meant a larger mean subgroup size, owing to more sharing of items of equipment in group play. The combined effect of these two factors is such that the amount of equipment is likely to be the actual covariant with mean subgroup size. For a given amount of equipment, an increase in the number of children will tend both to decrease mean subgroup size (effect of N) and to increase mean subgroup size (effect of D_p). These two effects may well cancel each other out, though to be sure of this a third type of study, an ND study, varying number of children with constant resources, would have to be carried out.

So although amount of play equipment seems unlikely to affect mean subgroup size in a direct, or causal sense, it may in practice be the variable of importance. If larger subgroups of children were wanted – children playing more in groups of three, four, or five, rather than in pairs – then the amount of play equipment would have to be decreased. It would not matter whether the number of children remained constant or not (at least, within a range of ten to thirty children).

The results also suggest that amount of play equipment affects the amount of use made of the tricycle; the tricycle was so popular that it was mainly the absolute number of tricycles, rather than the number per child, which affected its usage. An increased amount of play equipment also meant more gross object manipulation, and less watching of other children. More equipment has some effect on reducing aggressive behaviour, although play equipment density seems to be the more important parameter here. Finally, there are fewer records of children not engaging in any activity.

Effects of number of children

Results obtained from the NR studies of Chapter 4, but not from the DR studies of Chapter 5, can be attributed to the parameter N, or number of children present in the group.

There are two main effects of the number of children, which are largely independent of density and resource factors. First, larger numbers of children tend to bring about more same-sex interactions. Second, there is less fantasy or imaginative play. These findings are more accurately put in the converse form. While observable when comparing groups of thirty to twenty or fifteen children, it is when one has small groups of about ten children, with a close-knit sociometric structure, that an increase in cross-sex friendships and in fantasy or sociodramatic play becomes noticeable and important. These might well be considered positive advantages of small groups. This assumes of course that the groups are constant in composition, not changing subdivisions of a larger group, for example.

The results also suggest that with larger numbers of children there will be more table play. There is less play at sandpits, and a decrease in exchange of objects. Conversely, when numbers are small, especially falling to about ten children, there is less rough-and-tumble and chasing play.

Effects of kinds of play equipment

Changes in the kind of equipment provided may produce changes which other kinds of manipulation of the physical environment are unlikely to achieve. The evidence here must be qualified by the short duration of the investigation, but a greater ratio of large apparatus to smaller manipulative toys is likely to increase gross motor activity, to increase the amount and level of cooperative group play between children, and to encourage unusual and inventive uses of the apparatus available (especially if chairs and tables can be used for play purposes). Conversely, a greater ratio of smaller manipulative toys to large apparatus will encourage more fine object manipulation and table play. In addition, probably because of increased object manipulation, there will be fewer automanipulative behaviours (such as ear-tugging, clothes-fumbling, nose-picking, hair-grooming) observed in the children. It seems likely that temporary reductions in the variety of equipment available (e.g. by removing small toys or large apparatus) may encourage certain children to participate in play activities they would normally not indulge in, and hence 'stretch' their behaviours possibly in a creative fashion. There may also be more rough-and-tumble play, and possibly signs of stress in some children, when reductions in variety of play equipment are introduced; this would suggest the need for increased vigilance and, if necessary, reassurance by staff in such conditions.

Comparison with previous research

In Chapter 3 the relevant previous research on the effects of density and crowding on young children was briefly reviewed. The experimental studies at preschool institutions were summarised in Table 3.1, which indicates that the previous research falls into three types. These studies are now considered in more detail in relation to our own experimental findings.

Studies varying N, D_p, and D_s

The study by Hutt and Vaizey was unusual in that some of the subjects were either classified as brain-damaged, or as autistic, the research being carried out in a hospital playroom. These children were observed in a larger group, the size of which varied. The observations reported were on time spent in aggressive/destructive behaviour (throwing, banging, breaking, or kicking toys, hitting, pushing, pinching, or kicking an adult or a child), social interaction (approach, contact, or converse with adult or child; cuddled by adult), and at the boundary of the room (within 3 ft of the periphery). These definitions are given in Hutt and Hutt (1970).

The results indicate that as group size increased, the normal children (i.e. those who were only in-patients or day-patients at the hospital) spent more time in aggressive behaviours, and less time in social interaction. Time at the boundary did not change significantly.

The hospital playroom situation was clearly very different from that which we investigated. Not only were the groups heterogeneous, but the variations in group size may well have meant the introduction of quite unfamiliar children to those under observation. In so far as comparison is made with our own findings, the increase in aggressive behaviour might well be due, in part at least, to the reduced amount of play equipment per child when more children were present. Our results would also lead us to expect fewer physical contacts with other children in such circumstances (Table 5.6). As physical contacts count as social interaction by the Hutts' definition, the decrease in social interaction could also be due to the amount of play equipment per child. Thus despite the difference in circumstances, the results of the Hutt and Vaizey study are what we would predict on the basis of our own results, but we would attribute them to D_p rather than to N. This leads to the predictions that aggressive/destructive behaviour would not increase if play equipment was increased proportionately to the size of group; and that the decrease in social interactions was limited to physical contacts, and would not hold for verbal interactions or group play.

The study by Bates (1970) was made in a private nursery school for 2-and 3-year-old children in Oregon, a context much more closely comparable to our own. Natural variations due to absences were used to examine effects of varying N, and therefore D_p and D_s.

Both boys and girls increased the percentage of interactions which were of a conflict nature when density was increased. As with the Hutt and Vaizey results, this is consistent with our own findings if ascribed to D_p rather than to N.

Bates's other results differed for boys and girls. For one variable, opposite results were obtained for the two sexes. Boys were reported to play in larger groups, girls in smaller groups, as density increased.

From our own findings we would expect subgroup size in group play to decrease with N, but increase with D_p, the two effects probably approximately cancelling one another out (see earlier discussion, p. 186). We did not find significant sex interactions here. Table 4.12 indicates an overall decrease with N (averaged over the separate experiments) of -4.1 per cent for boys and -9.1 per cent for girls. A similar calculation for the percentage change in mean subgroup size from three-toy to one-toy conditions gave figures of $+14.5$ per cent for boys and $+10.4$ per cent for girls. Although not differing significantly, the trends shown here are congruent with Bates's findings. However, Bates's study was on only one group of children, so it is also possible that his findings are peculiar to the children in that group.

Bates's other findings are specific to either boys or girls; in the absence of a fuller report, it is not clear whether or not the other sex showed a corresponding but non-significant tendency. Boys were reported to show less locomotion in the more crowded conditions. We would expect this to be due to the reduced amount of both space and play equipment per child (D_s and D_p), but to hold true for girls as well. Girls were reported to spend more time alone, with members of the same sex, and in the least-used area of the room. The finding concerning times spent alone is contrary to our results; we would expect less time to be spent alone by both sexes, owing to less play equipment per child. The finding concerning more same-sex companions agrees with our results, and is one we would attribute to number of children, as Bates does. We would also expect more time to be spent with less popular items, or room fitments, when there was less play equipment per child, and this may correspond to Bates's finding concerning the least-used, therefore presumably least popular, area of the room.

The study by the McGrews (McGrew, P. L., 1970; McGrew, W. C., 1972) was carried out in a nursery class in Edinburgh, with 3- and 4-year-old children. P. L. McGrew recorded four proximity measures at frequent intervals. W. C. McGrew recorded twelve different behaviours by event sampling. This may have been difficult to do accurately, but no measures of observer reliability are reported. The number of children was varied by sending half the children outside for certain sessions; the children remaining indoors had either the same or reduced space, but the same amount of play equipment as previously. The only results found significant for both space conditions were a decrease in negative expletives with more children, a decrease in solitary position, and an increase in proximity to adults.

Our results (and those of Hutt and Vaizey, and Bates) would predict more aggressive or conflict behaviour with more children, which we would attribute to D_p. McGrew found the opposite effect with negative expletives, which must, however, be weighed against inconsistent or non-significant findings for other behaviours such as object struggle, hit, push, and destructive. We would regard McGrew's findings as inconclusive, given that only one nursery group was observed and that the reliability of sampling may be in question. Event sampling might well be biased to give apparently more incidents in a small group than in a large one, because of easier scanning of the children. This could be a plausible alternative explanation of McGrew's failure to record an increase in the number of aggressive behaviours per child when more children were present.

With more children McGrew found a decrease in solitary position; this is consistent with our own findings, and we would attribute it to D_p, the amount of play equipment per child being less. The increase in proximity to adults is not expected on the basis of our results.

In summary, of the three previous studies which varied N, D_p, and D_s together, most of the results are comparable to our own, and most we would ascribe to the amount of play equipment per child (D_p), in particular, the changes in aggressive behaviour reported by Hutt and Vaizey (1966), and Bates (1970). A few results are in disagreement, or suggest sex-specific effects we did not find.

Studies varying D_s and R_s

Of the five studies in this category, three – those of McGrew (1972), Gilligan (1970), and Preiser (1972) – examined a range of spatial densities less crowded than 25 sq. ft per child; two, those of Price (1971) and Loo (1972), examined a range which extended to more crowded conditions than 25 sq. ft per child. This distinction is important, given the evidence we obtained for threshold effects. The studies by Price and Loo are also the most substantial, in terms of range of behaviours and number of groups observed.

The study by the McGrews (1970, 1972) was carried out as another aspect of their study on group size discussed in the previous section. The effects of reducing available space by a factor of 4 : 5 were examined for both small and large groups of children. The only results found to be significant for both group size conditions were a decrease in running when less space was available, and an increase in peer proximity. The decrease in running is in accord with our own findings, which we attribute to D_s. We did not measure peer proximity, but did find an increase in physical contacts between children (also a consistent trend from McGrew, P. L., 1970). The absence of effects on aggressive behaviours, crying, sucking, or auto-manipulation, is in agreement with our own findings, within the range of spatial densities the McGrews investigated.

Gilligan's study was on 4- and 5-year-old children. Three separate groups experienced outdoor playgrounds of three different sizes. Each group was observed daily for 15 days, for periods of 45 minutes, and the whole group was rated for social participation and leadership on Parten's (1932, 1933) scales. There were no significant effects of playground size. Gilligan's recording methods differ greatly from our own, but her not finding any effect of D_s or R_s on social participation is in agreement with our own results as we would extrapolate them to more spacious conditions.

Preiser studied one group of 3- and 4-year-old children in a nursery school. Either 67 or 100 per cent of the floor space was available to the 15 children. Some change in usage of different areas was reported. The account of the findings is very brief, but does suggest a lack of appreciable changes – or changes consistent for all the children – for social contacts and aggressive behaviour. This would be consistent with our own findings for the range of spatial density which Preiser investigated.

In summary, the findings of these three studies are in agreement with our own, that is, that changes in social and aggressive behaviour are not observed with variations of D_s above 25 sq. ft per child. McGrew's finding of reduced running as space per child gets less is supported by our own results.

The studies by Price (1971) and Loo (1972) require more detailed consideration. Price (1971) observed 22 groups of preschool and first-grade children, aged from 3 years 6 months to 6 years 8 months, in New York City. They were observed in free play in their classrooms, either in crowded or non-crowded conditions, each for two days. The non-crowded condition was the ordinary classroom. In the crowded condition part of the class was blocked off by furniture; an attempt was made to keep the materials the same by moving them into the smaller area. Actual spatial densities varied in the different groups. The range for non-crowded conditions was 47.3–9.2 sq. ft per child, mean 26.2 sq. ft per child; for the crowded conditions it was 13.1–4.6 sq. ft per child, mean 9.1 sq. ft per child. The amount of space in the non-crowded conditions from 1,804 to 298 sq. ft, mean 677 sq. ft, and in the crowded conditions from 496 to 102 sq. ft, mean 220 sq. ft. Observers took 10-second observations of each child, scoring 33 behaviour categories on an all-or-none basis.

This study is one of the $D_s R_s$ type, in which the range of variation crosses the threshold of 25 sq. ft per child we found in our own work. The observation of 22 separate groups is a very strong point of the study. Unfortunately, the two sessions of crowded conditions were clearly novel to the children. Thus novelty is confounded with spatial factors (probably more than in our own study reported in Chapter 6, since our children were used to spatial variations). It should also be noted that variation in D_p was not entirely avoided, because only an *attempt* was made to keep the same materials in the much smaller space. Finally, some of the observers combined aggression with rough-and-tumble play, although others apparently did not.

Price's most substantial result was reduced locomotor activity in the crowded conditions. There were noticeably fewer occurrences of running, walking, and crawling. This is in agreement with our own findings, and we attribute it to D_s. Price also found that the crowded conditions produced more solitary play (from 26 to 30 per cent, in 19 out of 22 classes) and less social play (from 29 to 26.5 per cent, in 16 out of 22 classes), with less frequent talking between children. The reduction in social play and talking agrees with our own results. Unlike Price, we found a corresponding increase in parallel play, rather than playing alone. This might reflect the older average age of her sample (mean age 4 years 9 months), since parallel play tends to be a feature specific to preschool children.

Finally, Price reported more automanipulation in the crowded conditions. This we did not find in our study, but if more children or more groups were examined it might emerge. An alternative possibility is that the increase in automanipulation in Price's study was due more to the novelty of the crowded condition than to the spatial crowding itself (cf. McGrew, 1972; Smith, 1974c).

Price reported no significant effect of the spatial variations on the occurrence of aggressive behaviour. It did, however, rise by 15 per cent in the crowded conditions, 13 out of her 22 classes showing an increase. Inter-observer agreement was low for this category, and some observers included rough-and-tumble play. The latter behaviour we found to be less frequent in very crowded conditions (e.g. Table 6.4). It may well be that if occurrences of rough-and-tumble play were removed from the records of aggressive behaviour in Price's study, then the slight trend for an increase in aggression with severe crowding would become significant. Her findings do not contradict our own, which suggest such an increase.

Price did not find significant interactions of sex with spatial density in her study. This agrees with our findings, but contradicts somewhat the findings reported by Loo (1972).

Loo observed 10 groups, each comprising three boys and three girls, aged 4 and 5 years. The children met in a room which provided either 265.1 sq. ft, or, by means of a portable wooden wall, only 90 sq. ft, and spatial densities were either 44.2 or 15 sq. ft per child. The same toys were present in each condition. Each group met for one session of free play, lasting 48 minutes, in each condition (order effects being counterbalanced). Ratings of behaviour for each child were provided, by six observers. Ratings were for aggressive behaviour, dominance, interruptions, nurturant behaviour, resistance, submission, number of children interacted with, solitary play, onlooker, and group involvement. Although inter-rater agreement was satisfactory, it is not entirely clear how ratings were carried out, and it would have been preferable to have used a specified sampling procedure, especially as six observers were available.

Like Price, Loo was able to carry out tests of significance using group totals rather than individual totals as statistics. This is a strong point of the study. It must be noted, however, that the children were not in natural groups (they were collected from school), and as only one session was given in each condition, their behaviour would be that appropriate to a novel environment with children they did not know very well. This limits generalisability to usual preschool settings. Loo found no significant main effect of density, or trends, for nurturant behaviour, resistance, submission, or onlooker. Her significant findings were that both boys and girls interacted with fewer children in the crowded conditions, that boys showed less aggressive behaviour, and that girls showed more dominance. There were non-significant trends for both boys and girls to show less group activity and more solitary activity, and for more interruptions.

Our own results (reported in Chapter 6) in very crowded spatial conditions, designed to be similar to Loo's, suggested smaller subgroup sizes of cooperative groups, which would be consistent with Loo's findings of fewer children interacting with each other. Our results are also consistent with her finding of a trend for less group play in the crowded conditions. We found an increase in parallel play rather than playing alone. Since Loo did not have a category of parallel play, such instances might have been included in solitary activity. At any rate, it is not certain whether our results agree or disagree with hers on this point.

We do not have any data to compare with Loo's results concerning frequency of interruptions.

Loo's finding of less aggressive behaviour in boys in the crowded conditions seems surprising, and certainly conflicts with our own results. However, in Loo's study, too, rough-and-tumble play was included in aggressive behaviour (Loo, personal communication). Loo found a very large sex difference in aggressive behaviour, and it is quite possible that some of this is due to the inclusion of rough-and-tumble play with aggressive behaviour. Rough-and-tumble play could be expected to be almost absent when spatial density reached 15 sq. ft per child (see Table 6.4), and this would spuriously appear as a decrease in aggressive behaviour, especially for the boys. It is worth noting that Loo found an increase in dominance behaviour in girls in the crowded conditions. It is therefore appropriate to question the validity of Loo's finding concerning decreased aggression in boys, and attribute this rather to a decrease in rough-and-tumble play. If this is done, her results do not argue against an increase in aggressive or dominative behaviour in very crowded conditions.

It is noteworthy that the three studies by McGrew, Gilligan, and Preiser found no effects of space on social or aggressive behaviour, while those of Price and Loo did. This supports our finding that there is a threshold around 25 sq. ft per child, such that in more crowded conditions effects on social and aggressive behaviour begin to appear.

The precise nature of these effects must await clarification, as all three studies – our own in Chapter 6, and those of Price and Loo – have defects, notably in the short number of sessions and hence the novelty of the conditions. However, all three studies tend to agree in finding less social or group play, and a corresponding increase in either parallel or solitary play. The effects on aggressive behaviour remain uncertain. Both Price and Loo confused aggression and rough-and-tumble play, but examined many more groups than we did. Nevertheless we have argued that on balance the evidence suggests an increase in aggressive behaviour in very spatially crowded conditions.

Studies varying D_p and R_p

Only the research by Johnson (1935) varied the amount of play equipment experimentally with children of about the age group we are considering.

Johnson reports the results of studies at three elementary schools in

Michigan. The first study was of a group of 16 boys and 15 girls, aged 3, 4, and 5 years. Behaviour in the school playground was observed for three days before and three days after the removal of most of the items of equipment, leaving only slides, swings, climbing apparatus, jungle gym, and sandpit.

The second study was of a group of 24 boys and 22 girls, and the third study of a group of 15 boys and 14 girls, all aged about 5 years. Each group was observed in its school playground for four days before and four days after the addition of a number of items of equipment to the few already present.

In Johnson's research the new conditions were novel to the children. However, in the first study the reduced equipment was novel, whereas in the second and third studies the additional equipment was novel. Effects of amount of equipment should therefore be distinguishable from effects of environmental novelty.

A more severe drawback to Johnson's design is that *variety* of equipment is confounded with *amount*. In all three studies a greater amount also meant a greatly increased variety. Our own results indicate that variety of equipment has very pronounced effects on children's behaviour, certainly in the short term.

Johnson obtained two results which were consistent across both the addition and reduction of equipment. Adding equipment reduced what she called undesirable behaviour – teasing, crying, quarrelling, and hitting – and reducing equipment increased it. This is consistent with our own findings for aggressive behaviour, and we would attribute it to the amount of play equipment per child, D_p. We did not find that variety of play equipment affected aggressive behaviour significantly.

Adding equipment led to fewer games being played, reducing it led to more. Johnson does not specify what kinds of games were observed, but if they were chasing games such as tag – generally one of the commonest games in primary school playgrounds – this is similar to our own findings for chasing and group running, attributable again to the amount of play equipment per child.

Johnson's other findings seem inconsistent when the effects of adding or reducing equipment are compared. In her first study she found that reducing equipment led to more social contacts, more play with materials (especially at the sandpit), and less vigorous bodily activity (especially climbing and jungle gym). In her second and third studies she found that increasing equipment also led to more play with materials, and less bodily activity, whether vigorous or not. No data on social contacts were reported for the latter studies.

Our own results would lead us to expect more visual and physical contacts with reduced play equipment per child, perhaps corresponding to Johnson's result in her first study. Her other findings regarding play with materials, and bodily exercise, are clearly contradictory as far as the effects of amount of play equipment are concerned. More probably, they reflect changes in the children's behaviour consequent on changes in the variety of equipment present – for example, much more play with the sandpit when that is the only remaining item available for play with materials.

We know of no other studies with which to compare our findings on effects of general variety of play equipment on behaviour. As Johnson remarked at the end of her report, 'Children are very resourceful in all situations, on meagerly as well as on generously equipped playgrounds.' This accords with the general conclusion we arrived at in the work discussed in Chapter 6.

Summary

Previous research on the effects of crowding on children presents a series of apparently discrepant findings (Table 3.1), which, however, make more sense when the different crowding parameters are considered separately. Taking this and other factors into account, a fairly consistent pattern emerges, most of which is in close agreement with our own findings.

In *ND* studies, where the number of children is varied, resources being constant, aggressive behaviour increases with crowding owing to competition over equipment. Increases in social behaviour with crowding are probably limited to visual and physical contacts.

In *DR* studies, where resources are varied for a fixed number of children, once again less play equipment per child leads to more aggression, as well as to more running and chasing games. Less space per child reduces gross motor activity, but does not affect social or aggressive behaviour until spatial density reaches about 25 sq. ft per child. If conditions are made even more crowded, there is less group play between children, and some evidence for more aggressive behaviour.

Reducing the variety of play equipment, at least in the short term, may not have detrimental effects in established playgroups or playgrounds. Rather, it may stimulate children to more use, perhaps more varied use, of materials or apparatus which previously they paid little attention to. In some circumstances this may increase social contacts.

8 Studies of preschool curricula and staff:child ratio: a review

Studies of preschool curricula and the educational environment of the preschool span some forty or fifty years, even if much of the most relevant research has been carried out within the last twenty. A general review of the effects of preschool experience was made by Swift in 1964. This covered areas such as the effects of nursery attendance on intellectual, social, and physical development; studies of teacher behaviour and teacher–child relationships; and effects of different nursery programmes. A fuller review is provided by Sears and Dowley (1963), in Gage's *Handbook of Research on Teaching*. More recent reviews are available in the *Second Handbook of Research on Teaching*, edited by Travers (1973). Gordon and Jester (1973) discuss techniques of observing the teaching of young children and the outcomes of particular procedures; Beller (1973) has reviewed research on organised programmes of early education. Research on early childhood education in Britain has been reviewed by B. Tizard (1974), and that on the effects of preschool education by Smith and James (1975). A general review of school environments, including the preschool, has been made by Gump (1978).

General issues such as whether preschool experience has beneficial effects, how long-term any such effects are, and how nursery schools, day nurseries, day care, and childminding compare with home rearing conditions, are carefully considered in the above reviews and will not be discussed further here. This chapter will focus particularly on work comparing the effects of preschool curricula on the behaviour and development of children in a nursery or playgroup. In particular, research on staff:child ratio and teacher distribution of attention will be considered. The majority of these studies have been done in the USA; the exceptions will be specified.

The effects of different preschool curricula: correlational studies

Most of the studies examining different preschool curricula have been correlational; that is to say, several preschools, with different programmes, have been compared with regard to the behaviour of the children, or their

197

scores on standard assessment procedures. The difficulty with these sorts of data lies in untangling the effects of other variables which may interact or be confounded with the programme variables. These could include physical environment variables such as those considered earlier in this book, teacher:child ratio, the age and sex distribution, and background of the children involved. Nevertheless, replications can lend credence to certain inferences, while discrediting others.

The Montessori method has attracted considerable research attention. Although the philosophy of Dr Montessori underlies the programme in all Montessori schools, its interpretation in practice can take different forms. Banta (1966; cited in Beller, 1973) compared two different Montessori classrooms; in one, the teacher interpreted the Montessori method to imply that structure and controls are necessary before freedom can be permitted, while in the other the teacher felt that the child must learn to set his or her own limit or controls on choice of activities and behaviour. Thus the actual ethos of the two classes and the behaviour of the children differed considerably. As Beller (1973) comments, 'one needs to get a sample of Montessori classrooms if one wants to generalise concerning the effect of the Montessori method on the development of children' (p. 563). Usually, however, researchers have not had the resources to do this. Thus if only a few classes are studied, it is all the more important to specify actual details of the programme, and of the staff and children involved. Dreyer and Rigler (1969) compared both parental attitudes and child achievement in a Montessori programme and a traditional nursery school. The Montessori children appeared more task orientated, and in their drawings produced more abstract geometric forms and fewer human forms than did the traditional nursery school children. They scored less well on a non-verbal test of creative thinking. This study tends to emphasise the more structured and cognitively-orientated, less imaginative or spontaneous nature of a Montessori programme. This is also true of the research by Berk (1971). Berk compared a middle-class Montessori school, with a fairly structured regime, with a more unstructured or free-play-orientated university nursery school. In the former there were more 'environmental force units' (Schoggen, 1963), and in particular there was more impact of teacher expectations and more child compliance in the Montessori school. In the university nursery school children had fewer demands from or conflict with teachers, but met more difficulties in actually managing task materials (which tend to be carefully graded in a Montessori programme). They were, however, more persistent in the face of difficulties. Berk also compared both these middle-class preschools with two preschools taking lower-class children, and differing in physical area and teacher:child ratio. She found that the comparison of the structured and unstructured programmes of the Montessori and university nursery schools yielded more effects on the children's behaviour than did teacher:child ratio and social class comparisons.

Beller, Zimmie and Aiken (1971; cited in Beller, 1973) compared the levels of play shown by the children in two Montessori classrooms, two 'adult-centred' classrooms, and two 'child-centred' classrooms. They found less play generally in the Montessori classes, but especially less symbolic play. Complex symbolic play occurred least in the Montessori classes, and most in the 'child-centred' classes. Beller (1973) concludes that 'Montessori nursery programmes tend to facilitate discrimination learning, while child-centred programmes, with an emphasis on self-initiated and self-directed spontaneous activity on the part of the children, appeared to be most conducive to creativity and free symbolic expression in the play behaviour of children.' In these respects, the 'adult-centred' classes Beller studied seem to have been intermediate.

A rather different picture emerges from a study by Reuter and Yunik (1973). They compared a Montessori school, a university laboratory preschool on a token economy programme, and a parent cooperative preschool run on traditional lines. They found most child–child interaction in the Montessori school, least in the university preschool; an inverse relationship held for frequency of adult–child interactions. In this study, therefore, the Montessori environment was the closest to a child-centred or free-play environment. However, the teacher:child ratio was much worse in this Montessori school (1:12) than in the other two preschools (1:3.5), and this might explain the results.

Evidence of such an effect of different teacher:child ratios comes from a study by O'Connor (1975). Two preschools had similar, largely child-centred programmes, but one had a ratio of 1:3.5, the other 1:7. In the first school there was more social exchange between children and adults, in the second, more between children. This suggests that Reuter and Yunik's findings might be due to different teacher:child ratios rather than to different programmes. This suggestion is supported by a study by Murphy and Goldner (1976), who compared two classes in a Montessori school with two classes in a nursery school, each with a teacher:child ratio of 1:8. With teacher:child ratio constant, Murphy and Goldner found little difference in the amount of time children spent in social interaction with peers and adults in the classes, although the overall duration of social interactions was longer in the Montessori school.

It is clear that terms such as 'Montessori programme' and 'traditional programme' are vague, unless supplemented by further descriptions of how many teachers are available (per child), and what they do. A common distinction, based on observations of such programmes in practice, is to what extent the staff or teachers direct children to certain activities, or alternatively leave them to make their own choices. These are sometimes referred to as adult-centred and child-centred, or structured and unstructured programmes. Indeed a dimension of this kind emerged as the most important factor from a survey by Soar (1970; cited by Gordon and Jester, 1973), who observed teacher practices in classrooms, carrying out a factor analysis of the 62 items on the *Teacher Practices Observation Record*. Factor One was labelled 'Teacher-directed activity versus pupil-selected activity'. A similar dimension occurs in many of the preschool studies.

For example, Huston-Stein *et al.* (1977) compared five preschool centres (13 classes) for the 'degree to which the educational programme involved adult-directed activities'. Correlated with *less* structure, as thus defined, were more 'prosocial behaviour' to peers, more imaginative play, and (with only marginal significance) more 'prosocial aggression' and 'hostile aggression'. The children conformed less to teacher requests at 'circle' time and during 'clean-up' periods. No differences were found in task persistence.

Fagot (1973) carried out three replicate studies in middle-class nurseries and preschools. The main finding from all the studies was that the amount of task behaviour a class engaged in varied greatly, and that classes with high task behaviour had teachers who were less directive, and used praise rather than criticism of children's behaviour.

Prescott (1973) compared seven 'open structure' and seven 'closed structure' day care programmes. Structure was determined by 'the administrator's policies on teacher versus child initiation of activities'. Children in the open structure facilities scored higher on total 'thrusting behaviour', 'receiving help', and 'tactile/sensory exploring'; they scored less highly than the closed structure children on 'meets (teacher) expectations', 'receives frustration', 'rejection or pain', 'tentative behaviour', 'not attending to external stimuli', and 'ignores intrusion'. Direction of children's attention was naturally more to other children, and less to adults, in the open structure classes.

In all of these studies the nature of the programme may be confounded with other factors. One way to overcome this problem of interpretation in a single study is to examine within-nursery differences. Few studies of this kind have been made. Cooper (1976) related children's behaviour in nursery schools to the presence or absence of a teacher. When the teacher was absent there was more peer interaction, and talking to self. Zern and Taylor (1973) compared 'rhythmic behaviours' (generally, automanipulative or stereotypic activities with no clear goal) during free and structured activities in one middle-class nursery school; both oral and non-oral rhythmic behaviours were seen more in the latter.

In studies such as these, factors influenced by differences between preschools (such as age and background of children) do not confound the results. It is still possible, however, that teacher-present/absent sessions, or free/structured sessions, show some non-random or systematic variation with other uncontrolled factors (such as time of day, number of children present, etc.). Basically, such difficulties are best overcome by introducing more experimental control. Experimental work on preschool environments is more difficult to carry out, and fewer investigations have been made. As with any experimental work, the danger is that too much control of variables renders the situation being studied unnatural, and hence strictly limits the extent to which findings may be generalised to other real-life situations. Nevertheless, the clearer inference to the causal effects of particular variables means that experimental studies are at the very least an important and necessary complement to the more correlational studies just reviewed.

The effects of different preschool curricula: experimental studies

Perhaps not surprisingly, some of the experimental studies of preschool facilities have been within the perspective of behaviour analysis and modification. The Living Environments Group at Kansas (Risley, 1977) has carried out a number of studies on day care and nursery facilities, usually examining relatively discrete aspects of the preschool ecology.

For example, Lelaurin and Risley (1972) examined the effectiveness of 'Zone' and 'Man-to-Man' staffing procedures in a large day care centre. Previously, the staff had used the 'Man-to-Man' procedure, in which a teacher shepherded a particular group of children from one area to the next; thus after lunch the children were seen to the washroom, supervised taking off their shoes, and then taken to the bed area. For an experimental period this was changed to a 'Zone' procedure, with one teacher in each of these four areas, processing children through. Later a temporary return to 'Man-to-Man' was made for comparison. Using measures of how often children were engaged in task behaviour, as compared with being unoccupied or waiting for other children to finish, the 'Zone' procedure was found superior. Less time was wasted than in 'Man-to-Man', where a teacher had to delay movement from one area to the next until all the children were ready.

Doke and Risley (1972), working with 14 children in a preschool for poverty-level families, compared environments with required and with optional activities. The preschool had a number of activity areas. In the options schedule, several different activities were simultaneously available. In the required or no-options schedule, only one activity was open at any given time of the day (these usually changed every quarter hour). The authors measured the time spent by the children participating in planned activities. This was as high in the no-options as in the options schedule, but only if there was a sufficient abundance of materials for each activity, and if each child could start the next activity as soon as the preceding one was finished (not being forced to wait for other children). Doke and Risley suggested that, with one teacher supervising children finishing one activity, while the other supervised those starting the next, high participation could be achieved by having no options.

A more general measure of teacher involvement was considered by Shores *et al.* (1976) in a study of nine children with psychological or behavioural problems. Following an ABCAB design, the authors compared A (active teacher involvement), B (no teacher involvement), and C (teacher-structured free play, in which teachers prompted or initiated activities but subsequently kept a low profile). For these children, it was found that significantly more teacher–child interaction occurred in condition A, naturally enough, but that the more significant changes were in levels of child–child interaction. These were higher in B than A, but were higher still in C. This suggests that a lack of teacher involvement will be sub-optimal for such children (who had a variety of language problems as well as social behaviour disorders). Of course this finding cannot necessarily be generalised to non-handicapped children.

An experimental study comparing high and low teacher involvement in normal preschool children was made by Thompson in 1944. Working at the Iowa Child Welfare Research Station, Thompson assigned twenty-three 4-year-old children to two experimental conditions; one group, meeting from 1 to 3 o'clock each afternoon, experienced programme A, while a second group, meeting in the same building from 3 to 5 o'clock, experienced programme B. The same materials were available to both groups, but in programme A teacher involvement was low. Essentially, children were left free to choose their own activities. In programme B teacher involvement was higher, not to the extent of directing children to activities, but rather by establishing friendly relationships with the children and guiding them. It also seems as though the same materials were arranged more conspicuously, and grouped more prominently into activity centres in programme B.

After a few drop-outs and changes, there were 11 children in programme A and 8 in programme B. Pre-tests revealed no differences between the two groups. The two programmes lasted eight months, and observations during this period confirmed that in programme B the teachers were giving more information and help to the children, more structured suggestions, and asking more leading questions of them. There was no significant difference in teacher restrictive contacts, such as prohibitions or telling off.

No significant differences were seen in friendly social contacts between the children, but there were more restrictive (unfriendly) contacts in programme A. Since these process variables were not pre-tested, such effects might have been pre-existing and not attributable to the programme. After the eight-month period, post-tests were carried out. These showed that the programme B children, who had had the friendly and involved teacher contacts, were now more constructive when faced with possible failure, more ascendant, had higher social participation scores, and showed more leadership. There were no differences in nervous habits (automanipulation or stereotypic behaviour), and no difference on Stanford–Binet intelligence scores, between the two groups.

Sears and Dowley (1963) describe Thompson's study as 'unique in research on teaching in the nursery school'. Its well-controlled experimental design suggests fairly clear inferences as to the impact of the difference between the two programmes, and it has been an influential report. Its main limitation is clearly sample size, as 11 and 8 children provide rather small groups within which individual personalities may play a large role.

In this respect, it is a pity that the groups could not be equated on observational measures of social and aggressive behaviour as well as on the tests given before the programme commenced. It also seems as though programme A children, who clearly did less well in terms of the assessments made in the project, not only experienced less teacher involvement but also had less attractively or suggestively presented materials. Nevertheless the study is a very interesting one, and it provides by far the closest model to the project we carried out, comparing structured and free-play programmes (reported in Chapter 9).

Tightly controlled experimental studies such as those of Thompson (1944), and our own, even when they succeed in maintaining a naturalistic ecology, are often limited by small to moderate sample size by reason of the time, resources, and organisation needed for mounting a study of this kind. An alternative is to relax some of the experimental control, and some researchers have done this, thus gaining larger samples. Typically, children are still assigned randomly or semi-randomly to programme conditions, but the programmes are not so closely matched (e.g. for building, teachers, materials) as in a study such as Thompson's.

Karnes (1969; cited in Beller, 1973) evaluated the differential effects of different preschool intervention programmes, which varied in structure (intensity and specificity of teacher–child interaction). Two traditional nursery programmes represented the less structured end of the continuum, a Montessori programme was intermediate, and two highly structured intervention programmes (Ameliorative, and Direct Verbal) were also studied. Ninety-one children were assigned randomly (subject to matching IQ scores) to different programmes. At the end of the preschool period, no differences were found between groups on the Peabody Picture Vocabulary Test, but the more structured groups showed some superiority on, for example, Metropolitan Number Readiness. The Direct Verbal group children came out best on the Stanford–Binet intelligence scores and the Illinois Test of Psycholinguistic Abilities, but not significantly better than one of the traditional nursery groups. As Beller (1973) points out, however, such results might be due to differences in the training and supervision of teachers, and pupil:teacher ratios, since these factors were confounded with the specified programme conditions.

Perhaps the most thorough, fairly large-scale study of preschool programmes is that by Miller and Dyer (1975). Over two hundred children (black, working-class 4-year-olds) were assigned randomly to one of four preschool programmes. These consisted of two Montessori classes, four traditional enrichment classes (more emphasis on free play), four Bereiter–Engelmann classes (academic skills approach), and four Darcee classes (emphasis on language and attitudes). The different programmes were monitored by observation. These showed that Montessori and traditional programmes could be described as relatively child centred and slow paced, with children in the traditional classes showing more role play, those in the Montessori classes showing more conversation and manipulation of materials. The Bereiter–Engelmann and Darcee programmes could be described as relatively teacher directed and fast paced.

Results were obtained after eight weeks and after six months; they were varied, indicating different effects of different programmes. The children in structured programmes did better in cognitive and academic areas such as Stanford–Binet scores, while the children in traditional classes scored well on curiosity and verbal–social participation. The Montessori children did better on inventiveness and curiosity. Although this might suggest that the most important impact, at least cognitively, is made by the more didactic programmes, the most stable effect found four years later when the children were in Follow Through was in non-cognitive areas; the cognitive gains in the didactic programmes appeared to have been relatively transient.

Staff participation and teacher:child ratios

Correlational, semi-controlled, and controlled experimental studies of the effects of preschool curricula can clearly complement each other, and probably all three kinds of research programme are necessary. As our own research project was, in this context, small-scale but well controlled experimentally, we considered which aspects might most profitably be subject to experimental variation.

One obvious dimension to emerge from the previous work is that of active versus passive staff participation, or teacher-directed versus pupil-selected activity. This was more or less the dimension studied experimentally by Thompson (1944). As already pointed out, Thompson's sample size was very small, and there were other drawbacks. A project along similar lines, experimentally comparing a 'structured-activities' and a 'free-play' regime, seemed well worthwhile, and this was carried out in the second year of our research programme and is reported in Chapter 9.

Another important factor, especially for preschools in which staff take an active, participatory role, is that of staff:child ratio. Some evidence as to the effects of this emerged from the studies by Reuter and Yunik (1973) and O'Connor (1975), although only in the latter was this factor not confounded with the preschool programme. The results of both studies are consistent with the conclusion that a lower staff:child ratio means more child–child interaction and less staff–child interaction per child.

Such results are naturally to be expected. What is not clear, however, is the effect of different staff:child ratios on the overall level of staff interaction with children, and their distribution of attention. It could be that staff in part compensate for larger numbers of children by increasing their rate of interaction. Also, the distribution of contacts amongst children in a class has been found to be markedly unequal, and this inequality could be affected, perhaps worsened, with lower teacher:child ratios.

Studies of teacher–child contacts and their unequal distribution in classrooms

Some studies of teacher–child contacts in nursery schools were made in the 1930s. For example, Moore (1938) examined the use of commands, suggestions, and requests by nursery school and kindergarten teachers. More comprehensive analyses were later made by Landreth *et al.* (1943). These investigations provide some basic information on the frequency of occurrence of different types of contacts, and variation with age of the child, and with training of the teacher. Foster (1930) analysed the distribution of teachers' time generally in nursery and kindergarten. She found that the teachers spent more time with younger children, especially in teacher-initiated contacts. The ratio of child-initiated to teacher-initiated contacts increased with age of the child and was higher for girls than boys. Foster's study is especially interesting, however, as being probably the first to focus attention on the inequality of distribution of teacher contacts. Good agreement was found between the teachers' own rankings of time spent with individual children, and observational records.

From interviews with the teachers it appeared that children receiving more than the average number of teacher contacts might either be children with certain difficulties – such as being aggressive and disobedient, or having some particular problem such as immature speech or nail-biting; or children who were very talkative, and liked being near adults and interacting with them. Children receiving fewer than the average number of contacts were either likely to be independent children who only asked for teacher assistance occasionally; or else shy, retiring children who avoided teacher contact. These findings, whilst lacking external validation, are not of course surprising; but they do make the point that those children who actually receive fewest contacts are not necessarily those who would least benefit from teacher involvement. This seems particularly true of the shy child, who is all too easily neglected, especially perhaps when teacher:child ratios are poor.

Turning to more recent work, Stevenson (1975) considered amounts and kinds of verbal contact between teachers and children in preschool classes in Britain, though mainly in the context of evaluation of the Peabody Language Development Kit. Other work has been done in British infant and junior school classrooms, and as these have had a relatively informal teaching structure, the findings are relevant to the discussion of nursery school environments. Boydell (1974) examined and described categories of teacher conversation with pupils in six junior school classrooms. Private, work-orientated contact was found to be predominant, but this was mainly task supervision with relatively little emphasis on the substantial content of children's activities. Boydell's impressions are not entirely consistent with those from Resnick's observations (1971, 1972) in four infant school classes. Resnick did indeed find that 80–90 per cent of teacher–pupil exchanges were brief (four utterances or less), and that many of these were 'management directives'. These tended often to be child initiated. However, the remaining 10–20 per cent of long exchanges provided about 50 per cent of actual remarks by teachers, and of these many were teacher initiated and were, for example, questions relating to the content of the child's activity. Resnick also reported an impression of unequal distribution of teacher contacts with children, but without quantitative support.

Earlier, Jackson and Lahaderne (1967) had reported very large inequalities in teacher–child contacts in sixth-grade classrooms in the USA. Their approach was applied by Garner and Bing (1973) to five junior school classes in England. Garner and Bing categorised verbal contacts as work, procedure, or discipline orientated, and as teacher or pupil initiated. Large inequalities were found in the distribution of contacts generally, there being a lack of compensation between different kinds of contact. On the basis of teacher ratings, it seemed that children who got most contacts were either active, bright, personable children, or active but duller miscreants. These results bear direct comparison to those of Foster (1930) in the USA some forty years earlier; these are apparently the only two studies of this kind.

Studies of teacher:child ratios

Little work has been done on the effects of variation of teacher:child ratios on either teacher–child contacts, the distribution of attention, or children's behaviour generally in the preschool. The studies by O'Connor (1975) and Reuter and Yunik (1973) have already been reviewed. An earlier small-scale experimental study is also worth mentioning. Williams and Mattson (1942) examined aspects of the language of preschool children when a child was either alone (with toys), with an experimenter, with an experimenter and one other child, or with an experimenter and two other children. There were only six children, aged 4 years, who experienced each condition. The results suggested that children used longer sentences and most social speech when with the experimenter and one other child, although the percentage of speech which was classified as friendly intercourse increased with an increase in the number of children.

There has been an appreciable amount of research on teacher:pupil ratios and class size in the context of secondary and further education (e.g. Fleming, 1959; Cottrell, 1962; De Cecco, 1964). Surprisingly, these studies and reviews do not point clearly to advantages of smaller classes. Indeed for academic purposes there even seems to be some slight advantage in large classes. Little *et al.* (1971) point to such an effect also for consideration of reading attainment in junior and infant school. As they make clear, it is difficult to separate out other factors from variation in size, but any effects of class size, whatever their direction, appear to be small. However, these generalisations may well not be extendable to the preschool, whose instructional contact usually depends much more on one-to-one or small-group contact than on the whole-class teaching approach more commonly used for older age groups.

Actual staff:child ratios in preschool institutions vary very considerably. In Reuter and Yunik's studies (1973) cited earlier, these varied from 1:3.5

to 1:12 for USA nursery classes. The OECD report on early childhood care and education (1977) indicates much poorer ratios for many day care institutions in different countries. For example, in France the *écoles maternelles* aim at a ratio of 1:35, but often achieve 1:40. Austria and Switzerland aim for 1:28, but often achieve between 1:30 and 1:40 in kindergartens. In the Netherlands a ratio of about 1:30 seems usual. However, in Denmark and Finland class sizes of around 20, with 2 teachers, hence a 1:10 ratio, are reported as typical. Many playgroups and nursery classes in Britain have similar ratios; for example, the Preschool Playgroups Association recommends a second staff member for groups of more than 15 children. In nursery schools the ratio of staff to children is about 1:13 (DES, 1973). The ratio of 1:3.5 reported by O'Connor, and by Reuter and Yunik seems to represent the most favourable end of this scale.

In Chapter 10 we report a study in which experimental variations of staff:child ratio were made during structured-activities sessions in the experimental playgroups. The ratios varied from 3:12 (1:4) to 2:28 (1:14). This represents the spread of ratios characteristically found in Britain and the USA, although it does not extend to the ratios of 1:30 or worse apparently obtaining in some day-care centres in Continental Europe. Chapter 11 summarises the results of the studies carried out in Chapters 9 and 10, and compares them with the results from studies reviewed in this chapter.

9 A comparison of structured-activities and free-play conditions

The purpose of this investigation was to compare the effects of different organisational regimes on the behaviour of young children. Group One experienced a structured, organised-activities regime for most of a two-term period, whereas Group Two experienced a free-play regime for the same period. In order to examine for cumulative effects which might occur, it was necessary for each group to experience a consistent organisational regime. This requirement ruled out a design in which each group experienced both regimes alternately. Given the design used, it was essential to be satisfied that the two groups were closely similar in significant initial characteristics. Inevitably, the built in replication employed in the other studies was not possible here, and this investigation is best seen as an intensive, detailed case-study.

Population sample

The study started in September 1972. At this time Group One contained 23 children (11 boys, 12 girls) and Group Two contained 23 children (12 boys, 11 girls). However, some children were due to leave for school at the end of the first term – two boys and two girls from Group One, and three boys and one girl from Group Two. As the project was to last two terms, it was decided not to make any systematic observations on the children who were leaving after one term.

At the November half-term one new boy and two new girls were admitted to each group. These children were included in the samples, extra records for them being obtained where necessary. Excluding the children who left in December, therefore, each group contained 22 children, 10 boys and 12 girls, all of whom remained in the playgroups until at least April of the following year.

These children constituted the observed samples in the study. Ideally, we would have had equal numbers of boys and girls in each group, but this was not possible owing to a lack of boys of suitable age on our waiting list. However, the two groups of children who were observed were very

Table 9.1. *Age and sex composition of structured-activities group (Group One) and free-play group (Group Two)*

	Number of children	Mean age at start of project (months)	Age range (months)
Group One: overall	22	41.8	32–50
Group One: boys' subgroup	10	42.6	33–50
Group One: girls' subgroup	10	42.0	33–49
Group Two: overall	22	41.6	31–49
Group Two: boys' subgroup	10	42.4	34–49
Group Two: girls' subgroup	10	41.8	32–49

closely matched in age and sex composition. Each child could be paired with a child of the same sex in the other group, of closely similar age – usually within one or two months, and in no case was there more than a three-month difference. Also, within each group, the 10 boys and 10 of the girls could be paired for age (within three months). These pairings were used in subsequent data analysis. Details of the groups and subgroups are given in Table 9.1. Background details for each child are available in Appendix A.

Each group attended two mornings per week during school terms, which comprised 13 weeks from September to December and 14 weeks from January to April. Attendance was just above 90 per cent for both Groups One and Two.

Structured-activities and free-play regimes

The two regimes whose effects were to be compared were differentiated by the amount and kind of intervention from the staff in the choice of activity by the children. One regime, labelled 'structured-activities', or 'adult-choice', involved a high level of intervention. The other regime, labelled 'free-play', or 'child-choice', involved a low level of staff activity with children. The intention was to simulate two degrees of staff involvement along a general scale of this kind which previous work (see Chapter 8) suggested was an important one in preschool institutions. The two regimes to be adopted were intended to be well separated along this scale, while not being so extreme as to be unrepresentative in the context of current practice in British preschool institutions.

The organised or structured-activities regime was designed to represent a fairly high degree of adult involvement and structuring of activities, such as might be found in a traditional kind of nursery class. The three playgroup staff were instructed to involve themselves actively in the children's play, using every opportunity to talk with the children, develop play constructively, bring out concepts of number, shape, and colour, and so on. As a ready vehicle for this involvement, two or three main activities were arranged for each half-morning (other toys were also available), a different set of two or three main activities being presented for the two halves of each morning. For example, one half-morning might incorporate the three activities of making cakes, playing with a plastic train set and rails, and work with paper and plasticine. After the milk break three new activities might be water play, picture dominoes, and making models with plastic shapes. Each activity would be localised in an area of the room (on a couple of tables if appropriate), and would have one member of the playgroup staff primarily responsible for it.

Each adult would use her intervention flexibly, as a means of interacting with the children and guiding their play. thus an adult supervising water play would suggest different activities such as washing a doll, pouring water through a funnel, sucking or blowing water through tubes, floating and sinking objects, and so on. These activities naturally provided a focus for interaction and conversation between adult and children. Children were encouraged but not forced to engage in certain activities and to talk about them, and those not engaged in any organised activity were also invited (but not forced) to take part. In general, staff aimed to see that each child spent some time at each of the two or three activities each half-morning, although clearly it was unrealistic to expect this to be rigidly adhered to. The general intention was that children, although occasionally in self-directed activity with the other toys available, should for the majority of the time be circulating among the staff-supervised activities for that session.

The free-play regime was designed to represent a fairly low degree of adult involvement and structuring of activities, such as might be found in some playgroups or day nurseries. The staff were asked *not* to involve themselves with the children unless a child specifically asked them (in which case they should terminate the interaction once the initial request was satisfied), or unless behaviour which might be harmful to other children or to property had to be prevented. Essentially, the staff had a 'caretaking' rather than an 'educational' role. The overall objective was to minimise staff–child interactions and to leave children with the responsibility of developing their own activities, within a framework of security from disruption, and knowledge of the potential play material.

The exact working out of these two regimes was discussed amongst the research staff and the playgroup staff, and its execution was monitored by the researchers. An instruction handout given to the playgroup staff, giving more details of the two regimes, is reproduced in Appendix E. The overall distinction between the two regimes in terms of amount of adult–child interaction was verified quantitatively, using observational procedures.

Although clearly distinct, the two regimes were not thought to be extreme. On the one hand, children in the organised-activities group were not *forced* to take part in these activities, although they were encouraged to do so, in a few cases quite firmly. On the other hand, children in the free-play group were introduced to new materials, or given some help if they asked for it; they were not left completely on their own. Nevertheless, the difference between the two regimes was felt to be substantial.

Clearly, the two regimes adopted are only two from an immense spectrum of possibilities. In particular, it might be felt that the dimensions of adult *involvement* and adult *direction* in the structuring of activities could be independent. However, it was not possible to do more than compare two conditions, and we chose to compare two which contrasted well and appeared to be realistic and important. We recognise that this by no means exhausts the kinds of possible variations that might be investigated. Equally clearly, generalisations from the present study must be tentative.

Although varied regarding the amount of adult involvement and structuring, the conditions of the two groups were made as similar as possible in other respects. The matching of the groups in terms of their age and sex composition has already been mentioned. The two groups met in the same premises, had the same overall timetable, and had the same three staff supervising them. In addition, the same toys and apparatus were available on corresponding mornings. If, for instance, Group One met on a Tuesday morning and had the organised activities mentioned earlier (p. 211), then on the next (Wednesday) morning the same toys or equipment would be out for Group Two. In the examples given, dough and pastry rollers, the plastic train equipment, and plasticine and paper, would all be available in the first half of the morning, and water bowls and accessories, picture dominoes, and plastic shapes in the second half. In addition, on both mornings other equipment such as a Wendy house, climbing-frame and slide, rocking-boat, and easel would be available. The actual amount of additional equipment varied during the term but approximated one basic set of equipment. On any particular pair of mornings, the layout of toys was also approximately the same for both groups.

Timetabling of differing regimes

The introduction of the two contrasting regimes did not start immediately. The first two weeks of the September term were allowed as a period for settling in to the new premises, with the staff adopting an intermediate approach in which a lot of free play was allowed but with fairly frequent intervention to help children settle and become familiar with the range of toys and equipment available. This condition continued into the third and fourth weeks, which were used as an initial baseline condition, common to both groups of children, in which observations were made of their levels of behaviour and choice of activity. For the remaining eight weeks of the first term and the twelve weeks of the next term, the two groups experienced the two contrasting regimes. Finally, in the last two weeks of the final term, both groups experienced a similar final baseline condition to give clearer information on differences between the two groups at the end of the experiment. This final baseline conditions was intended to be similar to the initial baseline conditions, although as by now all the children were well settled, the final baseline conditions was fairly similar to the free-play regime.

Observational methods and assessment procedures

The observer moved around quietly in the playroom to watch the behaviour of the target child. Most of the children were already fully accustomed to the observer's presence from the previous year. The two-week settling-in period, used by the observer as practice sessions, ensured further habituation so that very little notice was taken of him by the time basic data gathering began.

It was considered desirable to get a broad picture of the effect of the two differing regimes, which we expected might influence a wider range of behaviours and abilities than had the variations in the physical environment considered earlier. For example, differential effects on cognitive and linguistic abilities, activity spans, and social skills, might all be expected. In consequence, we used a much wider range of assessment procedures than in the other projects. In all, seven kinds of assessment were used, five of which were observational.

Timetabling of observational procedures

For each group, the observational data were obtained in eight consecutive blocks. These comprised an initial baseline block, six consecutive experi-

Table 9.2. *Observational procedures within each data block*

	First half-morning	Second half-morning
First day (Tues., Wed.)	Time samples of companions, activities, and behaviours	Event sampling of aggressive incidents
Second day (Thurs., Fri.)	Scan sampling of activities	Staff verbalisations *or* event sampling of fantasy and rough-and-tumble play
Third day (Tues., Wed.)	Event sampling of fantasy and rough-and-tumble play *or* staff verbalisations	Scan sampling of activities
Fourth day (Thurs., Fri.)	Event sampling of aggressive incidents	Time samples of companions, activities, and behaviours

mental blocks, and a final baseline block. Within each block a set of records was made, as shown in Table 9.2. This arrangement of data collection was intended to balance out any effects of time of day or day of week. An identical procedure was followed for both groups. Each block of data took two weeks to collect.

Extra observations were made in the remaining time to obtain a complete set of time-sample and activity-scan data for children who were absent during any observational session.

Time sampling of companions, activities, and behaviours

Data were gathered using the standard 40-second time-sampling technique described in Chapter 2. In a half-morning session, two time samples were obtained for each child in the group, giving a total of 4 samples per child in each data block. Details of the categories used and inter-observer agreement are given in Appendix B.

The time-sampling data on companions allowed the construction of sociograms, while the data on activities and behaviours allowed estimates of the probability of their being observed in the different regimes. However, some kinds of behaviour were known to occur relatively infrequently so that focal-child sampling did not give sufficient data for satisfactory statistical reliability. This was particularly so for aggressive behaviour and rough-

and-tumble play, and data for these behaviours were supplemented by event sampling. Event sampling was also made of fantasy play sequences. These were often of long duration, far exceeding the 40-second sample period, and it was desirable to get a broader picture of the nature and duration of fantasy play episodes from an event-sampling procedure.

Event sampling of aggressive incidents

The observer scanned the room, looking for any incident of aggressive behaviour. An aggressive incident was defined operationally as occurring when a child behaved (either physically, verbally, or both) in a way which hurt or clearly conflicted with the interest of another child. When in doubt as to whether the incident was, or would become, aggressive, the observer recorded the details and made a judgement later. Details of any incident (context of conflict, children involved, result of encounter) were recorded on a small portable tape-recorder and later transcribed. It was not possible to obtain a realistic measure of inter-observer agreement for this, since only the principal observer was both well-acquainted with the children and virtually ignored by them. However, a session with a second observer in a different playgroup gave an 85 per cent concordance on number of aggressive incidents observed using the event-sampling technique (Smith and Green, 1974).

Event sampling of aggressive behaviour was carried out for two half-morning sessions for each group.

Event sampling of fantasy play and rough-and-tumble play

The observer scanned the room looking for any incident of fantasy play or rough-and-tumble play. Ideally, event sampling of these two kinds of behaviours would have been done separately, but the tight timetabling of observations precluded this. However, it was found relatively easy to sample rough-and-tumble play with fantasy play (as compared, for example, with aggressive incidents), since most of the rough-and-tumble incidents were of a fantasy nature, occurring in an imaginative context of monster or Dalek[1] play, cowboys and indians, or similar.

Fantasy play was defined as play in which the child showed evidence of non-literal or make-believe use of objects, actions, or verbalisations. Rough-and-tumble play was taken to include play-fighting, play-chasing, and group running. In describing incidents the observer concentrated on

[1] Daleks are a race of fierce robots which appeared in a popular and long-running television serial, 'Dr Who'.

recording the identities of the children in the episode and the nature of the sequence – in fantasy play, the objects used or pretended, apparatus utilised, gross motor patterns, roles assigned or accepted. Often only one fantasy episode was occurring, in which case much more detail could be given. If two or three separate episodes were occurring (generally the maximum in a group of 22 children) then only the broad details mentioned above could be recorded, the observer switching attention fairly frequently from one episode to another. The time was noted every minute so that the duration of episodes could be estimated.

The observer concentrated primarily on noting fantasy play episodes, in the sense that these were sometimes quiet or unobtrusive, whereas rough-and-tumble episodes were generally noisy and easily seen. As with aggressive behaviour, the event-sampling technique was facilitated in this case by the great familiarity of the children to the observer, and his ease of movement without causing disruption. Generally it was found possible to forecast the beginning of a fantasy play episode (e.g. a particular child going into a Wendy house probably meant the beginning of a 'family' episode; another child creeping under a table probably meant the beginning of a 'monster' episode) and to move up to observe more closely without affecting the children. In these circumstances, a measure of inter-observer agreement would have been difficult and unrealistic. However, the accuracy of recognition of fantasy play and rough-and-tumble play was assessed by inter-observer agreement based on focal samples in another playgroup (Smith and Dodsworth, 1978). Concordances of 87 per cent for fantasy play and 75 per cent for rough-and-tumble play were obtained for occurrence in a sample. Given agreement that fantasy play occurred, concordance of duration over 15-second intervals was 91 per cent, and concordance over number of participants per one-minute period was 96 per cent.

One half-morning of event sampling for fantasy play and rough-and-tumble play was made in each data block.

Scan sampling of activities

Scan sampling of activities was used to get an estimate of the length of time children continued at a given activity, and also the number of different activities in which they engaged during a half-morning. Scans were made through a 40-minute period, at 2-minute intervals. At the start of each 2-minute interval, the observer scanned the room, noting which activity each child was engaged in. The categorisation of activities was the same as that used in the time-sampling procedure detailed in Appendix B, although in the case of table play or more specialised activities, further details were given (e.g. play with beads and string; picture dominoes; train set). A child could be scored for more than one activity category at a time – for example, books, Wendy house, and fantasy play. The scan was made as rapidly as possible, consistent with reliable assessment of activities, so that children would not have moved around appreciably while the scan was being made. It was found possible to make the scan in about 1 minute 15 seconds. This allowed a 45-second 'break' before the next scan began. The observations were dictated on a to a small portable tape-recorder.

Twenty consecutive scan samples were made during a half-morning. This was virtually the whole duration of the 45-minute period, starting a few minutes after the playgroup had begun, so as to allow the children to settle at activities and to give the observer time to get the feel of ongoing groups and activity selection. Scans were obtained from two such half-mornings during each data block.

Three sets of information were extracted from the data. First, the number of different activities in which a child engaged in a 45-minute period. Second, the number of scans in which a child was not observed in any activity. Third, when a child did continue an activity over more than one scan, the mean attention span was calculated for the child for that period, taking attention span as the number of additional consecutive scans in which a common activity was observed. In absolute terms, the attention span in minutes would be about twice the attention span in scans, since the scans were 2 minutes apart. (Strictly speaking, this would be an average estimate, as the actual attention span might vary by about one minute either way; also, it is assumed that the child does not effectively discontinue, then recommence, an activity within a 2-minute interval.)

Staff language to children

Records of staff verbalisations to children were made to provide a check that there was indeed more staff contact with children in the organised-activities than in the free-play regime, and that this greater degree of contact was mainly in the context of initiating and developing play activities.

Focal-staff sampling was used, one member of staff being observed for 5 minutes. Each separate utterance by the staff member to a child was recorded and categorised. An utterance was taken as a group of words linked together by a speaker, meaningful in itself and generally demarcated by a pause. One-word utterances, and non-verbal signals such as head nods, were not scored. Utterances to other staff members or adults were also ignored.

Each utterance was recorded on a prepared record-sheet, a tick being placed under one of seven categories which had been developed during pilot work at the beginning of the study. The categories used were *play invite* ('what shall we do?'; 'shall we make a man?'); *play develop* ('has he got legs?'; 'can you find a card like that?'; 'perhaps Keith will help you draw it'); *information/help* ('here's a bit'; 'that's a square'; 'perhaps Keith will help you'); *miscellaneous question* ('what's that?'; 'did you make that?'; 'what did you see yesterday?'); *comment* ('look at what Penny's made'; 'that's nice'; 'all right, you do that'); *command* ('bring that close'; 'be careful'); and *prohibition* ('that's enough of that'; 'don't be so noisy'). No inter-observer agreement for these category definitions was obtained. It was anticipated (and was indeed the case) that the differences between the two groups would be so great for most categories that even low concordances would scarcely cast any doubt on the results.

During a half-morning when staff verbalisations were being recorded, two 5-minute samples were obtained for each of the three staff members in the playgroup. The two samples for a particular member of staff were taken at widely separated times. Two samples for each staff member were obtained during each data block.

Cognitive and linguistic tests

The main emphasis of the assessment procedure in this study was on observational measures of the children both before, during, and after the operation of the two different nursery regimes. However, we also obtained some measure of the children's performance on standardised tests at the beginning and end of the project. This served both to check that the two groups were reasonably well matched for ability at the beginning of the study, and to see whether one group improved more than the other in some respects by the time the study was concluded.

Two standard tests of ability for preschool children, one primarily cognitive and one primarily linguistic, were employed. The Caldwell Preschool Inventory[1] provided an overall assessment of the child's general knowledge, and ability to deal with colours, shapes, numbers, and concepts such as 'inside' and 'behind', using small objects. The Peabody Picture Vocabulary test[2] gives an assessment of the child's vocabulary in terms of recognition and selection of a picture of a normal object from four pictures presented. A cumulative series of picture sets is presented, becoming progressively more difficult. Each test took about twenty minutes to

[1] Cooperative Tests and Services, Educational Testing Service, Princeton, New Jersey, USA.
[2] NFER Publishing Company, 2 Oxford Road East, Windsor, Berks, UK.

administer. The tests were given individually to each child. All the children were tested at the start of the first term, and again at the end of the second term. However, with three of the children in Group Two testing could not be successfully completed because of their shyness and non-cooperation.

Staff ratings and comments

At the end of the project staff were asked for open-ended comments on how the two groups of children differed in behaviour over the two terms, and whether either of the two regimes was in any way better, or more suitable for any particular children.

More structured rating assessments were also obtained. Both at the end of the initial baseline period, and again at the end of the experimental period in the second term (before the final baseline period), each member of the playgroup staff was asked to rate on a continuous scale each of the two groups, as a whole, according to the following five characteristics: noisy/quiet; creative/uncreative in play; easy/difficult to control; fight a lot/few fights; pleasant/quite a strain to be with.

At the end of the experimental period each staff member also rated (on a numerical five-point scale) each child according to the following eight characteristics: cooperative/uncooperative; plays mostly alone/with other children; aggressive/not agressive; often/not often at table play; independent/can cope well; needs help/at a loss by himself; noisy/quiet in play; affectionate/not particularly affectionate to adults and children. these eight characteristics were considered important and probably relevant to the effects of the differing regimes; in previous work they had been found to be salient constructs in the perception of children by nursery and preschool staff.

Methods of analysis

Analysis was based initially on the blocks of data described on p. 214. The data blocks formed the following array:

organised-activities group	B1	E1	E2	E3	E4	E5	E6	B2
free-play group	b1	e1	e2	e3	e4	e5	e6	b2

where capitals are used for the organised-activities group and lower-case for the free-play group. B and b refer to the common baseline condition at the beginning and end of the study, while E and e refer to the two differing (experimental) regimes. Each block contains a basic set of data from all the different observational assessment measures, although in some cases the amount of data is not very large and more reliable results are obtained from summing over blocks.

A number of possible analyses present themselves with this data configuration. The most obvious analysis for comparison of the overall ongoing consequences of the two regimes is to compare $E(1-6)$ with $e(1-6)$. In the case of the time-sample data, analysis of variance was used. A two-way analysis of variance – regime (two factors) and time (six factors) – was employed, with a separate print-out and time analysis for boys ($N = 10$) and girls ($N = 12$) separately.

However, in evaluating the results from this kind of analysis, other comparisons and analyses also need to be borne in mind. First, a difference between $E(1-6)$ and $e(1-6)$ might be due to initial differences between the groups, rather than to the differing regimes. This could be indicated, or counter-indicated, by a comparison of B1 and b1. Any cumulative effects of the two regimes would be indicated by the time analysis of $E(1-6)$ and $e(1-6)$, but whether such differences tended to persist in the common conditions of the final baseline would be indicated by comparing B2 and b2.

Generally, Wilcoxon matched-pairs signed-ranks tests were used for these comparisons, as children could be paired across the two groups for sex and age. In addition, sex differences within and between groups were examined using the Wilcoxon test and the reduced sample of 10 boys and 10 girls matched for age within and between groups.

In the case of staff language to children, binomial tests were used to compare particular half-morning sessions (summing over staff).

Results

Staff language to children

The measurements of the language used by staff to children were designed to check quantitatively that the staff did indeed behave differently to the children in the two regimes, and along the lines proposed to them. The results were quite clear-cut, and were very similar for each of the three staff members. The data for the two groups were compared by means of binomial tests on each focal-adult sample (six per data block). Overall totals for the experimental and baseline conditions are given (summed over the three adults) in Table 9.3. In addition, the experimental data are broken down into three periods to give an indication of the stability of the differences over time.

Table 9.3. *Categorisations of language used by staff to children, in baseline and experimental conditions*

Significance levels for differences between Groups One and Two from binomial tests

(*) $P < 0.1$ *** $P < 0.001$ ** $P < 0.005$ * $P < 0.05$

		Baseline overall	Experimental overall E/e(1–6)	Sequential experimental blocks E/e(1,2)	E/e(3,4)	E/e(5,6)
Play invite	Group One	5	107	33	44	30
	Group Two	7	11 ***	1 (*)	4 **	6 *
Play develop	Group One	7 (*)	767 ***	235 ***	286 ***	246 ***
	Group Two	26	43	7	17	19
Information help	Group One	43 (*)	393 ***	133 ***	134 ***	126
	Group Two	25	80	6	28	46 **
Miscellaneous questions	Group One	14	141 **	34 *	57 *	50
	Group Two	13	45	5	12	28
Comments	Group One	8	204 ***	55 **	86 ***	63 *
	Group Two	14	46	4	18	24
Commands	Group One	25	100 ***	37 (*)	33	30
	Group Two	6 (*)	32	8	9	15
Prohibitions	Group One	9	30	8	11	11
	Group Two	3	22	9	4	9

In examining the baseline conditions, it can be seen that the staff language did not differ significantly for any of the seven categories. It approached significance ($P < 0.1$) for three categories, but with no consistent direction of difference between the two groups. The overall number of utterances was 111 in Group One, and 94 in Group Two – a non-significant difference.

By contrast, looking at verbalisations in the experimental conditions, there was a total of 1,742 in the Group One samples, and 279 in the Group Two samples. Furthermore, this difference was appreciable, and highly significant ($P < 0.005$), for all the categories of verbalisation except *prohibition*. In terms of a ratio of Group One to Group Two, the biggest difference was in *play develop* (18:1) and *play invite* (10:1), followed by *information/help* (5:1) and *comments* (4:1). The difference was also large for *miscellaneous questions* (3:1) and *commands* (3:1). With the possible exception of *commands*, these are all types of verbalisation to be expected to occur most in the involvement with the children through activities, which was intended to characterise the organised-activities regime. It is clear that this expectation was fulfilled, and that the greater difference was indeed in inviting children to activities and developing and helping their play in that context.

The incidence of *prohibitions* such as 'don't be so noisy', 'stop that, it's dangerous', was expected to be approximately equal in the two regimes. On the one hand, the chance of noisy play being prohibited might be more frequent in the organised-activities regime. On the other hand, the incidence of what might be considered noisy or dangerous play itself would probably be higher in the free-play regime. Overall, the level of prohibitions was very similar for the two groups.

The sequential presentation of data blocks E,e(1,2), E,e(3,4), and E,e(5,6) shows that the difference between the groups was maintained at a fairly constant level throughout the experimental period.

Sociometric analyses

Figures 9.1 and 9.2 present the friendship networks, calculated on both the baseline and experimental time-sample data on companions. They are constructed as described on p. 70, but including the three staff as well as the children. The few children who left in December, and therefore were not part of the observed sample, are not included in these sociograms.

Figure 9.1 gives the overall sociometric network for Group One which, for most of the samples used, was in the organised-activities condition. It makes sense here to include the three staff, Mrs B. (supervisor), Mrs X, and

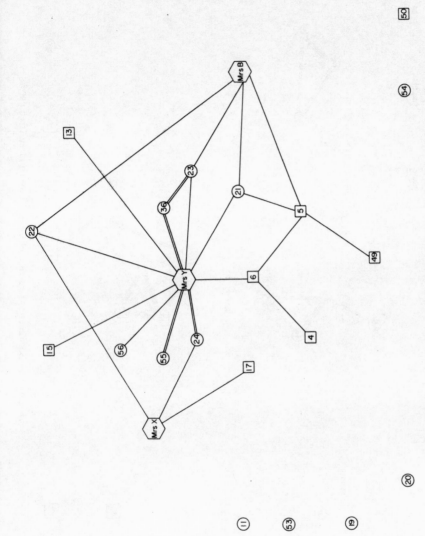

Figure 9.1. Sociometric structure of Group One children (structured activities)

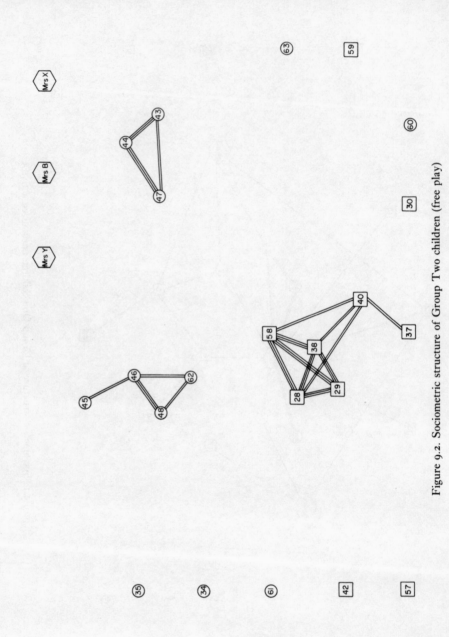

Figure 9.2. Sociometric structure of Group Two children (free play)

Mrs Y (assistants). (Mrs X left in March, after block 4 of the experimental sequence, and was replaced temporarily by Mrs W; her data were included with Mrs X's for simplicity.) As expected, all three occupied central places in the association network, and certain children also had clear preferences for certain staff members. There were only five links between children (as compared with seventeen in Figure 9.2). Twelve of the children had a close association with at least one staff member, but ten others did not; all of the latter, however, were seen associated with a member of the staff for at least 15 per cent of the scans, but not to this extent for any particular one of the three staff.

Figure 9.2 shows the overall association network for Group Two, which, for most of the samples used, was in the free-play condition. This gives a similar sort of picture to those seen in Chapters 4 and 5, though with marked sex segregation. There was a large 'gang' of boys 28, 29, 38, 58, and 40, with 37 more loosely associated. A group of girls, 46, 48, and 62, had 45 more loosely associated; and there was another triad of girls, 43, 44, and 47. Nine of the children were isolates by the 15 per cent criterion, and the three subgroups mentioned were independent of each other.

Choice of companions

The results for the ten categories of companion choice, plus two combined categories, together with results for mean subgroup size (with other children) and percentage same-sex choice, are shown in Table 9.4. Differences between the two groups for either B/b(1) or B/b(2) – initial and final baseline conditions – were tested for by Wilcoxon matched-pairs signed-rank tests. For the experimental blocks, analyses of variance were used, the two factors being treatment (organised-activities/free-play) and time (blocks 1 and 2, 3 and 4, 5 and 6). Significance levels for differences between groups on the total experimental blocks, and time effects, are based on these analyses.

The comparison of the first baseline conditions shows no appreciable difference between the two groups at the beginning of the study. The only significant result is that there were fewer *opposite-sex pairs* in Group Two (compare discussion of sociograms); but there is no difference in overall *group play* (with children).

The comparison of the experimental conditions shows very marked and significant differences. When in organised activities, Group One had many more occurrences of group or parallel associations with adults; conversely, Group Two in free play had many more occurrences of both *parallel play* and *group play* with children. Even when the Group One children were in *group play* with other children, the *mean subgroup size* was less.

Table 9.4. *Companions: baseline and experimental conditions*

Mean occurrence per block, and significance levels, for Group One (upper line) and Group Two (lower line)
* $P < 0.05$ ** $P < 0.01$ *** $P < 0.001$.

	B/b(1)	B/b(2)	E/e(1–6)		Time effects and interactions
Alone	31	14	9.3		
	24	17	14.5	**	
Parallel (adult + children)	0	0	22.3		
	4	0	1.5	***	
Group adult	2	0	26.3		Time**
	4	0	1.8	***	Time × treatment*
Group (adult + children)	0	0	7.2		
	0	0	0	***	
Small parallel subgroup	13	12	3.8		
	13	19	10.7	***	
Large parallel subgroup	9	13	3.2		
	8	4	11.7	***	
Same-sex pair	11	14	8.3		
	18	20	17.5	***	
Opposite-sex pair	11	8	2.7		
	2	5	4.3	*	
Subgroup of three	7	11	4.3		
	11	12	11.2	***	Time**
Subgroup of four or more	4	16	0.8		
	4	11	14.8	***	
Parallel play	22	25	7.0		
	21	23	22.4	***	
Group play	33	49	16.1		
	35	48	47.8	***	Time**

Table 9.4. (*cont.*)

	B/b(1)	B/b(2)	E/e(1–6)	Time effects and interactions
Mean subgroup size	2.54	3.19	2.20	
	2.71	2.81	2.91 ***	Time**
Percentage same-sex companions	56.6	75.8	69.7	
	82.1 *	72.5	78.2	

These results were to be expected. The children were encouraged to associate with the adults, so child-only groups would be expected to be less frequent. As fewer children were available at any particular time for these groups, their mean subgroup size would be smaller.

There was also less play *alone* in the organised-activities condition. The staff clearly succeeded in getting children who usually played alone into group activity with them, as well as the otherwise more sociable children.

An examination of sex differences revealed these to be non-significant except that in Group One, during organised activities, more boys than girls played in *same-sex pairs* ($P < 0.05$) and in *subgroups of three* ($P < 0.05$) and altogether in *group play* ($P < 0.01$); the mean occurrence per child for this last category through the experimental condition was 6.7 for boys and 2.5 for girls. However, more girls than boys were seen in *parallel play* or *group play with adults and children* ($P < 0.05$ in each case). For the three categories covering adult association, the mean occurrence per child was 13.7 for boys and 16.5 for girls. This indicates some tendency for the girls to be more attracted to the staff-organised activities and for the boys to remain more in independent group play (for example, boys 4, 5, 6, and 49 in figure 9.1).

Most of the time effects were non-significant. There was, however, an increase in *group play* and *mean subgroup size* in both groups through the experimental period. The effect found for *group adult* is due solely to a low score for this category in block E(3).

Choice of activities ✓

The results for 23 categories of activities are shown in Table 9.5, together with significance levels. The main interest is in the differences between the organised-activities and free-play conditions during the experimental blocks, E/e (1–6). In interpreting these results, it should be borne in mind that the same materials were available in each condition, on corresponding days.

Twelve activities were chosen about equally in the two conditions. In order of overall occurrence, these were *clay, miscellaneous play, shopping, jigsaws, books, easel, blocks, miscellaneous organised activities, water, doll's house, unusual uses of apparatus,* and *room fitments* (last three very rare).

The Group One children, in organised activities, were much more frequently seen at *table play*. This included games such as picture lotto or picture dominoes, as well as building activities with Lego or plastic shapes, threading cotton-reels, etc. This composite category was the most frequent for both groups, but occurred twice as frequently in organised activities. The only other category more frequent in organised activities was,

Table 9.5. *Activities: baseline and experimental conditions*

Mean occurrence per block, and significance levels, for Group One (upper line) and Group Two (lower line)
* $P < 0.05$ ** $P < 0.01$ *** $P < 0.001$

	B/b(1)	B/b(2)	E/e(1–6)		Time effects and interactions
Table play	14	25	25.2		Time***
		*		***	Time × condition*
	7	19	12.3		
Sandpit	7	8	4.0		
				*	Time***
	13	9	6.7		
Easel	12	2	3.3		
		**			
	1	1	2.3		
Wendy house	9	14	2.2		
				**	Time*
	7	15	5.8		
Doll	6	10	1.8		
				***	
	7	3	5.5		
Dressing-up clothes	1	2	0.3		Time***
				*	Time × condition**
	4	2	1.3		
Climbing-frame	16	7	4.2		
				***	
	8	4	10.8		
Rocking-boat	4	8	1.7		
				***	Time*
	4	4	5.7		

Table 9.5. (*cont.*)

	B/b(1)	B/b(2)	E/e(1–6)	Time effects and interactions
Toy chest	0	0	1.0	
	0	1	2.3	*
Rough-and-tumble play	4	5	1.5	
	13	11	9.0	***
Books	7	4	3.2	Time**
	4	4	3.0	Time × condition**
Blocks	0	2	1.7	
	1	1	3.2	
Doll's house	0	2	0.3	
	2	3	1.2	
Jigsaw	3	0	4.3	
	2	1	2.8	Time***
Water	0	1	1.0	
	0	1	1.3	Time***
Shopping	0	0	3.8	
	0	0	4.2	Time***
Clay	0	0	9.0	
	0	0	7.2	
Miscellaneous organised activities	0	0	2.8	
	0	0	1.3	Time***
Miscellaneous play	6	10	5.2	
	11	10	5.8	Time*
Fantasy play	10	12	4.2	
	7	13	9.0	***
Unusual uses of apparatus	2	4	0.3	
	8	0	1.2	Time × condition*
Room fitments	0	0	0	
	0	2	0.2	
No activity	10	8	14.5	
	7	14	7.5	*** Time*

Table 9.6. *Activities: significant sex differences between effects of organised-activities and free-play conditions*
Mean occurrence per block in experimental conditions, reduced subject samples

	Group One (organised activities)		Group Two (free play)	
	Boys	Girls	Boys	Girls
Table play	9.8	13.5	5.8	5.7
Wendy house	1.3	0.5	1.8	4.0
Rocking-boat	1.2	0.2	2.3	3.2
Doll	0.8	0.8	0.8	4.2

surprisingly perhaps, *no activity*. This was scored for times when a child was, for example, sitting at a table and nominally in an activity, but not taking any part in it or apparently showing any interest in it. More data on this aspect of behaviour are available later from the activity-scan data.

The Group Two children, in free play, were seen more frequently in nine activities; in order of frequency for this group, these were *climbing-frame*, *rough-and-tumble play*, *fantasy play*, *sandpit*, *Wendy house*, *rocking-boat*, *doll*, *toy chest*, *dressing-up clothes* (the last two were not common). These are the kinds of activities found to be popular in free play during the other years of the project, but which were not often utilised in organised activities in this project.

Thus there were clear differences in the activity choices during the experimental sessions. These were mostly to be expected, apart from the greater incidence of *no activity* in the organised-activities condition. Table 9.5 also gives figures for the base-line condition, but as numbers were small these are not so informative. Group Two tended to show more *rough-and-tumble play* in both baseline conditions; more information on this behaviour is presented later.

Most of the time, and time × condition, effects indicated in Table 9.5 are due to the changing popularity of particular items over time. For example, the *sandpit* was popular in blocks 3, 4, and 6; *jigsaws* in blocks 5 and 6; and so on. The only persistent tendency was for a decrease in *no activity* with time, for both groups, especially in the last two time blocks.

Some sex differences are noticeable in the effects of the two conditions. The significant effects are shown in Table 9.6, using the slightly reduced subject samples, balanced for sex. In each case, the girls seemed more affected by the difference in the two conditions than did the boys. In organised activities the girls especially spent more time at *table play*, but less time with the *Wendy house*, *rocking-boat*, or *doll*. These findings agree with the greater involvement of the girls in the organised activities, noted in the previous section.

Occurrence of behaviours

The results for the shorter list of 27 behaviour units are presented in Table 9.7, together with significance levels. Fuller results for 89 behaviour units are given in Appendix D.

By and large, the baseline scores for the two groups were similar. In the experimental conditions, the scores for Group Two in free play did not differ greatly from the level of baseline scores. The main changes were for Group One, in organised activities.

Table 9.7. *Behaviour units: baseline and experimental conditions*

Mean occurrence per block, and significance levels, for Group One (upper line) and Group Two (lower line); list of 27 behaviour units
* $P < 0.05$ ** $P < 0.01$ ***$P < 0.001$

	B/b(1)	B/b(2)	E/e(1–6)		Time effects and interactions
Upper smile	22	20	17.3		
	19	17	20.7		
Open smile	11	22	7.3		
	11	12	12.2	**	
Play noise	7	10	5.7		
	14	16	13.2	***	
Talking between children	46	59	29.0		
	47	64	53.7	***	Time***
Talking to/from adult	7	8	38.7		Time***
	12	4	9.5	***	Time × condition*
Look around/ distance	6	2	7.2		
	9	4	5.0		
Watch	34	30	35.8		
	29	22	22.2	***	
Visual contact child	53	50	41.0		
	55	59	53.7	***	

Table 9.7. (*cont.*)

	B/b(1)	B/b(2)	E/e(1–6)		Time effects and interactions
Visual contact adult	11	7	36.7		
	19	6	12.0	***	Time***
Contact apparatus	57	58	61.5		
	48	55	55.8	*	
Physical contact between children	26	26	20.2		
	25	27	28.0	***	Time***
Physical contact with adult	2	3	8.3		
	5	0	3.5	***	Time × condition**
Walk	35	40	22.3		
	46	46	39.3	***	
Run	17	18	9.0		
	20	18	19.0	***	
Climb/slide	15	10	5.0		
	12	8	11.8	***	
Chase/flee/group run	3	2	0.5		
	12	3	5.8	***	
Object exchange	8	17	16.3		
	9	14	11.0	**	Time*
Push/pull	12	18	8.2		
	8	8	11.8	*	
Kick/throw/hit	5	6	2.2		
	9	10	4.8	*	
Pedal/propel	1	0	0.7		
	1	0	0.3		
Fine manipulation	42	46	45.8		
	38	41	45.7		
Gross manipulation	5	9	3.0		
	10	6	5.8	*	

Note: for Chase/flee/group run an asterisk (*) appears between the B/b(1) values; for Push/pull an asterisk (*) appears between the B/b(2) values.

Table 9.7. (*cont.*)

	B/b(1)	B/b(2)	E/e(1–6)	Time effects and interactions
Physical aggression	2	2	2.7	
	2	2	1.3	
Agonistic behaviour	8	8	7.3	
	7	9	5.5	
Suck	5	6	6.0	Time***
	9	6	4.3	
Face contact	18	15	12.0	
	8 *	13	9.8	
Auto-manipulation	39	31	28.2	
	29	27	27.7	

In organised activities there was more *talking to/from adult, visual contact adult, physical contact adult*, and *contact apparatus*. There were more occurrences of *watch* (particularly adults, or groups of adults and children), *sit*, and *object exchange*.

By contrast, there was less *talking between children, visual contact child, physical contact between children, open smile, play noise, walk, run, climb/slide, chase/flee/group run, push/pull, kick/throw/hit*, and *gross manipulation of objects*.

These findings agree with those for choice of companions and activities. In organised activities the children were more likely to be sitting at table play with adults, watching or interacting with them; they were less likely to be in contact with other children, or engaging in free motor activity or gross physical play with objects.

No difference was found for *fine manipulation of objects*, which was high for both groups. There was also no significant difference in *agonistic behaviour*; however, this was relatively infrequent, and more data are presented from event sampling in the next section.

Significant sex differences in the effects of the organised-activities/free-play conditions are shown in Table 9.8. It was again found that girls especially increased their contacts with adults in the organised-activities conditions, while there was less running and chasing play by boys (the girls' scores for these being anyway relatively low). Only the boys increased their scores for *object exchange*, a finding which is difficult to fit into the general pattern of results.

Table 9.8. *Behaviour units: significant sex differences between effects of organised-activities and free-play conditions*

Mean occurrence per block in experimental conditions, reduced subject samples

	Group One (organised activities)		Group Two (free play)	
	Boys	Girls	Boys	Girls
Talk to/from adult	15.7	18.3	4.5	4.2
Visual contact adult	14.8	18.7	5.3	5.8
Contact apparatus	25.8	30.5	26.8	25.7
Walk	11.7	8.5	18.0	18.3
Object exchange	8.8	6.0	3.7	6.3
Run	3.8	4.3	11.8	6.3
Chase/flee/ group run	0.5	0.0	4.3	0.5

Of the time effects indicated in Table 9.7, the noticeable ones are that contacts with adults tended to increase or stay the same in Group One, but stayed the same or decreased in Group Two. Contacts with children tended to increase in both groups during the experimental blocks. Sucking tended to decrease.

Aggressive behaviour

In addition to the records of aggressive behaviour obtained from the time-sampling records, some event-sampling records were made of aggressive (or, more generally, agonistic) behaviour for the whole group. Two separate half-mornings of event sampling were made in both the initial and final baseline blocks, and for each of the six experimental blocks. Procedural details are given above.

For purposes of subsequent analysis, any incidents which had been initiated by the few children not in the main sample of 22 children in each group (see p. 209) were excluded from the analysis. After this, there was a total of 168 incidents recorded for Group One, and 132 for Group Two. A Wilcoxon matched-pairs test between individual children in the two groups gave a non-significant result.

Most of these incidents went unnoticed by staff. Intervention by a member of staff during the course of a dispute did not differ between the

Table 9.9. *Percentage staff intervention in aggressive incidents*

	Baseline blocks	Experimental blocks
Group One	17	19
Group Two	2	3

Table 9.10. *Mean occurrence per child, per session, of initiation of aggressive incidents*

	B/b(1)	E/e(1–3)	E/e(4–6)	B/b(2)
Group One				
Boys	0.25	0.62	0.65	0.90
Girls	0.25	0.21	0.33	1.00
Overall	0.25	0.39	0.48	0.95
Group Two				
Boys	0.40	0.58	0.35	0.70
Girls	0.33	0.21	0.36	0.21
Overall	0.36	0.38	0.36	0.43

baseline and experimental sessions, but did differ between the two groups (Table 9.9). Group One experienced on average 18 per cent intervention, Group Two only 2 per cent. This is significant at $P < 0.01$ (Wilcoxon test, matched sessions). Although both values are small, it seems likely that right from the start of the project the staff were either less vigilant, or less inclined to intervene (probably both) in the group consistently experiencing the free play conditions.

The mean occurrence of initiation of aggressive incidents per child, per half-morning, is shown in Table 9.10 for boys and girls in each group. The results are averaged for the two half-mornings of the first baseline block of observations, the six half-mornings of the first three experimental blocks, the six half-mornings of the last three experimental blocks, and the two half-mornings of the last baseline blocks.

Overall, there was no difference between the groups in the incidence of aggression in the experimental or the baseline conditions on Wilcoxon tests. However, for the second baseline, the difference did reach significance at the 10 per cent level. Also, the Group One children showed an appreciable increase in the number of aggressive incidents as the experiment progressed. These children initiated more aggressive incidents in the final than in the initial baseline block ($P < 0.001$), and in the second half of the project than in the first ($P < 0.02$, Wilcoxon tests). The difference between the first and second cluster of experimental blocks did not reach significance. By

Table 9.11. *Mean occurrence per child, per session, of initiation of three categories of aggression*

Group One upper line; Group Two lower line

	B/b(1)	E/e(1–3)	E/e(4–6)	B/b(2)
Specific hostility	0.20	0.27	0.30	0.55
	0.27	0.33	0.24	0.34
Harassment	0.05	0.08	0.14	0.27
	0.05	0.05	0.08	0.07
Games hostility	0.00	0.05	0.05	0.14
	0.05	0.01	0.03	0.02

contrast, there were no appreciable or significant time differences for Group Two.

The results were examined further by subdividing the aggressive incidents according to a classification proposed by Manning *et al.* (1978). Manning's main categories of aggression or hostility are (a) specific hostility (mainly property or territorial disputes), (b) harassment (in which the hostility seems deliberately directed at a person), and (c) games hostility (hostile behaviour in the context of a rough-and-tumble or make-believe activity). Fuller definitions are provided by Manning, who quotes a figure of 90 per cent for coding consistency. Without being finally committed to the validity of this scheme of classification, we found that most of the observed incidents could be fairly readily classified according to Manning's criteria. Table 9.11 gives the mean number of initiations per child, per session, for each group of the three categories of aggression mentioned above. It is clear that the pattern of increase in Group One and no change in Group Two is found for all three classes of aggression or hostility. Proportionately, the increase in Group One is most marked for games hostility and harassment, but it is significant only for specific hostility ($P < 0.05$, comparing first and second halves of the project), probably because of the much larger number of incidents in this category; the increase for harassment approaches significance ($P < 0.10$).

Sex differences in these three categories of aggression, and in overall initiation of any aggressive incident, are shown in Table 9.12. Here, the reduced age-matched samples of 10 boys and 10 girls from each group were used for analysis. The sex differences are similar for both groups, but approach significance (on Wilcoxon tests) only when the children in both groups are combined. The overall differences in initiation of aggression still only approaches significance ($P < 0.06$). However, the sex difference in harassment (greater for boys) is significant ($P < 0.01$).

Table 9.12. *Sex differences in aggression*

Mean occurrence per child for boys ($N = 10$) and girls ($N = 10$), of matched ages, over all sessions, of initiation of aggression; Group One upper line; Group Two lower line
** $P < 0.01$

	Boys	Girls
Specific hostility	6.1	4.3
	5.9	4.0
Overall	6.0	4.2
Harassment	3.1	0.9
	1.6	0.6
Overall	2.4	0.8
Games hostility	0.7	1.2
	0.3	0.5
Overall	0.5	0.9
Total aggressive incidents	9.9	6.4
	7.8	5.1
Overall	8.9	5.8

This finding shows some concordance with the findings of Manning, which were based on a smaller group of Scottish children but with many more records per child. Our results are in agreement in finding a relatively small sex difference in specific hostility, but a large sex difference in harassment; but in contrast to her findings, no sex difference in games hostility was found.

In summary, both groups showed a consistent pattern of sex differences in type of aggression or hostility, and in agreement with the earlier time-sample results, Group One showed a slightly, but not significantly, higher rate of aggression overall. Group One experienced a somewhat higher rate of staff intervention in aggressive incidents as well, and there was also a steady increase in rates of all three types of aggression throughout the project. The corresponding lack of increase for Group Two suggests that this was neither a change in the observer's criteria or vigilance, nor an age-related change. the increase for Group One is particularly marked when the final base-line (free-play) sessions are compared with the initial ones, though it must be borne in mind that here there were only two sessions in each block. Clearly any inferences must be tentative, but the pattern of results does suggest that the decrease in peer interactions in the experimental condition for Group One may have adversely affected the children's ability to interact in a non-hostile way, especially when they were once again in a free-play situation.

Table 9.13. *Mean number of scans per child, per session, of rough-and-tumble play*

	B/b(1)	E/e(1–2)	E/e(3–4)	E/e(5–6)	B/b(2)
Group One					
Boys	1.45	1.00	0.23	0.30	1.75
Girls	0.46	0.27	0.13	0.06	0.63
Overall	0.91	0.60	0.17	0.17	1.14
Group Two					
Boys	3.40	2.90	3.83	2.73	3.30
Girls	0.17	0.67	0.23	1.40	0.50
Overall	1.64	1.68	1.86	2.00	1.77

Rough-and-tumble play

In addition to the data from time sampling, further information on rough-and-tumble and fantasy play were available from both the activity scans and event sampling. The data from the scans are the most useful with regard to time spent in an activity, while the event-sampling data yield more information on aspects such as duration of each episode and number of children involved. In the event sampling, priority was given to the recording of fantasy play episodes; the recording of rough-and-tumble episodes was not considered reliable enough to warrant further analysis, so for rough-and-tumble play only the scan data are presented. These results are shown in Table 9.13.

The numerical results in Table 9.13 are for scans, but these can be converted to an estimate of time spent in an activity by multiplying by 2 (the scan interval being 2 minutes). Thus, in Group One each child spent on average about two minutes in rough-and-tumble play in each session of 40 minutes during the baseline blocks. During the experimental blocks, the average was reduced to just over half a minute. The difference between the rate of occurrence in the base-line and experimental blocks, overall, is significant ($P < 0.002$, Wilcoxon test; $P < 0.05$ for boys, not significant for girls).

For Group Two, the rate of occurrence of rough-and-tumble play was fairly steady through the project. There is no significant difference between the baseline and experimental blocks overall (Wilcoxon tests; not significant for boys, $P < 0.01$ for girls).

Despite some differences between Group One and Two in the initial baseline, it is clear that the organised-activities condition results in much less rough-and tumble play; this is in accord with the time-sample data.

Table 9.14. *Mean number of scans per child, per session, of fantasy play*

	B/b(1)	E/e(1–2)	E/e(3–4)	E/e(5–6)	B/b(2)
Group One					
Boys	3.85	1.13	1.00	2.03	3.60
Girls	2.25	0.85	0.83	0.73	4.50
Overall	2.98	1.09	0.91	1.32	4.09
Group Two					
Boys	2.60	1.75	2.50	1.45	2.75
Girls	2.17	0.71	2.48	2.02	3.33
Overall	2.36	1.18	2.49	1.76	3.07

Table 9.15. *Sex differences in rough-and-tumble play and fantasy play*

Mean number of scans for boys ($N = 10$) and girls ($N = 10$) of matched ages, over all sessions

	Boys	Girls
Rough-and-tumble play		
Group One	1.3	0.5
Group Two	5.1	1.2
Overall	3.2	0.8
Fantasy play		
Group One	3.2	2.1
Group Two	3.4	3.2
Overall	3.3	2.7

Fantasy play

The results from scan sampling for fantasy play are shown in Table 9.14. It can be seen that each child in Group One spent on average about six to eight minutes in fantasy play in each session of 40 minutes during the baseline blocks. During the experimental blocks, the average was reduced to about two minutes. The difference between the rate of occurrence in the baseline and experimental blocks overall is significant ($P < 0.002$, Wilcoxon test; $P < 0.02$ for both boys and girls).

Despite some overall differences between the two groups, and the fluctuations in Group Two, it is clear that the organised-activities condition results in appreciably less fantasy play; again this is in accord with the time-sample data.

Tables 9.13 and 9.14 suggest a strong sex difference in rough-and-tumble play, and a much less strong one for the occurrence of fantasy play. These are best examined using the reduced samples of 10 boys and 10 girls in

Table 9.16. *Amount of fantasy play from event sampling*

	Baseline blocks	Experimental blocks
Mean number of episodes per session		
Group One	10.5	5.7
Group Two	17.0	6.8
Mean number of times any child seen in episode, per session		
Group One	32.0	21.0
Group Two	53.0	27.5

Table 9.17. *Number of participants in fantasy play sequences, from event sampling*

	Baseline blocks	Experimental blocks
Mean number of participants for at least half the episode		
Group One	2.2	2.0
Group Two	2.4	3.0
Mean number of participants for each child taking part		
Group One	3.1	3.2
Group Two	3.2	4.5

each group, matched for age. The results are shown in Table 9.15. For rough-and-tumble play, the sex difference is significant overall ($P < 0.02$, Wilcoxon test; not significant for Group One, $P < 0.02$ for Group Two). For fantasy play the sex difference is not significant for either group, or overall. These are broadly in agreement with previous findings (Smith and Connolly, 1972; Smith, 1977).

The data obtained from event sampling probably give a less accurate record of time spent in fantasy play, since there were fewer sessions of recording, and the accuracy of the records is difficult to assess. Defining an episode as a coherent sequence of fantasy play, the mean number of episodes per half-morning for each group is shown in Table 9.16, together

Table 9.18. *Duration of fantasy play sequences from event sampling*

	Baseline blocks	Experimental blocks
Duration in minutes of episodes		
Group One	6.0	8.9
Group Two	4.5	7.0
Duration in minutes of each child's participation		
Group One	4.4	5.6
Group Two	3.4	5.7

with the mean number of times any child was seen in any episode. These numbers are larger for Group Two not only during the experimental blocks, agreeing with the earlier data, but also during the baseline blocks; this was not the case with the scan data. Since only two sessions of event sampling could be made for each group in the baseline blocks, variation between individual sessions may well account for this discrepancy.

Table 9.17 shows the data on number of participants, based on two measures: (a) the mean number of participants who took part in an episode for at least half its duration, and (b) the mean number of participants, averaged over each child taking part in an episode. The latter numbers are higher, as they include children who took part for only a short time. For both sets of figures, the differences between Groups One and Two are non-significant during the baseline blocks, but are significant on Mann–Whitney tests at the 5 per cent level during the experimental blocks.

Table 9.18 shows the duration, in minutes, of fantasy play sequences, based on two measures: (a) the mean duration of main episodes, and (b) the mean duration of a fantasy play sequence for each child taking part. The latter numbers are smaller as they include children who took part for only a short time. None of the differences between Groups One and Two is significant on Mann-Whitney tests.

The inferences from these data are none too clear, because there were insufficient data from the baseline blocks to give an accurate comparison with the experimental blocks. So far as the latter are concerned, the impact of the organised-activities condition seemed to be on the number of fantasy play sequences and on the number of participants, but not on the duration of episodes. The staff did discourage more episodes of fantasy play during

Table 9.19. *Mean number of different activities engaged in, per child, per session*

	B/b(1)	E/e(1–2)	E/e(3–4)	E/e(5–6)	B/b(2)
Group One					
Boys	6.5	5.1	4.9	5.0	5.5
Girls	6.1	4.2	4.2	4.0	5.3
Overall	6.3	4.6	4.5	4.5	5.4
Group Two					
Boys	6.4	5.5	6.9	6.7	7.5
Girls	5.6	4.9	6.3	6.3	6.2
Overall	6.0	5.2	6.6	6.4	6.8

Table 9.20. *Mean number of scans per child, per session, in which child was not engaged in any activity*

	B/b(1)	E/e(1–2)	E/e(3–6)	E/e(5–6)	B/b(2)
Group One					
Boys	3.1	1.9	1.0	0.7	0.3
Girls	1.5	2.3	1.1	0.7	0.7
Overall	2.3	2.1	1.0	0.7	0.5
Group Two					
Boys	3.5	2.3	1.1	0.7	0.5
Girls	2.6	1.8	0.9	0.9	0.8
Overall	3.0	2.0	1.0	0.8	0.7

Table 9.21. *Mean attention span per child, per session*

Attention span measured as mean number of consecutive scans in which child was engaged in same activity

	B/b(1)	E/e(1–2)	E/e(3–4)	E/e(5–6)	B/b(2)
Group One					
Boys	3.5	5.3	4.6	6.1	5.5
Girls	2.9	4.5	4.9	5.0	4.2
Overall	3.2	4.9	4.7	5.5	4.7
Group Two					
Boys	3.0	4.1	3.3	3.6	2.6
Girls	3.2	3.7	3.3	3.0	3.2
Overall	3.1	3.9	3.3	3.3	2.9

Table 9.22. *Means for three activity measures for each group*

	Baseline block	Experimental block
Number of different activities		
Group One	5.8	4.5
Group Two	6.4	6.1
Number of scans with no activity		
Group One	1.4	1.3
Group Two	1.8	1.3
Attention span		
Group One	4.3	5.5
Group Two	3.4	3.9

organised activities than during free play, the figures being 13 per cent and 7 per cent respectively, but these were mostly short, noisy episodes of 'monsters' or 'Daleks'. Quieter episodes of fantasy play, for example in the Wendy house, were generally left undisturbed by staff in the organised-activities condition, but fewer children were obviously available to join in as more of them were likely to be in staff-organised activities.

Scan sampling of activities ✓

Two half-morning sessions of scan sampling of activity choice were made in each block, each session consisting of scans at 2-minute intervals through a 40-minute period. Analysis of these data yielded three measures: the number of different activities each child engaged in, the number of scans in which a child was not observed in any activity, and the mean attention span (taken as mean time spent at an activity). Results are presented in tables 9.19, 9.20, and 9.21, and summarised in Table 9.22.

The data on the number of different activities engaged in are shown in detail in Table 9.19, and summarised in Table 9.22. Groups One and Two did not differ significantly in the baseline condition, but did differ ($P < 0.001$, Wilcoxon test across children) in the experimental blocks. For Group One there were significantly fewer activities engaged in per session in the experimental blocks compared with the baseline blocks ($P < 0.001$). This effect was present for boys and girls equally. For both groups there was a tendency for boys to engage in a greater number of activities per session than girls, but using the reduced subject sample this does not reach significance on Wilcoxon tests for either group or for both groups combined.

The data on the number of scans in which a child was not observed in any activity are shown in detail in Table 9.20, and summarised in Table 9.22. There were no clear or significant differences between groups, or between baseline and experimental blocks. Also, there were no consistent sex differences. There were, however, strong time effects for both groups. Children were less often observed in no activity as the project progressed, no doubt because of their increased age and experience. Comparing the first four with the last four blocks, the time effects are significant on Wilcoxon tests across children, at $P < 0.001$ for Group One and $P < 0.005$ for Group Two.

The lack of difference between the two groups for the number of scans with no activity is discrepant with the data from focal sampling, which suggests that no activity was more frequent in the organised-activity conditions of Group One. A possible explanation for this is that less stringent criteria were applied, during scan sampling, in deciding whether a child was at an activity. Since the scans had to be made quickly, a child seated with a group of children and an adult at a table activity, for example, might have been coded as at that activity in scan sampling, whereas focal sampling might have revealed so little involvement that no activity was scored. In this respect, the focal samples are probably more accurate, although the scan samples provide more in terms of absolute data. Nevertheless, given the discrepancy in results here, it would be incautious to put too much reliance on either set of findings.

The data for mean attention span are shown in detail in Table 9.21, and summarised in Table 9.22. The results are similar for both boys and girls, and are more complex than for the other two measures considered. The two groups did not differ significantly at the first baseline block, on a Wilcoxon test. However, during the experimental blocks, Group One showed a consistently longer mean attention span, significant at $P < 0.05$. This difference was maintained during the last baseline block, being significant at $P < 0.01$ (Wilcoxon tests). Although there was no overall difference between the baseline and experimental blocks for either group, the experimental sessions for Group One differed significantly from the first baseline block ($P < 0.05$).

The results for the first baseline block are probably reasonably typical, given the similar figures for both boys and girls, and the similarity to Group Two's results through the project. If this is so, then it may be concluded that the organised-activities conditions experienced by Group One brought about a general increase in the time children spent at particular activities,

Table 9.23. *Mean test scores per child on Caldwell Preschool Inventory and Peabody Picture Vocabulary test*
*** $P < 0.001$

	Mean score before	Mean score after	Mean change	Significance level before/after
Caldwell				
Group One	33.5	45.1	11.6	***
Group Two	36.8	46.7	9.9	***
		non-significant		
Peabody				
Group One	37.2	44.0	6.8	***
Group Two	38.2	45.4	7.3	***
		non-significant		

and that this increase was maintained, at least for a while, after the organised-activities condition finished and both groups experienced similar staff regimes.

Cognitive and linguistic tests

Although the main emphasis of the project was on the observation of ongoing behaviour patterns in the two kinds of nursery regime, the opportunity was also taken of administering some standardised tests to both groups of children. These were given just before the start of the first term, and again at the end of the second term. The tests used were the Caldwell Preschool Inventory and the Peabody Picture Vocabulary Test (see p. 218). The results in terms of raw scores are shown in Table 9.23. These are based on $N = 19$, because three children in Group Two had to be excluded from testing owing to shyness and non-cooperation; the three matched children in Group One were thus also dropped from the analysis. Significance levels are from Wilcoxon matched-pairs tests.

Naturally enough, over the eight-month period almost all the children showed substantial gains in scores on both tests, so that for each group, the change in 'before' and 'after' scores is highly significant. There were no significant differences between Groups One and Two, although Group Two scored slightly higher both before and after the project. Group One improved slightly more than Group Two on the Caldwell test, but slightly less on the Peabody test; neither difference approaches significance. There is therefore no clear evidence for any differential cognitive or linguistic gain by either group during the project.

Staff comments and ratings

Open-ended comments were obtained at the end of the project from Mrs B (supervisor), Mrs X, and Mrs Y (assistants). Mrs X's comments and ratings were obtained by the time she left in March, shortly before the end of the project. Staff were asked to describe their impressions of how the two groups of children had come to differ in their behaviour over the past two terms, and whether either of the programmes was 'better' in any way. Their replies are reproduced below.

Mrs B. (supervisor):

The children in organised activities have come to expect that certain demands will be made of them as regards conforming, in some measure, to the wishes of the teachers. Some of the children are extremely cooperative and possibly regard this as a special form of link and added security which they did not experience previously. A small number of children, mainly the older boys, prefer on the whole to be given a free choice, although they occasionally enjoy group games, e.g. lotto, dominoes, or activities such as pastry play and construction kits.

The children in free play seem on the whole quite happy left to their own devices, with the exception of one or two children who seemed, especially at the beginning, to need very much the close contact of an adult. In this group, activities requiring a great deal of direction from an adult, e.g. lotto, dominoes, are often neglected; the exception being when one child very familiar with the activity tries to direct it. This is not usually successful for a very long period.

On the whole I consider the free-play condition to be slightly better, in that the children select spontaneously from the activities offered, thus presumably satisfying their needs more adequately. In this way some conflict of wills is obviously avoided between staff and pupils. I feel that ideally this programme should be modified to afford the pupils periods of rougher play with large equipment, alternating with periods of quieter play with table toys, painting, etc.

Mrs X (assistant):

Group One children have grown to accept the more 'disciplined' system compared with last year's free play. Because staff are communicating with them, they now eagerly talk to staff; Group Two do not; they discuss things amongst themselves. Group One children turn to an adult with a comment or problem. Group Two children do not. The Group Two children seem more aware of themselves as a group – more socially concerned about one another – as a group they seem happier; this might be a continuation from last year, or a result of this year's conditions.

Both programmes have good points, e.g. in Group One some children benefit from adult contact if their home conditions offer little adult communication. Other children perhaps get more from a free-play group like Group Two. A mixture of both programmes would best cater for most of the children – so much depends on the individual's home situation and the kind of play and learning done there.

Mrs Y (assistant):

(More creative work seems to come from the Group Two children, when they are allowed a freer scope with the materials provided.) The girls in particular are more boisterous in this group.

I think that both programmes have something to offer but I don't feel that one is better than another. Rather, I feel that a mixture of the two programmes is ideal.

Each staff member also mentioned some children to whom the organised-activities programme was most suited, and others to whom the free-play programme was most suited. Out of 29 mentions, there were three pairs of agreement, all concerning children who were best in the free-play programme; however, there were five pairs of disagreement, mostly between Mrs B and Mrs Y. Fourteen children were mentioned only by one member of staff. In general, therefore, agreement as to which children would benefit most from which programme was not good. In particular, there seemed to be a lack of consensus as to whether a child who spent a lot of time in a particular activity or mode of behaviour should be encouraged in that, or rather encouraged to develop other aspects of his or her personality.

At the beginning and end of the project, each member of staff rated Group One and Group Two, as a whole, according to five characteristics. (All three rated Group One as *more difficult to control*, and *less pleasant to be with,* both before and after the project. At the beginning of the project, all three rated Group One as *more noisy*, and having more fights, and two rated Group One as *more creative at play*; however, by the end of the project, all three staff rated (Group One as *less noisy, having fewer fights, and less creative at play.*)

Each staff member also rated each child, on a five-point scale, for eight characteristics. The results are shown in Table 9.24, a lower rating indicating more of the labelled characteristic. Differences between groups are assessed for significance by Wilcoxon tests, for ratings from each member of staff separately.

As these results were obtained only after the project was completed, any differences could be due to initial differences between the groups, rather

Table 9.24. *Mean ratings for each group by the three staff on the project*
Results for Group One on upper line and Group Two on lower line, from 1 (high rating) to 5 (low rating)
* P < 0.05   ** P < 0.01   *** P < 0.001

	All staff	Mrs B		Mrs X	Mrs Y
Often at table play	2.82	3.05		2.72	2.68
	3.17	3.41		3.00	3.09
Aggressive	3.12	2.68	*	3.36	3.32
	3.27	3.32		3.41	3.09
Creative in play	3.00	3.23		2.88	2.91
	3.15	3.18		3.18	3.09
Plays mostly alone	3.11	3.32		3.27	2.73
	3.30	3.32		3.23	3.36
Noisy in play	3.16	2.77		3.27	3.45
	3.32	3.32		3.27	3.36
Independent, can cope	2.38	2.64		2.86	1.64
well	2.38	2.55		2.91	1.68
Affectionate to adults	3.26	3.27		3.14	3.36
and children	3.23	3.32		3.00	3.36
Cooperative	3.05	3.27	***	2.64	3.23 **
	2.05	1.64		2.50	2.00

than to the experimental conditions. In fact, however, most of the differences are non-significant. All three staff rated Group One children as being more *often at table play*, though not consistently enough for all children to reach significance. This is consistent with the observational measures, in which table play was much more frequent in Group One, though with appreciable individual differences.

Mrs B, the supervisor, also rated the Group One children as more *aggressive* at the end of the project. This is in accord with the observational data, especially those from event sampling, though not with the whole-group ratings mentioned earlier.

There are further discrepancies between the whole-group ratings and those based on individual children, with respect to being *creative in play* and *noisy in play*. The staff rated Group One as a whole as less noisy and creative at the end of the project, but the average individual ratings shown in Table 9.24 show opposite, if non-significant, trends.

No appreciable differences were found on the ratings for *playing mostly alone*, *being independent*, and *being affectionate*. However, there was general agreement that Group Two children were especially *cooperative*, more so than Group One children. This difference was significant for both Mrs B and Mrs Y. This agrees with the whole-group ratings of Group One as more difficult to control and less pleasant to be with, but these ratings were also made at the beginning of the project and thus may represent initial group differences, rather than effects of the experimental conditions.

In summary, the staff saw some benefits of both the free-play and the organised-activities conditions, and two explicitly stated that a mixture of the programmes would be desirable. All staff thought certain children would benefit particularly from one condition or the other, but with less agreement as to which children; this was probably because of differing judgments as to whether existing preferences should be strengthened in a child, or new ones encouraged.

Ratings suggested that staff perceived Group One as more troublesome and less cooperative; but this may well have been the case from the start and hence not a result of the experimental conditions. In most other cases the ratings of the two groups were not greatly different, and any trends were not very consistent across the three staff, or the two different rating methods applied.

Summary ✓

A battery of observational methods (focal, scan, and event sampling), standardised tests, and staff comments and ratings were used to assess the ongoing and cumulative effects of the regimes.

Observations of staff language showed that the three staff were interacting with the children as envisaged in the project design. They did not behave appreciably differently to the two groups in the baseline conditions, but during experimental sessions they directed very much more language to the Group One children; this was especially so in inviting children to activities and developing play ideas with them. All categories of staff language were more frequent in Group One, except for (relatively infrequent) prohibitions such as 'don't be so noisy'.

The group sociograms showed a fairly typical network of peer relationships in Group Two in the free-play regime. More than half the children had strong friendships with others, which in this group were quite markedly segregated by sex. By contrast, in Group One all the children spent an appreciable time playing with staff, many of them having particularly close relationships with one or more members of staff. Only a few children, rather more boys than girls, maintained any strong peer companionships.

Focal-sample data on companions and behaviour units substantiated this picture. In Group One there were many more verbal, visual, and physical contacts with staff, both initiated and received by children. There were correspondingly fewer verbal, visual, and physical contacts with other children. Both group and parallel play with other children were less frequent, and when group play did occur in the organised-activities condition, fewer participants tended to be involved. However, whatever the experimental conditions, the actual frequency of group play and mean subgroup size tended to increase over the two terms with the increasing age and nursery experience of the children.

Most of the increased contacts with staff made and received by children in Group One took place at the activities organised by staff for that session. Usually one or two of these three activities were sedentary table activities, and there was much more table play in Group One. The two groups did not differ in choice of many activities, such as clay, shopping, jigsaws, books, and painting, but in the organised-activities condition there was much less use of apparatus such as the climbing-frame and slide, rocking-boat, and toy chest, although these were equally often present in the two groups. Group One children were less physically active in organised activities, more often sitting at table play and exchanging objects, and less often walking, running, climbing or sliding, or engaging in gross object manipulation such as pushing and throwing. In general, they engaged in fewer different activities during a morning session.

The encouragement of Group One children to join in organised activities meant that fewer children played alone than was the case with Group Two children in free play. Sometimes, however, it seemed as though the joining in was fairly passive. Group One were more often seen watching adults, and from focal-sample data were more often scored as not being in any activity. This latter finding was not supported by scan-sample data, which may, however, have been scoring passive watching as, for example, table play. Both focal and scan data revealed a decrease in not being in any activity with time, which supports the validity of both data sets. It is suggested, however, that the increased involvement of children with staff in organised activities may not always be very active, although clearly much may depend on the particular staff involved, the number of children, and the activity in question.

As well as being less physically active generally, the Group One children in organised activities were less often laughing or making play noises, and engaged in less rough-and-tumble play. Despite a difference between the groups even in the initial baseline, both focal and scan data suggest that the further reduction during organised activities was a real one. This reduction was especially marked for the boys, who more often engage in active, rough-and-tumble play anyway. However, there is no indication of any lasting effect after the experimental conditions were over, when levels of rough-and-tumble play in Group One returned to normal levels.

Similar findings hold for the incidence of fantasy play. Both focal-and scan-sampling data agree in finding a decrease in fantasy play during organised activities (which themselves were very rarely of a fantasy nature). The event-sampling data also support this assessment; these latter data also suggest a difference in initial baseline levels, but the focal and scan data are probably more reliable here because only one period of event sampling for fantasy play was obtained in each block. The decrease in fantasy play ties in with the decrease in use of the Wendy house, and the doll and pram in the organised-activities conditions. These decreases were especially marked for girls; previous disagreement as to a possible sex difference in the frequency of fantasy play (Smith, 1977) may thus be explained by differences in staff involvement, as well as in equipment provided. The greater decrease in fantasy play for girls is probably explained by their greater attraction to the more sedentary staff activities such as table play. Noisier episodes of fantasy play, such as spacemen and monsters, were more often discouraged by staff during organised activities, but still for less than 20 per cent of such episodes. The main effect on fantasy play was not on the duration, but on the frequency of episodes, and on the number of participants.

Although most or all of these effects of the organised-activities condition seem to have been temporary, there is evidence for two more permanent effects, maintained during the final baseline period.

First, whereas aggressive behaviour remained at a fairly constant level in Group Two, there was a moderate but fairly steady increase in Group One through the experimental sessions, with a sharp increase in the final baseline session. Although based on fairly small sets of data, these trends are consistent for both sexes and for the three kinds of aggressive encounters – specific hostility, harassment, and games hostility – described by Manning *et al.* (1978). The data from focal sampling agree as to the general trend; the absence of a final baseline difference is probably ascribable to the small number of observations.

If the increase in aggression is a robust finding, it is tempting to link it to the much decreased level of peer interactions during the organised-activities session. Peer interactions increased sharply again in the final baseline, but perhaps without a matching ability to manage or avoid the escalation of minor disputes which then tended to occur.

Second, and suggesting a positive rather than a negative aspect to organised activities, the mean attention span at activities was considerably longer in this condition, and remained significantly longer in the final baseline period. Staff did indeed try to get children to concentrate at tasks during organised activities, and it seems as though this endeavour had an impact which was more than transient. Of course there is no virtue in a child spending excessive amounts of time at one activity, but there is a modest trend towards increased attention span in the preschool and early school years, and the modest but significant increase for Group One found here is of this order of magnitude.

It was also expected that the organised-activities group might show a differential increase in performance on cognitive and linguistic tests. No evidence for such an effect was found.

The two methods of obtaining staff ratings – on the whole group and on individual children – yielded rather mixed results. Group One was perceived as more difficult to control and less cooperative, but this may have been the case throughout the project, from the initial baseline, and hence not owing to the experimental conditions *per se*.

Staff comments on the practice of the two regimes suggested that a mixture of the two might well be best. Such a practice is of course often followed in nursery classes and other preschool institutions. Our findings offer some support for this view. The organised-activities condition has the advantage of greater verbal interaction with adults, encouragement of specific activities, and perhaps increased concentration. The free-play condition has the advantage of more child–child interaction, with more spontaneous fantasy play sequences, and larger subgroups of children engaged in group play. There is more gross physical activity, more rough-and-tumble play, and perhaps a more stable control of conflict situations with peers. This tends to point to a balance of advantages and disadvantages, centred around the differential choice of adults or peers for social interaction. A combination of both may well be the best.

However, the relative emphasis on adult or peer interaction in the preschool may also depend much on the backgrounds of children and their particular needs. A difficulty here is a possible lack of consensus on such needs. The staff working on our project all felt that certain children benefitted especially from one or the other condition, but showed very little agreement as to *which* children. Should one encourage strong aptitudes and preferences, or rather aim for a diversity of abilities? The further implications of the results of this study will be considered in more detail in Chapter 11, together with other relevant research reviewed in Chapter 8 and the results of research on staff:child ratio reported in Chapter 10.

10 Variations in staff:child ratio in structured-activities conditions

This chapter describes experiments designed to examine the effect of varying the staff:child ratio on communication between staff and children during structured-activities conditions. Two separate studies were carried out during consecutive terms, these being the first two terms of the third year of the project (see Chapter 2). Staff:child ratios were varied by changing both the number of children present (as in Chapter 4) and the number of staff available. Observations were mainly made on individual staff members, backed up by some shorter observations on children. Ratings from the staff of their impressions of these conditions were also obtained.

Population sample and variations in number of children

During the two terms the children present were those for whom details have already been given in Chapter 4; the only difference being that the investigation described earlier was based on data from the first half of each morning, used for free play, while the present investigation was based on data from the second half of each morning, used for structured activities. Only the main points are summarised again here. The numbers of children were varied by having a third group of children (Group Three) attending on Wednesday and Thursday mornings. Thus on Tuesdays only Group One children were present, but on Thursdays Groups One and Three together formed a larger group. Similarly, on Fridays only Group Two were present, but on Wednesdays Groups Two and Three together formed a larger group. During the first term Group One consisted of 20 children, Group Two had 22, while Group Three had 12. Mean attendance was 85 per cent. During the second term Groups One, Two and Three each had 14 children. Mean attendance was 88 per cent. Fuller details of group compositions can be seen in Tables 4.1 and 4.2. Background details for each child are available in Appendix A.

Organisation of activities and variations in numbers of staff

The organised-activities setting used in these studies varied somewhat from that described in Chapter 9, where a direct comparison with free-play conditions was made. In the present studies, the structured activities followed the free play, and took place in the second part of the morning, from 11.00 to 11.45. During the milk break, most of the large apparatus (climbing-frame, Wendy house, tricycle, toy chest, rocking-boat) available in free play was put away. At the end of the milk break, either two or three localised activity areas were organised, depending on whether two or three staff would be actively involved in the session.

It was decided to vary the number of staff, as well as number of children, in order to get a greater spread in the range of staff:child ratios studied. Either all three staff actively worked with the children during organised-activities, or, on other mornings, only two were available (the third worked on her own in the kitchen, away from the play area).

The activity areas organised remained constant for each half-morning, but varied from session to session as would naturally happen in preschool practice. However, to reduce the effects of variations in the actual activity materials on patterns of staff–child interaction, one activity area was kept fairly constant, and it was at this area that the staff member to be observed for that half-morning worked with the children. This activity area was necessarily fairly diversified, so as to maintain interest from session to session. It also provided a stable variety of interactional contexts for observation. The activity area consisted of a table or tables with either sand trays, water trays, or pastry; a painting area, either at easels or on the floor, perhaps painting boxes; and a table or tables with small toys, such as jigsaws, crayons and paper, Lego. The staff member concerned moved around these as she saw fit.

Each other member of staff (one or two, depending on the staffing condition) also had her own activity area in which to work with children. These tended to be more specialised than the general activity areas just described, but were of the kind often found in preschools; for example, making pictures with paper and glue; playing picture lotto; miming stories; making models with plastic straws and shapes.

Each staff member stayed at her activity area for the 45-minute period, and the children could choose which area they went to. However, staff were asked to encourage children to circulate now and then from one area to another, and not to allow too many children to concentrate on one activity. Usually circulation occurred naturally anyway, but occasionally staff had to ask some children to leave a popular activity until later in the morning;

Table 10.1. *Staff : child ratios in Terms One and Two*

	Mean number of children	Approximate staff : child ratio	
		Two staff	Three staff
Term One			
Tuesdays (Group One)	17.9	1 : 9	1 : 6
Fridays (Group Two)	19.3	1 : 10	1 : 6
Thursdays (Groups One and Three)	27.9	1 : 14	1 : 9
Wednesdays (Groups Two and Three)	28.6	1 : 14	1 : 10
Term Two			
Tuesdays (Group One)	12.3	1 : 6	1 : 4
Fridays (Group Two)	12.2	1 : 6	1 : 4
Thursdays (Groups One and Three)	24.4	1 : 12	1 : 8
Wednesdays (Groups Two and Three)	25.0	1 : 12	1 : 8

and although most children circulated, a few did tend to stay at one activity for the duration of the session. Clearly staff could only partially control this, so these factors produce some distortion in the results, probably small and fairly random in nature, which could not be avoided without introducing a quite unnatural degree of regimentation. The largest non-random effect is likely to be caused by preferences of certain children for certain staff members, but this would be offset if combined results for all staff members are considered.

The amount of equipment available in the activity areas – for example, the number of tables put out for small toys, the number of easels, etc. – was varied so as to be roughly commensurate with the number of children present. In Term one this meant a ratio of 2 : 3 for small and large groups, and for Term two, a ratio of 1 : 2. As the activities were generally fairly sedentary (the children having had plenty of active play in the first half of the morning) it was not felt necessary to vary space proportionately, and the whole hall was always available for use.

Staff : child ratios and observational schedules

Considering the actual numbers of children present (i.e. taking mean attendance into account), the range of staff : child ratios obtained from the variations in both numbers of children and numbers of staff is shown in Table 10.1. The range was from about 1:14 to 1:6 in Term One, and from 1:12 to 1:4 in Term Two. This was felt to correspond to a reasonably characteristic range of ratios as found in many British and American nursery and preschool institutions (see Chapter 8).

The main source of data was based on focal samples of individual staff members, through the duration of a half-morning. This procedure was used because it was felt that there might be appreciable changes in the 'load' a particular staff member would have during this session. If variations during a half-morning were likely to be larger than variations between half-mornings (remembering that the staff member observed was always at the same, mixed-activity area), then samples taken through the duration of entire half-mornings were judged to be the most appropriate method.

No observations were made during the first three weeks of the first term, to allow adequate time for the children to settle in; similarly for the first week of the second term. Six weeks of each term were taken up with observations on staff, two weeks for each staff member. Thus each of the three staff members was observed once, in each staffing condition (two or three), per group size condition, and for each group. This meant a total of eight observations of each staff member each term. Each observation lasted 40 minutes, from about 11.05 to 11.45.

Another four weeks of each term were set aside for observations on children. The observations on the staff could give only a partial view of the impact of staff:child ratios, as some children might interact very little with staff even when ratios were very high. A complementary record of observations on children seemed necessary. Because of the large numbers of children in some conditions, these samples had to be short. One-minute focal samples on individual children were used; in this way it was possible to get two such 1-minute samples for each child, in each staffing condition, per group size condition. This was done for each term.

At the end of each half-morning, each member of staff who had participated rated the session according to three characteristics. In addition, at the end of each term, each member of staff rated all the children according to five characteristics.

Observational methods and rating procedures

Observations of staff communications to children

The observer positioned himself in the mixed activities area, and remained reasonably close to the staff member being observed. As in other studies, the children were used to the observer's presence, and paid very little attention to him.

The staff member was observed for the 40-minute period described earlier, and her communications with the children were noted. The observational procedure was piloted and practised during the first three weeks of the first term. In order actually to record what was said, a radio microphone would have been necessary, and while perhaps desirable, the time needed to transcribe the recordings would have been prohibitive, given the volume of data to be collected. Given time considerations, a pen-and-paper recording method was used. This meant that actual speech could not be recorded, but it was possible to record which children a staff member spoke to, and which children spoke to her, together with information on the number of conversational bouts and the broad subject matter of the conversation.

Preprinted sheets having five vertical columns were used to record the conversations; an example of a completed sheet is given in Appendix C. Typically, one such sheet covered one or two minutes of the sample period. The time was recorded in the left-hand column. The second column from the left was used to record an utterance by the staff member, and the third column from the left to record utterances by a child or children, directed to the staff member. The initials of the children concerned were written in so that they could be identified.

An *utterance* was taken as a group of words linked together by the speaker, meaningful in itself and generally demarcated by a pause; typically it was a statement or a sentence. A one-word utterance on its own, such as 'yes' or 'look', was included as a separate utterance if it was judged to affect the sequence of interaction, or to be very clearly intended to do so. A clear head nod or head shake was also regarded in this way. For example, if a child said 'shall I paint this blue?', looking at the staff member, who then nodded her head, followed by the child saying 'where's the blue paint?', then the head nod was regarded as fully equivalent to a spoken 'yes' and was treated as such in data recording and analysis.

On the other hand, some short, usually one-word utterances, did not seem to affect the sequence of interaction or even be likely to do so. Vocal 'yes' or 'um' made while a child was in the process of speaking, and not serving to interrupt the child or to move the child to a new utterance, were disregarded.

Repeated utterances or repetitions of meaning were regarded as separate, provided a gap of some several seconds intervened. (It was obviously not possible to time this exactly, so the observer made a judgment on this sort of criterion.) A direct sentence, 'that's blue, isn't it?', would be scored as one utterance. However, if the staff member said 'that's blue' followed by a pause in which the child said nothing, followed by 'isn't it?', this would be scored as two successive utterances.

Consecutive utterances by a staff member to a child, without reply, were indicated by vertical lines with a horizontal stroke for each utterance, in the second column. Consecutive utterances by a child to a staff member, without reply, were indicated by vertical lines with a horizontal stroke for each utterance, in the third column.

A number of consecutive utterances between a staff member and a child, judged to be continuous by virtue of the short time intervals and by the position and orientation of both, was regarded as a *conversation* of linked utterances. Conversations were indicated by zigzag lines between the second and third columns (from staff member to child, and vice versa).

While often a staff member talked to only one child, sometimes more than one child was addressed. If each child was named separately, as in 'Simon, Emma, take the boxes back', this was scored as two utterances, one to Simon and one to Emma. Usually this was not the case. The utterance was then labelled as a *general* utterance. It could be replied to by a specific child, of course, in which case the reply was linked to the general utterance by an oblique line, and could start a zigzag conversation record.

It was also possible to record the broad context of the utterances and conversations. The great majority of these were concerned with the ongoing activities, and were considered as being in a *play* context. Two exceptions were noted on the record-sheets, however. If a conversation was about routine matters, such as washing hands (after painting), changing aprons, going to the toilet, changing activities, then these utterances were labelled as a *routine* context. If a conversation involved direct prohibitions, for example to stop making a noise, or making a mess, this was labelled as a *prohibition* context. Such utterances were indicated by writing R or P in the fourth column of the record sheets.

The fifth column of the sheets was used for noting which children were currently with the staff member, and what activity was involved. However, recording these details was given low priority, the main intention being to record the utterances accurately. Thus although these extra details were often obtained, they were not considered systematic or accurate enough to use. Similar considerations applied to the time records in the first column.

Each 40-minute focal sample provided some thirty completed record-sheets to analyse. In initial coding of these sheets, seven categories of statement or conversation were distinguished:

general statement: a general utterance, or series of utterances, made by staff and not replied to;

staff statement: an utterance, or series of utterances, made by staff to a particular child, and not replied to;

staff-initiated conversation: a conversation initiated by staff to a particular child, with at least one reply;

general conversation: a conversation initiated from a general utterance by staff, replied to by particular child and then by staff to that child;

child-initiated conversation: a conversation initiated by particular child to staff, with at least one reply;

child comment: an utterance made by child in response to a general utterance by staff, or utterance made to another child, and not replied to by staff;

child statement: an utterance, or series of utterances, made by particular child to staff, and not replied to.

For each category, it was noted (a) which child was involved, (b) the number of separate utterances made by staff and child in a statement or conversation, and (c) whether the context was play, routine, or prohibition. All record-sheets were categorised by one person, and careful checks were made on the consistency of coding.

All the observations were made by one observer. The main observer effect is likely to be one of drift, i.e. of becoming more strict or more lenient about scoring certain categories, or more practised at noticing certain utterances, during the two-term duration of the project. This could affect comparisons between the two terms, and could also affect comparisons between the three staff members (observations not being balanced between them for time of term). However, observer drift should not affect comparisons of staff:child ratio *per se*, since for a given staff member comparisons of small and large numbers of children were made in the same week, and comparisons of different staffing conditions usually in successive weeks.

The observer making all the records knew the children very well, so the recording of their initials was very rapid. It was possible to carry out a test of inter-observer concordance with another observer during a 20 minute period at the end of the first term (mid-point of study). The second observer had also spent some time in the playgroup, and knew the children well. Records were made simultaneously but separately by the two observers, each record being coded independently at different times by a third person coding all the record-sheets.

Concordance was assessed as percentage agreement, divided by agreement

Table 10.2. *Inter-observer concordance (percentage) for categories of staff–child communication, from focal-staff samples*

Figures in brackets for agreement on particular child addressed, in addition to category of communication

	Concordance (per cent)		
	Number of occurrences	Number of staff utterances	Number of child utterances
General statement	50(50)	33(33)	—
Staff statement	78(50)	96(35)	—
Staff-initiated conversation	100(69)	98(78)	100(79)
General conversation		Insufficient data for calculation	
Child-initiated conversation	96(96)	100(89)	93(79)
Child comment		Insufficient data for calculation	
Child statement	45(45)	—	60(60)

plus disagreement, both for overall occurrence of categories, and for occurrence of categories with specific children. The overall agreement over the seven categories was 87 per cent. Concordances for specific categories, and taking children's identities into account, is shown in Table 10.2. It is very satisfactory for *staff-* and *child-initiated conversations.* Here a staff member is conversing with one child, and there is relatively little ambiguity in recording. Concordance for *general conversations* and for *child comment*, was not calculated as too few instances were observed for results to be meaningful; these categories were also relatively rare in the general data and little analysis was done on them. Concordance for *staff statements* is satisfactory. Concordance for *general statements* and *child statements* is lower; not surprisingly, it is easier to miscode a general utterance, or to miss a child's statement, if one is focussed on the staff member.

Concordance for the context of each category, given agreement on the category, was 98 per cent for *play*, and 86 per cent for *routine*. Concordance for *prohibition* was 100 per cent, but was based on only two occurrences.

Observations of children's communications

While making the 1-minute focal samples of children, the observer positioned himself close to the child concerned. Usually this had no discernible effect on the child's behaviour. The children were sampled in random order.

Records were made on the same record-sheets as were used for the focal-staff samples. However, the second column was now used for utterances made by the focal child, and the third column for utterances made by other children, or a staff member, to the focal child. Play noises, or vocalisations not directed to any one child, were disregarded. The context was noted as play, routine, or prohibition, as before. In addition, at the end of each sample the number of other children present with the focal child at a given activity was noted. This included both children in group play and those in parallel play with that child (i.e. close by, and using the same materials).

In the coding of the sheets, eight categories were used:

> *statement to staff*: an utterance, or series of utterances, made by focal child to staff, and not replied to;
> *conversation to staff*: a conversation initiated by focal child to staff, with at least one reply;
> *conversation from staff*: a conversation initiated by staff member to focal child, with at least one reply;
> *statement from staff*: an utterance, or series of utterances, made by staff member to focal child, and not replied to;
> *statement to child*: an utterance, or series of utterances, made by focal child to other child, and not replied to;
> *conversation to child*: a conversation initiated by focal child to other child, with at least one reply;
> *conversation from child*: a conversation initiated by other child to focal child, with at least one reply;
> *statement from child*: an utterance, or series of utterances, made by other child to focal child, and not replied to.

For each category it was noted (a) which other child or staff member was involved, (b) the number of separate utterances made by each child or staff member, and (c) whether the context was play, routine, or prohibition.

All the observations were made by one observer. A session of inter-observer concordance was carried out at the end of the first term with a second observer, during which twenty 1-minute samples were made simultaneously but separately. Concordance was assessed as for the focal staff samples. Although twenty samples were obtained, numbers per category were still rather small, so concordance was averaged for all categories involving *statements* without replies and for all categories involving *conversations*.

For *statements* without replies, concordance for number of occurrences was 80 per cent. this was reduced to 40 per cent if the identity of the other person was also taken into account. Concordance for number of utterances was 67 per cent, reduced to 33 per cent if identity of the other person was also taken into account.

For *conversations*, concordance for number of occurrences was 89 per cent, reduced to 70 per cent if identity of the other person was taken into account. Concordance for number of utterances by the focal child was 85 per cent, and for number of utterances by the other person, 79 per cent; these were reduced to 60 per cent and 68 per cent if the identity of the other person was taken into account.

In all the samples, both observers agreed in classifying the communications as in a play context.

Staff ratings of differing staff: child ratio conditions

At the end of each morning session, each of the staff members was asked to rate her feelings about the structured-activities half of the morning, which had just finished, according to three characteristics. These were *enjoyable/not enjoyable, exhausting/not exhausting,* and *effective/not effective.* When rating a session, a tick was put somewhere along a 10 cm line between the two polar adjectives, and was later measured for its distance from the end point.

On occasions when only two staff members were actively involved with the children, only they were asked to rate the session. Otherwise all three rated the session.

Staff ratings of children

At the end of each term each of the three staff members was asked to rate each of the children from 1 to 5 according to three characteristics. The categories used were:

> *sociable/mature/enjoy group play – shy/easily upset/play alone;*
> *aggressive/naughty/possessive – quiet/docile/well-behaved;*
> *friendly/talkative to staff – not particularly friendly/talkative to staff;*

these were chosen as representing commonly recurring clusters of constructs used by nursery staff in describing children.

In addition, each staff member rated each child as getting either *more* or *less than their fair share of attention* in structured activities.

Results

Types of staff–child communication

The results are first presented briefly when averaged over all the sessions, for both terms and both groups, to give a baseline on which the effects of the experimental variations can be better assessed. Overall, children initiated 51.4 per cent of communications, and staff 48.6 per cent. However, the staff made 58.4 per cent of the utterances, the children only 41.6 per cent. As Table 10.3 shows, *child-initiated conversations* made up over one-third of the occurrences of communications and provided over half the number of utterances. *Staff-initiated conversations* were only about half as frequent, although on average they were slightly longer – involving about seven utterances rather than six. Of the 48 sessions observed, *staff-initiated conversations* were longer on average than *child-initiated conversations* in 35 of them; significant at $P < 0.01$ (sign test). The last column in Table 10.3 shows the ratio of staff to child utterances in conversations. From this it can be calculated that the average *child-initiated conversation* consisted of 2.9 child utterances and 3.2 staff utterances. The average *staff-initiated conversation* consisted of 4.9 staff utterances and 2.4 child utterances. The average *general conversation* had 2.6 staff utterances and 2.5 child utterances. The ratio of staff to child utterances was greater for *staff-initiated* than *child-initiated conversations* in all 48 of the sessions observed.

Conversations were of course longer than statements (which received no reply), although the latter were sometimes repeated, so that the mean number of utterances per statement exceeds one.

Two categories were relatively infrequent – *general conversation*, and *child comment*. These two categories were also of unknown reliability. It did not seem sensible to lump them together with other categories, but there were not enough data for meaningful analysis by groups, terms, and session conditions. The data in these two categories (totalling less than 8 per cent of occurrences, and less than 5 per cent of utterances) were dropped from any further analysis.

Table 10.4 shows the occurrence of the five main categories of communication, separately for Groups One and Two, and showing individual totals for terms and staff. The distribution of categories over Groups One and Two was similar. There was also not much change from Term One to Term Two. There were, however, fewer *child statements* (without reply) in Term Two, consistent for all three staff in both groups; this held for 20 out of 24 matched sessions between Terms One and Two, significant at $P < 0.01$ (sign test). There was also a tendency for *conversations* to get longer, but this was not so consistent over staff or sessions. The three staff members,

Table 10.3. *Totals for number of communications in each category, and number of utterances, from focal-staff samples*

	Communications		Utterances	Ratio of utterances to communications	Ratio of staff utterances to child utterances
	Number	(Percentage)			
Child-initiated conversation	3,617	(34.2)	22,188 (50.6)	6.13	1.095
Staff-initiated conversation	1,752	(16.6)	12,855 (29.3)	7.34	2.050
General conversation	266	(5.4)	1,359 (3.1)	5.11	1.050
Staff statement	1,837	(17.4)	3,247 (7.4)	1.77	—
Child statement	1,553	(14.7)	2,176 (5.0)	1.40	—
General statement	968	(9.2)	1,487 (3.4)	1.54	—
Child comment	569	(2.5)	590 (1.3)	1.04	—
Total	10,562		43,902		

Table 10.4. *Totals per term for number of communications in each category*

Separate totals for Groups One and Two, for Terms One and Two, and for the three staff members; mean numbers of utterances per communication in brackets

	Term One				Term Two			
	Overall	Miss C	Mrs Y	Mrs Z	Overall	Miss C	Mrs Y	Mrs Z
Group One								
Child-initiated conversation	959 (5.87)	277 (6.30)	290 (5.98)	392 (5.35)	838 (6.42)	238 (6.00)	301 (6.50)	299 (6.73)
Staff-initiated conversation	450 (6.67)	142 (6.43)	194 (7.25)	114 (6.35)	445 (7.55)	152 (6.83)	164 (9.05)	129 (6.73)
Staff statement	467 (1.79)	145 (1.70)	176 (1.82)	146 (1.83)	410 (1.80)	151 (1.62)	117 (1.72)	142 (2.06)
Child statement	482 (1.39)	172 (1.33)	149 (1.50)	161 (1.36)	306 (1.45)	95 (1.57)	132 (1.43)	79 (1.43)
General statement	202 (1.54)	77 (1.73)	77 (1.47)	48 (1.41)	270 (1.50)	142 (1.67)	64 (1.46)	64 (1.38)
Total communications	2,560	813	886	861	2,269	778	778	713
Total utterances	10,433	3,265	3,795	3,373	10,424	3,106	3,935	3,383
Group Two								
Child-initiated conversation	980 (5.75)	264 (5.63)	322 (6.10)	394 (5.50)	840 (6.60)	231 (6.50)	278 (6.68)	331 (6.58)
Staff-initiated conversation	412 (7.55)	116 (8.80)	185 (6.65)	111 (7.15)	445 (7.60)	143 (7.18)	162 (8.60)	140 (6.95)
Staff statement	507 (1.71)	122 (1.67)	166 (1.65)	219 (1.80)	453 (1.78)	140 (1.61)	165 (1.84)	148 (1.83)
Child statement	430 (1.41)	163 (1.31)	132 (1.63)	135 (1.35)	335 (1.36)	119 (1.40)	120 (1.38)	96 (1.26)
General statement	200 (1.56)	74 (1.78)	87 (1.46)	39 (1.31)	296 (1.54)	161 (1.62)	75 (1.43)	60 (1.24)
Total communications	2,529	739	892	898	2,369	794	800	775
Total utterances	10,444	3,053	3,807	3,584	10,642	3,186	3,833	3,623

Table 10.5. *Number of communications in each category from focal-staff samples*

Separate results for different sizes of group, for Groups One and Two, and Terms One and Two; mean number of utterances per communication in brackets

	Term One		Term Two		Term One		Term Two	
	Small group	Large group	Small group	Large group	Small group	Large group	Small group	Large group
Child-initiated conversation	460 (5.80)	499 (5.95)	385 (6.70)	453 (6.15)	473 (5.80)	507 (5.70)	395 (7.05)	445 (6.15)
Staff-initiated conversation	219 (6.65)	231 (6.70)	230 (8.20)	215 (6.90)	216 (9.05)	196 (6.05)	219 (9.20)	226 (6.00)
Staff statement	241 (1.81)	226 (1.78)	180 (1.75)	230 (1.85)	191 (1.80)	316 (1.62)	169 (1.83)	284 (1.74)
Child statement	228 (1.38)	254 (1.41)	126 (1.44)	180 (1.46)	195 (1.42)	235 (1.41)	138 (1.33)	197 (1.40)
General statement	118 (1.54)	84 (1.54)	132 (1.45)	138 (1.56)	99 (1.54)	101 (1.59)	98 (1.45)	198 (1.63)
Total communications	1,266	1,294	1,053	1,216	1,174	1,355	1,019	1,350
Total utterances	5,062	5,371	5,242	5,182	5,408	5,036	5,466	5,176

Miss C, Mrs Y, and Mrs Z, were also reasonably similar in the types of communication they engaged in; the most noticeable tendency was for Mrs Z to take part in relatively more *child-initiated* than *staff-initiated conversations*, compared with the other staff.

Table 10.5 shows the main analyses for size of group, and Table 10.7 for number of staff present, summing over the separate scores for the three staff members. The effects of the two variables of size of group and number of staff present are analysed separately, using sign tests over sessions matched for term, group, and staff member observed, giving 24 matched sessions for each variable.

Effects of size of group

The significant results for size of group can be summarised as follows from Table 10.5: there were more communications generally in larger group conditions (19 out of 24 sessions, $P < 0.01$, sign test), more *staff-initiated* communications (18 out of 24, $P < 0.05$), and more *child-initiated* communications (18 out of 24, $P < 0.05$). In particular, there were more *child statements* (20 out of 24, $P < 0.01$), the difference for other particular categories being non-significant.

Communications tended to be shorter in large group conditions [17 out of 24, $P < 0.1$), and this was most significant for *staff-initiated conversations* (18 out of 24, $P < 0.05$). As a result, although there were more communications, the number of utterances did not differ significantly for staff or children.

Thus although communications were more numerous in large groups compared with small groups, this was at the expense of the length of the conversations. Also, the increase in communications was small relative to the changes in staff:child ratio. In Term One the number of children increased by 50 per cent from the small to the large group, but the corresponding increase in number of communications was only 9 per cent (averaged over Groups One and Two). Staff-initiated communications (conversations and statements) increased by 6 per cent, and staff utterances actually fell by 2 per cent. In Term Two the number of children in the large group was twice that in the small group, but the corresponding increase in number of communications was only 24 per cent. Staff-initiated communications increased by 26 per cent, and staff utterances actually fell by 4 per cent.

All these figures, being based on observations of staff, mean that although the staff made more communications (albeit shorter ones) in large group conditions, individual children would on average have had fewer com-

Table 10.6. *Mean number of conversations with staff per child, and range for individual children*

Significance levels from *t* tests over children
* *P* < 0.05   ** *P* < 0.01

	Term One		Term Two	
	Small group	Large group	Small group	Large group
Group One				
Mean	34.2	28.4 **	44.3	26.6 *
Range	9–72	4–68	25–89	11–42
Group Two				
Mean	31.6	22.2 **	43.6	25.2 *
Range	10–66	2–59	9–77	10–44

munications with staff when in a larger group. This can best be brought out by tabulating data only for those children common to both the small and large group conditions. This has been done in Table 10.6 for the number of *conversations* (both *staff-* and *child-initiated*) which each child had with the staff members observed. The means are shown and also the range over children, indicating the considerable inequality in this measure. Some children clearly had many more conversations with staff than others.

The statistics in Table 10.6 are based on matched *t* tests across children, and show that an individual child would, on average, get fewer conversations with a staff member when in a large group, almost, although not quite, to the extent that the staff:child ratio had deteriorated.

A further question is whether the distribution of staff conversations with children is affected by the group size variations. Was the inequality magnified by worse staff:child ratios? This was examined by obtaining the variance ratio for numbers of conversations in the large group compared with that in the small group conditions (having normalised the two sets of scores in terms of means). A variance ratio greater than unity suggests greater inequality in a larger than in a smaller group. In Term One the *F* ratio was 1.32 for Group One and 1.53 for Group Two; in Term Two it was 1.06 for Group One and 0.79 for Group Two. None of these *F* ratios is significant. Three are greater than unity, notably those in Term One. Perhaps the staff were less experienced at coping with the group size variations earlier in the year, in terms of contacting the quieter children, but this interpretation is speculative. On the whole, the inequality of contacts was not greatly affected by the group size variations.

Effects of number of staff present

The significant results for number of staff can be summarised as follows from Table 10.7: there tended to be more communications generally when only two staff rather than three were present (17 sessions out of 24, $P < 0.1$), and particularly more *child-initiated* communications (18 sessions out of 24, $P < 0.05$). There tended to be more *child-initiated conversations* (17 sessions out of 24, $P < 0.1$), and there were more *child statements* (19 sessions out of 24, $P < 0.01$).

With fewer staff the number of utterances also increased, both for staff utterances (18 sessions out of 24, $P < 0.05$) and child utterances (18 sessions out of 24, $P < 0.05$). There was still a tendency for *staff-initiated conversations* to be shorter (17 sessions out of 24, $P < 0.1$).

As was the case with varying size of group, the increase in utterances when fewer staff were present did not compensate for the worsening of staff: child ratio by a factor of 33 per cent. In Term One the number of communications involving the member of staff observed increased by 20 per cent. Staff-initiated communications increased by 12 per cent, and staff utterances by only 5 per cent. In Term Two the number of communications increased by 11 per cent. Staff-initiated communications increased by 12 per cent and staff utterances by 12 per cent. While significant, these increases would not be enough to compensate for the decrease in staff numbers from three to two. Individual children would have fewer conversations when only two staff were present. The magnitude of the effect is more difficult to assess reliably, however, since further calculations would need to assume that the staff members were all equivalent and that communications per staff member could be multiplied by three or two to give indications of the total amount of staff–child communication in the playgroup. Since the observed staff member was in a somewhat different context of mixed activities from the other(s), this assumption might be questioned.

Content of staff–child communications

The content of communications had been classified as *play*, *routine*, or *prohibition*. The percentage of each of these categories, split between Groups One and Two and Terms One and Two, is shown in Table 10.8. Most communications were scored as *play*, which was interpreted in a broad

Table 10.7. *Number of communications per category from focal-staff samples for different number of staff present*
Separate results for Groups One and Two, and Terms One and Two; mean number of utterances per communication in brackets

| | Group One | | | | Group Two | | | |
| | Term One | | Term Two | | Term One | | Term Two | |
	Three staff	Two staff	Three staff	Two staff	Three staff	Two staff	Three staff	Two staff
Child-initiated conversation	433 (6.00)	526 (5.75)	419 (6.05)	419 (6.80)	426 (6.20)	554 (5.30)	407 (6.85)	433 (6.35)
Staff-initiated conversation	209 (6.55)	241 (6.80)	211 (7.80)	234 (7.30)	203 (8.75)	209 (6.35)	208 (7.60)	237 (7.60)
Staff statement	215 (1.91)	252 (1.68)	174 (1.83)	236 (1.77)	246 (1.71)	261 (1.71)	176 (1.87)	277 (1.76)
Child statement	206 (1.47)	276 (1.31)	143 (1.29)	163 (1.61)	191 (1.41)	239 (1.42)	133 (1.34)	202 (1.39)
General statement	106 (1.66)	96 (1.42)	163 (1.43)	107 (1.58)	76 (1.59)	124 (1.54)	161 (1.61)	135 (1.48)
Total communications	1,169	1,391	1,110	1,159	1,142	1,387	1,085	1,284
Total utterances	4,865	5,568	4,946	5,478	5,199	5,245	5,076	5,566

Table 10.8. *Percentage play, routine, or prohibition communications*

	Term One			Term Two		
	Play	Routine	Prohibition	Play	Routine	Prohibition
Group One	87.3	8.5	4.2	89.6	6.8	3.6
Group Two	84.5	10.0	5.5	90.6	6.0	3.4
Overall	85.9	9.2	4.9	90.1	6.4	3.5

sense. *Routine* communications were 10 per cent or less, and *prohibitions* usually under 5 per cent of the total. It should be borne in mind here that recordings were made only after equipment was out and before it was put away; in other circumstances the percentages might well be higher.

The relatively small numbers of *routine* and *prohibition* communications make it unrealistic to examine separate staff totals. These are added, for purposes of comparing the content of communications in the different sizes of group and staffing conditions, results for which are shown in Table 10.9.

It is clear from Table 10.9 that both *routine* and *prohibition* communications showed a proportionate increase when the staff:child ratio worsened, either by larger group size or fewer staff. By comparing 24 matched sessions as before, the overall trend for an increase in *routine* communications was significant for group size (19 sessions out of 24, $P < 0.01$), and nearly so for staffing condition (17 out of 24, $P < 0.1$). In the case of *prohibitions*, it was also significant for group size (19 out of 24, $P < 0.01$), and nearly so for staffing condition (17 out of 24, $P < 0.1$). These increases were broadly similar for Groups One and Two and for the two terms.

Individual differences among children

Individual children varied greatly not only in how often they communicated with staff, but also in the content of the communications. Some children seemed to receive prohibitions especially often, for example. To examine this in more detail, correlations were made across six variables separately for the small and large group sizes, of Groups One and Two, in Terms One and Two; this gave eight correlation matrices; results are shown in Table 10.10.

Older children generally initiated more communications to staff; the mean correlation is 0.41, and all eight separate coefficients are positive, four being significant. They also tended to receive more communications from staff; the mean correlation is 0.28, seven coefficients being positive, three

Table 10.9. *Percentage of routine or prohibition communications for different sizes of group and staffing conditions*

	Term One		Term Two		Term One		Term Two	
	Small group	Large group	Small group	Large group	Three staff	Two staff	Three staff	Two staff
Group One								
Routine	7.2	9.8	5.2	8.3	6.8	10.0	5.0	8.6
Prohibition	2.3	6.1	4.7	7.3	3.9	4.5	2.8	4.5
Group Two								
Routine	7.7	12.5	3.1	4.1	8.0	12.1	5.3	6.9
Prohibition	6.6	4.5	2.3	4.4	5.0	5.8	2.7	4.2

significant. There was no consistent relationship between age and receiving routine or prohibition communications.

There was a very slight but consistent tendency for girls to make more communications to staff than boys; although the mean correlation is only −0.09, it is negative in seven out of eight cases. Girls did not receive more communications from staff, however. Boys received more prohibitions, the mean correlation being 0.24; seven coefficients are positive, three significant.

Most of the remaining between-category correlations are positive, suggesting that on the whole children who make many communications to staff also tend to receive many, including routine and prohibition communications. This suggests an overall factor of verbal interaction. Some children interacted verbally with staff a lot, in all ways; these tended to be older children. Between the sexes, there was a slight tendency for girls to initiate more communications with staff, but not to receive more; boys tended to receive more prohibitions.

Types of communication: focal-child samples

The focal-child samples give data on both staff–child and child–child communications. The results for staff–child communications will have a different perspective from the corresponding results obtained from focal-staff samples, since the latter considered staff equally and identified mainly the children who interacted a lot with the staff, whereas the focal-child samples considered all the children equally.

The overall results from the focal-child samples, for all the sessions and groups, and both terms, are shown in Table 10.11. All eight categories occurred reasonably frequently, but communications with staff were more frequent than with other children – 55.2 per cent compared with 44.7 per cent. *Conversations with staff* tended to be a little longer than *conversations with children*, and in terms of utterances, those to or from staff constituted 64.3 per cent of the total, those to or from other children 35.7 per cent.

The number of utterances observed in conversations averaged less than the corresponding data from Table 10.3 using focal-staff samples. The sample period of 1 minute meant that long conversations were not picked up, and this may well explain this discrepancy.

As the number of occurrences in particular categories became relatively small when split between groups, terms, and staff:child ratio, it was decided to collapse the eight categories into four for further analysis, by ignoring distinctions as to who initiated a communication. The four categories thus were: *statements to/from staff, conversations to/from staff, statements to/from*

Table 10.10. Correlations between age, sex, and types of communication, for eight separate groups

Age in months
Sex coded as dichotomous variable (1 for boy, 0 for girl)
* P < 0.05 ** P < 0.01

	Mean correlation	Term One				Term Two			
		Group One		Group Two		Group One		Group Two	
		Small group	Large group	Small group	Large group	Small group	Large group	Small group	Large group
Age and child initiate	0.41	0.55*	0.52**	0.30	0.42*	0.45	0.16	0.47	0.41*
Age and staff initiate	0.28	0.35	0.36*	0.65**	0.38*	0.20	0.10	0.31	-0.10
Age and routine	0.08	-0.51*	0.06	0.06	0.23	0.16	-0.08	0.52	0.22
Age and prohibition	0.07	0.14	0.26	0.32	0.03	-0.42	0.09	0.37	-0.22
Sex and child initiate	-0.09	-0.14	-0.07	-0.04	-0.12	-0.04	0.09	-0.20	-0.20
Sex and staff initiate	-0.08	-0.10	-0.00	-0.00	-0.21	-0.29	0.08	0.09	-0.18
Sex and routine	-0.05	0.41	0.22	-0.20	-0.02	-0.32	-0.11	0.23	-0.51**
Sex and prohibition	0.24	0.19	0.25	0.44*	0.24	0.57**	0.51**	-0.40	0.11
Child initiate	0.39	0.10	0.62**	0.34	0.38*	0.32	0.52**	0.51	0.31

and staff

and routine								
Child initiate and prohibition	0.27	0.31	0.39*	0.53*	0.32	−0.11	0.01	0.48	0.21
Staff initiate and routine	0.23	−0.18	0.31	0.27	0.14	0.62*	−0.04	0.27	0.42*
Staff initiate and prohibition	0.33	0.37	0.64**	0.50*	0.32	−0.30	0.04	0.51	0.52**
Routine and prohibition	0.12	0.27	0.43*	0.27	−0.03	−0.17	−0.04	0.08	0.11

Table 10.11. *Totals over all sessions for number of communications in each category and number of utterances, from focal-child samples*

	Communications		Utterances		Ratio of utterances to communications	Ratio of staff/other child utterances to focal-child utterances
	No.	(%)	No.	(%)		
Statement to staff	119	(9.0)	156	(4.3)	1.31	—
Conversation to staff	202	(15.3)	935	(25.5)	4.63	1.078
Conversation from staff	266	(20.1)	1,052	(28.7)	3.95	1.430
Statement from staff	143	(10.8)	212	(5.8)	1.48	—
Statement to child	204	(15.4)	250	(6.8)	1.23	—
Conversation to child	114	(8.6)	423	(11.5)	3.71	0.748
Conversation from child	119	(9.0)	445	(12.1)	3.74	1.099
Statement from child	155	(11.7)	196	(5.3)	1.26	—
Total	1,322		3,669			

child, and *conversations to/from child*. The paired sets of data presented for different sizes of group, and for number of staff present, were matched for the children on which they were based; however, as child totals were small, it seemed inappropriate to use parametric statistics, and the significance of differences was therefore assessed by a simple binomial comparison (sign test).

Effects of size of group

Results for these sets of comparisons are shown in Table 10.12. These ignore the Group Three children (only present in the large group conditions). The children consistently had more other children in group or parallel activity with them, when in the large group conditions. This did not seem to make much difference to the total number of communications or utterances for Group One children, though for Group Two children utterances were less frequent in the large groups. *Conversations to/from staff* tended to be fewer in larger groups (significant or nearly so in two out of four comparisons), and *statements to/from child* (without reply) tended to be more frequent (significant in three out of four comparisons). *Conversations to/from child* did not show much variation.

Effects of number of staff present

Results for these sets of comparisons are shown in Table 10.13. These include the data from the Group Three children with the Group One and Group Two children, as appropriate, as the former also experienced both staffing conditions.

When only two staff were present, a given child was likely to be with appreciably more children in group or parallel activity. This did not make much difference to the total number of communications; utterances were less frequent in Term Two only. *Conversations to/from staff* consistently tended to be less frequent (significant in one out of four comparisons), and *statements to/from child* were consistently more frequent (significant or nearly so in two out of four comparisons). Also, *conversations to/from child* were consistently more frequent (significant in one comparison).

Staff ratings of different conditions

The three staff members rated each session as to how *enjoyable*, *exhausting*, and *effective* it was. The ratings were scored from 0 up to a maximum of 10, for sessions which were very enjoyable, exhausting, or effective. Mean

Table 10.12. *Number of communications in each category from focal-child samples for different sizes of group*

Separate results for Groups One and Two, and Terms One and Two; significance level of differences from binomial tests across children; mean number of utterances per communication in brackets

(*) $P < 0.1$ * $P < 0.05$ ** $P < 0.01$

	Group One				Group Two			
	Term One		Term Two		Term One		Term Two	
	Small group	Large group	Small group	Large group	Small group	Large group	Small group	Large group
Statement to/from staff	38 (1.45)	19 (1.11)	9 (1.44)	26** (1.54)	34 (1.24)	23 (1.22)	22 (1.32)	16 (1.88)
Conversation to/from staff	49 (3.82)	51 (3.43)	62 (3.71)	33(*) (5.15)	54 (3.15)	42 (3.55)	55 (6.07)	29** (4.45)
Statement to/from child	37 (1.11)	63* (1.30)	9 (1.56)	25* (1.36)	47 (1.17)	46 (1.20)	10 (1.10)	26* (1.19)
Conversation to/from child	31 (3.84)	34 (3.56)	9 (4.78)	13 (4.31)	22 (4.23)	21 (3.57)	20 (3.05)	16 (3.44)
Total communications	155	167	89	97	157	132	107	87
Total utterances	402	399	300	300	360	307*	435	245**
Mean number of other children with focal child	7.9	11.3**	5.2	9.7**	7.4	10.1**	4.1	9.7**

Table 10.13. *Number of communications in each category, from focal-child samples, for different numbers of staff present*

Separate results for Group One (including Group Three children when with Group One) and for Group Two (including Group Three children when with Group Two), and for Terms One and Two; significance level of differences from binomial tests across children; mean number of utterances per communication in brackets

(*) P < 0.1 * P < 0.05 ** P < 0.01

| | Group One (including Group Three) | | | | Group Two (including Group Three) | | | |
| | Term One | | Term Two | | Term One | | Term Two | |
	Three staff	Two staff	Three staff	Two staff	Three staff	Two staff	Three staff	Two staff
Statement to/from staff	41 (1.15)	31 (1.42)	29 (1.38)	22 (1.68)	37 (1.24)	43 (1.51)	24 (1.79)	35 (1.31)
Conversation to/from staff	74 (4.14)	42 (3.60)	78 (4.82)	51* (4.10)	68 (3.06)	44 (4.07)	65 (6.28)	46 (3.96)
Statement to/from child	42 (1.19)	84* (1.24)	25 (1.28)	30 (1.43)	47 (1.21)	76(*) (1.17)	21 (1.38)	34 (1.24)
Conversation to/from child	26 (3.42)	57* (3.77)	18 (3.94)	24 (4.79)	19 (4.21)	35 (3.63)	23 (3.22)	31 (3.13)
Total communications	183	214	150	127	171	198	133	146
Total utterances	492	514	518	404*	391	460	553	367**
Mean number of other children with focal child	7.5	13.5**	7.6	10.5**	7.6	12.1**	7.5	8.8**

ratings for each staff member, divided by condition, group, and term, are shown in Table 10.14, together with overall means summed over the three staff and over the two groups. Significance levels are based on binomial tests.

There was considerable variation from one session to the next in the way staff checked the rating scales. Rather few of the staff: child ratio comparisons were significant for individual staff members. Taking the overall means, there was a small but fairly consistent tendency for the staff to rate larger groups and fewer staff as *less enjoyable*; this was significant, or nearly so, for three out of four comparisons. The pattern of results was similar for the ratings for how *effective* the session was; larger groups and fewer staff produced ratings of *less effective*, and this was significant for three out of four comparisons, but the magnitude of the differences is small.

The ratings for how *exhausting* the sessions were show a more pronounced effect; all four comparisons were significant (or nearly so), and in Term Two especially the differences were fairly substantial, and consistent for the three staff members.

In summary, conditions of worse staff: child ratios, whether caused by more children or fewer staff, led to sessions being perceived as appreciably more exhausting. They also tended to be perceived as slightly less enjoyable and slightly less effective.

Staff ratings of children

Staff ratings of the children were obtained for each child in Groups One, Two, and Three, during Terms One and Two. Ratings were summed across the three staff members, and then correlated with each other and with certain of the observational measures. This was done in order to see which characteristics of the children correlated most significantly and consistently with staff perceptions. The results are shown in Table 10.15; correlations are shown separately for the three groups and the two terms.

Examining first the inter-relationships among the staff ratings, the children rated as *sociable* were also rated as *friendly*; all six correlations are positive, three significant. The children rated as *aggressive* tended, however, to be seen as *sociable*, but not *friendly*.

The children rated as *getting more attention* were consistently seen as being both more *sociable* and more *friendly* (all correlations positive, four significant in each case). There was no strong relationship with ratings of *aggression*.

Older children were rated as *getting more attention* (five correlations positive, three significant) and to a slight extent girls more than boys (five

Table 10.14. *Mean staff ratings of differing staff : child ratio conditions*
Group One upper line; Group Two lower line

(*) P < 0.1   * P < 0.05   ** P < 0.01   *** P < 0.001

	Term One		Term Two		Term One		Term Two	
	Small group	Large group	Small group	Large group	Three staff	Two staff	Three staff	Two staff
Enjoyable								
Miss C	6.45 / 7.18	5.85 / 6.78	7.81 / 6.73	5.66 / 6.56	6.32 / 7.26	5.87 / 6.50	6.80 / 6.78	6.65 / 6.47
Mrs X	9.00 / 7.46	7.16 / 7.91	8.13 / 9.49	8.51 / 7.81*	8.31 / 8.38	7.79 / 6.81	9.24 / 9.17	6.03 / 7.35
Mrs Z	5.93 / 5.50	5.19 / 5.70	8.01 / 8.15	7.56 / 6.32	5.84 / 6.23	5.19 / 4.77	7.80 / 8.00	6.45 / 7.52
Overall mean	6.92	6.43	8.05	7.07(*)	7.06	6.16*	7.92	6.75*
Exhausting								
Miss C	7.38 / 7.11	7.23 / 7.26	4.60 / 4.19	8.14 / 8.32**	6.57 / 6.17	8.52 / 8.89	6.46 / 6.07	6.26 / 6.49
Mrs X	2.65 / 1.65	5.28 / 4.14	1.46 / 0.94	3.36 / 3.71	3.73 / 2.86	4.26 / 2.95	1.05 / 1.62	5.80 / 4.10
Mrs Z	3.86 / 3.16	5.50 / 6.24	2.86 / 2.52	6.73** / 6.40**	5.14 / 4.48	4.07 / 5.00	3.78 / 3.50	6.09** / 5.66
Overall mean	4.30	5.94*	2.76	6.11***	4.83	5.62(*)	3.75	5.73*
Effective								
Miss C	6.15 / 6.96	5.99 / 6.29	7.86 / 7.06	4.83 / 5.70	6.19 / 7.27	5.87 / 5.55	6.47 / 6.96	6.19 / 5.66
Mrs X	7.96 / 7.50	6.48 / 7.14	6.64 / 7.27	6.77 / 6.16	7.78 / 7.83	6.51 / 6.69	6.92 / 6.69	6.12 / 6.53
Mrs Z	5.83 / 5.81	5.37 / 5.94	7.62 / 7.33	6.09 / 6.32	5.62 / 6.20	5.57 / 5.45	7.49 / 6.77	6.06* / 6.90
Overall mean	6.70	6.20	7.30	5.98**	6.82	5.94*	6.90	6.24*

Table 10.15. *Correlations between staff ratings of children and observational measures, for three groups, each term*

Age in months
Sex coded as dichotomous variable (1 for boy, 0 for girl)
* P < 0.05 ** P < 0.01 *** P < 0.001

	Mean correlation	Term One			Term Two		
		Group One	Group Two	Group Three	Group One	Group Two	Group Three
Friendly and sociable	0.59	0.73***	0.23	0.34	0.89***	0.81***	0.51
Friendly and aggressive	−0.89	0.00	−0.40	−0.38	−0.37	0.42	−0.37
Sociable and aggressive	0.31	0.46*	0.59**	0.22	−0.30	0.60*	0.29
More attention and friendly	0.53	0.80***	0.26	0.64*	0.63**	0.71**	0.12
More attention and sociable	0.56	0.86***	0.70***	0.27	0.74**	0.68**	0.10
More attention and aggressive	0.22	0.34	0.42	−0.10	0.16	0.35	0.13
More attention and age	0.44	0.78***	0.73***	0.25	0.60*	0.52	−0.27
More attention and sex	−0.27	−0.51*	−0.02	0.14	−0.45	−0.62*	−0.14
More attention and total communications	0.47	0.78***	0.35	0.36	0.47	0.56*	0.28
More attention and child initiate	0.42	0.72***	0.25	0.35	0.37	0.62*	0.22
More attention and staff initiate	0.36	0.53*	0.51*	0.14	0.57*	0.08	0.30
More attention and routine	0.02	−0.18	0.20	−0.19	0.27	0.12	−0.10
More attention and prohibition	0.12	0.35	0.15	−0.15	−0.26	0.38	0.25

correlations negative, two significant). Examining the children's actual communications with staff, as assessed by the focal-staff samples, the highest correlations with ratings of attention generally come from the measure of the total number of communications engaged in with staff (all correlations positive, two significant). There are similar correlations with both the number of *child-initiated* and the number of *staff-initiated* communications. However, there was little or no relationship between a child's rating for attention and the number of *routine* communications or *prohibitions* he or she received.

Overall, then, children who did communicate a lot with staff were rated as getting more attention, the mean correlation being 0.47. These children were also rated as more friendly and sociable, but not more aggressive. They tended to be older children, and were slightly more likely to be girls than boys.

Summary

Considering the overall data on the kinds of communications recorded, over 85 per cent of the communications between staff and children were concerned with the activity materials or were generally conversational. Less than 10 per cent were about routine matters, and less than 5 per cent were prohibitive. From the point of view of a particular staff member, staff were about equally likely to initiate a communication with a child as vice versa, but were relatively less likely to receive a reply. So far as conversations were concerned, child initiation was almost twice as frequent as staff initiation. Conversations averaged about six utterances, with staff-initiated conversations being slightly but fairly consistently longer than child-initiated conversations. Data from observing individual children showed that on average children communicated slightly more with staff than with each other; and that conversations with staff were longer than conversations with another child.

Individual children varied greatly in how much they interacted verbally with the staff. Generally speaking, children who initiated communications with staff tended to be those who received communications, and these included more of the older children, naturally enough as they would be more verbally competent. Staff rated children who got more attention (in the sense of verbal interaction) from them reasonably accurately. These children were also rated as friendly and sociable or mature. They rated girls as getting slightly more attention than boys, but observations showed that although girls initiated communications to staff slightly more frequently, they did not receive more. This is in part because boys more frequently received prohibitions from staff. In general, the children who received many routine or prohibitive communications, or who were rated as aggressive, were not those who got a great deal of attention. In the kind of activity arrangement prevailing, and for the periods of time observed, it seems that most interactions were pleasurable and activity centred, and that the children who interacted most with staff tended to be those who were older and more verbally competent or more interested in the activities. Boys received more prohibitions, but the overall level was very low.

The types of communication used by the three staff members were reasonably similar, the most obvious variation being in readiness to initiate (rather than respond to) conversations with children. There are some indications that staff communications were more efficient in the second term than in the first (longer conversations, fewer child statements without reply, perhaps less inequality of distribution of contacts). However, between-term comparisons are affected by possible trends in observer criteria; in addition, the average sizes of group were smaller, so whether such trends were due to either of these factors, or to increased staff competence in the kinds of setting used, cannot be decided.

Examination of the effects of the different staff:child ratio conditions, shows that the findings were, not surprisingly, fairly similar for the comparisons of different sizes of group, and the comparisons of different numbers of staff. The data for the focal-child samples confirmed that with more children, or fewer staff, the number of companions of the target child (in either group or parallel activity) was appreciably greater, roughly in proportion to the worsening of the staff:child ratio. Most of the children were taking part in one of the two or three activity areas organised by staff, and these loose conglomerations of children were obviously larger in the above circumstances.

In these conditions, there were more communications between staff and children, but many fewer than would compensate for the reduced probability of verbal contact between staff and any particular child. Staff were talking for much of the time anyway, even in the most favourable conditions, so scope for compensation was obviously limited.

In particular, staff were faced with more communications coming from children when the staff:child ratio worsened. Children made more statements to staff which received no reply, and initiated more communications generally. Staff also tended to initiate more communications to children, this being found more reliably when there were more children, rather than when there were fewer staff.

Although communications increased somewhat when the staff:child ratio was worse, the number of utterances per communication did not increase proportionately – indeed did not increase at all in the larger group conditions. As a result, conversations – especially staff-initiated conversations – were shorter.

The records obtained on individual children confirmed that from the child's point of view, there were fewer conversations with staff when there were more children around, or fewer staff to talk to. There was some tendency for more conversations with other children to occur when fewer staff were present, and there was a general trend for children to make more statements to other children which received no reply.

The proportion of routine and prohibitive communications by staff increased when staff:child ratios were worse. The increases are substantial on a proportional basis, if not in absolute terms. Since the observation periods did not include setting out or putting away the equipment, when such types of communication might be more frequent, the effects of the worsened staff:child ratios may if anything be underestimated in this respect.

Sessions with more children or fewer staff were rated as slightly less enjoyable, and slightly less effective, by the three staff involved. However, there was much variation in this measure, and the overall effects are small. Staff rated almost all the sessions as reasonably enjoyable and effective; as we have seen, from their point of view they had maintained or increased verbal communications with children, albeit with shorter conversations, and the absolute increase in routine or prohibitive communications was small. Staff did note these sessions as appreciably more exhausting, which presumably reflected the increased effort demanded in coping with a greater number of children.

From the point of view of a particular child, the effectiveness of the sessions with poorer staff:child ratios, considered in terms of communication with staff, may be less than the data from the staff ratings imply. While a member of staff might have felt, with reason, that she was coping well with such a situation, an individual child would have, on average, appreciably less contact with her, approaching if not quite equalling numerically the actual worsening of the ratio. This would probably have been experienced by most or all of the children, as the inequality of distribution of contacts with staff did not change very greatly in the different group size conditions (where it could best be estimated).

11 Structured activities in the preschool: comparison of present studies with previous research

The general theme of the studies in this section of the book concerns the nature of the preschool curriculum. In particular we are concerned with the issue of the extent to which staff should actively structure children's activities, and their effectiveness in doing so in differing staff:child ratio conditions.

The results we obtained in regard to these questions are on the whole clear and consistent, but some definite provisos must be made about the extent to which they can safely be generalised to other preschool institutions. In particular, the investigation reported in Chapter 9, comparing structured-activities and free-play conditions, must be considered a case-study; it is possible that the results obtained were peculiar to the particular groups of children taking part in the study. Also, the particular definitions of structured activities and free play are only two from a range of possible modes of staff–child interaction. this is less true of the study reported in Chapter 10, where quite consistent results were obtained for both the groups taking part, but nevertheless more general reservations must be made. Our findings are on children from mixed social class backgrounds, but few if any of the sample would be classed as deprived. The results might be different with children from very different backgrounds, or with different expectations about how preschool staff behave. Perhaps the strongest proviso relates to the fact that our studies were carried out with only three members of staff. Clearly the personality and training of staff could greatly affect the kinds of interactions with children in a preschool institution, and this was an area of investigation outside the scope of our enquiry.

Structured and unstructured activities in the preschool

It was argued in Chapter 8 that a general scale of structured to unstructured activities, or adult-centred to child-centred programmes, is one of the most important differences between preschools. The research by Thompson (1944) provides the closest parallel to our study presented in Chapter 9, being an experimental comparison limited to two preschool groups, one in each condition. The results of the two investigations are not in very good agreement. The only measures of agreement are on the negative findings; Thompson failed to find any effect of teacher involvement in the programmes on either the children's nervous habits, or on Stanford–Binet intelligence scores. This corresponds reasonably well with our own findings of no effects on sucking or automanipulative behaviour; and of no effects on scores on the Caldwell Preschool Inventory and the Peabody Picture Vocabulary Test.

Although there is agreement on the lack of effect on test scores, nevertheless this was an unexpected finding; at least, we felt it to be the most unexpected of our results. It seems reasonable to expect greater staff–child interaction to result in greater improvements in test scores of the kinds employed. Some of the larger-scale studies reviewed in Chapter 8 (e.g. Karnes, 1969; cited in Beller, 1973; Miller and Dyer, 1975) tend to support this supposition, and of course the general philosophy underlying preschool intervention programmes is that properly structured staff–child interaction can have cognitive and linguistic benefits for the children, certainly in the short if not in the long term. However, the background of the children is a most important consideration here. Few, if any, of the children in our groups could have been classed as 'disadvantaged'. Thompson (1944) drew his children from 'the upper two socio-economic strata of a university city', their Stanford–Binet scores ranging from 102 to 158. The impact of staff–child interaction, relative to the child's experience in the home or other behaviour settings, may well be less in such cases.

Thompson found a number of positive results favouring the group with more teacher involvement. His findings relating to constructive behaviour when faced with failure, and ascendant behaviour, cannot be compared with our results since comparable measures were not made. Thompson also reported more leadership and higher social participation scores, in the group having more teacher involvement, by the end of the study. Thompson here used Parten's measures, and since Parten and Newhall (1943) reported a very high correlation between these two measures, they were probably also very similar in Thompson's study.

However, our own study found a decrease in peer play and an increase in solitary activity in the teacher–involved (structured-activities) condition – apparently the opposite finding from Thompson's. It is possible that this disagreement is more apparent than real; Thompson (1944, p. 6) describes Parten's observations as being made 'during the free play of young children', so that Parten did not explicitly categorise children interacting with staff. It seems that Thompson applied Parten's scheme without modification to his 'teacher-involvement' group, and thus would have counted our categories of involvement with staff as either associative or cooperative activity on Parten's scale (the two 'highest' categories). It is therefore not certain whether Thompson is applying the criteria of a child's social participation to other children only, or to other children and staff.

In the process analysis of his two conditions, Thompson also reported no difference in friendly social contacts between children, except, surprisingly, that giving help to another child was more common in the teacher-directed group. The correlational study by Huston-Stein *et al.* (1977) also reported no correlation between positive social interaction with peers, and degree of structuring of activities; though they did report a negative correlation with prosocial behaviour towards peers (cooperation and helping), which is the opposite of Thompson's result.

In interpreting this disagreement, it must be remembered that Thompson's groups were small (11 and 8 children), and also that these process measures were not pre-tested and therefore cannot be unambiguously ascribed to the effects of the experimental conditions. Also, the review of studies on staff:child ratio strongly suggests that worse staff:child ratios – and hence less staff–child involvement – lead to more peer interaction. We are therefore inclined to have confidence in our own finding that less structured activities will promote peer interaction, whilst recognising that this in itself does not say much about the kind or quality of such interaction, or the overall social participation level with other persons (children and staff).

The main findings of our own study in these latter respects related to aggressive behaviour, rough-and-tumble play, and fantasy play. These will be considered in turn.

Aggressive behaviour

Our results suggested that the reduced level of peer interaction in the structured-activities condition did have some impact on the ability of the children to manage conflict situations among themselves. The children in the structured-activities condition increased their level of aggression gradually over the two terms, and quite sharply at the end in free play, whereas the group which was always in free-play conditions maintained a constant level of aggresion. While these changes cannot be unambiguously ascribed to differences in the levels of normal peer interaction, the connection is certainly suggestive. The increase in aggression in the structured-activities group was particularly marked for games hostility and harassment, the two categories of hostile behaviour which Manning *et al.* (1978), on the basis of data on home background and school prognosis, believe to be particularly related to difficulties in relationships with peers.

There are few other studies with which to compare our findings. Thompson (1944) reported a higher general level of hostile contacts between children in his group without teacher involvement, but difficulties in the interpretation of his findings have already been mentioned. Huston-Stein *et al.* (1977) reported both more prosocial aggression and more hostile aggression in preschools with fewer structured activities, but the results fall short of conventional levels of statistical significance.

However, the monograph by Jersild and Markey (1935) on children's conflicts does yield an interesting comparison with our result. These authors observed conflicts among children in three nursery groups, with a follow-up of many of the children nine months later, and a further follow-up of 12 children in kindergarten. The first follow-up revealed a general increase in the number of conflicts. However, the data on the second follow-up provide the more interesting comparison. Seven of these 12 children moved from Nursery B, where they had experienced teacher intervention in 35 per cent of conflicts, to kindergarten, where they experienced intervention in only 17 per cent; these children's level of conflicts was higher in the kindergarten. Five of the 12 children moved from Nursery C, where they experienced 23 per cent teacher intervention, to kindergarten, where it was 20 per cent. The level of these children's conflicts showed some decline. Although based on small numbers, the results suggest that high teacher intervention may have little short-term effect on levels of peer conflict, and may actually lead to an increase if teacher intervention is subsequently and quite abruptly relaxed. This is very similar to our own findings, in which the structured-activities group received 18 per cent teacher intervention, but the free-play group only 2 per cent.

Clearly no conclusive generalisation can emerge from these results. Again, the background of the children may be very important, and it certainly seems likely that a few children will very definitely require teacher intervention in their initiation of conflicts with others, if only to protect the other child involved. However, such cases may usually be a very small minority. Often when preschool staff intervene in a conflict, they do not know the background leading up to the encounter, so the intervention may be less effective (in the sense of fair or impartial) than it seems. Staff often take the side of the weaker child who would otherwise lose (e.g. Jersild and Markey, 1935; Smith and Green, 1974), and while this may seem a fair policy, it is worth considering whether it disrupts the dominance relationships among the children in the group. Children at this age show fairly linear dominance relationships, and are quite aware of them (Strayer and Strayer, 1976; Sluckin and Smith, 1977).

It is therefore suggested as a hypothesis for further investigation that in most cases free-play experience with little teacher interference will have better results for subsequent conflict levels among the children than much higher levels of teacher interference in more structured conditions. Either the amount of unrestricted peer interaction, or the level of teacher interference specifically in conflict situations, might be the important variable in the hypothesised effect.

Rough-and-tumble play

Rough-and-tumble play, in boys especially, was less frequent in the structured-activities condition of our study. None of the related studies provides comparable data to confirm this result, but it is a natural concomitant of the generally reduced level of free peer interaction in this condition. Preschool staff often discourage rough-and-tumble play because it tends to be noisy and disruptive (Smith, 1977), and this would be more obvious or more annoying to staff when they were trying to keep children's attention on quieter activities. The reduction observed in rough-and-tumble play was most marked for boys, who usually engage more frequently in this kind of play anyway, but it was observed for both sexes.

At present not enough is known about the developmental importance of rough-and-tumble play to say with any confidence whether it matters a great deal if opportunities for this kind of play are available or not in preschools. In most mammals rough-and-tumble provides the predominant kind of playful activity, especially in males. It has often been argued that it has socialising functions; for example, Poirier and Smith (1974) argue that young monkeys get to know each other and form social bonds through rough-and-tumble play. However, Symons (1978) regards the primary function of rough-and-tumble as being practise for fighting and predation skills. Fagen (1976) argues that it serves to strengthen muscle development and general bodily stamina during a critical period in infancy. These three main kinds of function are not necessarily mutually exclusive; nor can we assume that if they apply to mammals such as monkeys they necessarily apply to human children. Play-fighting in children has been discussed in detail by Aldis (1975), but as he points out, it has been little studied in the past and we do not have much evidence to go on.

If rough-and-tumble play merely developed competitive fighting skills in boys – which it may do, though we have no evidence – then it might or might not be thought best to discourage it, apart from any inconvenience that it causes to other activities. If it encouraged the development of social bonds, then this would generally be thought a more positive function. It could be argued that children have many other ways to make friends apart from play-fighting and -chasing, but nevertheless some children do seem to get especial pleasure and enjoyment out of this sort of activity, and it may be that it does provide an effective way for such children to interact with others.

Finally, if rough-and-tumble provides exercise for physical stamina, this again would seem beneficial, although there are other ways of exercising such as using climbing-frames and other large apparatus. Our structured-activities condition did in fact seem to reduce physical activity in the children generally – not just rough-and-tumble play. However, it is quite likely that most children had adequate opportunities for physical exercise outside the preschool. Thus the value attached to free motor activity will depend on whether the children have enough of this in other contexts; it may be very valuable for children from high-rise flats to have ample scope for physical exercise in their preschool. So far as the specific value of rough-and-tumble play is concerned, at present there seems not to be much argument for encouraging it, and some grounds for discouraging it; but further research might provide a firmer basis for making such decisions.

Fantasy play

Fantasy play was less frequent, and had fewer participants in our organised-activities condition compared with the free-play condition. This finding is in good agreement with two comparable studies. Huston-Stein *et al.* (1977) found a significant negative correlation between degree of structuring in their five preschools and frequency of imaginative play. Beller *et al.* (1971; cited in Beller, 1973) reported more complex symbolic play in two 'child-centred' preschool classes, less in two 'adult-centred' classes, and least in two Montessori classrooms (which were the most adult-directed in their investigation).

This suggests that traditional ways of structuring preschool activities may decrease opportunities for children to engage spontaneously in fantasy or imaginative play. However, the involvement of staff with children's activities need not have this effect. The staff can specifically initiate and encourage fantasy and sociodramatic play, and if done sensitively this has a substantial impact. A considerable number of studies in the USA, Britain, and Israel, have shown that fantasy play tutoring of this kind – usually done with children who do not engage in a great deal of fantasy play to start with – is not only enjoyable for the children but can boost levels of spontaneous fantasy play in the children once the tutoring has ceased.

How valuable is it to encourage fantasy play in preschool age children? The interviews by the Newsons (Newson and Newson, 1968) showed that in their sample of mothers, opinions were divided as to children's fantasies. Middle-class mothers often encouraged and enjoyed such activities in their children, but there was more of a tendency in working-class mothers to be doubtful about the value or appropriateness of play so divorced from reality. This has been confirmed by observations in the home (Wootton, 1974; Dunn and Wooding, 1977). Fantasy play in preschools also seems to be less frequently observed among children from working-class backgrounds (Tizard *et al.*, 1976; Smith and Dodsworth, 1978).

The play-tutoring studies mentioned above have been used as a way of ascertaining, by experimental means, the effects of increasing fantasy play in children from 'disadvantaged' backgrounds. Typically, children given play tutoring have been matched with other, control, children who were not given play tutoring. Both groups of children are assessed on a number of measures – such as language skills, creativity, intellectual and social development – both before and after the play-tutoring sessions. About a dozen such studies have been made and generally they tend to show that the play-tutored children show larger gains on the assessment measures than the control children.

This could be taken to indicate that the increase in spontaneous play shown by the children was responsible for these gains. However, the play-tutored children in the course of the tutoring programme also received a considerable amount of extra attention from an adult, and this could reasonably be expected to benefit linguistic and intellectual skill, especially in children from 'disadvantaged' backgrounds. Some studies attempted to exclude this possibility, by arranging for the control group children to receive tutoring also, but in a non-fantasy play context. Unfortunately no measurements were made of the amount of tutoring, or adult–child contact, occurring in either the play-tutored or control groups, so we cannot be sure that these controls were adequate.

These studies have been reviewed by Smith and Syddall (1978), who conducted a similar study in which one group of children received play tutoring, and another group skills tutoring. Observations made during all the tutoring sessions showed that both groups of children received equal amounts of tutor–child contact, although the contexts differed. Assessments before and after the tutoring revealed improvements in both groups, but to approximately the same extent. The only particular benefits to the play-tutored children, apart from an increase in subsequent spontaneous fantasy play, was an increase in social play generally, and higher scores on one test of role-taking ability.

A subsequent study undertaken by Smith *et al.* (1978) was on a larger scale, and embodied an additional follow-up assessment in the design. Again both play-tutored and skills-tutored groups showed roughly equal gains on a number of observational and test measures; the most consistent advantage found only in the play-tutored group was, once more, an increase in social or group play, especially in large subgroups.

These two reports suggest that the benefits of play tutoring reside mainly in the tutoring contact, particularly in so far as language and cognitive skills are concerned. Tutoring in the particular context of encouraging fantasy play – at least when this is done with several children, so that sociodramatic play is – does, however, benefit the children by increasing their subsequent level of social participation.

To return now to our original findings: we found that the structured-activities condition tended to decrease the amount of fantasy play, and the number of children taking part, relative to the free-play condition. Two independent reports confirmed this finding. The structured-activities condition corresponded quite well to the skills-tutoring conditions mentioned above; fantasy activities were not entirely absent in structured activities, but were infrequent.

A structured-activities regime could, however, include a much larger play-tutoring component, in which fantasy activities were encouraged. In some senses, more play tutoring would move this condition closer to free play, in that fairly spontaneous play by the children is encouraged, and more social play in larger subgroups occurs as a consequence. The experimental studies mentioned above demonstrate that play tutoring could benefit the language development and cognitive skills of the children as much as would skills tutoring; thus play tutoring would seem to have both the cognitive benefits from the tutoring, and the social benefits from the play. Certainly, if an objective is to increase social skills and social participation in preschool children, then sociodramatic play tutoring seems an effective and enjoyable way to go about achieving this end.

In summary, free-play conditions seem conducive to children's spontaneous fantasy play, and to rough-and-tumble play (which often has fantasy elements); structuring activities will tend to reduce these behaviours, if structuring means generally encouraging quieter, more cognitive or skilful tasks. Less sociodramatic and rough-and-tumble play, as well as perhaps less practice in uninterrupted management of conflict situations, seem to be likely consequences of the general decrease in peer interactions which went with our structured-activities condition. More teacher involvement need not have these consequences, but is likely to in many contexts.

What about the other side of the coin, the increase in staff–child interactions which we observed in the structured-activities condition? Although we did not find any definite benefits from our test assessments, the results for attention span (activity span) were significant and durable; we found that the attention span of the structured-activities children increased compared with that of the free-play children, and that this increase was largely maintained when both groups were again in free play.

Attention span

A number of studies were made investigating the attention span or activity span of preschool children in the 1920s and 1930s. Some of these were laboratory studies, others were more naturalistic observations made in nurseries and preschools. There is some measure of agreement in the findings reported, limited by obvious differences in the circumstances of the study, the kinds of materials provided, and the definitions of attention span. Most studies did agree, however, in finding an increase in attention span with age.

A study finding very short 'interest spans' was that of Herring and Koch (1930). They reported mean spans of 1.9 minutes for 2-year-olds and 2.2 minutes for 4-year-olds. These authors allowed up to one minute's distraction within an 'interest span', but their results probably give shorter spans than those of other studies because of the conditions they employed. Each child was alone with a limited set of fairly novel toys; this might well have led to more distractability than in the type of environment usually found in preschools. the kind of materials are also obviously important. Moyer and Haller Gilmer (1955) devised a 'distraction-free' setting, containing toys designed for 'maximum holding power', for children aged $1\frac{1}{2}$–7 years. They naturally obtained some very long attention spans, and this was one of the few studies not to report a regular increase in span with age. However, their experimental situation seems even further removed from that of the usual preschool setting.

Bott (1928) made observations of attention span ('total time to nearest minute occupied with that toy') with a small number of children. She found an increase from 2.5 minutes at 2 years, to 4.7 minutes at 3 years, and 5.6 minutes at 4 years. Bott also ignored distractions of less than one minute. These spans, while longer than those of Herring and Koch (1930), are still substantially less than in the two other studies to be discussed. However, as Bott analysed data from only three children at each age range, little reliance should be put on the figures, and they clearly do not provide norms for the ages concerned.

Van Alstyne (1932) carried out a study on a much larger scale. Altogether 112 children aged 2–5 years were observed in three nursery schools and four kindergartens. Scans were made at 1-minute intervals, over 45-minute periods. Attention spans averaged over the 12 kinds of play materials present through the age range were 6.9 minutes for 2-year-olds, 8.9 minutes for 3-year-olds, 11.4 minutes for 4-year-olds, and 12.6 minutes for 5-year-olds. The number of different activities sampled in a 45-minute period fell from 5.0 to 2.9 over the same age range.

Another large-scale study was carried out by Gutteridge (1935) in Australia. Altogether 417 children aged 2–5 years were observed in nursery schools and kindergartens. The definition of duration of attention is unclear, but breaks of up to one minute were ignored. Gutteridge obtained long spans, though again the increase with age was clear: means were 9.4 minutes at 2 years, 13.4 minutes at 3 years, 19.0 minutes at 4 years, and 23.8 minutes at 5 years.

More recently, Stodolsky (1974) reported findings on activity transitions in preschool children. Although her main interest was in reporting how children moved from one activity to another, data on average length of activity segments are provided. Altogether records were obtained for 65 children in four preschools. In a pilot study, the mean activity segment length increased from 4.6 minutes in 3-year-olds to 5.4 minutes in 4-year-olds and 5.1 minutes in 5-year-olds. In the main study the corresponding figures were 5.4 minutes for 3-year-olds, 6.5 minutes for 4-year-olds, and 7.2 minutes for 5-year-olds. Finally, in a smaller longitudinal study, mean activity length increased from 5.3 minutes to 6.3 minutes for 16 children over a one-year period. The longitudinal and main cross-sectional data yielded highly significant age effects.

The general conclusion from these studies is that attention span increases through the preschool years by a moderate amount. While the actual lengths of span found vary appreciably with observational methodology, definition of span, materials available, and general setting, it seems reasonable to assume that some increase in attention span is a sign of increasing maturity in the child. This argument could be carried too far – children need to sample different activities, and too much concentration on one activity might be considered less than optimal – but a modest increase in attention span as an index of greater concentration could well be considered desirable.

Our own findings were summarised in Tables 9.21 and 9.22. The figures given there must be doubled to give attention spans in minutes, since each scan lasted 2 minutes. This implies that our mean attention spans for 3-

and 4-year-old children were around six to twelve minutes. These spans are very similar to Van Alystyne's, shorter than Gutteridge's, and longer than Stodolsky's. Our estimate for number of different activities in a 40-minute period, namely, around five or six, is not very different from Van Alstyne's.

We found that the attention spans for the children in the free-play condition did not show much variation, whereas spans for the children in structured activities increased through the experimental period and remained at a significantly higher level in the final baseline period – the increase being from about six-and-a-half minutes to about nine minutes, on average. There are no other studies with directly comparable findings. Huston-Stein *et al.* (1977) reported no significant correlation between structuring in the preschool and task persistence; but this latter measure was essentially one of persistence or distractibility at the moment of observation, rather than activity span *per se*.

It is not surprising that structuring activities should act to increase activity span, since this tends to be one of the aims of the staff in such situations; attempts are made to interest a child in an activity and to sustain such interest over minor distractions or shifts of attention which might, in an unstructured setting, lead to a change of activity. Smith (1977), in an observational study of fantasy play in a nursery school, found that informal play tutoring by the staff resulted in longer fantasy play sequences for particular children than occurred in spontaneous play. Observing younger children aged $1\frac{1}{2}$–2 years in the home environment, Dunn and Wooding (1977) found that joint attention of mother and child on the object of the child's play resulted in significantly longer play bouts than when the mother was not paying attention. This seems to be an analogous finding to ours, in that an adult's interest is positively affecting the child's span of involvement in a particular type of play or activity.

Needless to say, such a generalisation should not be pushed too far. If done insensitively, adult-structuring could become interference, and the child's involvement passive. There was some slight indication of this from our study, where, from focal-sampling data, there were more cases of children doing nothing (often being passive, although associated with an organised activity) in the organised-activities than in the free-play condition. That this was not the main factor in the results is, however, shown by the fact that the increase in attention span persisted in the final baseline conditions when few organised activities were available.

Staff–child interaction and the effects of staff:child ratio

The research reported in Chapter 10 provided further data on the kind of staff–child communications occurring in a structured-activities condition, and the distribution of such communications. The first set of findings to be discussed relates to the overall data; following that, the variations in communication patterns with different staff:child ratio conditions will be considered.

Comparison of our investigation with others is limited by the small number of relevant studies, and the fact that several of these were carried out on older children than those in our own sample.

Kinds of staff–child interaction and their distribution

The verbal interactions of staff with children were classified as being broadly to do with play activities, routine activities, or prohibitions. These are, in general terms, similar to categories such as work, procedure, and discipline of Garner and Bing (1973), and instructional, managerial, and prohibitory of Jackson and Lahaderne (1967), granted the difference in age range of children these studies were concerned with; and approximate comparisons can also be made with other studies.

Our results indicated that some 86–90 per cent of teacher interactions were play (broadly unstructured), some 6–9 per cent routine, and some 3–5 per cent prohibitions. Also in the preschool age range, Moore (1938) found less than 1 per cent of 'negative commands', the examples of which correspond to our prohibitions category. Moore's study was carried out in one nursery school and one kindergarten in the USA. Studying infant school children aged 5–7 in Britain, Resnick (1971, 1972) found some 2 per cent of staff communications were 'negative statements'. However, Garner and Bing (1973), observing in five infant classes, found that disciplinary contacts totalled 17 per cent, compared with 18 per cent procedure and 65 per cent work and response opportunity. Also Boydell (1974) found 26 per cent of routine questions or statements in six classes of 5- to 8-year-olds; Boydell regards these categories as equivalent to Garner and Bing's disciplinary plus procedural ones. Jackson and Lahaderne's study (1967) on older sixth-grade children in the USA gave percentages fairly similar to those of Garner and Bing.

Our own results thus suggest slightly more prohibitions than found by Moore (1938) or Resnick (1971), but otherwise a considerably greater concentration on instructional play contacts than the other studies mentioned. The disagreements in these relative amounts of different types of contact could clearly be due to many variables: time and condition of study, age and background of children and staff, definitions of categories. It is probably more useful to compare other aspects of the teacher–child contacts, such as age and sex differences, and who initiates the communications.

Foster (1930), in her study of a nursery school and two kindergartens in the USA, reported that teacher-initiated contacts decreased with age of child, while child-initiated contacts increased. This was in a whole-day preschool setting, based on all activities including lunch and nap time. For conversational contacts only, teacher-initiated contacts also increased with age. This is broadly in agreement with our findings that both child-initiated and teacher-initiated communications correlated positively with age, though more highly for the former.

Foster also noted that girls initiated more communications than boys, but boys tended to receive more. We also found girls initiating slightly more communications than boys; the sex difference for receiving communications was not consistent. Not surprisingly, we did find boys receiving more prohibitions, as did Jackson and Lahaderne (1967) on a much older age group.

We found children and teachers initiating roughly equal percentages of communications; Garner and Bing (1973) with 5- and 6-year-olds reported 60 per cent teacher initiations and 40 per cent child initiations. We consistently found that staff-initiated communications were slightly longer than child-initiated communications, they also had a greater proportion of staff to child utterances. No other studies provide data to compare directly with this, but Resnick (1971) did report that children more frequently initiated brief contacts (four or fewer utterances) than extended contacts (more than four utterances), which is in agreement with our findings.

Several studies comment on the unequal distribution of teacher contacts, while providing little quantitative information (Foster, 1930; Jackson and Lahaderne, 1967; Resnick, 1971; Garner and Bing, 1973). Garner and Bing found generally positive correlations between their different communication categories, suggesting that the inequality of contacts applied fairly generally to all types of contact. We found exactly the same pattern of generally positive correlations. Older children who were rated as friendly and sociable by the staff both initiated and received more verbal contacts, and tended to be correctly identified by staff as getting more attention. Children receiving many routine or prohibitory contacts were not rated as getting more attention by the staff, although in fact there was a slight tendency for them to receive more contacts. However, these kinds of contact were relatively few, and the predominant factor influencing level of contact was probably the degree to which the child enjoyed joining in the staff-organised activities (as opposed to spontaneous peer-group activities). This was influenced appreciably by age and slightly by sex, these children tending to be seen by the staff as friendly and sociable or mature.

Effects of staff:child ratio on interactions and their distribution

Our study of staff:child ratios was carried out by varying both the number of staff and the number of children (Chapter 10). Only communications (mainly verbal) between staff and children were recorded. The effects of varying numbers of staff or children were similar, and held over the range of staff:child ratios studied, namely 1:4–1:14. Effects were evident both on the balance of staff–child to child–child interactions, and on the quality of staff–child interactions when they occurred.

From data obtained from watching individual children, it was clear that fewer staff or more children shifted the likelihood of interaction away from staff to other children, as would be expected. A given child was less likely to have conversations with a staff member, and more likely to give or receive statements from other children. Conversations with other children were more frequent when fewer staff were present. There was some trend towards children talking less in these conditions, but overall it would be fair to say that the relative frequency of staff–child and child–child interaction is in a reciprocal relationship; as one goes up, the other goes down.

This would be in agreement with the results of the study in which we compared free-play and structured-activities regimes (Chapter 9). The former facilitated more child–child interaction generally, the latter more staff–child interaction. In the study of staff:child ratios all the sessions were of a structured-activities nature, but it was obvious to an observer in the setting that as the staff:child ratio worsened, more children were effectively engaged in free play for considerable periods of time.

These conclusions concerning the reciprocal balance of staff–child and child–child interaction, and the factors affecting it, are supported by the few other relevant studies in preschools. Reuter and Yunik (1973) found most child–child interaction and least adult–child interaction in Montessori classes with ratios of 1:12, compared with other preschools with ratios of 1:35. Reuter and Yunik's study confounded staff:child ratio with teacher technique and ages of the children, but Murphy and Goldner (1976) found rather little difference in interaction patterns between Montessori classes and more structured nursery school classes which had the same ratio of 1:8. Indeed it could be concluded from this latter study that staff:child ratio was a more potent influence than degree of structuring of activities in affecting the relative balance of staff–child and child–child interactions, though clearly this could be argued too far on rather little evidence. The importance of the staff:child ratio is confirmed by O'Connor's report (1975), which compared two preschools fairly similar in curriculum, but with ratios of 1:3.5 and 1:7 respectively. The relative balance of social exchange, proximity, and interest went from staff to children in these two settings.

All these studies agree on what is, admittedly, an unsurprising finding. However, there is no agreement on the policy decisions to be made from it. Reuter and Yunik (1973) argue that the age trend in the 3- to 5-year-old age range is away from adult–child towards child–child interactions. They then infer that the children with low staff interaction and high peer interaction (Montessori) show a 'superiority of social interaction development'. While recognising the confounding of variables in their study, they suggest that there is a need to substantiate whether the high adult:child ratios aimed at in Headstart and other nursery school programmes are really necessary, or indeed whether they may even be counter-productive.

Murphy and Goldner (1976) also pursue this point, while recognising that the goals of a nursery school programme must ultimately decide the desirability of a high or low staff:child ratio. They also suggest that higher adult:child ratios may be unnecessary, considering that the consequent decrease in peer interaction 'may inhibit the development of peer-oriented interpersonal skills such as cooperation, leadership, and group problem-solving skills'. This latter statement is, however, speculative so far as their own study is concerned.

O'Connor (1975) presents what may be thought of as a more reasoned conclusion, namely, that the optimum balance of adult and child interaction for development is at present unknown. She agrees with the premise of Reuter and Yunik (1973) that the trend in this age range is from adult to peer interactions, but points out that two opposite inferences could be made from this. First, one could argue that too high an adult:child ratio means 'many adults eliciting and promoting adult interaction and excessive and immature dependency'; or second, one could argue that too low an adult:child ratio means 'too few adults forcing premature reliance on developmentally more advanced interaction and dependency'. She concludes that further research is needed in this respect.

We would agree that there is a balance to be drawn between facilitating peer interaction on the one hand and adult interaction on the other, and some of the different costs and benefits of the two approaches were indicated by our comparison of free play and structured activities (Chapter

9). The studies which we carried out on different staff:child ratios also indicate some of the qualitative as well as quantitative ways in which staff–child interaction varies as a function of the ratio. In particular, we found from observing staff members that they did not change their verbal output very much, however many children were present. This was understandable, as they were interacting with children most of the time; but the inevitable consequence was appreciably fewer conversations with any particular child (with the distribution of contacts across different children apparently not varying very much). Several findings indicated some deterioration in the quality of those interactions that did occur. First, conversations were shorter. Clearly shorter conversations mean less chance to develop themes; Resnick (1971) suggests that extended conversations are the most valuable in the infant classroom. Second, there were more statements made by children to staff which went unanswered; with many children around, a member of staff could often not cope with all the children wishing to talk with her at once. Third, a greater proportion of staff utterances were of a routine or prohibitive nature, rather than concerned with developing play. With more children per staff member there was naturally more need for management directives than was the case for lower child:adult ratios.

These results clearly suggest that more children per staff member will not only shift the balance from adult to peer interactions, but will also mean a deterioration in quality of those adult interactions which do take place. Even if the premise that adult interaction should get less frequent with age, used by Reuter and Yunik (1973) and Murphy and Goldner (1976), is accepted, this does not allow any inference that adult–child interactions in the preschool are unimportant or that their quality should be neglected.

Neither our study, nor any other, provides direct experimental evidence for the consequences of different staff:child ratios on children's linguistic or cognitive development. However, there is a large body of research indicating that for many children at least, structured adult interaction can have certain beneficial effects, at least in the short term. It therefore seems reasonable to infer that the amount and quality of such interaction will also be an important factor in such effects.

While O'Connor (1975) is right to reject as too simple the arguments against high adult:child ratios such as presented by Reuter and Yunik (1973) and Murphy and Goldner (1976), she is probably wrong to put the emphasis on the supposed developmental aspect of adult dependency. Adult interaction and peer interaction have *different* consequences for preschool children. Time budgeting means that increasing one probably decreases the other, but the desired emphasis on each will depend on the skills and competences most important for particular children, not on a general age shift which ignores qualitative differences. A few children may need prompting by staff into peer interactions and away from dependency; but most of the staff–child interactions we have observed were not 'dependent', but were concerned with genuine relationships and had implications for important developmental processes. O'Connor might profitably have put more emphasis on the concerns of Murphy and Goldner for the development of specifically peer competencies. This is a valid concern, which must be weighed against the concern for good staff–child interaction. Our study of a free-play setting indicated the possible importance of spontaneous peer interactions for rough-and-tumble and fantasy play, and for the control of conflict situations. While more can be found out about the consequences of more or less of each kind of interaction, the choice of balance can only come from knowing the background of the children in a particular preschool and assessing this in relation to the desired developmental goals.

Summary

One main dimension by which preschool organisation can be characterised is the degree to which it is 'adult-centred' or 'child-centred' in terms of the initiation or choice of activities. This will depend both on the overt actions and attitudes of the staff of a preschool, and on the staff:child ratio. Several studies report an approximate trade-off between the amount of adult intervention and the amount of peer interaction, with the balance being affected by both the previous factors.

Active adult involvement or structuring of activities will obviously increase the amount of staff–child interaction (assuming that the structuring is one of involvement in children's play or activities at an individual or small group level, rather than resorting to whole-class teaching methods). Our own work and that of others suggests that adult support can improve children's concentration and attention span at activities. Much of the preschool research literature also finds positive benefits for children's cognitive and language development, at least in the short term, especially for children who might be expected to underachieve at school.

If these kinds of benefits are important goals of a preschool programme, then our work on staff:child ratios indicates that improving the number of staff per child not only increases the number of conversations each child will have with an adult, but also the length of conversations and the efficiency of communication. Also, the number of routine and prohibitive communications by staff are reduced. These trends held over a range of from 1:14 to 1:4 staff per child. Putting it conversely, more children per staff member will not only shift the balance from adult to peer interaction; it may also adversely affect the quality of adult–child interaction which still does take place.

The important benefits of peer interaction must not be overlooked by any prevailing emphasis on the role of preschool staff. Such benefits are likely to be most important for children who, while perhaps getting enough adult stimulation at home, are lacking enough opportunity for spontaneous play with children of approximately the same age and developmental status. The likely benefits are mainly social. In so far as they are tangible, we can point to the possible greater control of aggressive and conflict situations when adult structuring or intervention in conflicts is not too frequent or strict (clearly sometimes adults must intervene); and the greater frequency of fantasy play and rough-and-tumble play in a free-play condition. These latter findings must be qualified. Fantasy and sociodramatic play *can* be encouraged sensitively by staff involvement, and this has been shown to have value for children who may initially engage in low levels of spontaneous fantasy play. The developmental importance of rough-and-tumble play is uncertain, though some children, especially boys, may find it a way of forming friendships. Possibly it is most valuable as physical exercise. Physical exercise can also, of course, be structured by staff, though that seems relatively infrequent in many preschools.

In most cases some kind of mixture or alternation between adult structuring of activities and spontaneous play may be suitable. It is also possible for staff to try to plan involvement so carefully and unobtrusively in terms of children's ongoing activities that something of the benefits of both peer interaction and adult involvement are retained – an approach such as that of 'structuring play in the early years at school' (Manning and Sharp, 1977). Ultimately, the backgrounds and needs of the children and the aims of the preschool must be the criteria for making such decisions.

12 Implications and applications

Doing research has its problems, and research on preschool organisations and facilities is no exception. There are difficulties in designing a feasible and satisfactory methodology, in selecting criteria for evaluation, and also in the interpretation of the results. While the first two sets of problems are particularly those of the researcher, the last set are as much those of anyone to whom the results may be of practical importance. In the human sciences, the interpretation of findings must be made within the context of the values and objectives of those persons seeking to make use of them.

In this final chapter we evaluate the general approach adopted in these studies, and consider the limits to the generality of our findings. We draw out implications of our findings and examine their bearing in the broader context of aims and values in the provision, expansion, and design of facilities for preschool children.

General approach and methodology: summary and evaluation

Amongst developmental psychologists, Bronfenbrenner (1977) in particular has made a plea that more research should be ecologically valid; that is to say, the research should be carried out in settings or situations which are familiar to the child and which elicit a normal range of responses. Although many of our children had not attended a playgroup before, nevertheless our research had ecological valididity in the sense that attending some form of preschool is usual for a substantial proportion of 3- and 4-year-olds. Naturally, the results of our research programme are only applicable to such preschool environments – we cannot infer much about space requirements or effects of toy variety in the home, for example. We have also examined the preschool environment purely on its own terms, and have not considered the 'exosystem' (Bronfenbrenner, 1977), the impact of the preschool on family life, and other aspects outside the immediate preschool setting.

Within these limitations, we felt ourselves fortunate in being able to achieve a generally good control of the variables we were specifically interested in, without sacrificing ecological validity. A very real and fundamental difficulty of research into many areas linked with social policy issues is that experimental control is not available, and hence inferences from research findings are difficult and contestable. The investigation of the effects of day care is a case in point (Belsky and Steinberg, 1978); for example, the comparability of day-care and home-reared samples in particular studies is open to question. If certain effects are found in one study, what particular aspects of the day-care system investigated might be responsible? These are inevitable kinds of question which do not remove the justification or the need for such research, but do render policy initiatives based closely on their results difficult to argue and agree upon.

A few of our environmental conditions were rather unusual, and would probably have been perceived as such by the parents and children. Notably, the conditions with a very high spatial density and the conditions when only large apparatus was available (see Chapter 6) were distinctly different from normal playgroup conditions. These conditions were only presented for a small number of sessions. The other variations which were made – in amounts of space and play equipment, in size of group, number of staff, and their degree of involvement – seemed well within the range of playgroups and preschool instructions. The regular variations, right from the start of the playgroup, meant that the children did not expect one standard routine and did not show surprise at the changes we made. (If anything they might have been atypical in being used to such changes.)

Ecological validity was assisted by the fact that we seldom tested the children individually – only at the beginning and end of the second year (Chapter 9). Otherwise, data on the children were obtained by observation, supplemented by staff ratings. The observer who made the bulk of the observations felt that the children largely ignored his presence, and this is borne out both by remarks of visitors to this effect, and by the very low frequencies recorded of talking to or contacting the observer.

Given the constraints of time and manpower, the use of short repeated time samples provided much information which seemed generally statistically reliable. At least for the major studies, sufficient samples per child were obtained in each condition; twenty or more 40-second samples seemed adequate (less for comparing free play and structured activities, where the differences in behaviour were larger than in the other studies). The shorter studies reported in Chapter 6 are not so adequate in this respect. Of course the number of samples needed depends on the frequency of the behaviour under investigation. The results are more reliable for frequent behaviours such as talking, looking at other children, object use, physical activity; less so for infrequent behaviours. Often, the formation of composite categories, such as agonistic behaviour, or automanipulative behaviour, provided a way of circumventing this problem.

The validity of the results also depends on the accuracy and stability of the observer's recording. This was discussed in more detail in Chapter 2, and was found to be satisfactory or good except for a few categories such as those involved in automanipulation, which were easy to miss. The categories themselves gave a wide overview of social, physical, and play behaviour. Within the constraints under which we operated it would have been difficult to cover more. However, some aspects of the children's behaviour obviously were not picked up by the observational scheme used. In relation to the kinds of results we obtained, two omissions spring to mind.

First, there were no measures of the complexity of play or activity. For example, while fantasy play was scored for occurrence or non-occurrence, no further indication of its complexity was obtained, although this would be feasible. In another study (Smith and Dodsworth, 1978), the existence of elaborated or replica use of objects in fantasy play was recorded. Other methods are possible. In the investigations reported here, the nearest measures are the length of the episode and the number of participants, and these were available for only one study (Chapter 9). It would have been nice to have known whether the size of group affected complexity of play, for example (Chapter 4).

Second, although special records were generally kept of any aggressive or agonistic encounters, similar records were not kept for episodes of 'prosocial' behaviour – examples of one child helping another, sharing things, or caring for another child. The study of prosocial behaviour in preschool children dates back to Murphy's investigations (1937) of 'sympathetic behaviour', and earlier, but until recently has not attracted the same interest as aggressive behaviour (Mussen and Eisenberg-Berg, 1977). At the time we planned the investigations, prosocial behaviour was not uppermost in our minds. We would probably plan differently now; for example, to investigate the relative bearing of structured activities or free play on children's prosocial behaviour. Given the findings for aggressive behaviour, the answer might be interesting; but we cannot infer it from our data. A difficulty with recording prosocial behaviour, however, is that it is more difficult to define and demarcate than aggressive behaviour. If one child plays together with another, or complies with a request, is this prosocial behaviour, or is some more active helping initiative required?

The observations made on the children were generally augmented by getting the playgroup staff to complete rating scales on features of the experimental conditions, and sometimes on the children as well. This information was useful, especially in contrast with the observational records. It indicated which aspects were most salient to staff, and how they felt about, for example, high or low staff:child ratios. However, they were by no means always accurate at assessing the impact on the children. For example, they reported more aggression in larger size classes (Chapter 4), although per child there was no increase in frequency of aggression. The value of the staff reports most emphatically did not mean that they could be used as a substitute for measures obtained from more time-consuming direct observation.

In retrospect, we might also have gained some valuable information by interviewing the children; at least, the older ones (4-year-olds). At this age range children can give reasons why they like friends (Hayes, 1978) and they can report accurately on class friendships (Smith and Delfosse, 1978) and dominance relationships (Sluckin and Smith, 1977). Possibly we could usefully have asked them about the different environmental conditions, or at least their awareness of them. For example, how aware were they of the small group and large group conditions? Our observations established very different sociometric patterns for large and small groups (Chapter 4). Given the importance of friendships for the young child, this could have provided a useful way of structuring an interview. We might have asked them whether they preferred mornings with a few well-known children, or mornings with many children and a wider choice of friends, including perhaps one or two they felt particularly close to.

Another important feature of most of our investigations – all except that comparing structured activities and free play – was that each study was replicated on independent groups of children. We believe this to be particularly important and valuable, and on the whole the pattern of results bears this out. Finding the same result in the two groups either puts an individually 'significant' result on a very firm footing, or makes strong trends in both groups a likely candidate for further investigation. Similarly, an absence of trends in both groups (as for example with spatial density and aggression, within the usual range of densities, Chapter 5) gives us further confidence in the finding. The possibility of spuriously accepting results as 'significant' or 'non-significant' is reduced, as was discussed in Chapter 2.

The two groups used for the studies in Chapters 4, 5, 6, and 10 were essentially similar. Thus, concordance of results gives us confidence in generalising the results to similar groups in similar conditions. It does not increase our confidence in generalising the results to different contexts. In considering the overall generality of our findings, the issue arises again as to how similar our own playgroups were to conditions in other preschool settings to which our results might be of relevance.

There are many factors here, such as the location in which we worked (Sheffield – a North Midlands industrial city), and the time of our investigation (early to mid-1970s). However, the factors which are probably the most important are the background of the children, the particular staff we employed, and the number and duration of playgroup sessions. In all these respects, other preschool institutions may be similar or they may be considerably different.

The social background of our children was reasonably varied, but it would certainly have been possible to find children with generally more impoverished or 'deprived' family circumstances, both in Sheffield and elsewhere. Whereas our composition was perhaps reasonably typical of many playgroups and nursery schools or classes, day nurseries often have a large proportion of children with difficult home circumstances. Again, some nursery schools are sited in areas where children are considered to be at severe educational disadvantage, as in the Educational Priority Areas. Decisions as to the best preschool curriculum are likely to be particularly affected by the previous experiences of the children and the ongoing home environment, and our results from Chapter 9 should be interpreted in this light. It seems less likely that results on, for example, spatial density would be so affected, but here again the possible effects of living in high-rise flats or other very cramped conditions should be considered. Children from such homes might be more in need of spacious preschool facilities, if only for vigorous motor activity to promote physical health and general motor coordination.

Our playgroup staff varied in background and training (see Chapter 2). Obviously, their particular personalities and ways of interacting with the children would have most bearing on the studies in Chapters 9 and 10, where structured-activities conditions were involved. In the studies on free-play conditions (Chapters 4, 5, and 6) there is little reason to qualify the results on these grounds.

The results for the free-play conditions might be especially affected by the number and duration of sessions. Two sessions of two-and-a-half hours a week, while not unusual for playgroups, is relatively modest compared with the time children spend in nursery schools, and especially in day nurseries. Possibly the effects of amount and variety of resources, such as space and play equipment, would be greater or more cumulative if children were meeting five times a week, for most of the day. To some extent this is counter-indicated by our failure to find time through session or time through year effects interacting significantly with the experimental variables (Chapters 4 and 5). However, in the case of full-time nurseries, the increase in the amount of time spent in the institution is so great that this qualification may not be relevant. Even if the trends found in our studies also held for full-time nurseries – as seems likely – the threshold of effects or their magnitude may be different (for example, the threshold for spatial density effects on aggression (Chapter 7) might be different). Also, effects which we failed to detect might become much more obvious and important.

These qualifications have been made before, but we do not apologise for making them again because of their significance. In this context, the findings from each of the studies are summarised.

Summary of results of separate studies

Number of children in the group

The behaviour of the same children was observed when by themselves (small group) or with other children (large group). Different ratios of small to large group size (2:3, 1:2, 1:3) were investigated over three successive terms. Resources (space, play equipment) were varied commensurately with overall group size.

The most noticeable results were on sociometric structure. Same-sex pairs of children playing together were more frequent in the larger classes. Table play was more common, and so were records of no activity. In classes with as few as ten children, the children all knew each other well, and most were involved in a close sociometric structure with large subgroups and more cross-sex friendships. More fantasy play was observed in the smaller classes. Aggressive behaviour did not vary with class size.

Playgroups staff preferred classes of a middle size (15–25) rather than either extreme (10 or 30).

Amounts of space and play equipment

Three space conditions and three equipment conditions were covaried independently over a nine-month period. Spatial densities were 25, 50, or 75 sq. ft per child. Either one, two, or three sets of play equipment were provided. Class size was constant at 24 children.

The main effects were on choices of activity. The amount of space available mainly affected the amount and kind of physical activity. In a larger space there was more running, chasing, and vigorous or unusual uses of apparatus. In a smaller space there was more use of the climbing-frame and slide. A smaller space also meant more physical contacts between children, but no substantial change in social or aggressive behaviour.

Effects of amount of play equipment were more wide-ranging. When more equipment was available, children played in smaller subgroups, or switched from large parallel subgroups to smaller parallel subgroups or solitary play. The more popular items such as the tricycles and Wendy houses were used extensively. Less popular items tended to be neglected. There was less sharing of equipment, but also less aggressive behaviour. Physical activity decreased, but there was little change in levels of social contact or interaction *per se*. There were some indications that conditions with more play equipment were less stressful for the children since less crying and sucking was observed.

Playgroup staff generally preferred the richer environments.

Subsidiary studies of physical resources

These studies were carried out over a relatively small number of sessions.

One investigation compared spatial densities of 15 and 60 sq. ft per child. At 15 sq. ft per child, physical activity was greatly inhibited and even walking was reduced. More parallel play in large subgroups took place in relatively stationary activities such as sandpits or tables. There was some evidence of less social interaction, and more aggressive behaviour – results which were not found for the less extreme spatial variations made previously.

A second study compared behaviour when one complete set of play equipment was available, with behaviour when half a set was available. Even with relatively little play equipment, the children still occupied themselves, with an increase in free motor activity. Much running and gross motor activity was also observed during short periods when no play equipment was present.

A third study compared the effects of having only large apparatus available, with the effects when mainly small manipulative toys were available. Having only large apparatus produced a marked increase in both social and physical activity in many children, with some very creative uses of the tables, chairs, toy chests, tricycles, and prams. Having mainly small toys produced an increase in object manipulation in many children, and a decrease in gross motor activity. Automanipulative behaviours were less frequent.

A comparison of structured-activities and free-play conditions

Starting from an initial comparable baseline, one class of children experienced a programme involving high staff interaction (structured activities) over a two-term period, whilst another class experienced a programme involving minimal staff interaction (free play). A final common baseline period was observed at the end of the project. The two classes were closely matched in composition and in the physical resources provided.

Structured activities resulted in children spending more time interacting with staff, and less with peers. They spent longer periods at fewer activities – those which staff were working with. Most children joined in activities, so few were alone; but for some, joining in was a rather passive business. There was less general physical activity, and less rough-and-tumble play. Fantasy play was also less frequent. The two most durable effects, which seemed to persist into the final baseline condition, were a continued increase in attention span at activities, and some increase in aggressive interactions with other children.

The playgroup staff generally felt that some mixture of the two conditions would be preferable. Each was felt to be of particularly benefit to some children, but there was little agreement amongst the staff as to which children benefitted from which condition.

Variations in staff: child ratio in the structured-activities condition

Staff:child ratios were varied from 1:4 to 1:10 by changing both the number of staff available and the number of children present at different sessions and over two terms. Verbal contacts and interactions between staff and children, and amongst children themselves, were recorded.

Most staff–child interactions were conversations about play activities, averaging about six utterances. These were generally longer than child–child conversations. Older children tended to make more contacts with staff, but there were great individual variations. Staff were fairly accurate at naming children who interacted with them a lot, and rated these children as sociable and friendly.

Variations caused by differing numbers of staff or children had similar effects. Worsening the staff:child ratio meant that staff slightly increased the frequency of their contacts, but not enough to compensate for the reduction in the amount of contact made with any individual child. Members of staff were faced with relatively more incoming verbal contacts from children, more of which went unanswered. Conversations tended to be shorter, and more staff verbalisations were about routine matters or were prohibitions. The inequality of staff contacts to different children did not change substantially. Children tended to talk more to other children.

Playgroup staff showed only a slight tendency to rate sessions with a worse staff:child ratio as less enjoyable or effective. Perhaps not surprisingly, they rated these sessions as appreciably more exhausting.

Implications of the findings

These will be considered in two sections, following the structure of the book. First, considerations of the free-play behaviour of preschool children in relation to numbers and resources. Second, the relative advantages and disadvantages of free play or structured activities in the preschool, and the effects of staff:child ratio in the structured-activities conditions.

Numbers and resources for free play

The studies of the free-play behaviour of the children considered the impact of the amount of space, the amount and variety of play equipment, and the number of children in the class on aspects of their behaviour. A detailed review of our own results and those of others is provided in Chapter 7.

The clearest implication from this work is that at least 25 sq. ft of free space should be available per child in preschool institutions. Three studies, including our own results (Chapter 6), indicate that social behaviour is less frequent in conditions more crowded than 25 sq. ft per child, and it is also likely that an increase in aggressive behaviour may occur. Staff are likely to find such conditions unpleasant, and movement is impeded. These are all undesirable effects, and there are no benefits to counterbalance them. A minimum of 25 sq. ft per child is often recommended, and we suggest that it is firmly followed. Above 25 sq. ft per child, we do not have evidence that the spatial provision is very important, except for the amount of free motor activity. This increases fairly sharply up to 50 sq. ft per child, then less rapidly.

Preschool staff may or may not greatly value free motor activity and the rough-and-tumble or chasing games which often accompany them. It is probably particularly important as physical exercise for children from cramped home environments, and it is a good way for some children (more often boys) to make friends. However, it is also noisy and occasionally disruptive of other activities.

Increasing the amount of space available per child will increase such free motor activity; putting more play equipment into the available space will reduce it. If physical exercise is valued, but staff do not particularly want much rough-and-tumble play, or do not have much space available, then provision of climbing apparatus in a moderately sized space will tend to encourage physical activity in a vertical rather than a horizontal plane. Removal of small toys will tend to increase both free motor activity and physical activity on apparatus. Small classes of around ten children may also decrease rough-and-tumble play without greatly affecting general physical activity.

It may be an aim to encourage social or cooperative play between children. Some decrease in the amount of play equipment available will encourage larger subgroups in cooperative play, and children who usually play alone may move into parallel play. However, the actual frequency of cooperative play is difficult to change. It has not been shown that decreasing play equipment affects this, nor has class size been found to have any clear effects. If class size is small – about ten or twelve children – a close-knit group can be expected in which all the children know each other well; cooperative subgroups will be large, and cross-sex friendships more common. In large classes children will on average know each other less well, and same-sex pairs will be the most common subgroups in cooperative play.

For at least a short-term increase in the frequency of cooperative play, temporary removal of small toys, leaving only large apparatus, could be tried. This would be feasible only if vigorous spontaneous play is tolerated and staff are available to reassure one or two children who may at first find the novel conditions unsettling.

Aggressive behaviour in free-play situations will be less frequent when more play equipment is available per child. There will also be fewer signs of stress such as crying or thumb-sucking, and fewer cases of children not engaging in any activity.

Providing more play equipment may mean that children tend to concentrate use on the particularly popular items. If a wider range of activities or different activities are to be encouraged in a free-play setting, then some reduction in the amount of equipment per child might be called for. Alternatively, the variety of equipment could be reduced. Removing small toys will encourage imaginative and unusual uses of the large apparatus, even amongst some children who are not usually interested in such active play. Conversely, removing large apparatus may encourage some children into quieter manipulative play with objects and table-based activities. Table play also seems to be encouraged in larger classes. Fantasy play can be encouraged by small classes.

Factors such as class size, available space, and amount and variety of play equipment, will often be only partially under the influence or control of staff or organisers of a preschool institution. Apart from any constraints imposed by finance or the building available, it is clearly not possible for us to recommend any optimal balance of these factors, apart from ensuring that space is not too constrained. Variations of class size and amount and variety of equipment will produce several effects, some of which may be considered beneficial, others not.

The summary above has been made in terms of which particular behaviours staff might or might not want to facilitate. However, it must be remembered that by influencing one type of behaviour changes may also be brought about in others. For example, reducing aggression by providing more toys may also reduce physical activity and size of subgroups. In practical circumstances it may be more useful to consider the likely effects of particular changes that might be planned.

If an increase or reduction in class size together with commensurate resources is planned (for example, by splitting a large classroom or two) the results of the study in Chapter 4 are particularly relevant.

If the size of a class is to be varied without changing resources, then the likely consequences of changing spatial and equipment densities may be gauged from the findings presented in Chapter 5.

Similarly, if for a given size of class the amount of play equipment is to be changed, the findings on the effects of amount and density of play equipment are relevant, and if the amount of space is to be changed, the findings on the effects of space and spatial density should be consulted. These are summarised in Chapters 5 and 7.

If the kind of equipment is to be varied by having mainly large apparatus or mainly small toys available the reader is referred to Chapter 6.

Free play and structured activities

The manner and extent to which staff should actively involved themselves in encouraging and/or structuring certain activities of children, or alternatively allow them to pursue their own objectives, is again dependent on the backgrounds of the children and the objectives of the preschool programme.

The main effect of staff involvement and interaction with children is that staff–child interaction increases, and conversely that child–child interaction decreases. The better the ratio of staff to children, the stronger this effect is likely to be. As a result, the main benefits of staff involvement are likely to be in terms of cognitive and linguistic stimulation. The main benefits of free play are likely to be in terms of the development of peer relationships.

There are a number of aspects of staff involvement, which were not considered separately in the study reported in Chapter 10. The following are presented as suggestions rather than as any definitive statement.

One aspect of staff involvement is that of general conversation with children about activities. This in itself might be an opportunity to improve language skills. Adult conversation may provide a model of appropriate language in the situation, as well as more directly teaching vocabulary. It may also improve cognitive skills, by using concepts such as relative size, shape, position, and by providing and eliciting from the child thoughts and statements about the immediate focus of activity and the wider world outside the preschool.

It is worth noting that neither our study nor that of Thompson (1944) found evidence for such effects in terms of standardised test scores. It may be that for children from average or advantaged backgrounds, such general linguistic and cognitive benefits are relatively small, especially since the time the child spends in nursery school or playgroup is small relative to the time spent at home. After all, even in a well-staffed preschool, the amount of interaction with staff which any one child will experience will be considerably less than the total time spent in the setting. If the home environment is also stimulating, the corresponding benefits of nursery school, while useful in terms of providing a variety of experience, may not be so great as to be highly salient in a small study.

However, the bulk of evidence with 'disadvantaged' children does point to such benefits. In his review of intervention programmes, Bronfenbrenner (1974) concluded that preschool intervention in group settings did result in 'substantial gains in IQ and other cognitive measures during the first year of the program', and that 'cognitively structured curricula produced greater gains than play-oriented nursery programs'.

A second aspect of staff involvement is that staff may encourage children to persist at activities. This could happen directly or indirectly. Directly, staff may ask a child to continue with or complete some as yet unfinished task. Indirectly, simply talking about the task, or giving occasional encouragement, may cause the child to take more interest in the activity and persist at it longer. Within limits, this seems a desirable aim, and we found that the structured-activities condition not only increased such activity spans while it was in operation, but also led to an increase in the children's persistence when back in a free-play setting.

A third aspect of staff involvement relates to encouraging certain activities in children and discouraging others. In part, this could be achieved by varying both the equipment and the space available, as discussed earlier. Also, staff may directly encourage certain activities, for example, table play or sociodramatic play, and discourage others, such as rough-and-tumble play.

If rough-and-tumble play and noisy games are actively discouraged, it may well be advisable to structure certain active games such as dancing and miming to give scope for physical activity. The actual developmental importance of rough-and-tumble activities, reviewed in Chapter 11, is still uncertain.

The traditional structuring of activities, by decreasing child–child interaction, may also decrease the frequency or complexity of fantasy and sociodramatic play sequences. However, this need not be the case. Sensitive staff involvement in such play episodes can increase their frequency amongst children who do not engage in such play often or at a high level; and this increase persists if such involvement subsequently ceases. The research evidence, reviewed in Chapter 11, suggests that the cognitive and linguistic benefits of this play tutoring, as it is usually called, are equal to those of more conventional skills tutoring. In addition, it seems to be one kind of staff involvement which may help, rather than hinder, the level of social interactions amongst the children themselves.

If the active involvement of staff for part or all of a preschool curriculum is a central aim, then the question of staff:child ratio arises. Our own research bears most on the first respect mentioned above, that of staff conversations with children. Even here, the evidence is indirect, since our data are about processes rather than products. We do not know the ultimate effects of poorer staff:child ratios, but the immediate effect is likely to be a worsening of both the amount and the equality of communication with staff that a particular child receives. Generally, there will be a limit to the extent to which staff are able to adapt or increase their contacts according to differing numbers of children. With more children present, any particular child will have fewer conversations with a member of staff, the conversations will be shorter, more communications to staff will go unanswered, and more conversations will be about routine or prohibitory matters rather than concerned with play activities. It seems highly likely that this would be detrimental to the cognitive or linguistic stimulation aimed for. Even if structured activities occupy only part of the preschool curriculum, it is arguable that that part should be of high quality, and that good staff:child ratios are a necessary condition for this.

Whatever the aims of actively involving the staff with children's activities, it is likely that the distribution of contacts over individual children will be highly non-uniform. Probably some older children, and perhaps more girls than boys, will get much more attention than others. Staff may be aware of this, and describe these children as being particularly friendly and sociable. it is not clear, however, whether these are the children who necessarily should be getting the most staff attention. Unfortunately, there is not much evidence that improved staff:child ratios will change such inequalities (though overall levels of interaction will of course improve).

Against any benefits of staff involvement must be weighed the possible costs of decreased peer interaction. These might be minimised if much staff interaction was done subtly, via the children's ongoing play activities

(Manning and Sharp, 1977), or via fantasy play tutoring. More traditional modes of staff involvement may not only mean less rough-and-tumble play, gross physical activity, and fantasy play, as described earlier. It may also be the case that children's abilities to manage conflict situations with peers get insufficient practice in a highly structured environment. This is certainly a speculative result which stands in need of further research; and clearly staff involvement in conflicts is necessary in some cases. However, it is reasonable to hypothesise at present that children can sort out most conflicts by themselves and that in doing so some important social and cognitive learning is taking place. The involvement of staff in conflicts, at least in a proportion of cases, may be insensitive to the reasons and context of the conflicts. It would clearly be wrong for staff to opt out of or ignore conflict resolution, but it may well be something they need not be especially vigilant about in the case of most children and most situations.

It seems likely that some alternation of free-play periods and more structured-activity periods may be a desirable compromise. This was suggested by our playgroup staff, and it is of course found in many preschools. However, in deciding the balance of free play to structured activities the advantages and disadvantages of each for the children concerned should be borne in mind. Play tutoring or similar subtle involvement deserves consideration as providing some benefits of staff involvement while not noticeably decreasing the level of peer interactions.

The provision of preschool facilities: aims, values, and areas for further research

The level of provision of institutional facilities for preschool children, and the nature of the provision required, continues to be an area of active debate in the industrialised countries. In Britain, reviews of this issue have been made by J. Tizard (1974), Pringle and Naidoo (1976), and Van der Eyken (1977).

The statistics of preschool provision in Britain are reviewed at the beginning of this book. The most obvious factor is the insufficient provision of full-time care for young children of working mothers. Many mothers who work for substantial periods of the week have to make private arrangements with childminders. Little is known about conditions of childminding and the experiences of the children with childminders who receive no training for this task. Mayall and Petrie (1977), on the basis of a small-scale study, indicate that few childminders appear to be motivated primarily by a concern for children, and that often an inadequate range of toys is available and opportunity for physical exercise is small. As presently constituted, and no doubt despite a minority of more dedicated and concerned individuals, childminding does not generally seem to be a suitable means of care for the under-fives.

The peak of provision for the under-fives in Britain was in the late nineteenth century. In 1875, nearly 20,000 under-threes were in elementary schools, and some 350,000 under-fives (out of an appreciably smaller total population than today). The reason for these large numbers seems to have been the lack of public nurseries for working-class mothers in full employment. The 1870 Education Act allowed school boards to make attendance compulsory for children of 'not less than five years'. As the majority of children over five years were compelled to attend school over the succeeding decades, they were often accompanied by younger brothers and sisters. 'Dame Schools gradually disappeared as these children were accommodated in babies' classes of elementary and infant schools' (Whitbread, 1972). The percentage of children aged 3–5 attending elementary schools in England and Wales increased from 24 per cent in 1870, to 29 per cent in 1880, 33 per cent in 1890, and 43 per cent in 1900. As these numbers built up in the elementary schools, the under-threes began to feel the squeeze. From the peak in 1875, their numbers at elementary school fell to 3,500 by 1895. However, 'infant education from three to seven was recognised in practice by the public, teachers and the inspectorate as the first stage in elementary education' (*ibid.*).

The educational ideas of Pestalozzi and Froebel had been influential, via the earlier middle-class kindergartens. But the curriculum of the elementary schools, providing mass infant education, had become one of stereotyped mechanical exercises under class instruction. Moves to reform this situation were fuelled by Montessori's work in Italy, and subsequently in Britain by educators and researchers such as Margaret McMillan and Susan Isaacs. Meanwhile the 1905 Code of Regulation for Public Elementary Schools allowed local education authorities to exclude children under five, if they wished – a response to increased pressure for places as the school leaving age increased. But very few nursery schools were built, and most nursery provision was private. The percentage of 3- and 4-year-olds in elementary schools fell to 23 per cent in 1910, 15 per cent in 1920, and 13 per cent by 1970. Despite contemporary social and medical evidence of the need for nursery schools, expansion of secondary education had priority.

There was some very limited expansion of nursery places in the 1930s, although it was in this period that the more child-centred infant school curriculum came to be accepted. The Second World War produced a temporary increase in nursery provision. 'Whenever the choice existed, mothers showed a clear preference for nurseries and nursery classes over child-minders' (*ibid.*). But again nursery expansion was squeezed by primary and secondary education in the post-war years, and casual childminding again increased.

The Plowden Report in 1967 recommended a large expansion of nursery education. The emphasis was by now on the educational needs of young children, and the possible importance of nursery education as a means of providing compensatory education for disadvantaged children. The Urban Aid programme of 1969 provided some extra nursery places in Educational Priority Areas. In 1972 the White Paper, *Education: A Framework for Expansion*, and the accompanying circular 2/73, *Nursery Education*, followed up the Plowden Report and recommended part-time provision for 35 per cent of 3-year-olds and 75 per cent of 4-year-olds, but full-time provision for only 15 per cent of this age range. The emphasis was mainly on the social and educational needs of the children. So far, expansion has been limited and these targets have not been met. Although full-time preschool provision is probably available for about 15 per cent of the age range, much of this is not nursery education; and the 15 per cent figure is too small compared with the needs of working mothers.

Historically, it is clear that working mothers have provided a major demand for well-run nursery places. This is probably still the case, if such facilities are adequately publicised (Halsey and Smith, 1976). On the educational side, many administrators have looked askance at the idea of providing full-time places for young children so that their mothers may work; but in the present economic situation, many mothers are working, and less satisfactory alternative care arrangements have to be found.

The effects of day care on young children continue to be debated, but by and large early reports of ill-effects seem to be unjustified. In a critical review, Belsky and Steinberg (1978) conclude that high-quality, centre-based day care has neither salutory nor deleterious effects upon the intellectual development of the child, and is not disruptive of the child's emotional bond with his or her mother. In a situation where many mothers of young children are at work, it is important that day-care facilities should be of high quality; the separation of the day nursery and nursery school tradition is illogical and deplorable, and recent schemes of integrated provision, providing day nursery hours and facilities, but with some nursery teachers on the staff, is an obvious step towards achieving the required provision.

The educational importance of the preschool should not be neglected, but equally it should not be overstated. Its use as a means of compensatory education seems to be limited (Tizard, J., 1974; Bronfenbrenner, 1974). Any educational gains accruing to nursery school children seem to be temporary. It is not a panacea for educational disadvantage which ultimately refers back to poor home conditions and to more profound and enduring social and economic factors. At the immediate educational level, home visiting and intervention with parents and children may be as important as or more important than specific nursery experience. At the broader level, ecological intervention is required (Bronfenbrenner, 1974).

The social importance of the preschool is highly valued by many parents, particularly those who send children to playgroups. In many modern urban settings, chances for under-fives to play with peers are not great. Indeed, a sample of nursery school teachers rate the social–emotional aims of nursery education as the most important, more so than intellectual aims, which were ranked second (Taylor *et al.* 1972). The social needs of mothers also require consideration; preschools affect the family, not only the child, and their objectives must take account of this. While working mothers may seek full-time care, many non-working mothers may find home life with one or two very young children a strain if the home conditions are poor and if not even part-time child-care facilities are available. Brown *et al.* (1975) found a high incidence of depression and psychiatric disturbance in working-class mothers in London; and for unemployed women, but not for employed women, having a young child at home was the significant factor affecting vulnerability.

The objectives of preschool provision are plainly partly educational and partly social, so far as the child is oncerned; they also aim partly to help parents, whether employed or not. The relative balance of these objectives will affect the kind of preschool provision and expansion which is most desirable. That some kind of expansion is desirable seems incontrovertible.

Research can do much to make future planning of preschool facilities as rational as possible in the light of the objectives decided upon. Much research still needs to be done on the factors mentioned. What kind of demand exists for what kind of facilities? More needs to be known about childminding, and whether training of childminders, and organised neighbourhood facilities, might be preferable to the traditional nursery school. Although we now know a good deal about the intellectual and social consequences of nursery schools and day care, there is scope for continuing research in these areas as conditions change, and research questions and methodology become more well focussed and subtle.

In this book we have been concerned with the ecology of the preschool itself. Whether the preschool be a day nursery, nursery class, playgroup, or neighbourhood centre, decisions need to be made on the size of classes and the amounts of space and play equipment to be provided. We believe we have provided some solid evidence by which to assess decisions on these matters. We have also broached the issue of the role of the adult in the preschool, and the ratio of adults to children in a structured situation. Much more work is needed in this area. Other research is being done on preschool curricula and their effects, some using process as well as product analysis (e.g. Miller and Dyer, 1975). We are not aware of any product studies which have systematically examined long-term results of different staff:child ratios.

We need to know more about the developmental significance of certain behaviours which may be either encouraged or inhibited by different ecological conditions. The real significance of rough-and-tumble play remains to be established. How much free motor activity is needed to provide adequate physical exercise? Are conflicts best sorted out by the children themselves, and what exceptions are there to this? These are questions raised by our own findings, and there are others which could be considered – for example, the encouragement of prosocial behaviour.

Although we varied class size in the research project, we were not able to vary either the sex or age distribution in the groups. These would both be interesting areas for investigation. A study of age distribution would have most immediate practical significance. The possible benefits of mixed-age groups has recently received attention (Hartup, 1976), and some nurseries and schools use a family-grouping policy. It is worth remembering, as Whitbread (1972) points out, that earlier this century the nursery–infant school was conceived of as catering for the 3- to 7-year-olds. At present, we have very little firm evidence of the benefits of same-aged or mixed-aged groupings of children in these age ranges.

Much research needs to be done, but this will always be the case as society changes, and research questions and areas of interest change with it. The incompleteness of research findings should not be taken as a justification for continuing to fall short of an adequate national policy on preschool provision. We already know a great deal about what is needed, and the detailed needs of parents and children in particular areas can be ascertained. Some workable consensus should be reached rapidly on the overall objectives of preschool institutions in our society. As financial circumstances permit, this should lead to an expansion and restructuring of facilities, hand in hand with continued research and the monitoring of the detailed consequences of such changes.

Details of age and family background of children

First year of project: study on amount of space and play equipment

Child	Age at September 1971 (months)	Father's and mother's occupations	Siblings (and babies born during year)
Group One: older boys			
1	46	Architect Housewife	Older brother
2	42	Company director Housewife	Younger sister
3	40	Lecturer Housewife	Younger brother
4	38	Miller Housewife	Younger sister
5	37	— Civil servant (divorced)	None
6	33	Schoolteacher Playgroup assistant	Older sister
Group One: older girls			
7	47	Salesman Housewife	Younger sister
8	44	— Housewife (divorced)	Older sister
9	40	Lecturer Housewife	Two older brothers; younger sister
10	39	Businessman Schoolteacher	Younger sister
11	37	Glazier Staff nurse	Younger brother
12	33	Grinder Housewife	Older brother; two older sisters
Group One: younger boys			
13	33	Administrator (Polytechnic) Housewife	Baby sister
14	33	TV engineer Housewife	Two older brothers; older sister

323

Child	Age at September 1971 (months)	Father's and mother's occupations	Siblings (and babies born during year)
15	32	Engineering inspector Housewife	Older sister; younger sister
16	32	Salesman Housewife	Older brother
17	31	Capstan turner Housewife	Younger brother
18	28	Grinder Housewife	Younger sister

Group One: younger girls

19	33	Machinist Nursing auxiliary	Older brother
20	32	Technical rep. Housewife	Older brother
21	31	Sales manager Housewife	None
22	31	Telephone engineer Nursing auxiliary	Older brother
23	30	Pharmacologist Housewife	Older brother; older sister
24	29	Surveyor Housewife	Baby brother

Group Two: older boys

25	45	— Ex-student (unmarried)	None
26	43	Manager Housewife	Older brother
27	41	Remand Home supervisor Laboratory assistant	Older brother
28	37	Design engineer Housewife	None
29	36	Clerk Housewife	Younger brother
30	36	Schoolteacher Housewife	Two older sisters

Group Two: older girls

31	48	University porter Housewife	Younger sister
32	44	Lecturer Housewife	Older brother
33	41	Manager Housewife	Three older brothers; two older sisters
34	37	Bookmaker Housewife	Older sister

Child	Age at September 1972 (months)	Father's and mother's occupations	Siblings (and babies born during year)
35	36	Fitter's mate Housewife	Older brother
36	36	Metal worker Housewife	Older brother
Group Two: younger boys			
37	33	Merchant seaman Housewife	Older brother; older sister
38	32	Civil Servant Housewife	Baby brother
39	32	Airforce electrician Housewife	None
40	31	Manager Housewife	Older sister
41	30	Bus driver Housewife	Older brother; twin to child 47
42	28	Scientific officer Housewife	None
Group Two: younger girls			
43	33	Metal worker Housewife	Younger sister
44	32	Plumber Housewife	Older brother
45	32	Driving instructor Housewife	None
46	31	Building worker Garage attendant	Three older sisters
47	30	Bus driver Housewife	Older brother; twin to child 41
48	29	Art teacher Playgroup assistant	None

Second year of project: study comparing free play and structured activities

Child	Age at September 1972 (months)	Father's and mother's occupations	Siblings (and babies born during year)
Group One: boys			
4	50	Miller Housewife	Younger sister

Child	Age at September 1972 (months)	Father's and mother's occupations	Siblings (and babies born during year)
5	49	— Civil servant (divorced)	None
6	45	Schoolteacher Playgroup assistant	Older sister
13	45	Administrator Housewife	Younger sister
15	44	Engineering inspector Housewife	Older sister; younger sister
17	43	Capstan turner Housewife	Younger brother
49	43	Printer Housewife	Three older brothers
50	38	Machine operator Housewife	None
51	36	Landscape contractor Housewife	None
52	33	Contractor Staff nurse	Younger sister
Group One: girls			
11	49	Glazier Staff nurse	Younger brother
36	48	Metal worker Housewife	Older brother
19	45	Machinist Nursing auxiliary	Younger brother
20	44	Technical rep. Housewife	Older brother
21	43	Sales manager Housewife	None
22	43	Telephone engineer Nursing auxiliary	Older brother
24	41	Surveyor Housewife	Younger brother
53	38	Accountant Housewife	Younger sister
54	36	Manager Housewife	Older brother; older sister
55	33	Copy reader Housewife	Baby sister
23	42	Pharmacologist Housewife	Older brother; older sister
56	32	Manager Teacher	Younger sister

Note: Children 3, 9, and 10 were also present in the group from September until December, when they left for school. They were not included in data collection.

Child	Age at September 1972 (months)	Father's and mother's occupations	Siblings (and babies born during year)
Group Two: boys			
28	49	Design engineer Housewife	None
29	48	Clerk Housewife	Younger brother
30	48	Schoolteacher Housewife	Two older sisters
37	45	Merchant seaman Housewife	Older brother; older sister
38	44	Civil servant Housewife	Younger brother
40	43	Manager Housewife	Older sister
42	40	Scientific officer Housewife	Baby sister
57	38	Excavator driver Housewife	Younger brother
58	35	Psychologist Housewife	Older brother; baby brother
59	34	Engineer Housewife	Two older brothers
Group Two: girls			
34	49	Bookmaker Housewife	Older sister
35	48	Fitter's mate Housewife	Older brother
43	45	Metal worker Housewife	Younger sister
44	44	Plumber Housewife	Older brother
45	44	Driving instructor Housewife	None
46	43	Building worker Housewife	Three older sisters
48	41	Art teacher Playgroup assistant	Baby sister
60	37	Telephone engineer Housewife	Younger sister
61	35	University porter Housewife	Older sister
62	32	Toolsetter Housewife	None
47	42	Bus driver Housewife	Older brother; twin brother
63	31	Decorator Domestic help	None

Note: Children 2, 26, 27, and 33 were also present in the group from September until December, when they left for school. They were not included in data collection.

Third year of project: study comparing different numbers of children in the group

Child	Age at September 1973 (months)	Father's and mother's occupations	Siblings (and babies born during year
Term One			
Group One: boys			
49	55	Printer Housewife	Three older brothers
17	55	Capstan turner Housewife	Younger brother
50	50	Machine operator Housewife	None
51	48	Landscape contractor Housewife	None
64	41	Lecturer Housewife	Younger sister
65	35	Chemical engraver Housewife	None
66	33	Glazier Nursing sister	Older sister
67	29	Capstan setter Domestic help	Older brother
68	28	Motor engineer Housewife	None
Group One: girls			
20	56	Technical rep. Housewife	Older brother; baby sister
21	55	Sales manager Housewife	None
22	55	Telephone engineer Nursing auxiliary	Older brother
23	54	Pharmacologist Housewife	Older brother; older sister
53	50	Accountant Housewife	Younger sister
54	48	Manager Housewife	Older brother; older sister
55	45	Copy reader Housewife	Younger sister
56	44	Manager Teacher	Younger sister
69	36	Salesman Shop manageress	Older sister
70	32	Transport driver Housewife	None
71	30	Machinist Housewife	Older brother

Child	Age at September 1973 (months)	Father's and mother's occupations	Siblings (and babies born during year)
Group Two: boys			
38	56	Civil servant Housewife	Younger brother
40	55	Manager Housewife	Older sister
72	53	Foreman welder Housewife	Younger brother
42	52	Scientific officer Housewife	Younger sister
57	50	Excavator driver Housewife	Younger brother
58	47	Psychologist Housewife	Older brother; younger brother
59	46	Engineer Housewife	Two older brothers
73	30	Excavator driver Housewife	Older brother
74	28	Design consultant Housewife	None
Group Two: girls			
45	56	Driving instructor Housewife	None
46	55	Building worker Housewife	Three older sisters
47	54	Bus driver Housewife	Older brother; twin brother
48	53	Art teacher Housewife	Younger sister
60	49	Telephone engineer Housewife	Younger sister
75	47	Market trader Housewife	Younger sister
61	47	University porter Housewife	Older sister
62	44	Tool setter Housewife	Baby sister
63	43	Decorator Housewife	Baby brother
76	37	Student Housewife	Older sister; younger sister
77	34	Lecturer Library assistant	None
78	33	Joiner Housewife	Younger brother
79	31	Stamper Housewife	Older sister

Child	Age at September 1973 (months)	Father's and mother's occupations	Siblings (and babies born during year)
Group Three: boys			
80	53	Salesman Housewife	Older brother
81	41	Computer programmer Housewife	None
82	41	Engineer Housewife	Older brother
83	39	Lecturer Housewife	Older brother; younger brother
84	37	Joiner Housewife	Older sister
85	32	Baker Housewife	Two older brothers; older sister
Group Three: girls			
86	50	Baker Housewife	Two older brothers; younger brother
87	49	Organ builder Housewife	Older sister
88	43	Garage manager Shopkeeper	Older sister
89	42	Shop owner Housewife	Older brother
90	40	Lecturer Housewife	Two older brothers; older sister
91	39	Engineering inspector Housewife	Older sister; older brother
January 1974 **Term Two** *Group One: boys*			
50	54	Machine operator Housewife	None
51	52	Landscape contractor Housewife	None
52	49	Contractor Staff nurse	Younger sister
64	45	Lecturer Housewife	Younger sister
65	39	Chemical engineer Housewife	None
66	37	Glazier Nursing sister	Older sister
67	33	Capstan setter Domestic help	Older brother
68	32	Motor engineer Housewife	None

Child	Age at January 1974 (months)	Father's and mother's occupations	Siblings (and babies born during year)
Group One: girls			
53	54	Accountant Housewife	Younger sister
55	49	Copy reader Housewife	Younger sister
56	48	Manager Teacher	Younger sister
69	40	Salesman Shop manageress	Older sister
70	36	Transport driver Housewife	None
71	34	Machinist Housewife	Older brother
Group Two: boys			
57	54	Excavator driver Housewife	Younger brother
58	51	Psychologist Housewife	Older brother; younger brother
59	50	Engineer Housewife	Two older brothers
92	47	Storeman Housewife	Older sister; younger sister
73	34	Excavator driver Housewife	Older brother
74	32	Design consultant Housewife	None
Group Two: girls			
60	53	Telephone engineer Housewife	Younger sister
75	51	Market trader Housewife	Younger sister
61	51	University porter Housewife	Older sister
62	48	Tool setter Housewife	Younger sister
63	47	Decorator Housewife	Younger brother
76	41	Student Housewife	Older sister, younger brother
77	38	Lecturer Housewife	Baby brother
78	37	Joiner Housewife	Younger brother

Child	Age at January 1974 (months)	Father's and mother's occupations	Siblings (and babies born during year)
Group Three: boys			
93	50	—	Older sister
		Shopkeeper	
82	45	Engineer	Older brother
		Housewife	
83	43	Lecturer	Older brother;
		Housewife	younger brother
84	41	Joiner	Older sister
		Housewife	
94	41	Research worker	Older brother;
		Housewife	younger sister
85	36	Baker	Two older brothers;
		Housewife	older sister
95	33	Driver	Two older brothers;
		Housewife	two older sisters
Group Three: girls			
86	54	Baker	Two older brothers;
		Housewife	younger brother
87	53	Organ builder	Older sister
		Housewife	
96	47	Gardener	Older sister;
		Housewife	Younger brother
88	47	Garage manager	Older sister
		Shopkeeper	
89	46	Shop owner	Older brother
		Housewife	
91	43	Engineering inspector	Older sister;
		Housewife	older brother
97	35	Motor mechanic	None
		Housewife	

April 1974
Term Three
Group One: boys

51	55	Landscape contractor	None
		Housewife	
52	52	Contractor	Younger sister
		Staff nurse	
65	42	Chemical engineer	None
		Housewife	
66	40	Glazier	Older sister
		Nursing sister	
67	36	Capstan setter	Older brother
		Domestic help	
68	35	Motor engineer	None
		Housewife	

Child	Age at April 1974 (months)	Father's and mother's occupations	Siblings (and babies born during year)
Group One: girls			
55	52	Copy reader Housewife	Younger sister
56	51	Manager Teacher	Younger sister
69	43	Salesman Manageress	Older sister
70	39	Transport driver Housewife	None
71	37	Machinist Housewife	Older brother
98	34	Telephone engineer Housewife	Older sister; younger sister
Group Two: boys			
58	54	Psychologist Housewife	Older brother; younger brother
92	50	Storeman Housewife	Older sister; younger sister
73	37	Excavator driver Housewife	Older brother
74	35	Design consultant Housewife	None
Group Two: girls			
75	54	Market trader Housewife	Younger sister
61	54	University porter Housewife	Older sister
62	51	Tool setter Housewife	Younger sister
63	50	Decorator Housewife	Younger brother; older sister
76	44	Student Housewife	Older sister; younger sister
77	41	Lecturer Housewife	Younger brother
78	40	Joiner Housewife	Younger brother
Group Three: boys			
93	53	— Shopkeeper	Older sister
99	49	Textile manager Housewife	Younger sister
82	48	Engineer Housewife	Older brother

Child	Age at April 1974 (months)	Father's and mother's occupations	Siblings (and babies born during year)
83	46	Lecturer Housewife	Older brother; younger brother
84	44	Joiner Housewife	Older sister
94	44	Research worker Housewife	Older brother; younger sister
100	42	Clerk Housewife	Older brother
85	39	Baker Housewife	Two older brothers; older sister
101	38	Builder Housewife	None
102	34	Company director Housewife	Younger sister
103	32	Social worker Housewife	None
Group Three: girls			
96	50	Gardener Housewife	Older sister; younger brother
88	50	Garage manager Shopkeeper	Older sister
89	49	Shop owner Housewife	Older brother
91	46	Engineering inspector Housewife	Older sister; older brother
104	44	Student Housewife	Older sister
105	42	Student Doctor	None
97	38	Motor mechanic Housewife	None
106	38	Fitter Housewife	None
107	38	— Housewife	None
108	36	Company director Housewife	Older brother
109	35	Joiner Housewife	Two older brothers
110	34	Cost accountant Assistant librarian	Older sister
111	34	Cooling tower erector Housewife	Older brother

Note: Child 108 attended Wednesdays only; child 111 attended Thursdays only.

Category definitions

Number and nature of companions

At the end of a time-sample period, the names of all the children or adults with whom the focal child played or interacted through the majority of the period were noted down, either as *group* or *parallel* companions.

The terms *group* and *parallel* were used in the same way as in Smith and Connolly (1972), based in turn on Parten (1932). *Group* companions interacted substantially with the child in the nature of the activity, either visually, verbally, through exchanging objects, or in the organisation of a game. *Parallel* companions did not interact with the child, or only fleetingly. They were engaged in a similar or identical activity to the child and were in close proximity, but their presence did not substantially affect his or her behaviour.

On this basis, nine mutually exclusive categories were defined. A child was always scored in one of these categories at the end of a sample period. Inter-observer agreement is given in brackets (see p. 40).

1   *Alone* (0.85). The child has no group or parallel companions.

2   *Small adult subgroup* (0.87). The child is in group activity with an adult and not more than two other children.

3   *Large adult subgroup* (0.77). The child is in group or parallel activity with an adult and three or more other children.

4   *Small parallel subgroup* (0.59). The child has no group companions but is in parallel activity with one or two other children.

5   *Large parallel subgroup* (0.61). The child has no group companions but is in parallel activity with three or more other children.

6   *Same-sex pair* (0.67). The child has one other child of the same sex as a group companion.

7   *Opposite-sex pair* (0.86). The child has one other child of the opposite sex as a group companion.

8   *Subgroup of three* (0.77). The child has two other children as group companions.

9   *Subgroup of four or more* (0.86). The child has three or more other children as group companions.

Two composite categories were defined as follows:

Parallel play (0.76). The child has no group companions but is in parallel activity with one or more other children. Categories 4 and 5 above.

Group play (0.88). The child has one or more other children as group companions. Categories 6, 7, 8, and 9 above.

In addition, two other statistics were calculated for each child from all of his or her sample data on companions:

Mean subgroup size (0.94). Mean size of subgroups (number of other children played with, plus one), when the child is in group play (categories 6, 7, 8, and 9 above).

Percentage same-sex companions (0.88). Number of same-sex companions as a percentage of total number of companions, when the child is in group play (categories 6, 7, 8, and 9 above).

In the comparison of organised-activity and free-play conditions (Chapter 9), categories 2 and 3 were replaced by categories 2a, 3a, and 3b, as follows:

2a   *Parallel (adult + children)*. The child is in parallel activity with an adult and one or more children.

3a   *Group adult*. The child is in group activity only with an adult; may be parallel to other children.

3b   *Group (adult + children)*. The child is in group activity with an adult and one or more children.

Toy or activity choice

At the end of a time sample period, all the activities engaged in or toys used by the focal child for about ten seconds or longer were recorded. The 22 categories defined below are comprehensive but not mutually exclusive; a child was always scored in one or more categories. Inter-observer agreement is given in brackets (see p. 40).

Use of a toy or apparatus was scored only if it was carried around, manipulated, or made use of. Merely holding an object, or being passively in contact with apparatus, was scored as *no activity*.

1   *Table play* (0.91). Play at table (e.g. with paper, scissors, crayons, beakers, beads, links, plasticine).

2   *Sandpit* (1.00). Play at sandpit, with sandpit toys. The sand bowls were sometimes filled with water, and water play was also included in this category.

3   *Easel* (1.00). Painting or chalking at the easel.

4   *Wendy house* (0.83). Play inside the Wendy house, or with the tea party toys (teapot, cups, small table) which were placed inside the Wendy house.

5   *Doll* (0.70). Use of doll or teddy bear, or of the pram or cradle (top part of pram).

6   *Dressing-up clothes* (1.00). Wearing clothes in addition to normal attire, e.g. cowboy hat, shawl. Wearing an apron for painting was not included. This category also included play with the clothes-horse on which the dressing-up clothes were usually hung.

7   *Climbing-frame* (1.00). Use of the climbing-frame, or the slide attached to it, or the mat at the bottom.

8   *Rocking-boat* (1.00). Use of the rocking-boat.
9   *Toy chest* (1.00). Use of the toy chest or toy chest lid.
10   *Tricycle* (1.00). use of the tricycle.
11   *Rough-and-tumble play* (0.75). Play-fighting, play-chasing, running in a group.
12   *Books* (1.00). Use of books or comics.
13   *Blocks* (0.83). Use of wooden blocks.
14   *Doll's house* (—). Use of the doll's house, or the small figures or furniture inside.
15   *Jigsaw* (1.00). Use of a jigsaw.
16   *Telephone* (1.00). Use of the telephone (an old GPO telephone placed near the Wendy house).
17   *Musical instruments* (1.00). Use of musical roller or other instrument such as cymbals, drum, bells, triangle.
18   *Miscellaneous play* (0.75). Play with toys not accounted for above. This category also includes conversational activity not involving objects or apparatus.
19   *Fantasy play* (0.80). Fantasy play was scored if there was clear evidence of actions, vocalisations, or object use occurring in a pretended or non-literal context. Examples are pretending to drive a car (arm movements), sound a horn (vocalisation), or sell tickets (object use). Behaviourally indicated use of imaginary objects is included. Use of miniature versions of real objects (e.g. toy cars, toy iron) was not scored as fantasy play unless there was additional evidence for the pretended nature of the activity. Any examples of role play, for example as mother, baby, monster, fireman, were scored as fantasy play.
20   *Unusual uses of apparatus* (—). Use of furniture or large apparatus (tables, chairs, rocking-boat, toy chest, tricycle) in unusual, non-obvious ways. Examples are putting chairs in a line to walk along of make a 'train'; spinning a rocking-boat upside-down; standing toy chest on end; sitting on inverted tricycles.
21   *Room fitments* (–). Manipulation of non-toy fixtures such as curtains or fire extinguisher.
22   *No activity* (0.94). The child is neither making active use of any object or apparatus, nor engaged in any substantial social interaction.

In the comparison of organised-activity and free-play conditions (Chapter 9), category 18 included categories 16 and 17 above. Category 3 included chalking on the floor. Category 14 included use of a puppet theatre. Four additional categories used were:

16a   *Water*. Play with water, washing dolls.
16b   *Shopping*. Use of cartons, boxes and scales.
17a   *Clay*. Use of clay or plasticine.
17b   *Miscellaneous organised activities*. Stories, dancing, bean bags and bucket, other organised activities not at table and not codable elsewhere.

The *tricycle* (category 10) was not used.

Behaviour units

Each unit was scored on an all-or-none (one–zero) basis of occurrence or non-occurrence in a sample period. In the case of contacts with other children or adults (verbal, visual, physical, object exchange, or agonistic) the name of each other person who made or received contacts during the sample period was recorded.

Many of the behaviour units were similar to or identical with units from Blurton Jones (1972b), Brannigan and Humphries (1972), Grant (1969), and W. C. McGrew (1970).

Units are grouped under the headings facial, vocal, visual, physical contact, postural, locomotor, object use, agonistic, and automanipulative.

The list contains a total of 89 units. This is a reduction from the 114 units originally scored from the time samples. Seven of the units are composites from 21 of the original units, which are listed subsequently. Also listed subsequently are eleven units which were scored but not analysed, owing to very infrequent occurrence or very low reliability. Following this, a shorter list of 27 units is presented, 16 of which are composites. This second list, which contains the behaviours of most interest, is used for ease of presentation of results in the main body of the text. Inter-observer agreement is given as a concordance in brackets (see p. 40).

List of 89 units

Facial units

1   *Simple smile* (0.61). Lips drawn slightly up and back, mouth closed or nearly so, no teeth visible. As Brannigan and Humphries 1,9; Grant 25,26.

2   *Upper smile* (0.65). Lips drawn up and back, only upper teeth visible. As Brannigan and Humphries 2,7,10; Grant 23,24.

3   *Open smile* (0.76). Lips drawn up and back, mouth opened. As Brannigan and Humphries 3,8; Grant 20,21,22.

4   *Pucker* (–). Tightening of muscles and wrinkling of skin around eyes and mouth. Brow puckered. As Blurton Jones 5.

Vocal units

5   *Cry/scream* (–). Any crying, whining, or screaming vocalisation, waaah, aaah-hah.

6   *Chuckle* (0.70). Explosive staccato explusion of breath, huh-huh-huh. As Grant 110.

7   *Squeal* (1.00). High-pitched squeal vocalisation, distinguished from scream by context and less dissonant sound. As Grant 112.

8   *Play noise* (0.71). Vocalisations made in play, such as brr-brrr, peep-peep; stereotyped repeated utterances such as bang-bang, I am a monster.

9   *Talking alone* (0.63). Talking means an utterance including recognisable

words, but excluding singing or repeated stereotyped play noises. This category was scored if a child was talking in the absence of companions.

10   *Talking parallel* (–). As above, but in the presence of parallel companions. The utterance is not directed to any particular person.

11   *Talking to child* (0.79). As above, but the utterance is directed to another child.

12   *Talking to adult* (0.91). As above, but the utterance is directed to an adult.

13   *Talk from child* (0.76). Another child talks to the focal child.

14   *Talk from adult* (0.71). An adult talks to the focal child.

Visual units

15   *Look around* (0.62). Looks around room without prolonged fixation.

16   *Look distance* (0.30). Prolonged fixation into distance, no obvious person or group being fixated.

17   *Watch child* (0.52). Visual following of activities of other child or children without making eye-to-eye contact.

18   *Watch adult* (0.63). As above, but following activities of adult.

19   *Watch group* (0.82). As above, but following activities of adult with child or children.

20   *Glance at child* (0.47). Visual gaze of one second or less directed to another child's face.

21   *Glance at adult* (0.53). As above, directed to adult.

22   *Glance at observer* (0.36). As above, directed to observer.

23   *Look at child* (0.62). Visual gaze lasting one to three seconds directed to another child's face.

24   *Look at adult* (0.62). As above, directed to adult.

25   *Look at observer* (0.46). As above, directed to observer.

26   *Stare at child* (0.50). Visual gaze lasting more than three seconds at another child's face.

27   *Stare at adult* (–). As above, directed to adult.

28   *Stare at observer* (–). As above, directed to observer.

Physical contact units

29   *Contact apparatus* (0.90). Any gross body contact with table, chairs, climbing-frame, slide, rocking-boat, Wendy house, easel. Contact by hands only, or lasting only a few seconds, was not scored.

30   *Hold hands with child* (–). Holding hands with another child.

31   *Hold hands with adult* (1.00). Holding hands with an adult.

32   *Physical contact to child* (0.66). Any physical contact to another child, other than holding hands or contact in an agonistic context.

33   *Physical contact to adult* (0.40). As above, but to an adult.

34   *Physical contact from child* (0.78). As above, but another child makes a contact to the focal child.

35   *Physical contact from adult* (0.63). As above, but an adult makes a contact to the focal child.

Postural units

36   *Stand* (0.93). Standing with both feet, weight mainly or wholly on feet.
37   *Sit* (0.93). Weight supported by buttocks which are in contact with substrate.
38   *Kneel* (0.78). Weight supported on one or both knees and lower legs.
39   *Croch* (0.61). Knees bent, but weight still on feet.
40   *Lie* (1.00). Weight supported by whole body on substrate.

Locomotor units

41   *Walk* (0.87). Moving the body forward at a moderate pace, alternating legs and placing one foot firmly on the substrate before lifting the other. As McGrew VIII, 14.

42   *Shuffle* (0.49). One or two slow steps, or shuffling the feet, knees or buttocks along the substrate without losing contact with it.

43   *Run* (0.88). Moving the body forward at a rapid pace, alternating legs and with both feet off the ground instantaneously during each stride. As McGrew VIII, 8.

44   *Jump/hop* (0.71). Moving suddenly upward by leg and foot extension, landing on two feet (jump) or one foot (hop). As McGrew V, 1 and 2, and VII, 5 and 6.

45   *Skip* (0.50). Moving the body forward by alternating legs, placing one foot on the substrate and hopping slightly on it before shifting the weight to the other foot to repeat the same movement. As McGrew VIII, 10.

46   *Climb* (1.00). Gross physical activity with three or four limbs resulting in vertical motion of whole body.

47   *Slide* (0.87). Moving the body in constant frictional contact down an inclined surface.

48   *Crawl* (1.00). Moving forward on hands and knees, propelled by the limbs. As McGrew VIII, 3.

49   *Wrestle/tumble* (1.00). Mock fighting and tumbling with another child, involving gross physical contact but no agonism. As Blurton Jones 14, but including play-pushing.

50   *Chase/flee/group run* (0.70). Pursues or is pursued by another child, but no agonism; or running around in a coordinated fashion with other children.

51   *Play beat* (–). Sharp downward movement of hand towards another child, usually from above shoulder level; no physical contact or agonism. As Blurton Jones 15.

52   *Point* (0.73). Arm extends outwards but not in contact with any object, index finger usually extended. As Blurton Jones 26.

53   *Approach adult* (0.67). Locomotion up to an adult terminated by sustained proximity or verbal or visual contact.

Object use units

54   *Show* (–). Holds object in hand, shows to another person.

55   *Hold out* (–). Holds object in hand, arm extension as if to give object to another person but object not taken.

56   *Give* (0.80). Holds object in hand, arm extension, and releases grip when object taken by another person, or places object on substrate in front of another person. As Blurton Jones 25.

57   *Receive* (0.67). Extends arm, takes in hand an object given by another, does not flex arm until other has released grip. As Blurton Jones 24.

58   *Pick up* (0.75). Lifts an object by grasping followed by continuous arm movement.

59   *Put down* (0.85). Releases an object on to substrate, or drops object, by loosening grip.

60   *Hold* (0.61). Grasps an object in the hands while stationary, without manipulating it.

61   *Carry* (0.82). Grasps an object in the hands while locomoting, without manipulating it.

62   *Push* (0.78). Applies force to an object by limb and trunk extension, causing it to move away from original position. As McGrew VI, 7.

63   *Pull* (0.60). Applies force to an object by arm and trunk flexion, causing it to move away from original position. As McGrew VI, 6.

64   *Kick* (–). Extends one leg suddenly, causing foot to make forceful contact with object. As McGrew III, 5.

65   *Throw* (1.00). Moves object through air by releasing from hand at end of explosive overarm extension with simultaneous trunk movement. As McGrew III, 22.

66   *Hit* (0.80). Moves an object suddenly and forcefully into contact with another object by arm extention. As McGrew III, 3.

67   *Pedal* (1.00). Moves tricycle by rotary movement of feet or hands on pedals.

68   *Propel* (1.00). Moves tricycle or other large object while sitting or lying on it by means of pushing feet or hands into contact with substrate.

69   *Fine manipulation* (0.97). Movement of object in the hands involving fine muscular activity of fingers or hands. Slow repetitive motions without visual attention to the object were not scored.

70   *Gross manipulation* (1.00). Sustained movement of an object by gross limb activity, such as pushing, pulling, kicking, throwing, hitting, pedalling, or propelling. A brief occurrence, e.g. one kick, was not scored.

Agonistic units

71   *Physical aggression* (0.86). Any actions likely to cause hurtful physical contact to another, including fight (gross contact), grab (limb or clothes), push (with hand or arm), kick (with leg), beat at or hit (with arm), and throw at (with object).

72   *Dominate* (0.50). Pursuing a fleeing child; or taking or keeping possession of an object or apparatus when another child was in possession or attempting to get possession of it. Includes Blurton Jones 11(1,2).

73   *Dispute object* (0.50). Attempts to retain an object in conflict for possession. As Blurton Jones 11(3).

74   *Fail take object* (–). Grasps object in attempt to take from another child, but then lets go.

75   *Submit* (0.76). Flees from a pursuing child; or loses possession of an object or apparatus to another child.

Automanipulative units

76   *Suck* (0.89). Finger or toy in contact with lips.

77   *Tongue/lips* (0.50). Tongue protrudes out or makes rotary movement on lips. Includes Grant 45,46.

78   *Rub eyes* (–). Rubs eyes with knuckle or fingers. As Grant 86.

79   *Nose contact* (0.50). Picks nose with finger in nostril, or wipes nose with brushing movement of hand or arm.

80   *Ear contact* (1.00). Pulls ear with hand, or puts finger in ear.

81   *Hand to face* (0.63). Brief hand contact to face areas other than eyes, nose, or ears.

82   *Brush hair* (0.67). Hand runs through or pulls hair at side or front of head.

83   *Groom* (0.67). Runs fingers backwards through hair, or places hand on back of head or neck. As Grant 69, 85.

84   *Scratch* (0.50). Hard motion of the fingers and nails on the body surface. As Grant 81, 84.

85.   *Genital contact* (–). Rubs or handles genital area.

86   *Hand-fumble* (0.25). Repetitive twisting, turning, kneading, or flexing motions of fingers or hands, not involving gross limb movements or object contact.

87   *Mouth-fumble* (0.38). Repetitive mouth motions such as biting lips, mouthing; not involving object contact.

88   *Clothes-fumble* (0.23). Repetitive or apparently aimless manipulation of clothes worn.

89   *Hitch* (0.60). Upward pull with hand at trousers or skirt, usually at hem or between knee and thigh and with slight fumbling of material.

Some behaviour units were initially scored separately but then combined for purposes of analysis, owing to low occurrence. These were *cry* and *scream; jump* and *hop; chase/flee* and *group run; fight, grab, push at, kick at, beat at/hit,* and *throw at; chase, take toy, keep toy,* and *dominate at apparatus; flee, lose toy,* and *submit at apparatus; tongue out* and *lick lips.*

Some behaviour units were initially scored but were later omitted from analysis because of very infrequent occurrence or very low reliability. These were: *sing; talking to observer; physical contact to observer; lean adult; lift arms adult; walk with adult; follow adult; turn round; swing; arms flap; rock.*

Shorter list of 27 units

A shorter list containing only 27 units is used for data presentation in the main body of the text. This list contains sixteen composite units. A composite unit was scored as occurring in a time sample if any of its constituent units occurred. Inter-observer agreement is given in brackets (see p. 40). Units are defined as in the longer list.

Upper smile (0.65)
Open smile (0.76)
Play noise (0.71)
Talking between children (0.78). Composite of 11 and 13.
Talking to/from adult (0.87). Composite of 12 and 14.
Look around/distance (0.67). Composite of 15 and 16.
Watch (0.71). Composite of 17, 18, and 18.
Visual contact child (0.75). Composite of 20, 23, and 26.
Visual contact adult (0.67). Composite of 21, 24, and 27.
Contact apparatus (0.90)
Physical contact between children (0.69). Composite of 30, 32, and 34.
Physical contact with adult (0.72). Composite of 31, 33, and 35.
Walk (0.87)
Run (0.88)
Climb/slide (0.97). Composite of 46 and 47.
Chase/flee/group run (0.70)
Object exchange (0.70). Composite of 54, 55, 56, and 57.
Push/pull (0.71). Composite of 62 and 63.
Kick/throw/hit (0.90). Composite of 64, 65, and 66.
Pedal/propel (1.00). Composite of 67 and 68.
Fine manipulation (0.97)
Gross manipulation (1.00)
Physical aggression (0.86)
Agonistic behaviour (0.77). Composite of 71, 72, 73, 74, and 75.
Suck (0.89)
Face contact (0.78). Composite of 78, 79, 80, 81, 82, and 83.
Automanipulation (0.66). Composite of 77 to 89 inclusive.

APPENDIX C
Sample records

Specimens of the narrative records spoken directly into the tape-recorder. The examples below are of 30-second samples from the study in Chapter 6, in which number of children in the class and spatial density were the factors considered. Other studies employed 40-second samples in exactly the same way. Four transcribed samples are given from two children, Henry and Joanne, obtained during the course of one half-morning session; these are followed by the corresponding score-sheets. All names are pseudonyms.

Narrative commentaries of observations of children (see p. 39).

Henry (1)

Sitting on a chair at the table with Lego. . .he looks at Michael. . .at the moment not doing anything. . .he glances at Michael, Michael talks to him, he simple smiles and talks to Michael, picks up a plastic spanner and holds it. . .watches other children, rubs his eye.

Henry was parallel with Michael, Steven, and Andrew; no activity.

Joanne (1)

Sitting on a chair in the book corner, Peter talks to her, she talks to Peter, manipulates a book, stares at Peter, glances at Peter, talks to Jenny, points, shows something in the book to her, looks at Jenny, Jenny talks to her. . .manipulates the book, sitting on a chair in the book corner.

Joanne was group with Peter and Jenny, parallel with Catherine; book corner.

Henry (2)

Standing on his own. . .shuffles, watching other children, hand fumbles. . .he stares at Steven. . .walks along by himself. . .standing.

Henry was alone; no activity.

Joanne (2)

Walking along with Jenny she talks to Jenny, Jenny talks to her. . .standing, walking into a Wendy house, she scratches her leg, swings on the Wendy house, contacting Jenny. Susan talks to her, she swings on the Wendy house with Jenny

344

and Peter, she talks to Jenny, contacts her, walks and then stands outside the Wendy house, walking along, bends down and picks up a hat.

Joanne was group with Jenny and Peter; Wendy house.

Henry (3)

Sitting on a chair at table, with plastic pin board, Helen talks to him, he talks to Helen...picks up, puts down, and manipulates pieces on the plastic pin board ...talking to Helen contacts Helen.

Henry was group with Helen; table play.

Joanne (3)

Wearing a cap on her head, upper smile, she's pushing and pulling a toy chest, gross manipulation, bend over, standing and walking with Peter and Jenny...she talks to Peter and running and walking along, chuckling, open smiling and upper smiling and she stares at Jenny, Jenny talks to her, she walks along, bends down, holds the roller stick with Peter and beats at Peter, finger to ear, standing.

Joanne was group with Peter and Jenny; toy chest.

Henry (4)

Standing, holding some plastic Meccano, he looks at Mrs Z, shuffles, manipulating the plastic meccano now...crouches down on the ground, manipulating the meccano by himself...stands up again and walks along.

Henry was alone; miscellaneous play.

Joanne (4)

Wearing dressing-up clothes, sitting in a toy chest contacting Peter. She squeals and open smiles with Peter, Louise, Ruth, and Jenny. Sitting in the toy chest which is being pushed around by Louise...manipulating the dresing-up clothes. Peter talks to her, she talks to Peter, play beats at Peter, open and upper smiles and looks at Peter.

Joanne was group with Peter, Louise, Ruth, and Jenny; fantasy play, toy chest, dressing-up clothes.

Standard score-sheet coded for observations of children (see p. 40)

A   adult   C   child   G   group   O   observer   P   parallel   S   solitary

	Sample 1		Sample 2		Sample 3		Sample 4	
	Group	Parallel	Group	Parallel Alone	Group	Parallel	Group Alone	Parallel
Henry: large group, large space								
Companions . . .		Michael Steven Andrew			Helen			
Behaviours								
Smile open/upper/simple	Simple							
Pucker								
Glance CAO	Michael							
Look CAO	Michael							
Stare CAO			Steven				Mrs Z	
Look around/distance								
Watch CAG	C		C					
Talk from CA	Michael				Helen			
Talk SPCAO	Michael				Helen			
Play noise								
Chuckle/squeal								
Scream/cry								
Stand			✓				✓	
Walk/shuffle			Walk, Shuffle				Walk, Shuffle	
Run								
Jump/hop/skip								
Climb								
Slide								

Subject: Helen

Behaviour	No activity	No activity	Table play	Misc. obj. play
Kneel				
Crouch/crawl				Crouch
Bend over/down				
Lie				
Pedal/propel				
Push/pull				
Kick/throw/hit				
Point				
Show/hold out object				
Give/receive object				
Pick up object			✓	
Hold/carry object	hold			hold
Put down object			✓✓	✓
Manipulate object	✓		✓	
Wear clothes				
Contact apparatus	✓			
Automanipulate	rub eye	hand		
Suck				
Wrestle/tumble				
Chase/flee/group run				
Play beat				
Physical aggression				
Fail take object				
Dispute object				
Dominate				
Submit				
Physical contact CAO				
Physical contact from CA				
Hold hands CA				
Approach A				
Activities	No activity	No activity	Table play	Misc. obj. play

Jenny: large group, large space

	Sample 1		Sample 2		Sample 3		Sample 4	
	Group	Parallel	Group	Parallel	Group	Parallel	Group	Parallel
Companions . . .	Peter Jenny	Catherine	Jenny Peter		Peter Jenny		Peter Louise Ruth Jenny	
Behaviours								
Smile open/upper/smile					upper open		open upper	
Pucker								
Glance CAO	Peter							
Look CAO	Jenny				Jenny		Peter	
Stare CAO	Peter							
Look around/distance								
Watch CAG								
Talk from CA	Peter, Jenny		Jenny, Susan		Jenny		Peter	
Talk SPCAO	Peter, Jenny		Jenny		Peter		Peter	
Play noise								
Chuckle/squeal					chuckle		squeal	
Scream/cry								
Stand								
Walk/shuffle			Walk		Walk			
Run								
Jump/hop/skip								
Climb								
Slide								
Sit	√							
Kneel							√	
Crouch, crawl								
Bend over/down								

	Books	Wendy house	Toy chest	Fantasy play, Toy chest, Dressing-up clothes
Pedal/propel				
Push/pull				push pull
Kick/throw/hit				
Point				
Show/hold out object	show (Jenny) ✓			
Give/receive object				
Pick up object				
Hold/carry object				
Put down object				
Manipulate object	✓		gross	✓
Wear clothes				
Contact apparatus				
Automanipulate	✓	scratch ✓	h-ear	✓✓
Suck				
Wrestle/tumble				
Chase/flee/group run				
Play beat			beat at Peter	play beat at Peter
Physical aggression			✓ (Peter)	
Fail take object				
Dispute object				
Dominate				
Submit				
Physical contact to CAO				
Physical contact from CA		Jenny		Peter
Hold hands CA				
Approach A				
Activities . . .	Books	Wendy house	Toy chest	Fantasy play, Toy chest, Dressing-up clothes

Standard record-sheet for staff–child communications (see pp. 257–8)
Adult: Miss C; Group: Two; Conditions: Small ($N = 14$)

Time	Staff to Child	Child to Staff	Context	Activity/companions

11·03 — TG ⊥ ... RD TG / AP HM

AP (zigzag)

Table play (Sticky paper)

TG ⊥

RD ⊥

AP

HM

⊥ ⊥

11·04 — TG ⊥   P

LH (zigzag)   ← LH

Total occurrences, and significance levels, for full list of 89 behaviour units

Results for the 11 units common to the shorter list of 27 units (see Appendix B) omitted
Group One upper line; Group Two lower line

A   Interaction with age
D   Interaction with project experience
E   Interaction with amount of play equipment
G   Interaction with group size
[*] $P < 0.25$
(*) $P < 0.1$
* $P < 0.05$

S   Interaction with amount of spac
T   Interaction with project experie
X   Interaction with sex

** $P < 0.01$
*** $P < 0.001$

	Number of children in group						Further spatial variation	
	Term One		Term Two		Term Three			
	Small (N = 20)	Large (N = 30)	Small (N = 12)	Large (N = 24)	Small (N = 10)	Large (N = 30)	15 sq. ft/ child	30 sq. ft/ child
1 Simple smile	60	50	42	28	31	33 S*	30	34 G*
	62	44	52	36	29	31	25	35
4 Pucker	3	1	1	0	1	1	1	1
	4	2	0	1	0	0	0	0
5 Cry/scream	4	0	2	1	2	1	1	2
	1	1	0	1	0	0	0	0
6 Chuckle	54	60	32	43	44	31	34	41
	44	62	38	30	27	34	24	37
7 Squeal	11	9	10	10	5	7	7	5
	8	8	7	5	3	7	2	8
9 Talking alone	18	28	14	23	15	8	5	18*
	15	13	12	15	8	16	15	9
10 Talking parallel	31	42	39	22*	44	23*	33	34
	36	40	18	41*	39	27	24	42*
11 Talking to child	258	266	215	189	223	227	224	226
	305	305	169	176	213	197	191	219*
12 Talking to adult	42	37	19	26	27	34	25	36
	33	26	20	14	19	9	16	12
13 Talk from child	278	251	203	182	237	214	217	234
	288	286	166	176	223	196	200	219
14 Talk from adult	46	41	28	31	36	39	34	41
	47	30	20	14	27	18 T*	23	22
15 Look around	13	15	6	10	6	11	4	13
	11	18	2	9*	0	11**	8	3
16 Look distance	4	11	2	8	0	4*	2	2
	11	9	5	12	1	8*	1	8*
17 Watch child	83	86	47	28*	53	43	60	36**
	117	98	69	53	59	52	60	51
18 Watch adult	8	6	2	4	3	9	7	5
	9	16	4	4	6	5	6	5
19 Watch group	7	4	5	8	7	10	10	7
	23	24	7	9	6	13	9	10
20 Glance at child	138	127	96	85	126	129	134	121
	159	151	82	118**	142	119	135	126
21 Glance at adult	15	25	10	13	14	9 T*	10	13
	25	20	10	7 T*	20	12	21	11
22 Glance at observer	29	39	17	12	10	8	5	13
	32	36	15	9	14	12	11	15
23 Look at child	270	267	169	156	157	188	178	167
	270	324**	146	156	146	159	136	169*

Amounts of space and play equipment

Space			Equipment			Structured-activities and free play			
1	2	3	1	2	3	B/b(1)	B/b(2)	E/e(1–6)	
42	158	170A*	147	169	154A*	6	7	8.1	
226	263	225A*	226	255	233X**	8	10	7.8	
30	27	22	25	37	17X**	3	0	0.3	
24	9	19	23	14	15	3	0	0.5	
29	22	24	28	35	12**	3	0	0.5	
14	8	14	15	10	11[*]	3	0	0.3	
24	119	130	131	138	104*	8	11	5.3	
23	109	118	121	122	107	7	8	9.0	
34	34	42	40	37	33	2	4	0.8	
24	26	24	32	27	15*	1	1	0.7	
98	126	110	99	117	118X*	2	3	3.3	
09	108	110X*	87	110	130**A*	6	4	5.8	
92	178	207	215	205	160**	9	3	10.2	
80	145	173	187	159	158	12	4	8.5	
588	595	622	629	565	611*	38	53	23.3	
27	566	540	544	541	548X*	38	47	43.7	***
68	264	249	262	264	255	5	3	29.7	***
03	199	210	207	203	202	3	4	4.7	
39	498	564*	538	519	544	28	37	20.8	***
03	485	504	488	509	495	27	49	38.3	
69	342	347	360	337	361	7	6	30.2	***
23	288	318	311	319	299	12	2	8.0	
94	99	113X**	96	107	109A*	5	0	4.0	
95	115	120	118	113	99	4	2	2.5	
14	155	165**	137	134	163	1	2	3.7	
47	154	190*	157	180	154	5	2	2.5	
290	317	313E*	321	315	284[*]S*	33	28	14.2	*
12	335	324E*	361	300	310**S*	20	21	18.5	
19	92	81**	109	89	94	0	1	9.2	***
01	108	118	117	121	89	4	2	2.7	
63	148	148	174	143	142A*	3	3	16.2	***
95	173	163	171	170	191D*	5	1	1.3	
303	305	333	352	302	287*	14	12	13.3	*
284	272	348**	315	309	280	13	20	18.2	
43	123	120	134	134	118	1	4	16.7	***
51	112	153*	140	146	132	6	1	4.0	
14	136	116	118	120	128	4	6	2.3	**
32	164	133	138	135	156	6	1	5.5	
90	738	725	741	710	702X*	45	43	29.0	***
709	777	723A**	759	725	725X*	44	45	42.0	

	Number of children in group						Further spatial variation	
	Term One		Term Two		Term Three			
	Small (N = 20)	Large (N = 30)	Small (N = 12)	Large (N = 24)	Small (N = 10)	Large (N = 30)	15 sq. ft/ child	30 sq. ft/ child
24 Look at adult	37	35	27	21	25	29	23	31
	44	32	21	14	18	17 T*	21	14
25 Look at observer	49	34	14	12	13	18	14	17
	30	35	16	15	3	9	5	7
26 Stare at child	78	95	83	58*	72	58	60	70
	113	132	70	79	61	75	68	68
27 Stare at adult	15	16	7	8	10	9	8	11
	16	11	10	10	8	7	9	6 T*
28 Stare at observer	6	10	7	1*	4	5	6	3
	6	13	7	4	7	3	6	4
30 Hold hands with child	6	9	3	13*	9	7	6	10
	27	9**	5	5	5	9	5	9
31 Hold hands with adults	1	1	0	0	0	1	0	1
	2	0	0	1	0	0	0	0
32 Physical contact to child	86	109	70	77	111	88* S*	112	87* G*
	127	120	75	68	83	102	78	107*
33 Physical contact to adult	3	5	1	3	2	4	4	2
	5	1	3	0	0	0	0	0
34 Physical contact from child	102	100	88	82	111	106	126	91**
	131	106	85	73	95	92	93	94
35 Physical contact from adult	11	8	6	6	7	5	4	8
	16	8	4	5	6	2	5	3
36 Stand	330	352	247	245 T*	312	342	321	333
	414	380*	249	236	298	285	293	290
37 Sit	208	232	147	154	164	162	177	149
	192	219	153	159	148	151	153	146
38 Kneel	95	74	62	60	41	34	35	38
	79	73	50	53	33	34	31	36
39 Crouch	41	53	35	27	48	47	41	54
	47	38	22	23	31	36	32	35
40 Lie	32	35	22	20	13	5 T**	5	13
	33	34	21	12	3	3	3	3
42 Shuffle	67	63	25	27	21	11	15	17
	81	83	27	27	17	26	23	20
44 Jump/Hop	16	14	13	8	8	12	7	13
	28	21	11	7	8	4	5	7
45 Skip	18	24	16	12	2	14** S*	2	14** G*
	19	19	10	16	4	3	2	5
46 Climb	50	54	46	32	12	11	15	8
	74	58	33	22	12	12	12	12
47 Slide	25	26	26	21	0	1	0	1
	24	26	35	16*	0	0	0	0
48 Crawl	12	12	6	3	9	7	3	13
	15	5*	4	2	1	3	2	2
49 Wrestle/ tumble	5	5	1	4	4	2	1	5
	20	14	6	4	1	1	1	1
51 Play beat	7	5	2	2	7	2	3	6
	11	8	3	4	2	1	2	1
52 Point	26	29 T**	16	20	21	15	14	22
	29	25	13	15	10	17	13	14
53 Approach adult	27	28	17	12	15	25	17	23
	22	20	11	7	8	4	4	8

...mounts of space and play equipment

...ace	2	3	Equipment 1	2	3	Structured-activities and free play B/b(1)	B/b(2)	E/e(1–6)	
02	271	259X*	280	293	259T*	9	3	22.8	***
83	280	252	279	275	261	13	4	8.0	
27	130	155	115	152	140	11	6	3.2	
60	163	149	146	158	168	10	4	5.3	
28	231	255	238	247	229	12	6	7.3	
45	244	269	262	261	235	17	11	10.2	
62	66	60	58	61	69	1	0	5.3	
69	64	66	78	61	60	4	1	1.8	***
41	38	64*	43	58	42	4	2	1.5	
51	48	52	46	51	54	4	0	1.7	
12	18	21X*	17	16	18	1	0	0.2	
13	11	15	20	12	7*	2	0	0.5	
22	18	6	11	18	17	1	0	0.2	
11	11	2A*	11	9	5*	1	0	0.2	
56	151	131	179	126	133**	14	16	10.7	***
63	161	143A**	192	147	128***	15	16	18.5	
37	43	33	35	35	43	0	0	2.2	*
17	18	17	15	21	16	0	0	0.7	
93	139	128***	184	154	122***,	16	15	13.7	
57	146	126(*)	175	145	109***	13	18	15.3	
15	87	88[*]	109	89	92	2	3	6.3	***
96	67	57**	88	78	54**	5	0	2.7	
04	1139	1167*	1196	1152	1162	51	56	48.0	***
97	1182	1201	1195	1192	1193	66	59	58.0	
26	719	697	680	722	740	46	42	46.0	
54	670	664	635	666	687	32	29	37.0	***
52	242	227	253	240	228	12	20	17.2	
18	234	219	233	230	208	11	17	16.3	
63	176	163	162	164	176	3	2	3.3	
17	138	121	130	121	125	5	5	5.3	
08	92	78	98	87	93	8	3	3.0	**
78	63	58X*	60	73	66	5	8	5.8	
15	383	386	433	376	375*	29	19	19.3	
06	390	440	415	434	387(*)	28	23	21.7	
68	72	70	82	63	65[*]	0	7	3.2	
33	54	55*	64	40	38*	3	3	3.5	
28	40	36	42	33	29[*]	3	3	1.8	
3	23	24A*	33	13	14**	5	5	2.0	
49	114	111*	120	135	119	13	10	4.7	
58	131	117*	133	145	128	11	8	11.2	***
94	78	47***	66	86	67	7	0	2.0	***
92	63	62*	56	83	78	4	0	5.2	
19	29	12	13	21	26	2	1	2.2	
24	24	23	27	21	22	1	2	4.0	
7	10	7	13	7	4	1	1	0.3	*
6	7	3	4	5	7	5	3	2.0	
5	11	5	9	7	5	0	2	0.3	
8	9	10	9	10	8	0	2	0	
75	72	79	81	68	77	6	3	3.0	
76	73	87	79	92	65	7	4	3.5	
95	109	125	112	107	110	3	0	2.8	
68	77	89	82	79	73	1	1	1.7	

	Number of children in group						Further spatial variation	
	Term One		Term Two		Term Three			
	Small (N = 20)	Large (N = 30)	Small (N = 12)	Large (N = 24)	Small (N = 10)	Large (N = 30)	15 sq. ft/ child	30 sq. ft/ child
54 Show object	8	7	6	4	14	9	15	8
	17	13	9	9	5	7	8	4
55 Hold out object	2	8*	8	6	8	8	12	4
	1	6	4	4	2	3	1	4
56 Give object	26	24	24	22	34	29	40	23*
	21	22	17	21	47	27*	39	35
57 Receive object	25	24	25	30	43	49	54	38
	37	26	23	17	47	29*S*	38	36G*
58 Pick up object	202	226	152	146	207	185	193	199
	212	201	147	157T**	163	172	175	160
59 Put down object	178	194	142	128	170	155	165	160
	164	166	125	139T*	156	153	158	151
60 Hold object	79	88	72	63	109	90	109	90
	104	85	66	68	96	70*	87	79
61 Carry object	77	76	57	59	61	58	56	63
	89	78	46	46	23	41	29	35
62 Push object	52	54	22	47**	22	23	19	26
	38	31	19	18	19	36*	16	39**
63 Pull object	57	65	27	38	13	27	23	17
	46	50	19	19	22	31	20	33T*
64 Kick object	4	1	3	2	1	4	0	5*
	2	6	4	2	2	0	2	0
65 Throw object	8	8	8	5T*	9	10	11	8
	12	16T*	8	4	5	6T*	2	9*
66 Hit object	11	13	10	10	25	23	31	17
	14	15	7	7	10	8	8	10T*
67 Pedal	29	38	21	24	0	0	0	0
	35	57*	9	12	0	0	0	0
68 Propel	22	37	8	15	0	0		
	30	51*	11	12	1	2		
72 Dominate	23	16	11	6	18	21	28	11*
	11	17	14	10	11	17	13	15
73 Dispute object	9	8	12	4*	8	13*T*	15	6
	14	3**	13	6	14	10	11	13
74 Fail take object	11	6	7	2	6	5	8	3
	6	2	5	3	5	6	4	7
75 Submit	15	9	8	5	12	11	14	9
	11	8	9	10	12	3*	8	7
77 Tongue/lips	42	40	48	43	36	26	29	33
	80	68	55	51	27	48*	38	37
78 Rub eyes	2	3	3	5	3	5	1	7*
	11	5	2	2	2	5	3	4
79 Nose contact	28	18	11	17	13	21	12	22
	25	28	14	10	14	17	12	19
80 Ear contact	5	4T*	0	1	3	1	1	3
	5	8	3	4	2	7	4	5
81 Hand to face	36	26T**	27	26T*	22	15	12	25*
	43	45	25	24	21	19	23	17
82 Brush hair	22	23	13	17	8	9	9	8
	17	22	16	13	13	13	14	12
83 Groom	3	4	3	2	2	2	2	2
	5	6	6	1	4	0	3	1

mounts of space and play equipment

ace	2	3	Equipment 1	2	3	Structured-activities and free play B/b(1)	B/b(2)	E/e(1–6)	
2	41	36	40	37	32	4	3	4.0	*
4	39	38A*	31	33	37	0	5	1.8	
5	22	24	19	23	29	0	2	1.8	
3	24	17	22	27	15	1	1	1.3	
I	76	95*	89	104	89	3	6	6.5	
2	58	70	52	63	65	5	8	5.8	
2	75	73	85	81	64X*	1	10	8.2	*
8	67	60	63	57	65	4	4	4.7	
3	735	782	697	754	799**	41	42	38.3	
0	686	661	640	679	718*	30	40	39.0	
8	620	673	606	651	694**	42	39	35.5	
4	573	580	540	572	635**	24	36	35.2	
5	487	453	504	450	501	21	24	23.0	
8	481	526**	472	492	490	18	22	23.8	
I	355	378(*)	352	330	392*	14	15	7.5	***
9	326	365***	298	325	347(*)	17	16	14.3	***
9	185	194	151	190	217**	9	13	3.7	***
I	155	201***X*	165	172	160A**	5	5	8.5	
8	172	159	140	161	198**	5	12	6.7	
3	133	163***	140	124	135	5	6	7.7	
9	12	6	7	14	6A*	0	0	0.2	
7	22	35*	31	31	12**X**	0	0	0.8	
8	38	32	31	32	35	0	3	1.3	
5	26	26	33	33	11***X*	2	1	1.7	
0	61	54	49	63	53	5	3	0.7	*
8	61	80	62	62	75	7	9	2.3	
6	100	107	62	106	125***	0	0	0	
7	110	107	56	114	154***A**X**	0	0	0	
5	83	76	36	83	115***				
9	77	71	45	77	105***				
6	68	63X***	78	57	72	3	6	1.7	
7	43	42	48	47	37	1	3	1.5	
4	20	22X*	23	22	21	2	3	1.5	
7	14	12A*	12	13	18	0	5	1.3	
8	17	16X*	21	19	11	0	0	0.8	
5	13	21	14	20	15	1	2	1.0	
3	33	45X*	52	48	31	4	4	1.5	
I	39	33	39	35	29	5	2	1.8	
7	136	147	147	128	135	9	9	3.8	*
6	169	175**A*	152	155	163	9	8	7.5	
6	13	13X*	14	12	16X*	3	0	2.0	
0	17	11	17	6	15*	2	2	1.7	
4	58	68	65	68	57	7	4	3.5	
6	48	65	53	55	51	3	3	3.0	
9	20	30	18	28	23	0	0	0.2	
6	15	16	17	13	17	0	0	0.2	
4	124	146	141	130	153	8	6	7.2	
6	138	155	152	146	141	3	6	5.5	
6	25	22	29	21	23	4	7	2.7	
4	25	37	27	36	33	1	1	4.0	
8	34	34	35	30	31	1	0	0.8	
4	42	32X*	35	46	37	0	2	0.8	

| | Number of children in group | | | | | | Further spatial variation | |
| | Term One | | Term Two | | Term Three | | | |
	Small (N = 20)	Large (N = 30)	Small (N = 12)	Large (N = 24)	Small (N = 10)	Large (N = 30)	15 sq. ft/ child	30 sq. ft/ child
84 Scratch	2	2	0	2	2	4	2	4
	7	6	1	3	2	4	5	1
85 Genital contact	3	4	1	4	1	0	0	1
	3	5 T*	4	3	2	1	2	1
86 Hand fumble	42	54	28	18	36	51	38	49
	61	77	38	36	32	40	44	28
87 Mouth fumble	38	30	35	32	46	35	36	45
	41	51	43	48	38	51	37	52 T*
88 Clothes fumble	11	8	6	6	12	14	4	22**
	14	18	4	4	4	10	9	5
89 Hitch	10	9	8	3	10	15	9	16
	22	20	6	8	12	16	14	14

nounts of space and play equipment

ace		Equipment			Structured-activities and free play		
2	3	1	2	3	B/b(1)	B/b(2)	E/e(1–6)
10	24*	8	22	17*	3	1	1.3
24	18	19	18	25	0	4	2.0
9	6	10	7	8A*	0	1	0.2
6	3	3	6	6	1	0	0
82	75	72	77	75	9	2	7.5
120	92	146	98	90***	10	5	4.7
52	56E*	46	73	49S*	5	8	5.2
91	84T*	75	82	97A*	2	0	4.0
33	31	38	27	35	1	1	2.0
45	61	56	51	44	3	2	1.0
33	41	36	40	38	0	0	0.8
43	49	50	49	29*	0	2	0.7

Copy of instructions to staff concerning the two playgroup regimes

St Augustine's playgroup – year two

The two groups will – for most of the year – follow different programmes; one group an ADULT-CHOICE programme, the other a CHILD-CHOICE programme. These programmes will start after the first two weeks and continue probably into the third term. The first two weeks of the first term there will be a common INTRODUCTORY programme for *both* groups.

Introductory programme – first two weeks

(1) *Settle the children in the new premises, and especially settle new children in the group.*
During this period new children – and old 'loners' – should be encouraged to do *something* rather than just standing about.

(2) *Make the children aware of the toys and equipment provided, and what can be done with them – without developing sustained interaction or play-teaching situations with them.*
Some new toys might be introduced in each of the four sessions in this period. Try to ensure that each child at least sees each new toy. Show them the toys informally, and encourage them a little to play/explore with them, but do not actively develop long sequences of play, or 'follow up' with ideas of number, colour, shape, etc., or imaginative extension of the play.

E.g.: Show the children the puppet theatre; show how to hold glove puppets and talk with them. *Do not* suggest that David play 'daddy' and Jenny play 'mummy' and have a family scene (but do not prevent this either *if* it happens spontaneously).

This period will mainly be one of free play and low staff–child interaction for both groups, but giving objectives (1) and (2) above attention as necessary. You must make sure that the children are settling and that they understand what they can do with the toys and equipment, but do not extend interaction more than you think necessary to do this.

After the first two weeks the two groups will have different programmes. *But certain features will still be common to both groups.* These are:

(1) The same toys and equipment should be available on consecutive days (Tuesday and Wednesday; Thursday and Friday). This is a general rule which

may have occasional exceptions. The layout of the toys and equipment need not be identical.

(2) Children should arrive before 9.30 a.m. and (once children are settled) parents should not be present after that time, or before 11.45.

(3) All staff should be present in the playroom from 9.30 to 10.15 and from 11.00 to 11.45. Routine (i.e. kitchen) chores should be done before 9.30 or during milk break.

(4) Staff should give overall priority to prevention of injury or damage to children or property.

Child-choice group

In the child-choice group, *do not actively initiate or develop play activities.* The only exception to this should normally be to give some prompting to a new or lonely child into participating in an activity.

Be available to help or advise a child if he or she approaches you, but do not prolong the interaction more than is required by the child's request. Think of yourself as a caretaker who is leaving a child to make the choice himself. Do not involve yourself in sustained interactions.

E.g.: In response to a request, staff may mix new paint, show how a piece of jigsaw fits, draw a circle, show how to hold a puppet. If a child asks you to cut out a paper figure, or play in a Wendy house, suggest that he does it himself or gets another child to help him. Give some help if necessary – e.g. give him scissors and perhaps draw a figure if he cannot do so; suggest asking another child to have a tea party. Do not get involved in making things yourself or acting in an imaginary situation (such as tea party) yourself.

If a child asks for a story, tell him that everyone will have a story during milk break. Of course children can sit at a book corner and read books, but reading of books by staff should not occur except in milk break.

The intention of this programme is to minimise staff–child interactions and to leave children with the responsibility of working out their own activities, within a framework of security from disruption, and knowledge of the potential play material.

During these sessions staff can be sitting unobtrusively (on the high chairs). Be on the look-out to prevent harmful or unnecessarily disruptive behaviour (see below). Subject to this, and to being available to answer children's requests, the time can be spent making or repairing toys or equipment. The experimenters would also appreciate a log record which staff might make of unusual or interesting behaviour.

Behaviours to be prevented: obviously any injury to children or property. Stop behaviour if it looks like getting out of hand and damaging to toys. Also indiscriminate kicking, throwing, etc. – e.g. kicking a doll's house, sweeping tea things off Wendy house table. Pushing tables upside-down on the floor should be stopped as this damages the table tops. Waste of materials – flicking paint, breaking crayons – should also be prevented.

Do not stop any activities which do not harm children or property. Allow flexible and unusual uses of equipment – 'chair-trains', for example – if this does no harm. Another example is using the tables for climbing on and jumping off (assuming soft shoes are worn). This does not mean that ongoing activities at a table or Wendy house for example can be broken up by other children, but that equipment not currently in use can be used in this way.

E.g.: Someone sweeps the tea things off the Wendy house table and takes it off to make a chair-train; you might tell him to be more careful with the tea things – to put them in a corner of the Wendy house, for example – but he should not be prevented from taking the little table *unless* another child was already using it.

The equipment provided may be varied from time to time – e.g. occasionally perhaps two Wendy houses – as you see fit in order to provide the children with some variety, and incentive to use different pieces of equipment. Remember to put the same equipment out for the corresponding ADULT-CHOICE day.

Adult-choice group

Each session should have a basic play programme of activities initiated and developed by staff. These activities might be such as to develop the children's abilities to concentrate, use their power of creativity and imagination, develop manipulative skills, language, and concepts such as number, colour, shape, Think of yourself as a guide or teacher to the child, a kind of benevolent leader, who uses active and subtle persuasion to get a child to encounter play experiences of these kinds.

A typical play programme might involve each member of staff developing one kind of skill or play experience with, say, eight children for some five to ten minutes or so. While it is important to have a well-planned guideline to follow in developing an activity, you can be flexible as regards timing, number of children in a group, and so on. Do not forcibly prevent a child from opting out of an activity, but do your best to interest him again later in some play relevant to the morning's play programme. Perhaps you will need one member of staff to concentrate on these 'floating' children. The details of this are up to you. The aim is to *take every opportunity to interact meaningfully with the children, developing a personal relationship with each, and doing so mainly by channelling their play activities as you consider best to fulfil the aims above.*

It will probably help to keep a brief record of what activities each child has done each session; try to ensure that each child encounters a full variety of play experiences each term.

Behaviour to be prevented: as in the CHILD-CHOICE programme, any harmful of disruptive behaviour should be prevented. *In addition, feel free actively and positively to discourage any activities which you feel are likely to interfere with the ongoing play programmes.* If you are using toys or equipment then they cannot be taken off for other purposes. You also may wish for example to discourage very noisy activities if they are preventing other children from pursuing the activity you are developing.

Free play in this group can occur from 9.00 to 9.20 a.m. At about 9.20 begin to bring out equipment for the morning's programme and present it attractively; over a ten-minute period this is brought out and children are involved in appropriate groups (in general, keep groups mixed and varied).

Any *organised whole-group activities* should normally only occur in the milk break.

Bibliography

Abramovitch, R. (1976). The relation of attention and proximity to rank in preschool children. In *The Social Structure of Attention*. Eds. M. R. A. Chance and R. R. Larsen, London: Wiley

Ainsworth, M. D. S. (1973). The development of infant–mother attachment. In *Review of Child Development Research*, vol. 3. Eds. B. M. Caldwell and H. N. Ricciutti, University of Chicago Press

Ainsworth, M. D. S., Bell, S. M., and Stayton, D. J. (1974). Infant–mother attachment and social development: Socialisation as a product of reciprocal responsiveness to signals. In *The Integration of a Child into a Social World*. Ed. M. P. M. Richards, Cambridge University Press

Alcock, J. (1975). *Animal Behavior: An Evolutionary Approach*. Sunderland, Mass.: Sinauer

Aldis, O. (1975). *Play Fighting*. New York: Academic Press

Alexander, B. K. and Roth, E. M. (1971). The effects of acute crowding on aggressive behaviour of Japanese monkeys. *Behaviour* **39**, 73–90

Altmann, J. (1974). Observational study of behavior: Sampling methods. *Behaviour* **49**, 227–65

Altmann, S. A. (1965). Primate behavior in review. *Science* **150**, 1440–2

Anderson, J. (1956). Child development: An historical perspective. *Child Develop.* **27**, 181–96

Archer, J. (1970). Effects of population density on behaviour in rodents. In *Social Behaviour in Birds and Mammals*. Ed. J. H. Crook, London: Academic Press

Aries, P. (1962). *Centuries of Childhood*. London: Jonathan Cape

Arrington, R. E. (1931). *Interrelations in the Behavior of Young Children*. New York: Teachers' College, Columbia University

Arrington, R. E. (1939). Time-sampling studies of child behavior. *Psychol. Monog.* **51**

Arrington, R. E. (1943). Time sampling in studies of social behavior: A critical review of techniques and results with research suggestions. *Psychol. Bull.* **40**, 81–124

Baldassare, M. (1975). Residential density, local ties and neighbourhood attitudes: Are the findings of micro-studies generalisable to urban areas? *Social. Symp.* **14**, 93–104

Bandura, A., Ross, D., and Ross, S. A. (1961). Transmission of aggression through imitation of aggressive models. *J. Abn. Soc. Psychol.* **62**, 575–82

Bandura, A., Ross, D., and Ross, S. A. (1963). Imitation of film-mediated aggressive models. *J. Abn. Soc. Psychol.* **66**, 3–11

363

Baratz, S. S., and Baratz, J. C. (1970). Early childhood intervention: The social science base of institutional racism. *Harvard Educ. Rev.* **40**, 29–50

Barker, R. G. (1968). *Ecological Psychology*. Stanford University Press

Barker, R. G., and Gump, P. V. (1964). *Big School, Small School*. Stanford University Press

Barkow, J. (1977). Human ethology and intra-individual systems. *Soc. Sci. Inform.* **16**, 133–45

Bates, B. C. (1970. Effects of social density on the behavior of nursery school children. Unpublished PhD dissertation, University of Oregon

Baum, A., Harpin, R. E., and Valins, S. (1975). The role of group phenomena in the experience of crowding. *Environ. Behav.* **7**, 185–98

Baxter, J. C., and Deanovich, B. F. (1970). Anxiety arousing effects of inappropriate crowding. *J. Consult. Clin. Psychol.* **35**, 174–8

Bealing, D. (1973). Issues in classroom observation research. *Res. in Educ.* **9**, 70–82

Beller, E. K. (1973). Research on organised programs of early education. In *Second Handbook of Research on Teaching*. Ed. R. M. W. Travers, Chicago: Rand McNally

Belsky, J., and Steinberg, L. D. (1978). The effects of day care: A critical review. *Child Develop.* **49**, 929–49

Bereiter, C., and Engelmann, S. (1966). *Teaching Disadvantaged Children in the Preschool*. Englewood Cliffs, N. J.: Prentice-Hall

Berk, L. E. (1971). Effects of variations in the nursery school setting on environmental constraints and children's modes of adaptation. *Child Develop.* **42**, 839–69

Berkson, G. (1967). Abnormal stereotyped motor acts. In *Comparative Psychopathology*. New York: American Psychopathological Association/Grune and Stratton Inc.

Bernstein, B. (1959). A public language: Some sociological implications of a linguistic form. *Brit. J. Sociol.* **10**, 311–26

Bernstein, B. (1960). Language and social class. *Brit. J. Sociol.* **11**, 271–6

Bernstein, B. (1962). Social class, linguistic codes and grammatical elements. *Lang. Speech* **5**, 221–40

Biehler, R. F. (1954). Companion choice behavior in the kindergarten. *Child Develop.* **25**, 45–50

Bjorklid-Chu, P. (1977). A survey of children's outdoor activities in two modern housing areas in Sweden. In *Biology of Play*. Eds. B. Tizard and D. Harvey, London: Spastics International Medical Publications/Heinemann

Blackstone, T. (1971). *A Fair Start: The Provision of Preschool Education*. London: Allen Lane, Penguin Press

Blank, M., and Solomon, F. (1968). A tutorial language program to develop abstract thinking in socially disadvantaged preschool children. *Child Develop.* **39**, 379–89

Blurton Jones, N. (1967). An ethological study of some aspects of social behaviour of children in nursery school. In *Primate Ethology*. Ed. D. Morris, London: Weidenfeld and Nicolson

Blurton Jones, N. (1972a). Ed. *Ethological Studies of Child Behaviour*. Cambridge University Press

Blurton Jones, N. (1972b). Categories of child–child interaction. In *Ethological Studies of Child Behaviour*. Ed. N. Blurton Jones, Cambridge University Press

Body, M. K. (1955). Patterns of aggression in the nursery school. *Child Develop.* **26**, 3–11

Bott, H. (1928). Observation of play activities in a nursery school. *Genet. Psychol. Monog.* **4**, 44–88

Bowlby, J. (1951). *Maternal Care and Mental Health*. Geneva: World Health Organisation

Bowlby, J. (1957). An ethological approach to research in child development. *Brit. J. Med. Psychol.* **30**, 230–40

Boydell, D. (1974). Teacher–pupil contact in junior classrooms. *Brit. J. Educ. Psychol.* **44**, 313–18

Boydell, D. (1975). Systematic observation in informal classrooms. In *Frontiers of Classroom Research*. Eds. G. Chanan and S. Delamont, Windsor: National Foundation for Educational Research

Brackbill, Y. (1967) (ed.). *Infancy and Early Experience*. London: Collier-Macmillan

Brannigan, C. R., and Humphries, D. A. (1972). Human non-verbal behaviour, a means of communication. In *Ethological Studies of Child Behaviour*. Ed. N. Blurton Jones, Cambridge University Press

Bridges, K. M. B. (1929). Occupational interests of four-year-old children. *J. Genet. Psychol.* **36**, 551–70

Bronfenbrenner, U. (1974). *Is Early Intervention Effective? A Report on Longitudinal Evaluation of Preschool Programs*. Washington, D.C.: Office of Child Development, Department of Health, Education, and Welfare

Bronfenbrenner, U. (1977). Toward an experimental ecology of human development. *Amer. Psychol.* **32**, 513–31

Brown, G. W., Bhrolchain, M. N., and Harris, T. (1975). Social class and psychiatric disturbance among women in an urban population. *Sociol.* **9**, 225–54

Brown, J. L. (1964). Goals and terminology in ethological motivation research. *Anim. Behav.* **12**, 538–41

Brunetti, F. A. (1972). Noise, distraction, and privacy in conventional and open school environments. In *Environmental Design: Research and Practice*. Ed. W. J. Mitchell, Los Angeles: University of California Press

Calhoun, J. B. (1962). Population density and social pathology. *Sci. Amer.* **206**(2), 139–48

Campbel, F. (1972). Preschool behaviour study. (Abstract). *Architect. Psychol. Newsletter*, **3**, 1.

Cattell, R. B., and Peterson, D. R. (1958). Personality structure in 4–5 years olds, by factoring observed, time-sampled behaviour. *Ras. Psico. Gen. Clin.* **3**, 1–21

Challman, R. C. (1932). Factors influencing friendships among preschool children. *Child Develop.* **3**, 146–58

Chanan, G., and Delamont, S. (1975). *Frontiers of Classroom Research*. Windsor: National Foundation for Educational Research

Chapanis, A. (1967). The relevance of laboratory studies to practical situations. *Ergonomics* **10**, 557–77

Chazan, M. (1975). Evaluation of pre-school education: Research in the United

Kingdom. In *Problems in the Evaluation of Pre-school Education*. Strasburg: Documentation Centre for Education in Europe, Council of Europe

Choldin, H. M., and McGinty, M. J. (1972). Population density, crowding, and social relations. *Man–Environment Systems* 2, 131–58

Christian, J. J., and Davis, D. E. (1964). Endocrines, behavior, and population. *Science* 146, 1550–60

Cicirelli, V. G. (1969). *The Impact of Head Start: An Evaluation of the Effects of Head Start on Children's Cognitive and Affective Development*. Washington, D.C.: Westinghouse Learning Corporation

Clark, A. H., Wyon, S. M., and Richards, M. P. M. (1969). Free-play in nursery school children. *J. Child Psychol. Psychiat.* 10, 205–16

Clarke, A. M., and Clarke, A. D. B. (1976). (Eds.) *Early Experience: Myth and Evidence*. London: Open Books

Clarke-Stewart, K. A. (1973). Interactions between mothers and their young children: Characteristics and consequences. *Monog. Soc. Res. Child Develop.* 38, Serial no. 153

Clem, P., Ahern, K., Bailey, N., Gay, M., and Scantlebury, M. (1974). A comparison of interaction patterns in an open space and a fixed plan school. *Man–Environment Systems* 4, 59–60

Cole, M., and Bruner, J. (1971). Cultural differences and inferences about psychological processes. *Amer. Psychol.* 26, 867–76

Coleman, J. S., Campbell, E. Q., Hobson, C. J., McPartland, J., Mood, A. M., Weinfeld, F. D., and York, R. L. (1966). *Equality of Educational Opportunity*. Washington, D.C.: US Government Printing Office

Connolly, K., and Smith, P. K. (1972). Reactions of preschool children to a strange observer. In *Ethological Studies of Child Behaviour*. Ed. N. Blurton Jones, Cambridge University Press

Cooper, M. G. (1976). Observational studies of nursery schools. Unpublished PhD thesis, University of Durham

Cottrell, T. L. (1962). The effect of size of tutorial group on teaching efficiency. *Univ. Edin. Gazette* 33, 20–1

Council of Europe. (1975). *Problems in the Evaluation of Pre-school Education*. Strasburg: Documentation Centre for Education in Europe

Crook, J. H. (1970) (ed.). *Social Behaviour in Birds and Mammals*. London: Academic Press

Crook, J. H., Ellis, J. E., and Goss-Custard, J. D. (1976). Mammalian social systems: Structure and function. *Anim. Behav.* 24, 261–74

D'Atri, D. A. (1975). Psychophysiological responses to crowding. *Environ. Behav.* 7, 237–52

Davie, R., Butler, N., and Goldstein, H. (1972). *From Birth to Seven*. London: National Children's Bureau/Longman

Dean, L. M., Pugh, W. M., and Gunderson, E. K. E. (1975). Spatial and perceptual components of crowding. *Environ. Behav.* 7, 225–36

De Cecco, J. P. (1964). Class size and co-ordinated instruction. *Brit. J. Educ. Psychol.* 34, 65–74

Dee, N., and Liebman, J. C. (1970). A statistical study of attendance at urban playgrounds. *J. Leis. Res.* 2, 145–59

Department of Education and Science (1972). *Education: A Framework for Expansion.* Cmnd. 5174. London: HMSO

Department of Education and Science (1973). *Nursery Education.* Circular no. 2/73. London: HMSO

Department of the Environment (1973). *Children at Play.* London: HMSO

Derman, A. (1974). Children's play: Design approaches and theoretical issues. *Man–Environment Systems* 4, 69–88

Desor, J. A. (1972). Toward a psychological theory of crowding. *J. Pers. Soc. Psychol.* 21, 79–83

Deutsch, M. (1967). *The Disadvantaged Child.* New York: Basic Books

Doke, L. A., and Risley, T. R. (1972). The organisation of day-care environments: Required vs optional activities. *J. App. Behav. Anal.* 5, 405–20

Douglas, J. W. B.(1964). *The Home and the School.* London: MacGibbon and Kee

Douglas, J. W. B., Ross, J. M., and Simpson, H. R. (1968). *All Our Future.* London: Peter Davies

Dreyer, A. S., and Rigler, D. (1969). Cognitive performance in Montessori and nursery school children. *J. Educ. Res.* 62, 411–16

Dunbar, R. I. M. (1976). Some aspects of research design and their implications in the observational study of behaviour. *Behaviour* 58, 78–98

Dunn, J., and Wooding, C. (1977). Play in the home and its implications for learning. In *Biology of Play.* Eds. B. Tizard and D. Harvey, London: Spastics International Medical Publications/Heinemann

Durlak, J., Beardsley, B., and Murray, J. (1972). Observation of user activity patterns in open and traditional plan school environments. In *Environmental Design: Research and Practice.* Ed. W. J. Mitchell, Los Angeles: University of California Press

Durlak, J. T., and Lehman, J. (1974). User awareness and sensitivity to open space: A study of traditional and open plan schools. In *Psychology and the Built Environment.* Eds. D. Canter and T. Lee, Tonbridge: Architectural Press

Eibl-Eibesfeldt, I. (1970). *Ethology: The Biology of Behavior.* New York: Holt, Rinehart, and Winston

Eifermann, R. (1970). Level of children's play as expressed in group size. *Brit. J. Educ. Psychol.* 40, 161–70

Evans, K. (1974). The spatial organization of infants' schools. *J. Architect. Res.* 3, 26–33

Fagen, R. M. (1976). Exercise, play, and physical training in animals. In *Perspectives in Ethology,* vol. 2. Eds. P. P. G. Bateson and P. H. Klopfer, New York: Plenum

Fagot, B. I. (1973). Influence of teacher behavior in the preschool. *Develop. Psychol.* 9, 198–206

Fagot, B. I. (1977). Variations in density: Effects on task and social behaviors of preschool children. *Develop. Psychol.* 13, 166–7

Farwell, L. (1930). Reactions of kindergarten, first- and second-grade children to constructive play materials. *Genet. Psychol. Monog.* 8, 431–562

Feshbach, S. (1970). Aggression. In *Carmichael's Manual of Child Psychology.* Third edition, ed. P. H. Mussen, New York: Wiley

Fleming, C. M. (1959). Class size as a variable in the teaching situation. *Educ. Res.* **1**, 35–48

Foster, J. C. (1930). Distribution of the teacher's time among children in the nursery school and kindergarten. *J. Educ. Res.* **22**, 172–83

Fox, R., and Fleising, U. (1976). Human ethology. *Ann. Rev. Anthrop.* **5**, 265–88

Freedman, D. G. (1961). The infant's fear of strangers and the flight response. *J. Child Psychol. Psychiat.* **2**, 242–8

Freedman, J. L. (1975). *Crowding and Behavior.* San Francisco: Freeman

Freedman, J. L., Klevansky, S., and Ehrlich, P. (1971). The effect of crowding on human task performance. *J. App. Soc. Psychol.* **1**, 7–25

Freedman, J. L., Levy, A. S., Buchanan, R. W., and Price, J. (1972). Crowding and human aggressiveness. *J. Exp. Soc. Psychol.* **8**, 528–48

Froebel, F. (1826). *The Education of Man.* Leipzig: Keilhau; English edition, New York: Appleton, 1887

Galle, O. R., Gove, W. R., and McPherson, J. M. (1972). Population density and pathology: What are the relations for man? *Science* **176**, 23–30

Garner, J., and Bing, M. (1973). Inequalities of teacher–pupil contacts. *Brit. J. Educ. Psychol.* **43**, 234–43

Garvey, C. (1974). Some properties of social play. *Merrill-Palmer Quart.* **20**, 163–80

Gilligan, M. C. (1970). The effects of varied playground space on certain behavioral aspects of four- and five-year-old children. Unpublished PhD dissertation, New York University

Goldberg, S., and Lewis, M. (1969). Play behavior in the year-old infant: Early sex differences. *Child Develop.* **40**, 21–31

Gordon, I. J., and Jester, R. E. (1973). Techniques of observing teaching in early childhood and outcomes of particular procedures. In *Second Handbook of Research on Teaching.* Ed. R. M. W. Travers, Chicago: Rand McNally

Gramza, A. F., and Scholtz, G. T. L. (1974). Children's responses to visual complexity in a play setting. *Psychol. Rep.* **35**, 895–9.

Grant, E. C. (1969). Human facial expression. *Man* **4**, 525–36

Gray, P. H. (1958). Theory and evidence of imprinting in human infants. *J. Psychol.* **46**, 155–6

Gray, S. W., and Klaus, R. A. (1965). An experimental preschool program for culturally deprived children. *Child Develop.* **36**, 887–98

Gump, P. V. (1975). Ecological psychology and children. In *Review of Child Development Research*, vol. 5. Ed. E. M. Hetherington, University of Chicago Press

Gump, P. V. (1978). School environments. In *Children's Environments.* Eds. I. Altman and J. Wohlwill, New York: Plenum

Gump, P. V., and James, E. V. (1975). *Child Development and the Man-Made Environment: A Literature Review and Commentary.* Washington, D.C.: National Institute of Child Health and Development.

Gutteridge, M. V. (1935). *The Duration of Attention in Young Children.* Melbourne University Press

Hagman, E. P. (1933). The companionships of preschool children. *University of Iowa Studies in Child Welfare* **7**(4), 1–69

Halsey, A. H., and Smith, T. (1976). Pre-school expansion: Its impact on parental involvement and on the structure of provision. Final Report to Social Science Research Council, London

Hamilton, D. and Delamont, S. (1974). Classroom research: A cautionary tale. *Res. in Educ.* 11, 1–15

Hamilton, W. J. III, and Watt, K. E. F. (1970). Refuging. *Ann. Rev. Ecol. Systematics* 1, 263–86

Hartup, W. W. (1970). Peer interaction and social organisation. In *Carmichael's Manual of Child Psychology*. Third edition, ed. P. H. Mussen, New York: Wiley

Hartup, W. W. (1976). Cross-age versus same-age peer interaction: Ethological and cross-cultural perspectives. In *Children as Teachers*. Ed. V. Allen, New York: Academic Press

Hayes, D. S. (1978). Cognitive bases for liking and disliking among preschool children. *Child Develop.* 49, 906–9

Hayward, G., Rothenberg, M., and Beasley, R. R. (1974). Children's play and urban playground environments. *Environ. Behav.* 6, 131–68

Heathers, G. (1954). The adjustment of two-year-olds in a novel social situation. *Child Develop.* 25, 147–58

Heinicke, C. M. (1956). Some effects of separating two-year-old children from their parents: A comparative study. *Hum. Relat.* 9, 105–76

Hellmuth, J. (1970) (ed.). *Disadvantaged Child*, vol. 3: *Compensatory Education – A National Debate*. New York: Brunner–Mazel

Herring, A., and Koch, H. L. (1930). A study of some factors influencing the interest span of preschool children. *J. Genet. Psychol.* 38, 249–79

Hess, R. D., and Shipman, V. (1965). Early experience and the socialisation of cognitive modes in children. *Child Develop.* 36, 869–86

Hinde, R. A. (1959a). Some recent trends in ethology. In *Psychology: A Study of a Science*, vol. 2. Ed. S. Koch, New York: McGraw-Hill

Hinde, R. A. (1959b). Unitary drives. *Anim. Behav.* 7, 130–41

Hold, B. C. L. (1976). Attention structure and rank specific behaviour in preschool children. In *The Social Structure of Attention*. Eds. M. R. A. Chance and R. R. Larsen, London: Wiley

Hole, V., and Miller, A. (1966). Children's play on housing estates: A summary of two BRS studies. *Arch. J.* 143, 1529–36

Holme, A., and Massie, P. (1970). *Children's Play: A Study of Needs and Opportunities*. London: Michael Joseph

Hollis, J. H. (1965). The effects of social and non-social stimuli on the behavior of profoundly retarded children. Part I: *Amer. J. Ment. Deficiency* 69, 755–71; Part II: 772–89

Hoving, K. L., Laforme, G. L., and Wallace, J. R. (1974). The development of children's interpersonal aggression in competitive task. In *Determinants and Origins of Aggressive Behavior*. Eds. J. de Wit and W. W. Hartup. The Hague: Mouton

Huston-Stein, A., Friedrich-Cofer, L., and Susman, E. J. (1977). The relation of classroom structure to social behavior, imaginative play, and self-regulation of economically disadvantaged children. *Child Develop.* 48, 908–16

Hutt, C., and McGrew, W. C. (1967). Effects of group density upon social behaviour in humans. Paper presented to Symposium on Changes in Behaviour with Population Density, Association for the Study of Animal Behaviour, Oxford

Hutt, C., and Vaizey, M. J. (1966). Differential effects of group density on social behaviour. *Nature* **209**, 1371–2

Hutt, S. J., and Hutt, C. (1970). (Eds.) *Direct Observation and Measurement of Behavior*. Springfield, Illinois: C. C. Thomas

Jackson, P. W., and Lahaderne, H. M. (1967). Inequalities of teacher–pupil contacts. *Psychol. in the Schools* **4**, 204–11

Jencks, C., Smith, M., Acland, H., Bane, M. J., Cohen, D., Gintis, H., Heyns, B., and Michelson, S. (1972). *Inequality: A Reassessment of the Effect of Family and Schooling in America*. New York: Basic Books

Jensen, A. R. (1969). How much can we boost IQ and scholastic achievement? *Harvard Educ. Rev.* **37**, 1–123

Jersild, A. T., and Markey, F. V. (1935). *Conflicts Between Preschool Children*. New York: Teachers' College, Columbia University

Johnson, M. W. (1935). The effect on behavior of variation in the amount of play equipment. *Child Develop.* **6**, 56–68

Kerr, M. K. S. (1976). Patterns of social group structure, interpersonal spacing and behavior in young children. Unpublished PhD dissertation, University of Minnesota

Kessen, W. (1965). *The Child*. New York: Wiley

Koluchova, J. (1976). The further development of twins after severe and prolonged deprivation: A second report, *J. Child Psychol. Psychiat.* **17**, 181–8

Kounin, J. S., and Gump, P. V. (1974). Signal systems in lesson settings and the task related behavior of preschool children. *J. Educ. Psychol.* **66**, 554–62

Krebs, C. J., Gaines, M. S., Keller, B. L., Myers, J. H., and Tomarin, R. H. (1973). Population cycles in small rodents. *Science* **179**, 35–41

Krebs, J. R., and Davies, N. B. (1978). *Behavioural Ecology: An Evolutionary Approach*. Oxford: Blackwell

Labov, W. (1970). The logic of non-standard English. In *Language and Poverty*. Ed. F. Williams, Chicago: Markham

Landreth, C., Gardner, G. M., Eckhardt, B. C., and Prugh, A. D. (1943). Teacher–child contacts in nursery schools. *J. Exp. Educ.* **12**, 65–91

Lawrence, J. E. S. (1974). Science and sentiment: Overview of research on crowding and human behavior. *Psychol. Bull.* **81**, 712–20

Lelaurin, K., and Risley, T. R. (1972). The organisation of day-care environments: 'Zone' versus 'man-to-man' staff assignments. *J. App. Behav. Anal.* **5**, 225–32

Lewis, M., and Rosenblum, L. (1975). Eds. *Friendship and peer relations*. New York: Wiley

Lewis, M., and Wilson, C. D. (1972). Infant development in lower-class American families. *Hum. Develop.* **15**, 112–27

Little, A., Mabey, C., and Russell, J. (1971). Do small classes help a pupil? *New Society* **18**, 769–71

Loo, C. M. (1972). The effects of spatial density on the social behavior of children. *J. App. Soc. Psychol.* **2**, 372–81

Lykken, D. T. (1968). Statistical significance in psychological research. *Psychol. Bull.* **70**, 151–9

Lytton, H. (1973). Three approaches to the study of parent–child interaction: Ethological, interview and experimental. *J. Child Psychol. Psychiat.* **14**, 1–17

McCain, G., Cox, V. C., and Paulus, P. B. (1976). The relationship between illness complaints and degree of crowding in a prison environment. *Environ. Behav.* **8**, 283–90

McCandless, B. R., and Marshall, H. R. (1957). Sex differences in social acceptance and social participation of preschool children. *Child Develop.* **28**, 421–5

Maccoby, E. E., and Jacklin, C. M. (1974). *The Psychology of Sex Differences*. Stanford University Press

McDowell, M. S. (1937). Frequency of choice of play materials by preschool children. *Child Develop.* **8**, 305–10

McGrew, P. L. (1970). Social and spatial density effects on spacing behaviour in preschool children. *J. Child Psychol. Psychiat.* **11**, 197–205

McGrew, W. C. (1970). Glossary of motor patterns of four-year-old nursery school children. In *Direct Observation and Measurement of Behaviour*. Eds. S. J. Hutt and C. Hutt, Springfield, Illinois: C. C. Thomas

McGrew, W. C. (1972). *An Ethological Study of Children's Behaviour*. London: Academic Press

McPherson, J. M. (1975). Population density and social pathology: A reexamination. *Sociol. Symp.* **14**, 77–90

Manning, K., and Sharp, A. (1977). *Structuring Play in the Early Years at School*. London: Ward Lock Educational

Manning, M., Heron, J., and Marshall, T. (1978). Styles of hostility and social interactions at nursery, at school, and at home: An extended study of children. In *Aggression and Anti-Social Behaviour in Childhood and Adolescence*. Eds. L. A. Hersov and M. Berger, Oxford: Pergamon

Marshall, H. R. (1957). An evaluation of sociometric–social behavior research with preschool children. *Child Develop.* **28**, 131–7

Marshall, H. R., and McCandless, B. R. (1957). A study in prediction of social behavior of preschool children. *Child Develop.* **28**, 149–59

Marshall, J. E., and Heslin, R. (1975). Boys and girls together: Sexual composition and the effect of density and group size on cohesiveness. *J. Pers. Soc. Psychol.* **31**, 952–61

Martin, W. E. (1964). Singularity and stability of profiles of social behavior. In *Readings in Child Behavior and Development*. Ed. C. B. Stendler, New York: Harcourt, Brace, and World

Martlew, M., Connolly, K., and McCleod, C. (1978). Language use, role and context in a five-year-old. *J. Child Lang.* **5**, 81–99

Mayall, B., and Petrie, P. (1977). *Minder, Mother and Child*. University of London, Institute of Education

Medley, D. M., and Mitzel, H. E. (1963). Measuring classroom behavior by systematic observation. In *Handbook of Research on Teaching*. Ed. N. Gage, Chicago: Rand McNally

Milgram, S. (1970). The experience of living in cities. *Science* **167**, 1461–8

Miller, L. B., and Dyer, J. L. (1975). Four preschool programs: Their dimensions and effects. *Monog. Soc. Res. Child Develop.* **40**, Serial no. 162

Mitchell, R. E. (1971). Some social implications of high density housing. *Amer. Sociol. Rev.* **36**, 18–29

Moore, R. C. (1974). Patterns of activity in time and space: The ecology of a neighbourhood playground. In *Psychology and the Built Environment*. Eds. D. Canter and T. Lee, Tonbridge: Architectural Press

Moore, S. B. (1938). The use of commands, suggestions, and requests by nursery school and kindergarten teachers. *Child Develop.* **9**, 185–201

Moyer, K. E., and Haller Gilmer, B. von (1955). Attention spans of children for experimentally designed toys. *J. Genet. Psychol.* **87**, 187–201

Murphy, L. B. (1937). *Social Behavior and Child Personality*. New York: Columbia University Press

Murphy, M. J., and Goldner, R. P. (1976). Effects of teaching orientation on social interaction in nursery school. *J. Educ. Psychol.* **68**, 725–8

Murray, R. (1974). The influence of crowding on children's behaviour. in *Psychology and the Built Environment*. Eds. D. Canter and T. Lee, Tonbridge: Architectural Press

Mussen, P., and Eisenberg-Berg, N. (1977). *Roots of Caring, Sharing and Helping*. San Francisco: W. H. Freeman and Co

Neill, S. R. St J. (1976). Aggressive and non-aggressive fighting in twelve-to-thirteen year old pre-adolescent boys. *J. Child Psychol. Psychiat.* **17**, 213–20

Nelson, J. D., Gelfand, D. M., and Hartman, D. P. (1969). Children's aggression following competition and exposure to an aggressive model. *Child Develop.* **40**, 1085–99

Nelson, K. (1973). Structure and strategy in learning to talk. *Monog. Soc. Res. Child Develop.* **38**, Serial no. 149

Newson, J., and Newson, E. (1968). *Four Years Old in an Urban Community*. London: George Allen and Unwin

O'Connor, M. (1975). The nursery school environment. *Develop. Psychol.* **11**, 556–61

Oetzel, R. M. (1966). Classified summary of research in sex differences. In *The Development of Sex Differences*. Ed. E. E. Maccoby, Stanford University Press

Olson, W. C., and Cunningham, E. M. (1934). Time-sampling techniques. *Child Develop.* **5**, 41–58

Organisation for Economic Cooperation and Development (1977). *Early Child Care and Education: Objectives and Issues*. London: HMSO

Orne, M. T. (1962). On the social psychology of the psychological experiment: With particular reference to demand characteristics and their implications. *Amer. Psychol.* **17**, 776–83

Parten, M. B. (1932). Social participation among preschool children. *J. Abn. Soc. Psychol.* **27**, 243–69

Parten, M. B. (1933). Social play among preschool children. *J. Abn. Soc. Psychol.* **28**, 136–47

Parten, M., and Newhall, S. M. (1943). Social behaviour of preschool children. In *Child Behavior and Development*. Eds. R. G. Barker, J. S. Kounin, and H. F. Wright, New York: McGraw-Hill

Paulus, P., Cox, V., McCain, G., and Chandler, J. (1975). Some effects of crowding in a prison environment. *J. App. Soc. Psychol.* 5, 86–91

Poirier, F. E. (1972) (ed.). *Primate Socialisation.* New York: Random House

Poirier, F. E., and Smith, E. O. (1974). Socialising functions of primate play. *Amer. Zool.* 14, 275–87

Preiser, W. F. E. (1972). Behavior of nursery school children under different spatial densities. *Man–Environment Systems* 2, 247–50

Prescott, E. (1973). A comparison of three types of day care and nursery school/home care. Paper presented at Biennial Meeting of Society for Research in Child Development, Philadelphia

Price, J. M. (1971). The effects of crowding on the social behavior of children. Unpublished PhD dissertation, Columbia University, New York

Pringle, M. K., and Naidoo, S. (1976). *Early Child Care in Britain.* London: Gordon and Breech

Proshansky, H. M., Ittelson, W. H., and Rivlin, L. G. (1970). (Eds.) *Environmental Psychology: Man and his Physical Setting.* New York: Holt, Rinehart and Winston

Rafferty, J. E., Tyler, B. B., and Tyler, F. B. (1960). Personality assessment from free play observations. *Child Develop.* 31, 691–702

Ramey, C. T., Finkelstein, N. W., and O'Brien, C. (1976). Toys and infant behavior in the first year of life. *J. Genet. Psychol.* 129, 341–2

Resnick, L. B. (1971). *Teacher Behavior in an Informal British Infant School.* Pittsburgh: Learning Research and Development Center, University of Pittsburgh

Resnick, L. B. (1972). Teacher behaviour in the informal classroom. *J. Curriculum Stud.* 4, 99–109

Reuter, J., and Yunik, G. (1973). Social interaction in nursery schools. *Develop. Psychol.* 9, 319–25

Richer, J. M., and Nicoll, S. (1971). A playroom for autistic children, and its companion therapy project. *Brit. J. Ment. Subnorm.* 17, 1–12

Risley, T. R. (1977). The ecology of applied behavior analysis. In *Ecological Perspectives in Behavior Analysis.* Eds. A. Rogers-Warren and S. F. Warren, Baltimore: University Park Press

Rosenshine, B., and Furst, N. (1973). The use of direct observations to study teaching. In *Second Handbook of Research on Teaching.* Ed. R. M. W. Travers, Chicago: Rand McNally

Ross, M., Layton, B., Erickson, B. M., and Schopler, J. (1973). Affect, facial regard, and reactions to crowding. *J. Pers. Soc. Psychol.* 28, 69–76

Rutter, M. (1972). *Maternal Deprivation Reassessed.* Harmondsworth: Penguin

Saegert, S., Mackintosh, B., and West, S. (1975). Two studies of crowding in urban public places. *Environ. Behav.* 7, 159–84

Schmitt, R. (1957). Density, delinquency and crime in Honolulu. *Sociol. Soc. Res.* 41, 274–6

Shoggen, P. (1963). Environmental forces in the everyday lives of children. In *The Stream of Behavior.* Ed. R. Barker, New York: Appleton–Century–Crofts

Sears, P. S., and Dowley, E. M. (1963). Research on teaching in the nursery school. In *Handbook of Research on Teaching.* Ed. N. Gage, Chicago: Rand McNally

Senn, M. J. E. (1975). Insights on the child development movement in the United States. *Monog. Soc. Res. Child Develop.* **40**, Serial no. 161

Shores, R. E., Hester, P., and Strain, P. S. (1976). The effects of amount and type of teacher–child interaction on child–child interaction during free-play. *Psychol. in the Schools* **13**, 171–5

Shure, M. B. (1963). Psychological ecology of a nursery school. *Child Develop.* **34**, 979–92

Simon, A., and Boyer, E. G. (1967, 1970a, 1970b) (eds.). *Mirrors for Behavior: Anthology of Classroom Observation Instruments.* Vols. 1–6, 7–14, and Summary; Supplementary vols. A and B. Philadelphia: Research for Better Schools Inc.

Simon, A., and Boyer, E. G. (1974) (eds.). *Mirrors for Behavior III: An Anthology of Observation Instruments.* Wyncote, Pennsylvania: Communication materials Center

Sluckin, A. M., and Smith, P. K. (1977). Two approaches to the concept of dominance in preschool children. *Child Develop.* **48**, 917–23

Smilansky, S. (1968). *The Effects of Sociodramatic Play on Disadvantaged Preschool Children.* New York: Wiley

Smith, G., and James, T. (1975). The effects of preschool education: Some American and British evidence. *Oxford Rev. Educ.* **1**, 223–40

Smith, L. M., and Geoffrey, W. (1968). *The Complexities of an Urban Classroom: An Analysis Toward a General Theory of Teaching.* New York: Holt, Rinehart, and Winston

Smith, P. K. (1972). Social and play behaviour of preschool children. *Man–Environment Systems*, **2**, 90–1

Smith, P. K. (1973). Temporal clusters and individual differences in the behaviour of preschool children. In *Comparative Ecology and Behaviour of Primates.* Eds. R. P. Michael and J. H. Crook, London: Academic Press

Smith, P. K. (1974a). Ethological methods. In *New Perspectives in Child Development.* Ed. B. M. Foss, Harmondsworth: Penguin

Smith, P. K. (1974b). Aspects of the playgroup environment. In *Psychology and the Built Environment.* Eds. D. Canter and T. Lee, Tonbridge: Architectural Press

Smith, P. K. (1974c). Social and situational determinants of fear in the playgroup. In *The Origins of Fear.* Eds. M. Lewis and L. A. Rosenblum, New York: Wiley

Smith, P. K. (1977). Social and fantasy play in young children. In *Biology of Play.* Eds. B. Tizard and D. Harvey, London: Spastics International Medical Publications, Heinemann

Smith, P. K., and Connolly, K. J. (1972). Patterns of play and social interaction in pre-school children. In *Ethological Studies of Child Behaviour.* Ed. N. Blurton Jones, Cambridge University Press

Smith, P. K., Dalgleish, M., and Herzmark, G. (1978). A comparison of 'play' and 'skills' tutoring in nursery classes. Final Report to Social Science Research Council, London

Smith, P. K., and Delfosse, P. (1978). How children report friendships, and what friends they have. *Bull. Brit. Psychol. Soc.* **31**, 189

Smith, P. K., and Dodsworth, C. (1978). Social class differences in the fantasy play of preschool children. *J. Genet. Psychol.* **133**, 183–190

Smith, P. K., and Green, M. (1974). Aggressive behavior in English nurseries and playgroups: Sex differences and response of adults. *Child Develop.* **45**, 211–14

Smith, P. K., and Syddall, S. (1978). Play and non-play tutoring in preschool children: Is it play or tutoring which matters? *Brit. J. Educ. Psychol.* **48**, 315–25

Social Trends (1974). London: HMSO

Southwick, C. H. (1967). An experimental study of intragroup agonistic behavior in rhesus monkeys (Macaca mulatta). *Behaviour* **28**, 182–209

Stevenson, J. (1975). The nursery school language work. In *Educational Priority*, vol. 3. London: HMSO

Stodolsky, S. S. (1974). How children find something to do in preschools. *Genet. Psychol. Monog.* **90**, 245–303

Stokols, D., Rall, M., Pinner, B., and Schopler, J. (1973). Physical, social, and personal determinants of the perception of crowding. *Environ. Behav.* **5**, 87–115

Strayer, F. F., and Strayer, J. (1976). An ethological analysis of social agonism and dominance relations among preschool children. *Child Develop.* **47**, 980–9

Swift, J. W. (1964). Effects of early group experience: The nursery school and day nursery. In *Review of Child Development Research*, vol. 1. Eds. M. L. Hoffman and L. W. Hoffman, New York: Russell Sage Foundation

Symons, D. (1978). *Play and Aggression: A Study of Rhesus Monkeys*. New York: Columbia University Press

Taylor, P. H., Exon, G., and Holley, B. (1972). *A Study of Nursery Education*. London: Evans/Methuen Educational

Thompson, G. G. (1944). The social and emotional development of preschool children under two types of educational program. *Psychol. Monog.* **56**, no. 5

Tinbergen, N. (1969). Ethology. In *Scientific Thought 1900–1960: A Selective Survey*. Ed. R. Harré, Oxford University Press

Tizard, B. (1974). *Early Childhood Education*. Windsor: National Foundation for Educational Research

Tizard, B., Cooperman, O., Joseph, A., and Tizard, J. (1972). Environmental effects on language development: A study of young children in long-stay residential nurseries. *Child Develop.* **43**, 337–58

Tizard, B., Philps, J., and Plewis, I. (1976). Play in pre-school centres – II. Effects on play of the child's social class and of the educational orientation of the centre. *J. Child Psychol. Psychiat.* **17**, 265–74

Tizard, B., and Rees, J. (1975). The effect of early institutional rearing on the behaviour problems and affectional relationships of four-year-old children. *J. Child Psychol. Psychiat.* **16**, 61–73

Tizard, J. (1974). The upbringing of other people's children: Implications of research and for research. *J. Child Psychol. Psychiat.* **15**, 161–74

Tizard, J. (1975). The objectives and organisation of educational day care services for young children. *Oxford Rev. Educ.* **1**, 211–21

Travers, R. M. W. (1973) (ed.). *Second Handbook of Research on Teaching*. Chicago: Rand McNally

Tulkin, S. R. (1972). An analysis of the concept of cultural deprivation. *Develop. Psychol.* **8**, 326–39

Tulkin, S. R., and Kagan, J. (1972). Mother–child interaction in the first year of life. *Child Develop.* 43, 31–41

Updegraff, R., and Herbst, E. K. (1933). An experimental study of the social behavior stimulated in young children by certain play materials. *J. Genet. Psychol.* 42, 372–91

Van Alstyne, D. (1932). *Play Behavior and Choice of Play Materials of Preschool Children.* University of Chicago Press

Van der Eyken, W. (1977). *The Pre-School Years.* Fourth edition. Harmondsworth: Penguin

Walters, J., Pearce, D., and Dahms, L. (1957). Affectional and aggressive behavior of preschool children. *Child Develop.* 28, 15–26

Weikart, D. P. (1967). Preschool programs: Preliminary findings. *J. Spec. Educ.* 1, 163–82

Welch, S. and Booth, A. (1975). The effect of crowding on aggression. *Sociol. Symp.* 15, 105–28

Whitbread, N. (1972). *The Evolution of the Nursery–Infant School.* London: Routledge and Kegan Paul

Winsborough, H. H. (1965). The social consequences of high population density. *Law and Contemporary Problems* 30, 120–6

Williams, R. M., and Mattson, M. L. (1942). The effect of social groupings upon the language of preschool children. *Child Develop.* 13, 233–45

Witt, P. A., and Gramza, A. F. (1970). Position effects in play equipment preferences of nursery school children. *Percept. Mot. Skills* 31, 431–4

Wolfe, M. (1975). Room size, group size, and density: Behavior patterns in a children's psychiatric facility. *Environ. Behav.* 7, 199–224

Wootton, A. J. (1974). Talk in the homes of young children. *Sociol.* 8, 277–95

Wright, H. F. (1967). *Recording and Analyzing Child Behavior.* New York: Harper and Row

Zern, D., and Taylor, A. L. (1973). Rhythmic behavior in the hierarchy of responses of preschool children. *Merrill–Palmer Quart.* 19, 137–45

Author index

Italic page numbers refer to the Bibliography

Subject index